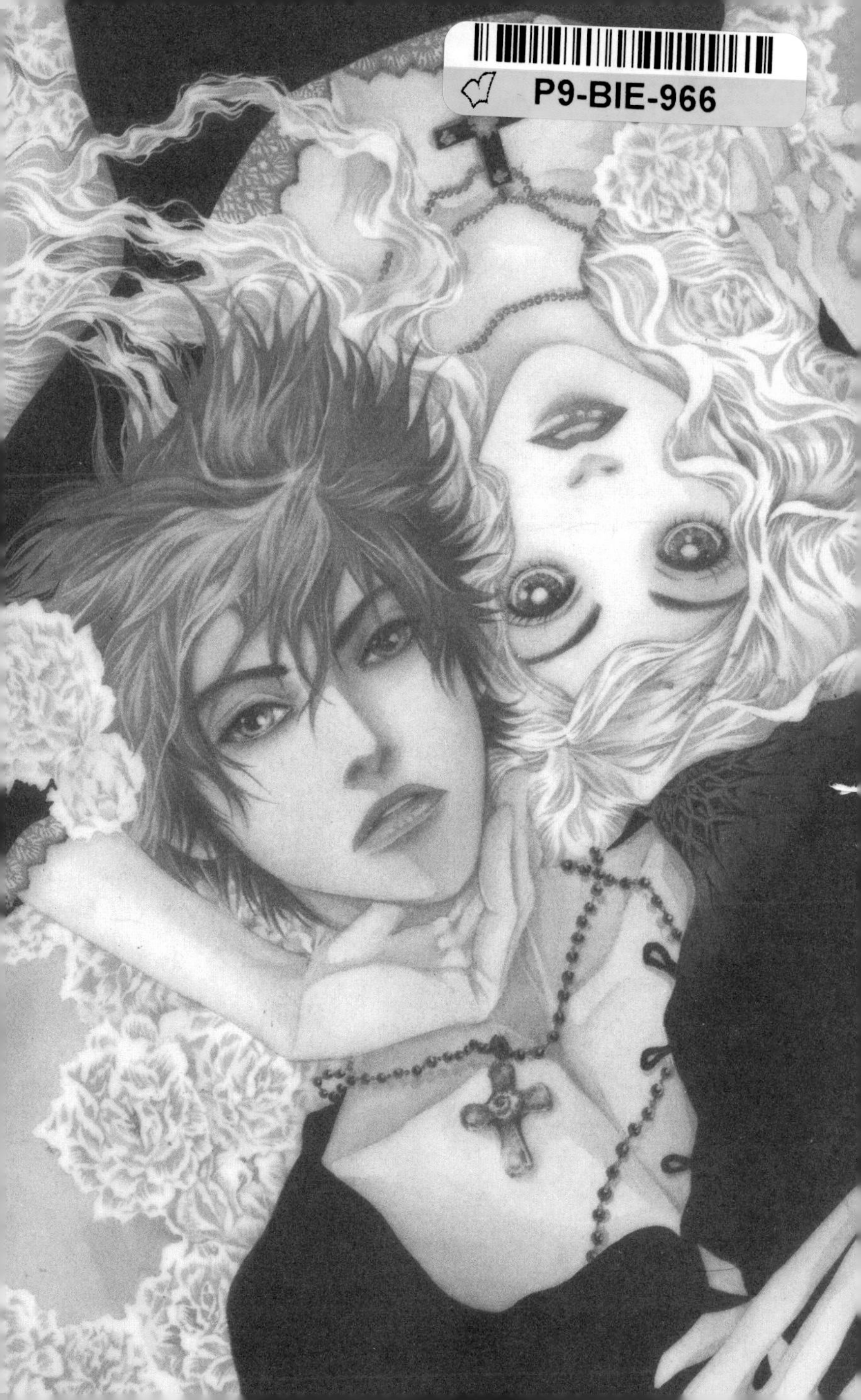

Fever Volume 2
Created by Hee Jung Park

Translation - Hye Young Im
English Adaptation - Ailen Lujo
Copy Editor - Shannon Watters
Retouch and Lettering - Star Print Brokers
Production Artist - Jennifer M. Sanchez
Graphic Designer - Chelsea Windlinger

Editor - Hyun Joo Kim
Digital Imaging Manager - Chris Buford
Pre-Production Supervisor - Lucas Rivera
Production Manager - Elisabeth Brizzi
Managing Editor - Vy Nguyen
Creative Director - Anne Marie Horne
Editor-in-Chief - Rob Tokar
Publisher - Mike Kiley
President and C.O.O. - John Parker
C.E.O. and Chief Creative Officer - Stu Levy

A  Manga

TOKYOPOP Inc.
5900 Wilshire Blvd. Suite 2000
Los Angeles, CA 90036

E-mail: info@TOKYOPOP.com
Come visit us online at www.TOKYOPOP.com

ISBN: 978-1-4278-0533-1

First TOKYOPOP printing: July 2008
10 9 8 7 6 5 4 3 2 1
Printed in the USA

-fever-

VOL. 2

CREATED BY
HEE JUNG PARK

HAMBURG // LONDON // LOS ANGELES // TOKYO

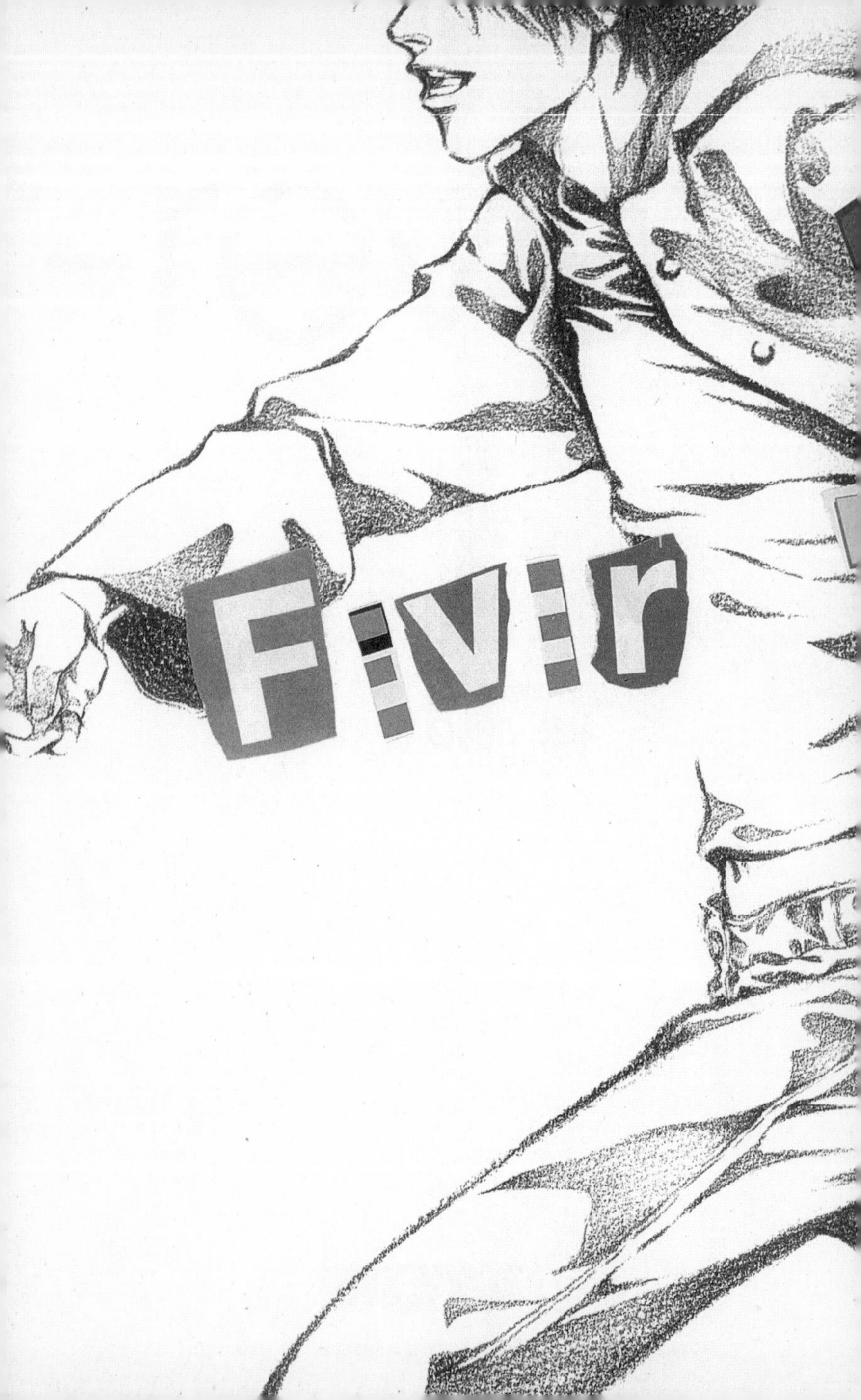
Fever

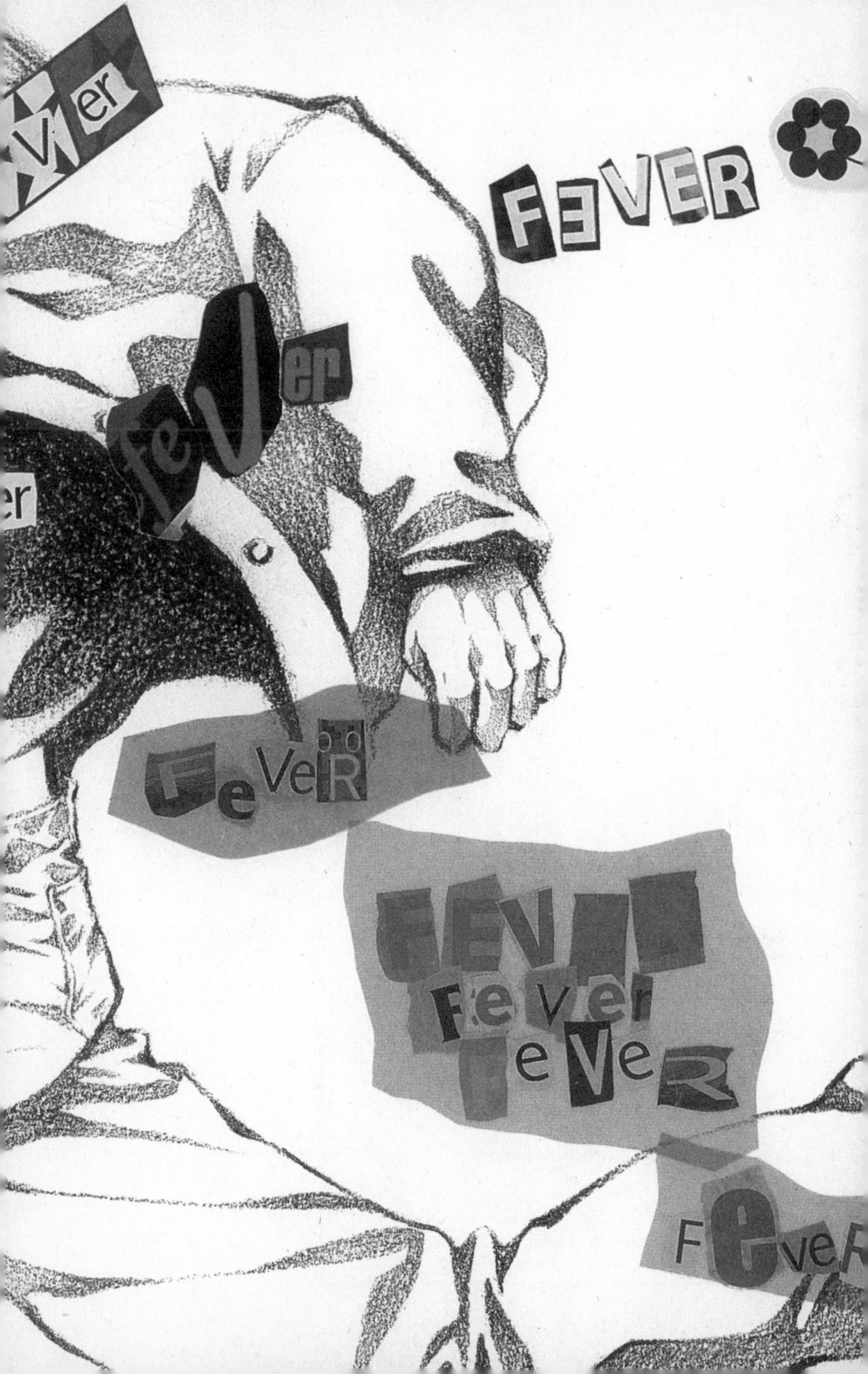

FEVER
fever
er
FeVeR
Fever
eVeR
FeveR

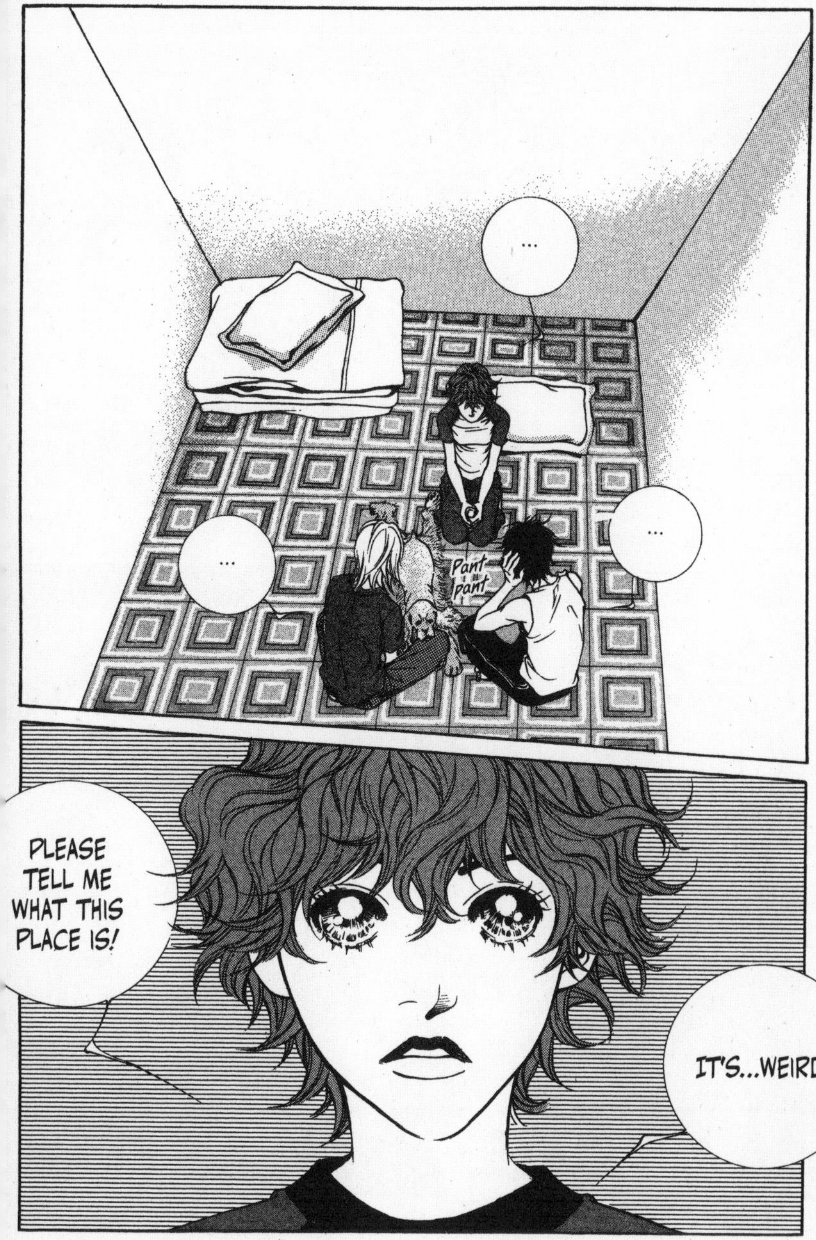
...
...
Pant pant
...
PLEASE TELL ME WHAT THIS PLACE IS!
IT'S...WEIRD.

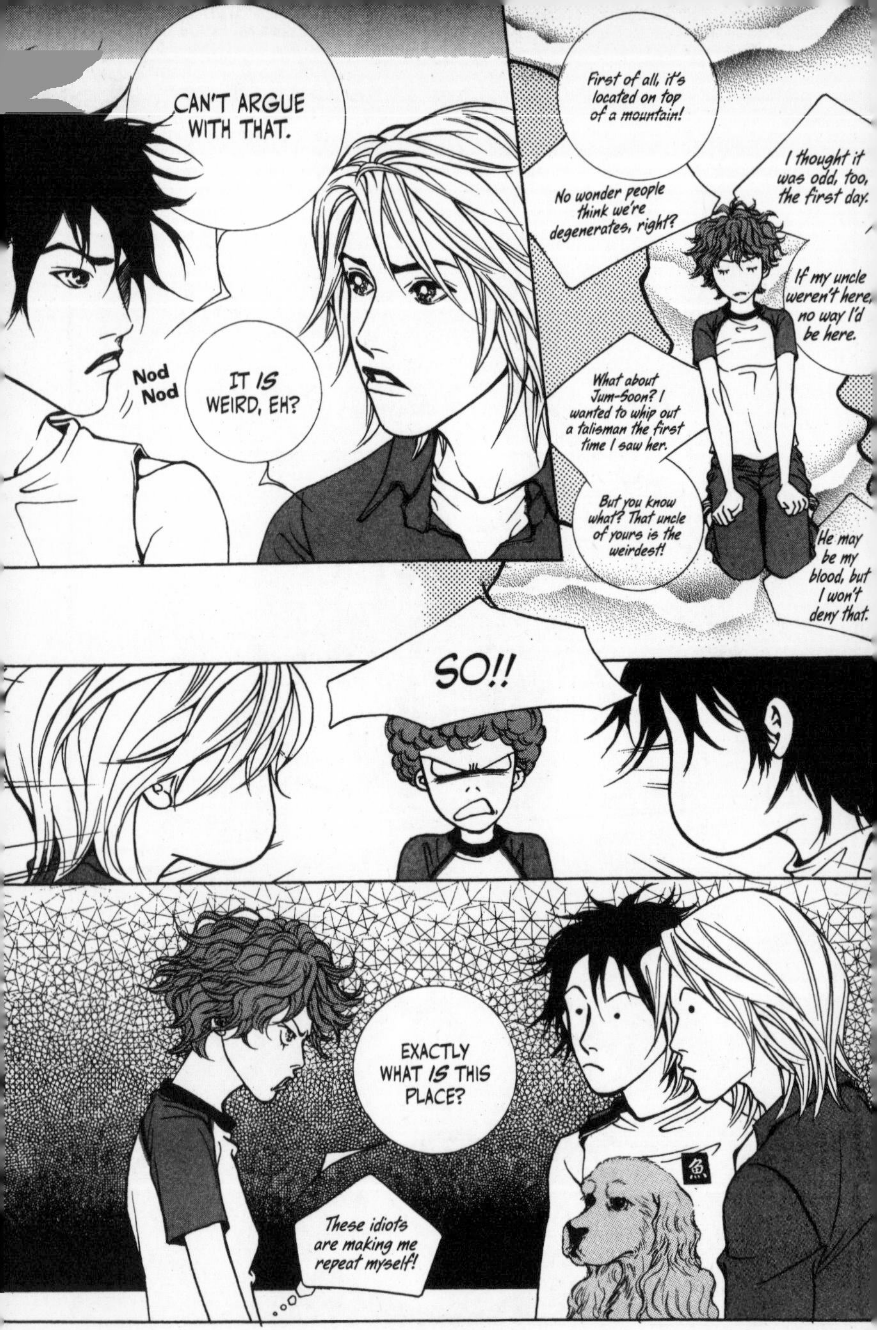
CAN'T ARGUE WITH THAT.
Nod Nod
IT IS WEIRD, EH?
First of all, it's located on top of a mountain!
No wonder people think we're degenerates, right?
I thought it was odd, too, the first day.
If my uncle weren't here, no way I'd be here.
What about Jum-Soon? I wanted to whip out a talisman the first time I saw her.
But you know what? That uncle of yours is the weirdest!
He may be my blood, but I won't deny that.
SO!!
EXACTLY WHAT IS THIS PLACE?
These idiots are making me repeat myself!

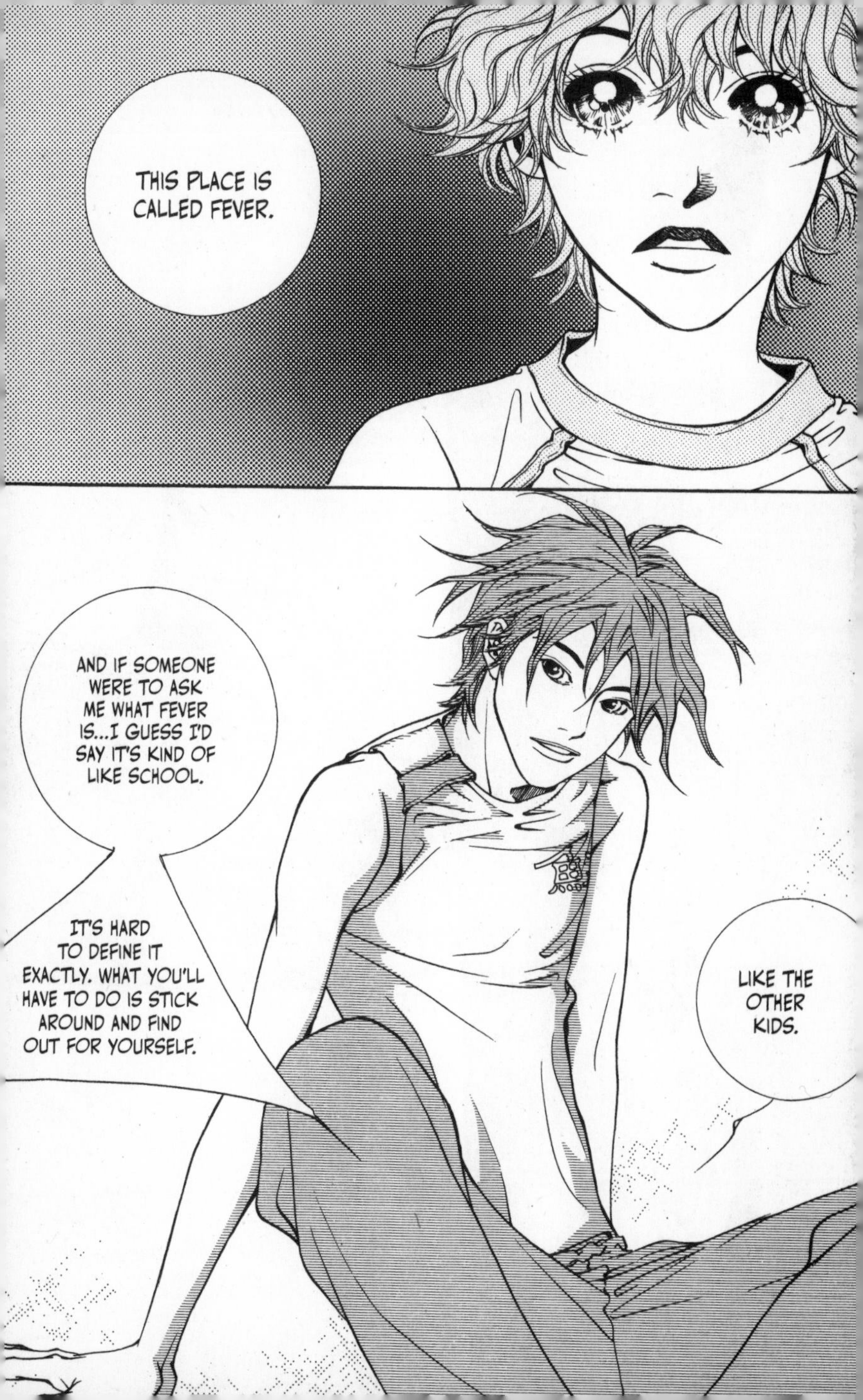
THIS PLACE IS CALLED FEVER.
AND IF SOMEONE WERE TO ASK ME WHAT FEVER IS...I GUESS I'D SAY IT'S KIND OF LIKE SCHOOL.
IT'S HARD TO DEFINE IT EXACTLY. WHAT YOU'LL HAVE TO DO IS STICK AROUND AND FIND OUT FOR YOURSELF.
LIKE THE OTHER KIDS.

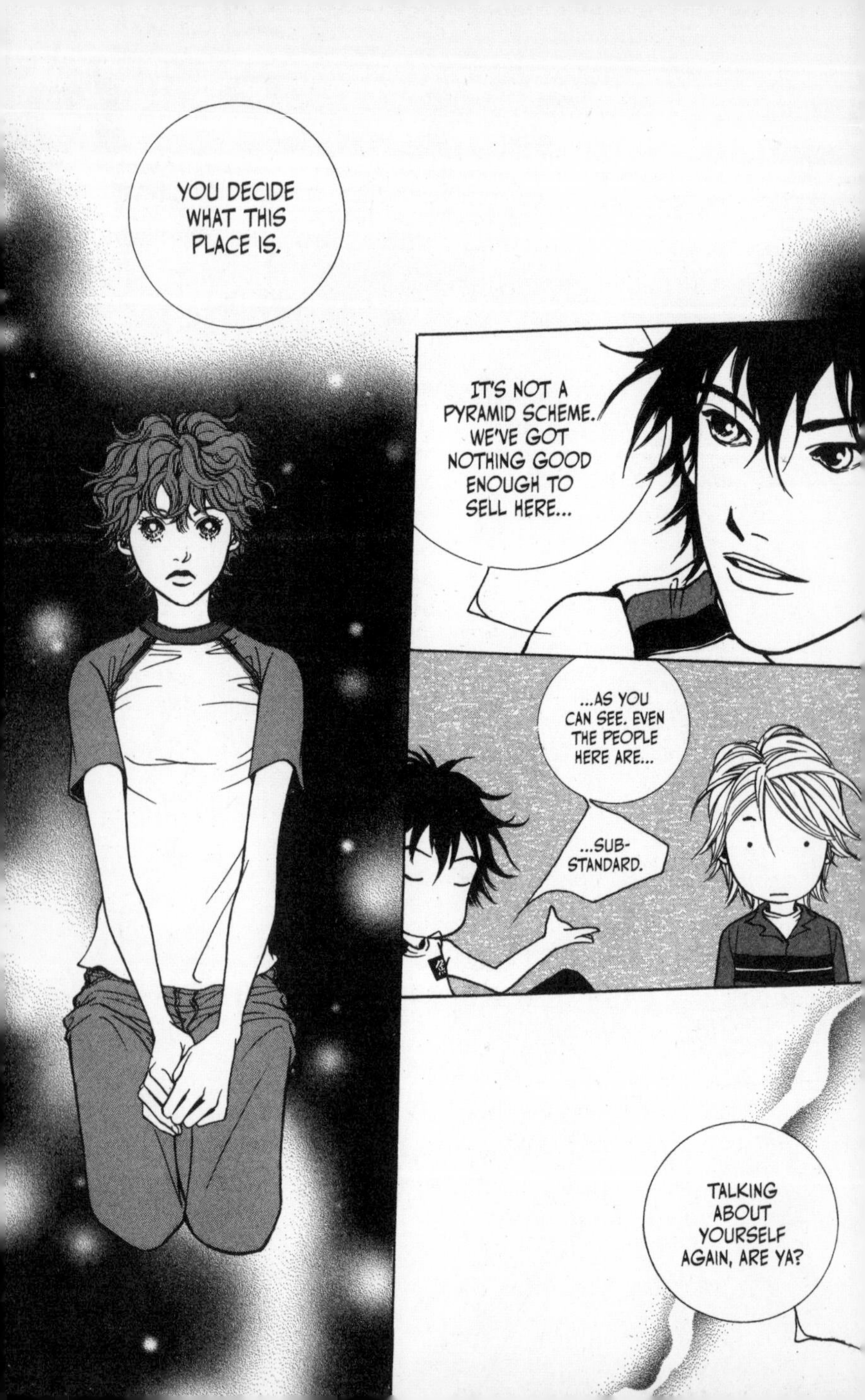

YOU DECIDE WHAT THIS PLACE IS.
IT'S NOT A PYRAMID SCHEME. WE'VE GOT NOTHING GOOD ENOUGH TO SELL HERE...
...AS YOU CAN SEE. EVEN THE PEOPLE HERE ARE...
...SUB-STANDARD.
TALKING ABOUT YOURSELF AGAIN, ARE YA?

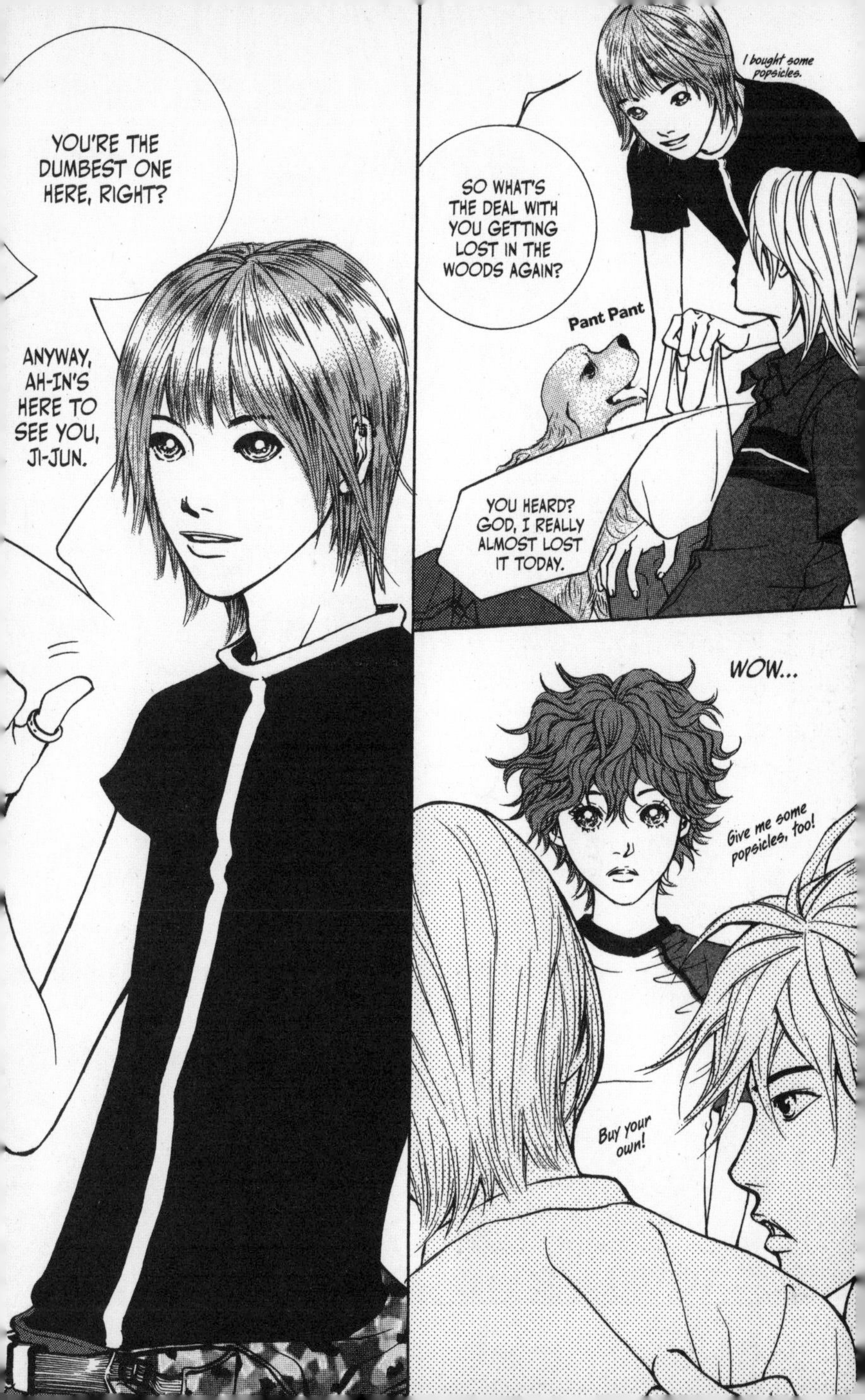

YOU'RE THE DUMBEST ONE HERE, RIGHT?
ANYWAY, AH-IN'S HERE TO SEE YOU, JI-JUN.
I bought some popsicles.
SO WHAT'S THE DEAL WITH YOU GETTING LOST IN THE WOODS AGAIN?
Pant Pant
YOU HEARD? GOD, I REALLY ALMOST LOST IT TODAY.
WOW...
Give me some popsicles, too!
Buy your own!

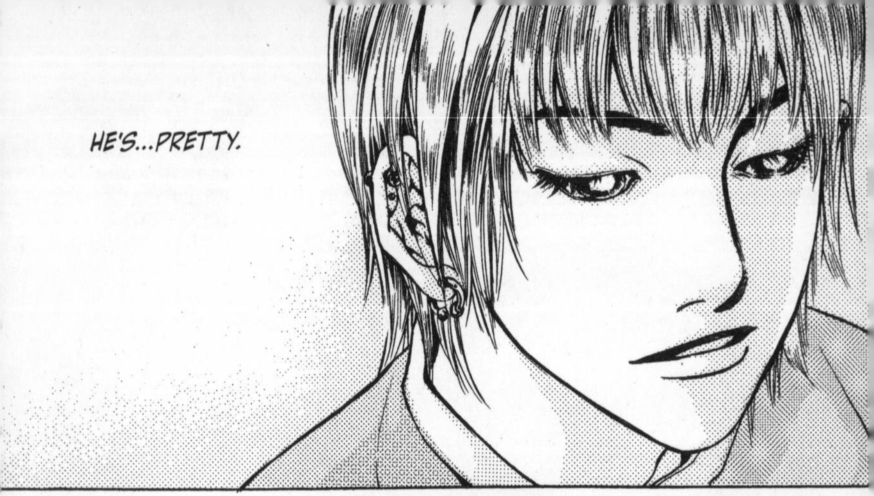
HE'S...PRETTY.

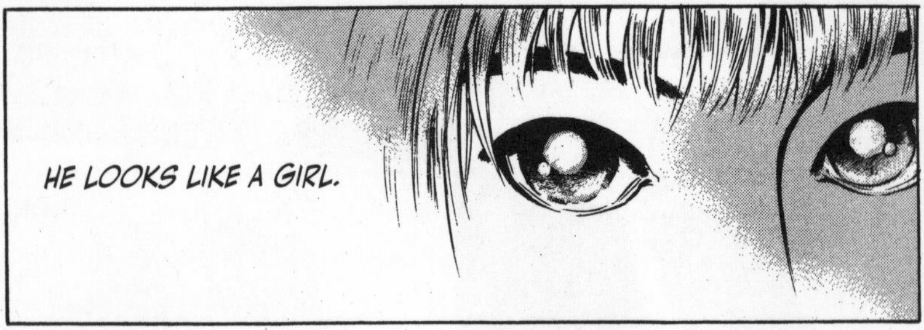
HE LOOKS LIKE A GIRL.

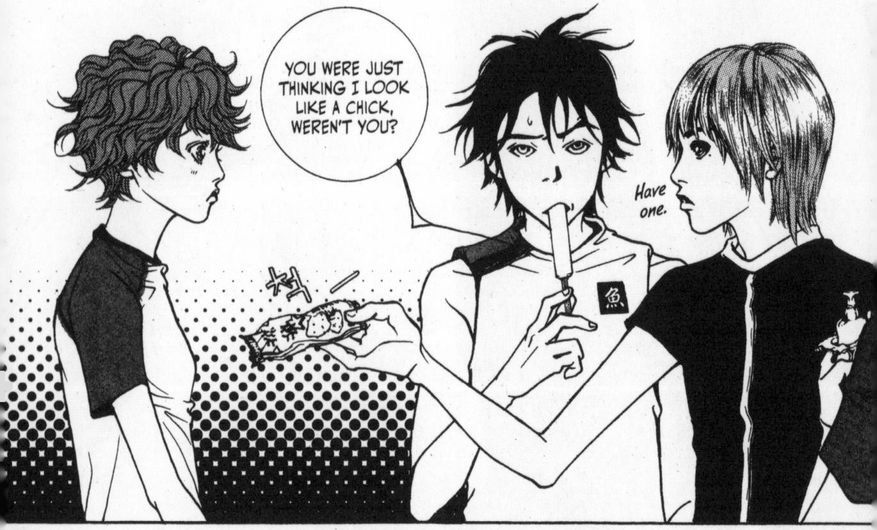
YOU WERE JUST THINKING I LOOK LIKE A CHICK, WEREN'T YOU?
Have one.

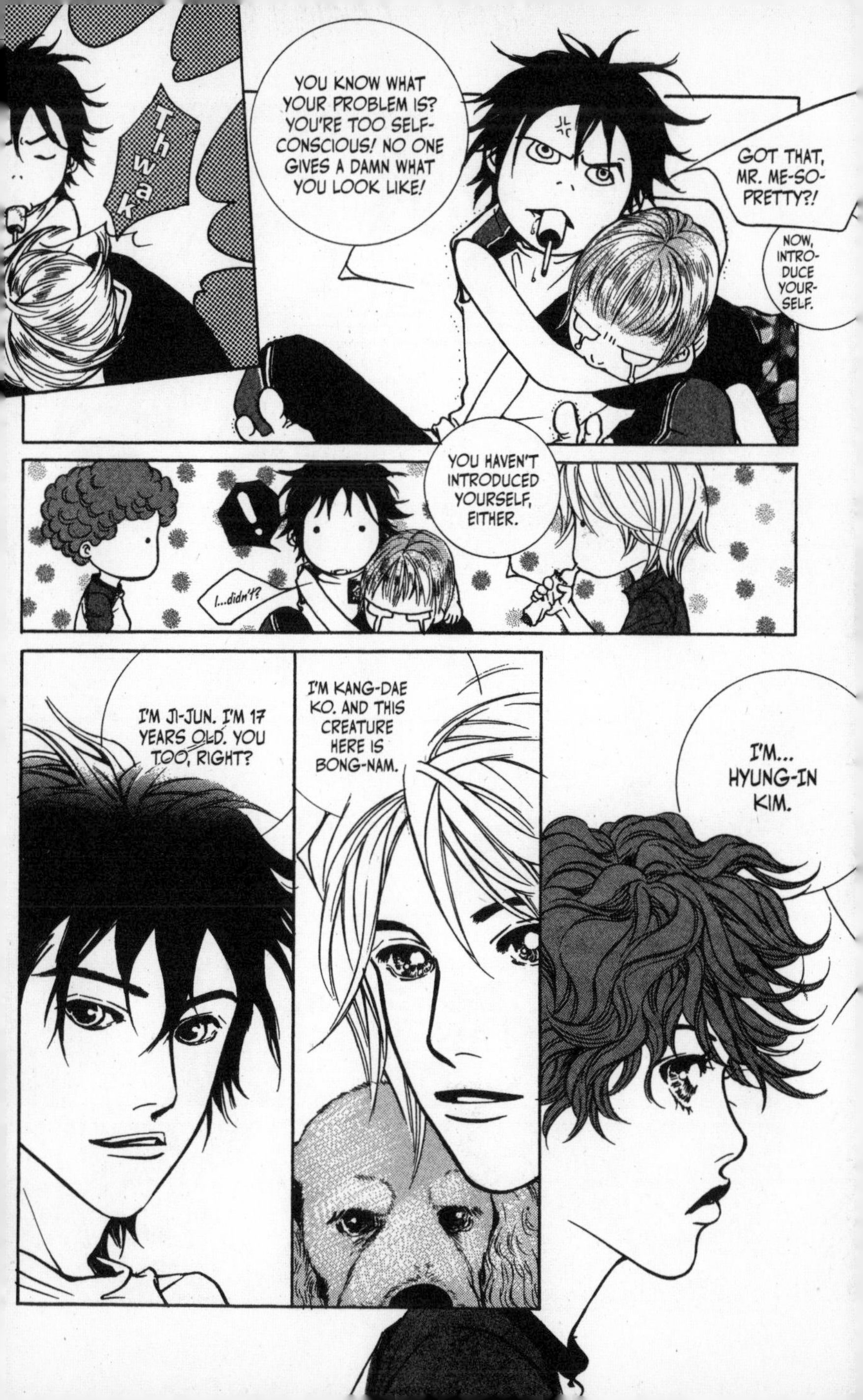
Thwak
YOU KNOW WHAT YOUR PROBLEM IS? YOU'RE TOO SELF-CONSCIOUS! NO ONE GIVES A DAMN WHAT YOU LOOK LIKE!
GOT THAT, MR. ME-SO-PRETTY?!
NOW, INTRODUCE YOURSELF.
!
I...didn't?
YOU HAVEN'T INTRODUCED YOURSELF, EITHER.
I'M JI-JUN. I'M 17 YEARS OLD. YOU TOO, RIGHT?
I'M KANG-DAE KO. AND THIS CREATURE HERE IS BONG-NAM.
I'M... HYUNG-IN KIM.

JI-HO
LEE.

OOH, HE'S SO CUTE!

Ah-ha!

You just thought, "Ooh, he's so cute!" Right?!

That does it!

I'll take this weirdo off your hands! Take your time, Kang-Dae!

Waaah, noooo!

Can he read minds?

O-okay.

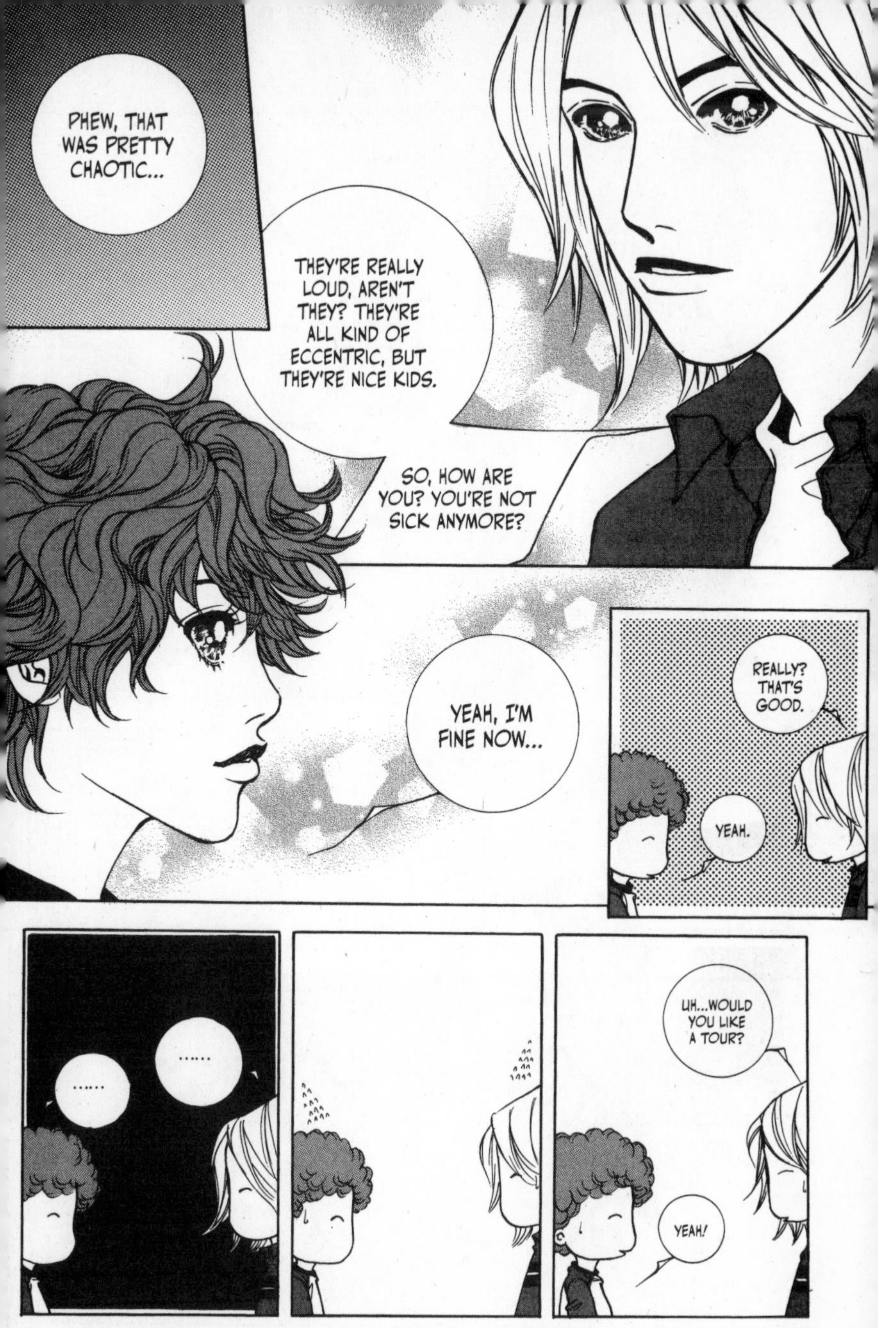
PHEW, THAT WAS PRETTY CHAOTIC...
THEY'RE REALLY LOUD, AREN'T THEY? THEY'RE ALL KIND OF ECCENTRIC, BUT THEY'RE NICE KIDS.
SO, HOW ARE YOU? YOU'RE NOT SICK ANYMORE?
YEAH, I'M FINE NOW...
REALLY? THAT'S GOOD.
YEAH.
......
......
UH...WOULD YOU LIKE A TOUR?
YEAH!

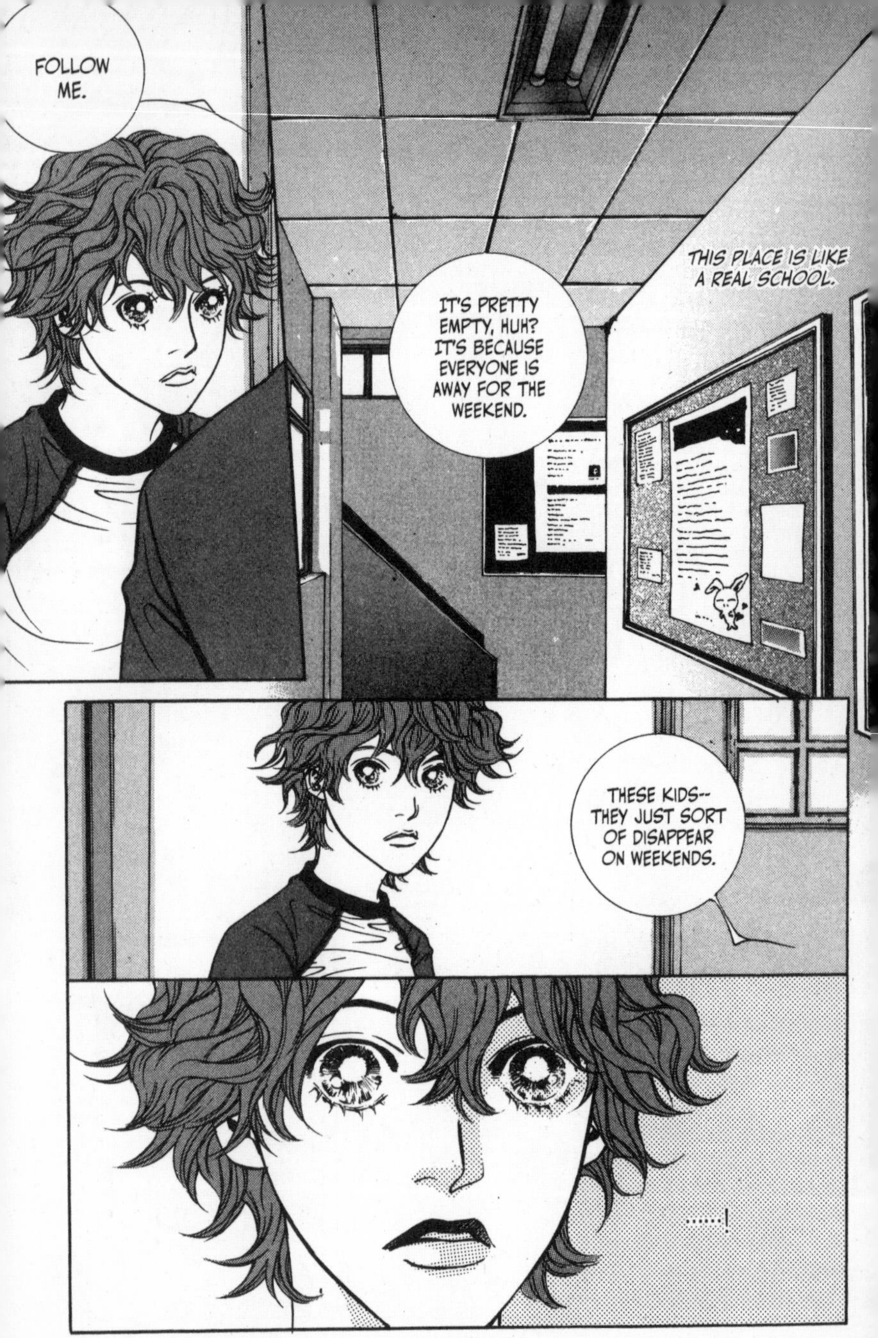
FOLLOW ME.
IT'S PRETTY EMPTY, HUH? IT'S BECAUSE EVERYONE IS AWAY FOR THE WEEKEND.
THIS PLACE IS LIKE A REAL SCHOOL.
THESE KIDS-- THEY JUST SORT OF DISAPPEAR ON WEEKENDS.
......!

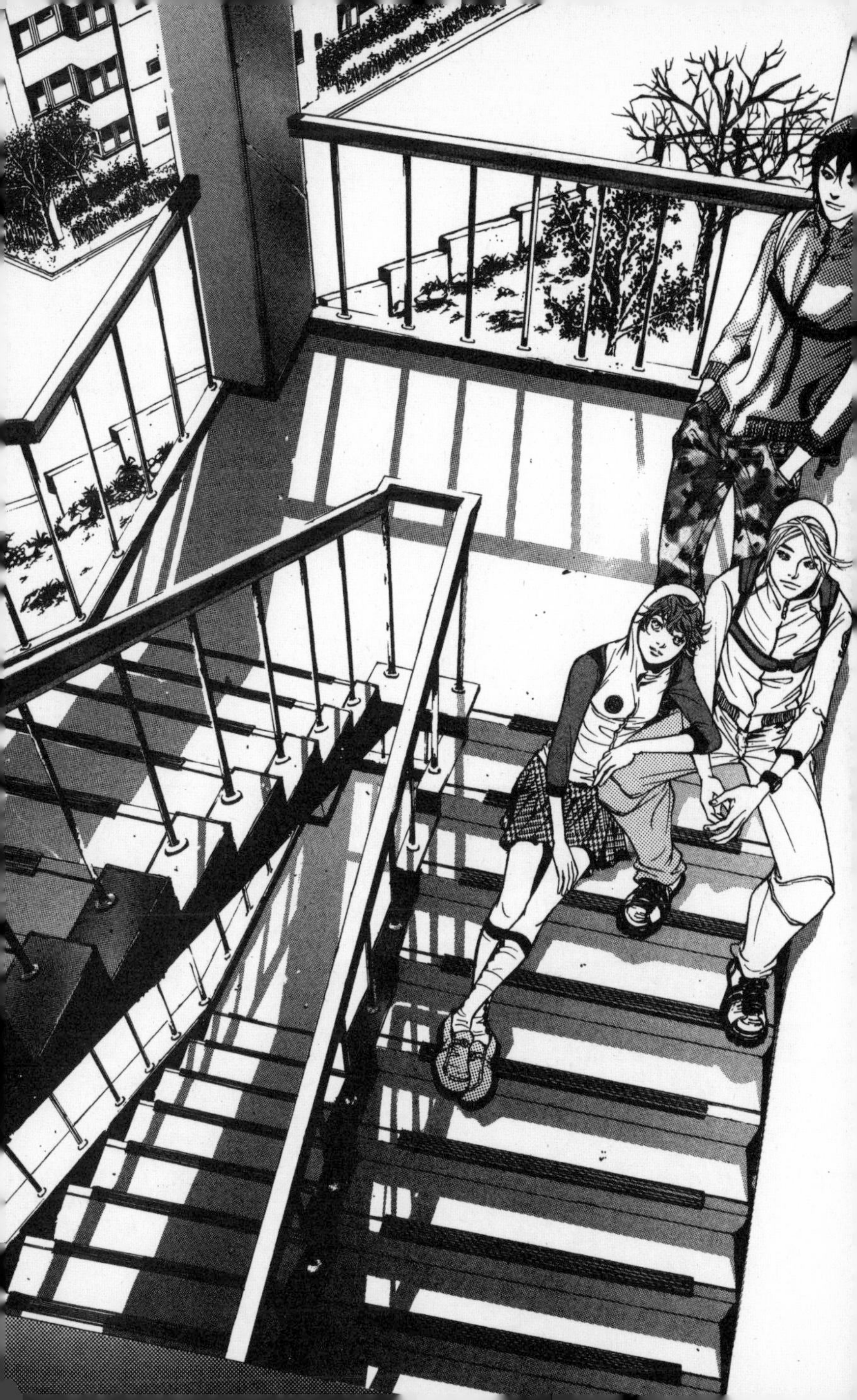

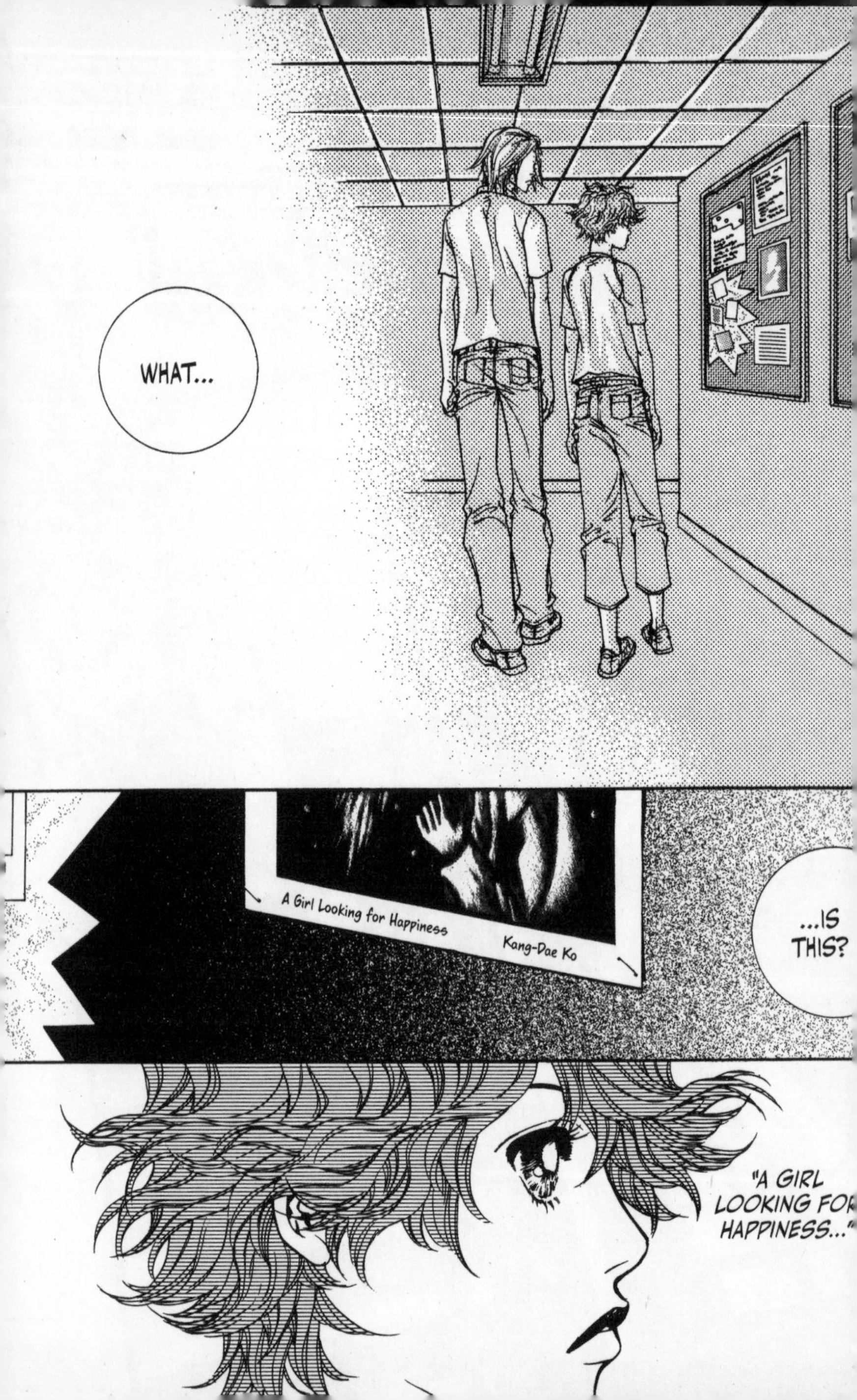
WHAT...
A Girl Looking for Happiness
Kang-Dae Ko
...IS THIS?
"A GIRL LOOKING FOR HAPPINESS..."

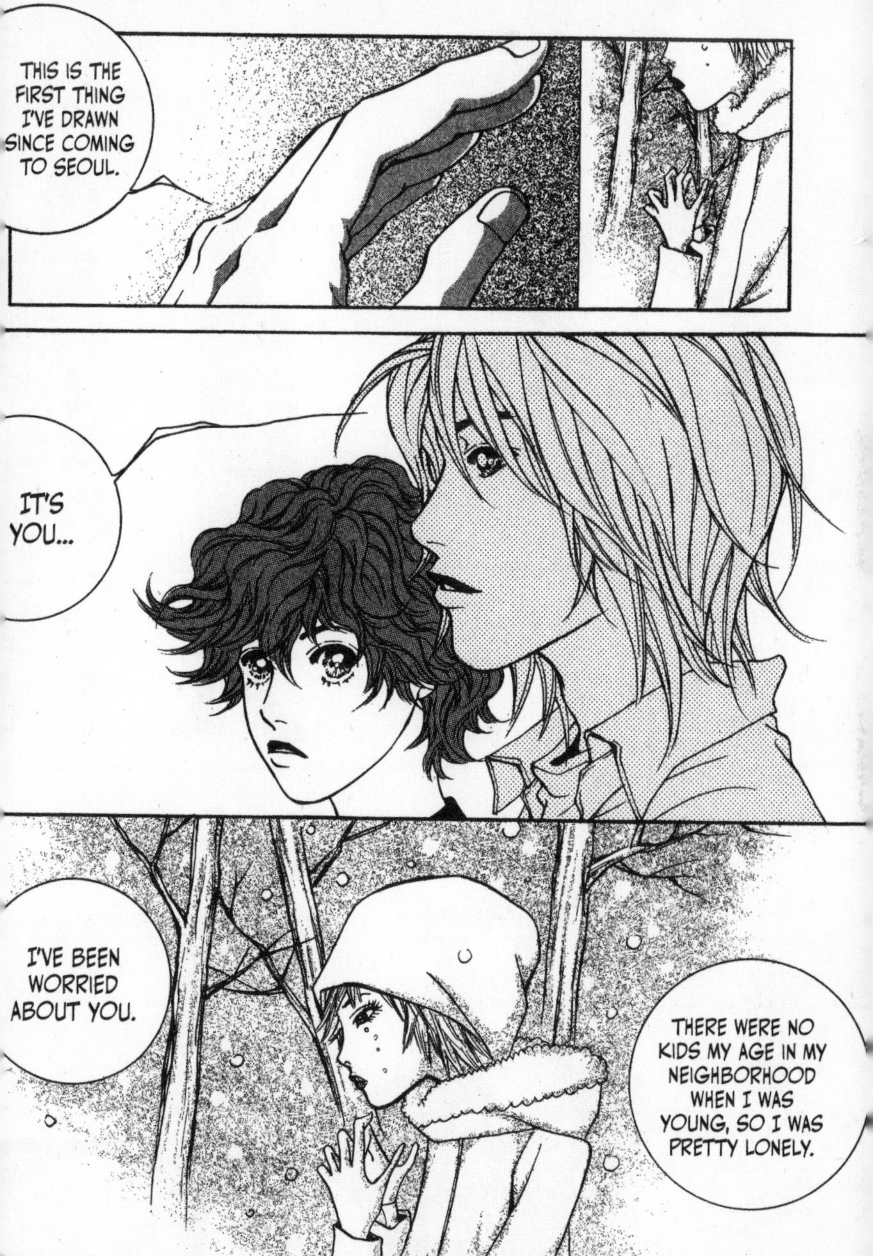
THIS IS THE FIRST THING I'VE DRAWN SINCE COMING TO SEOUL.
IT'S YOU...
I'VE BEEN WORRIED ABOUT YOU.
THERE WERE NO KIDS MY AGE IN MY NEIGHBORHOOD WHEN I WAS YOUNG, SO I WAS PRETTY LONELY.

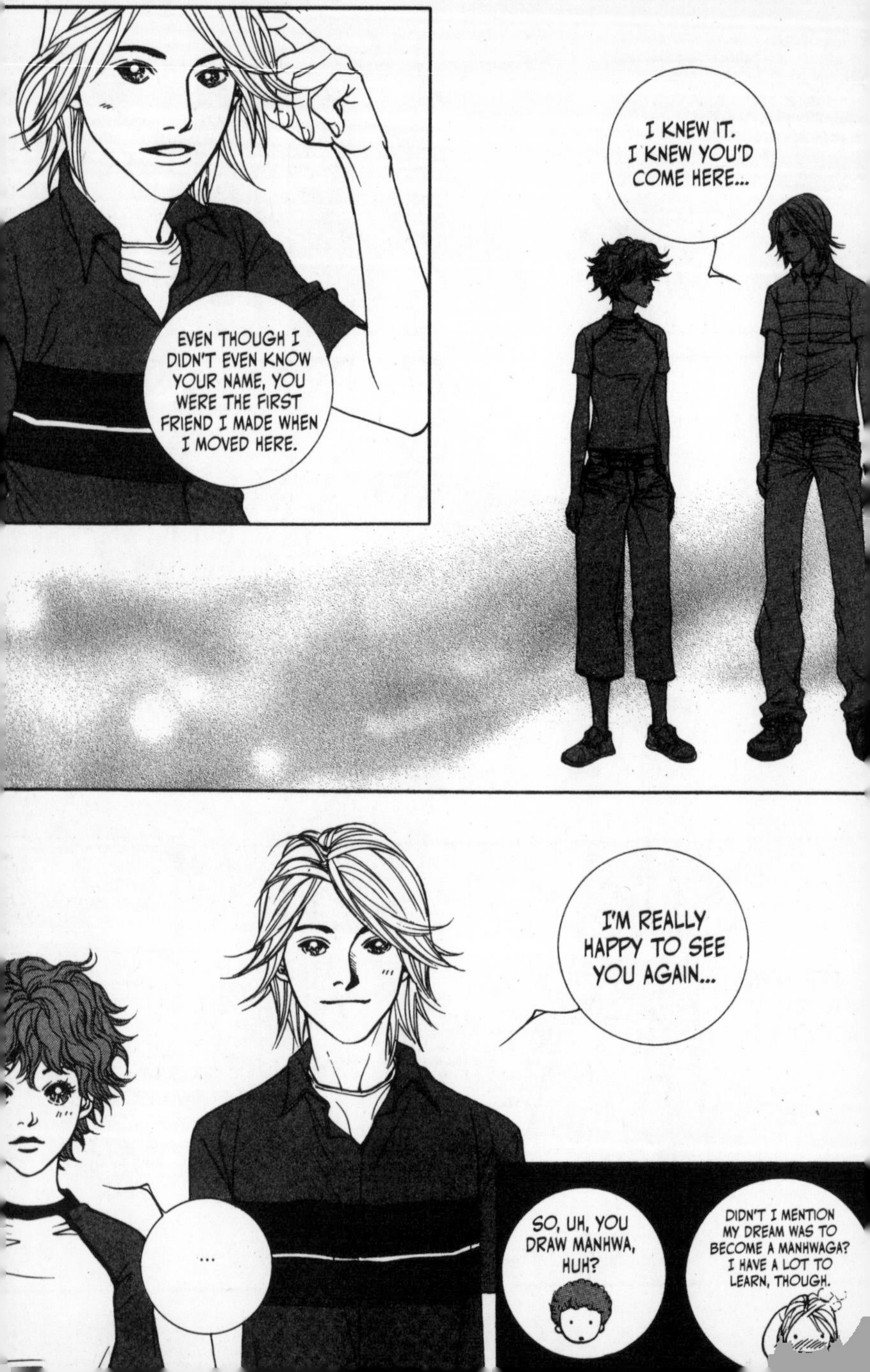
EVEN THOUGH I DIDN'T EVEN KNOW YOUR NAME, YOU WERE THE FIRST FRIEND I MADE WHEN I MOVED HERE.
I KNEW IT. I KNEW YOU'D COME HERE...
I'M REALLY HAPPY TO SEE YOU AGAIN...
...
SO, UH, YOU DRAW MANHWA, HUH?
DIDN'T I MENTION MY DREAM WAS TO BECOME A MANHWAGA? I HAVE A LOT TO LEARN, THOUGH.

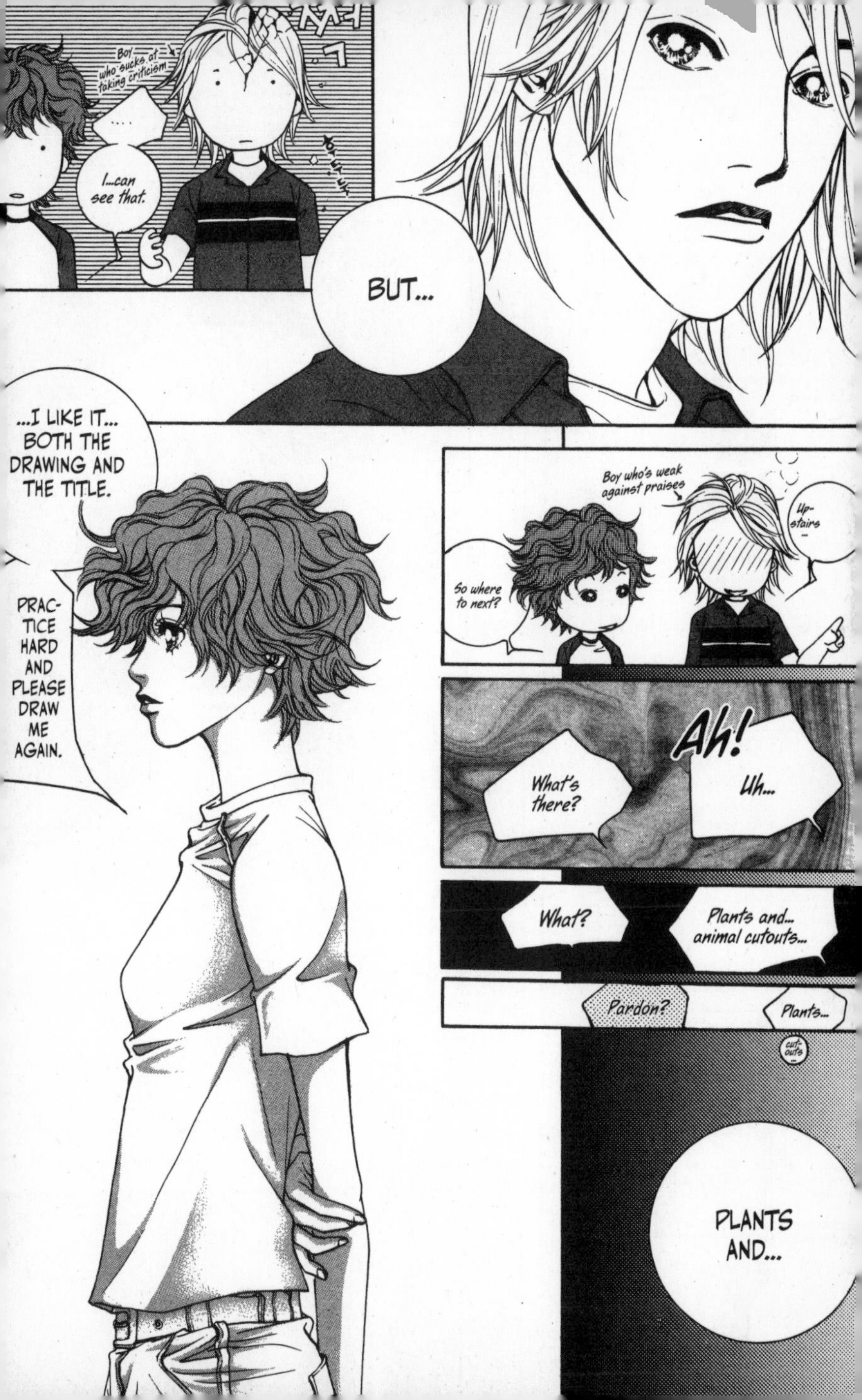
Boy who sucks at taking criticism
....
I...can see that.
BUT...
...I LIKE IT... BOTH THE DRAWING AND THE TITLE.
PRAC-TICE HARD AND PLEASE DRAW ME AGAIN.
Boy who's weak against praises
So where to next?
Up-stairs...
Ah!
What's there?
Uh...
What?
Plants and... animal cutouts...
Pardon?
Plants...
cut-outs...
PLANTS AND...

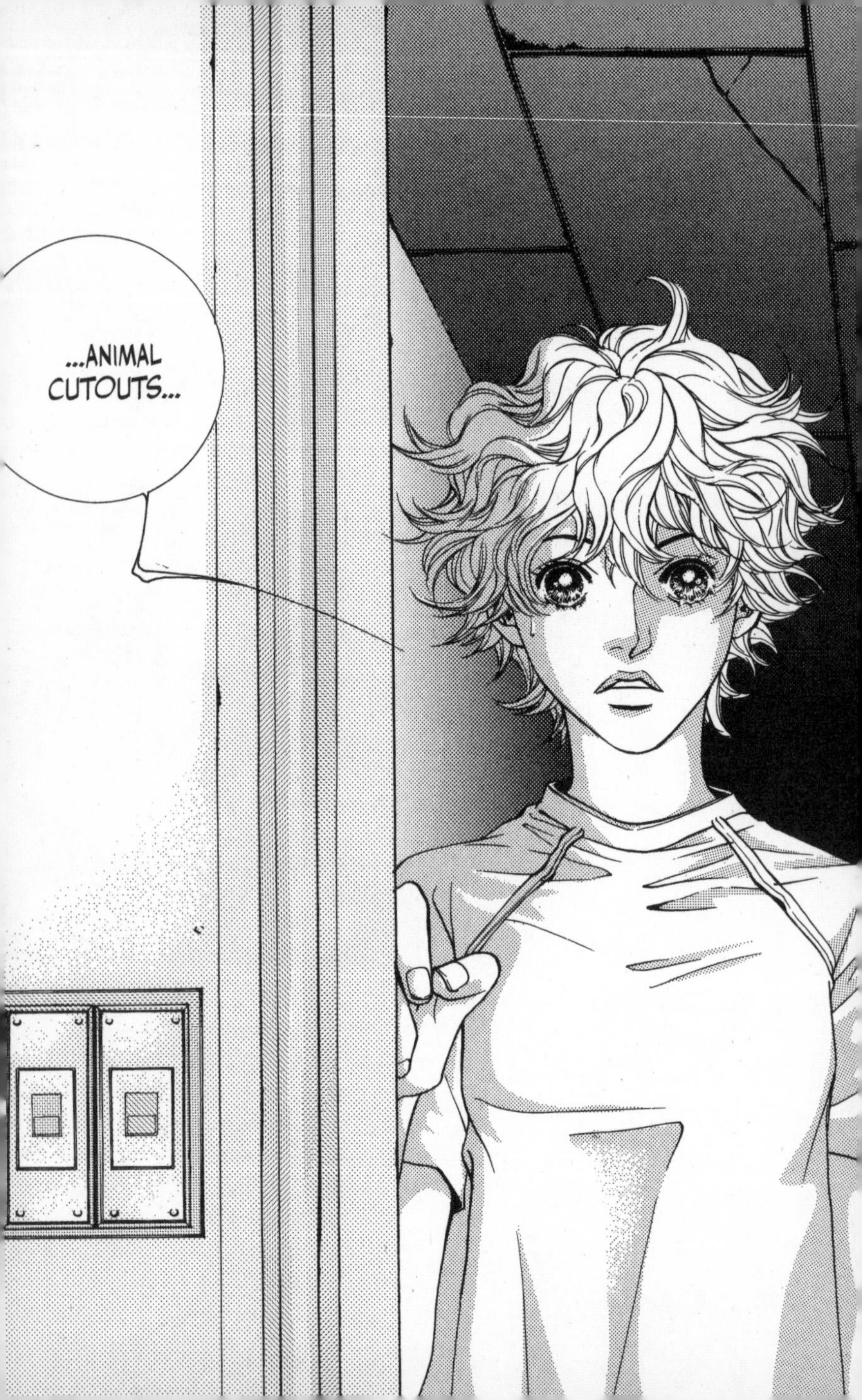
...ANIMAL CUTOUTS...

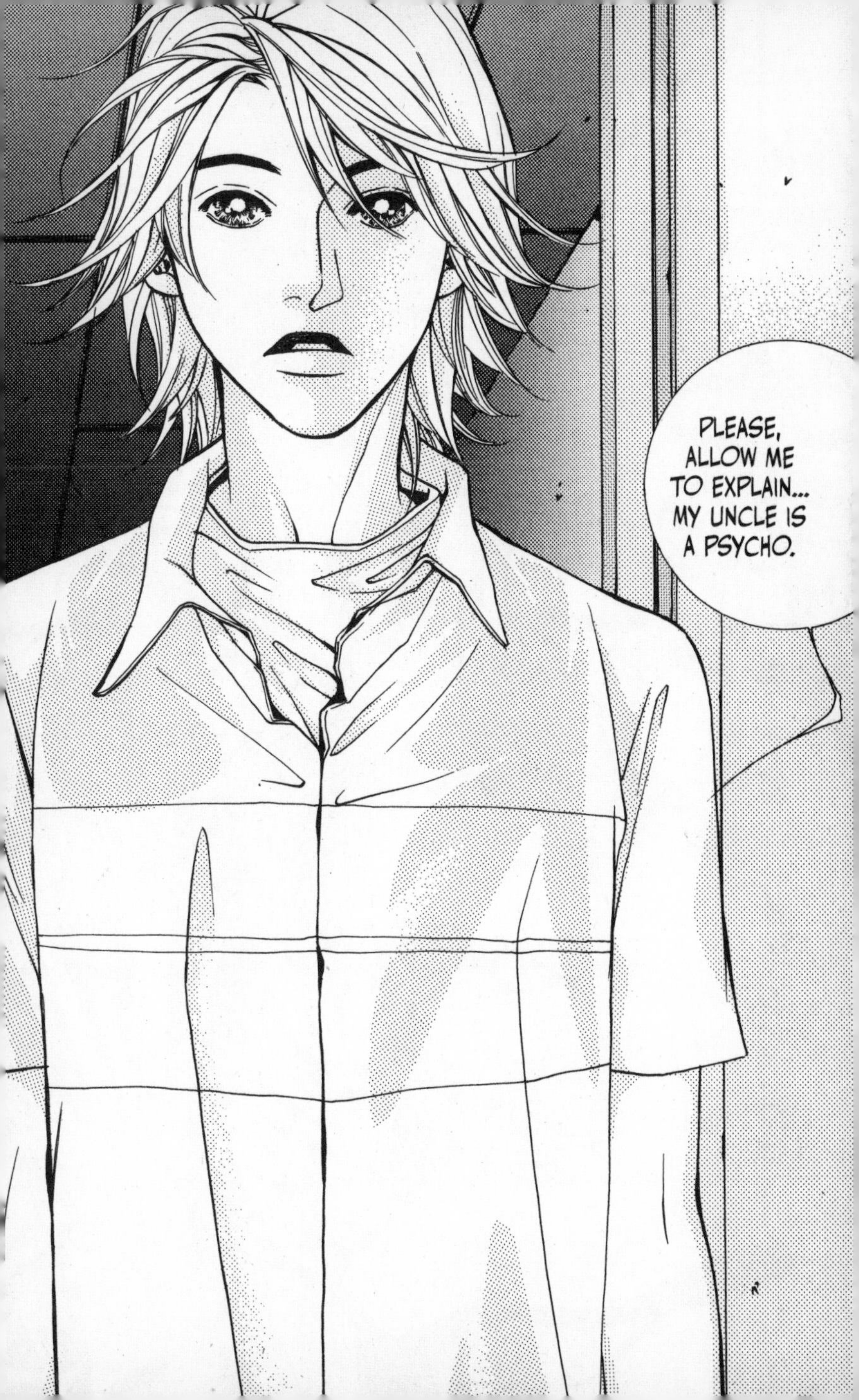
PLEASE, ALLOW ME TO EXPLAIN... MY UNCLE IS A PSYCHO.

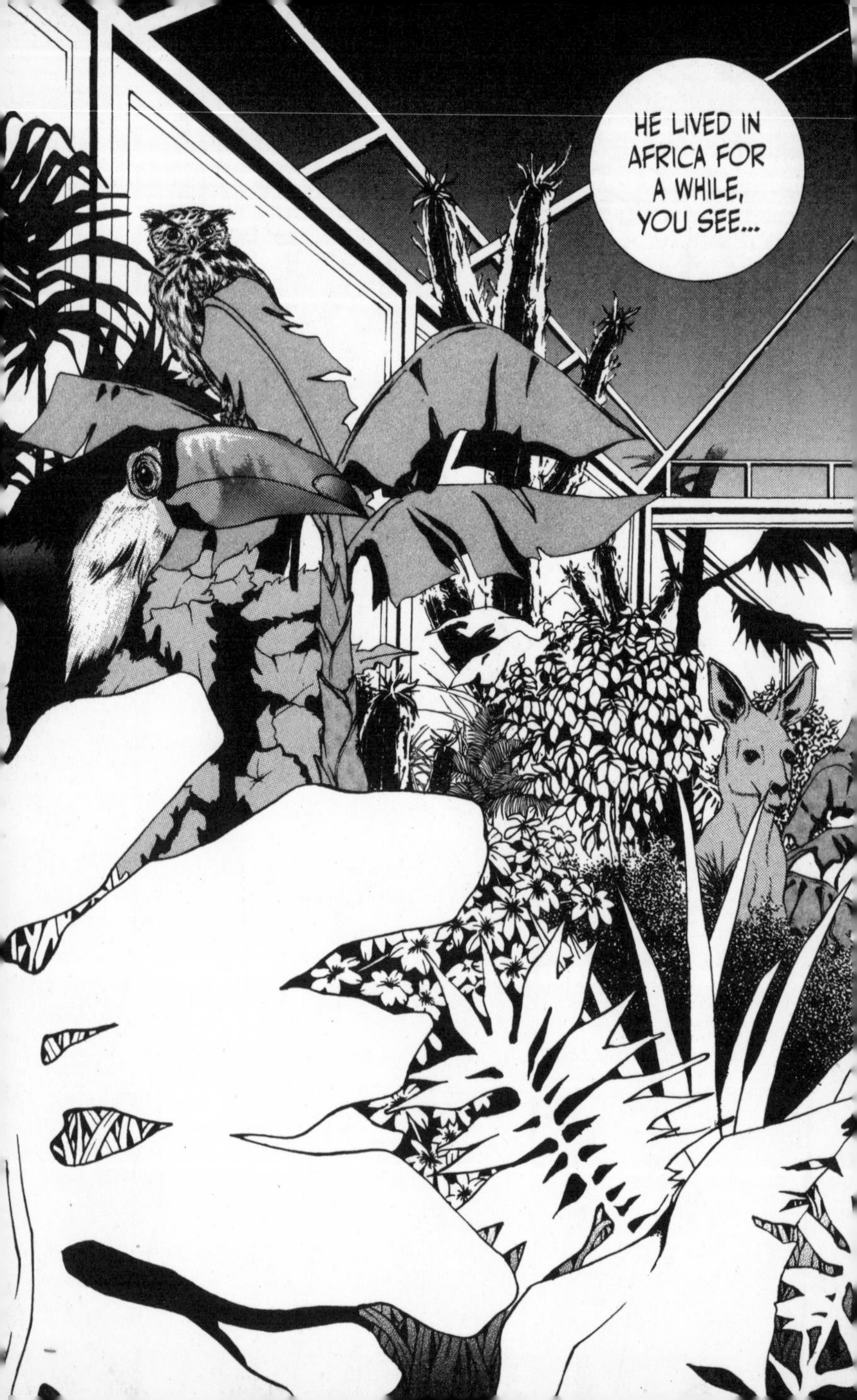
HE LIVED IN AFRICA FOR A WHILE, YOU SEE...

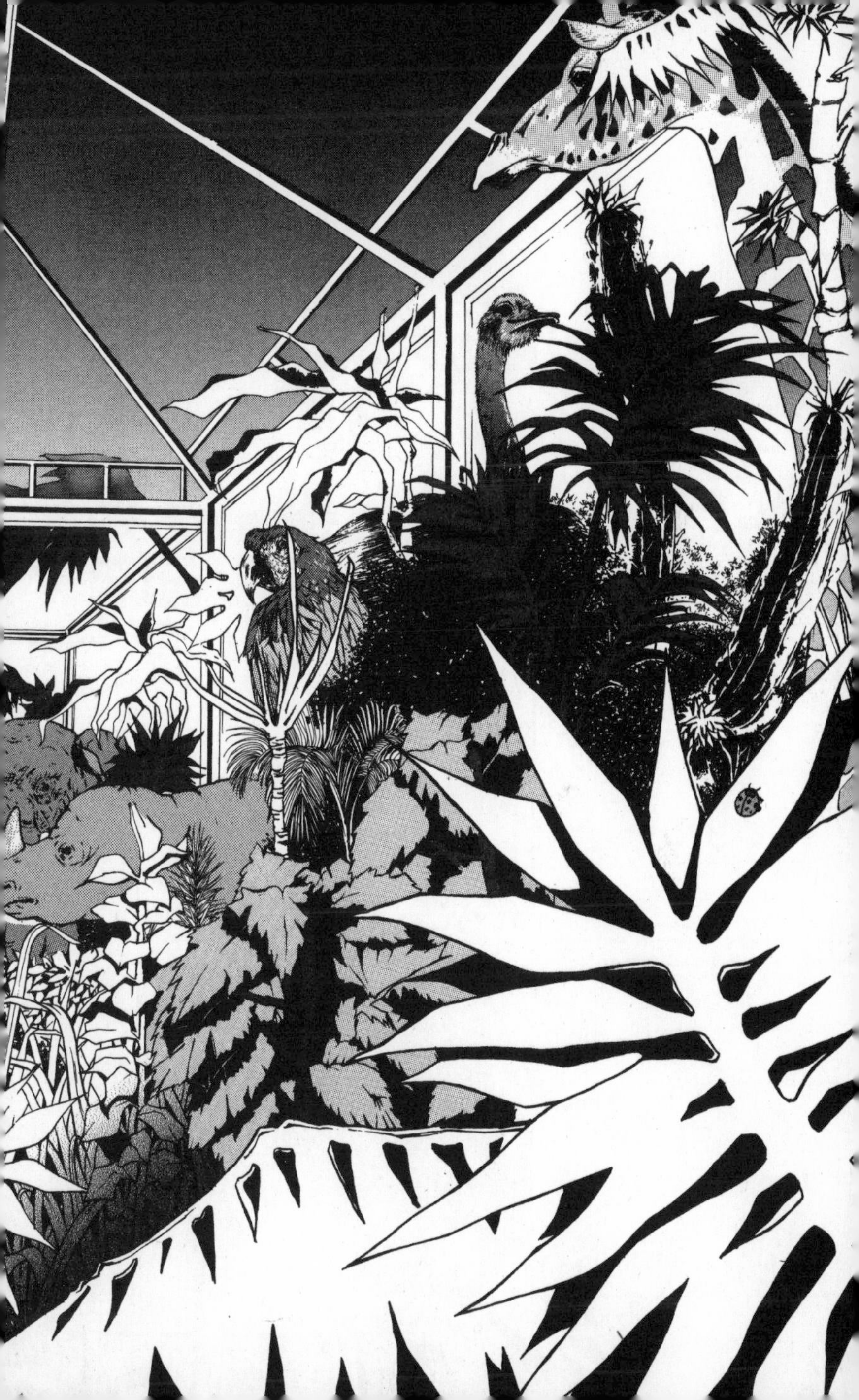

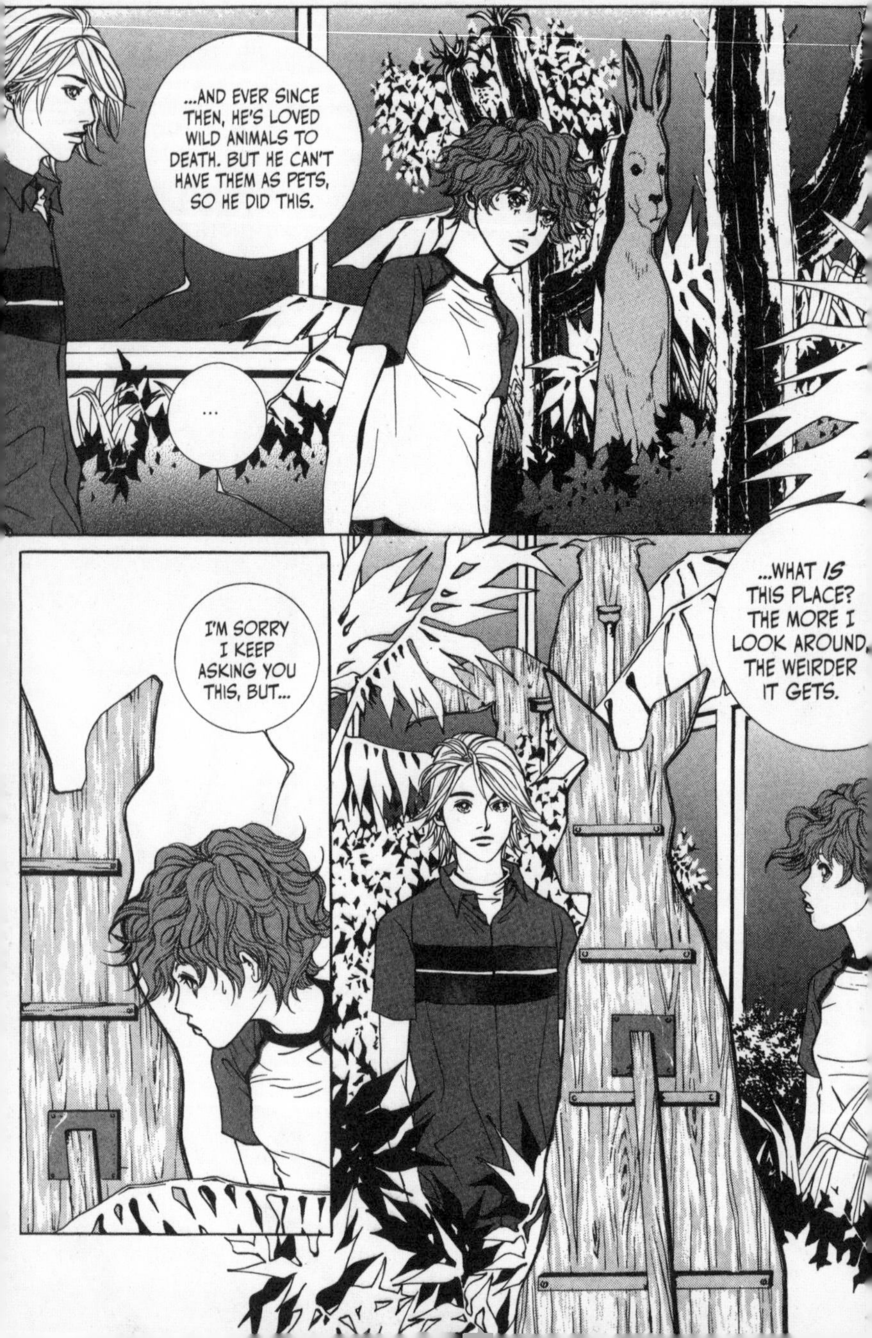
...AND EVER SINCE THEN, HE'S LOVED WILD ANIMALS TO DEATH. BUT HE CAN'T HAVE THEM AS PETS, SO HE DID THIS.
...
I'M SORRY I KEEP ASKING YOU THIS, BUT...
...WHAT *IS* THIS PLACE? THE MORE I LOOK AROUND, THE WEIRDER IT GETS.

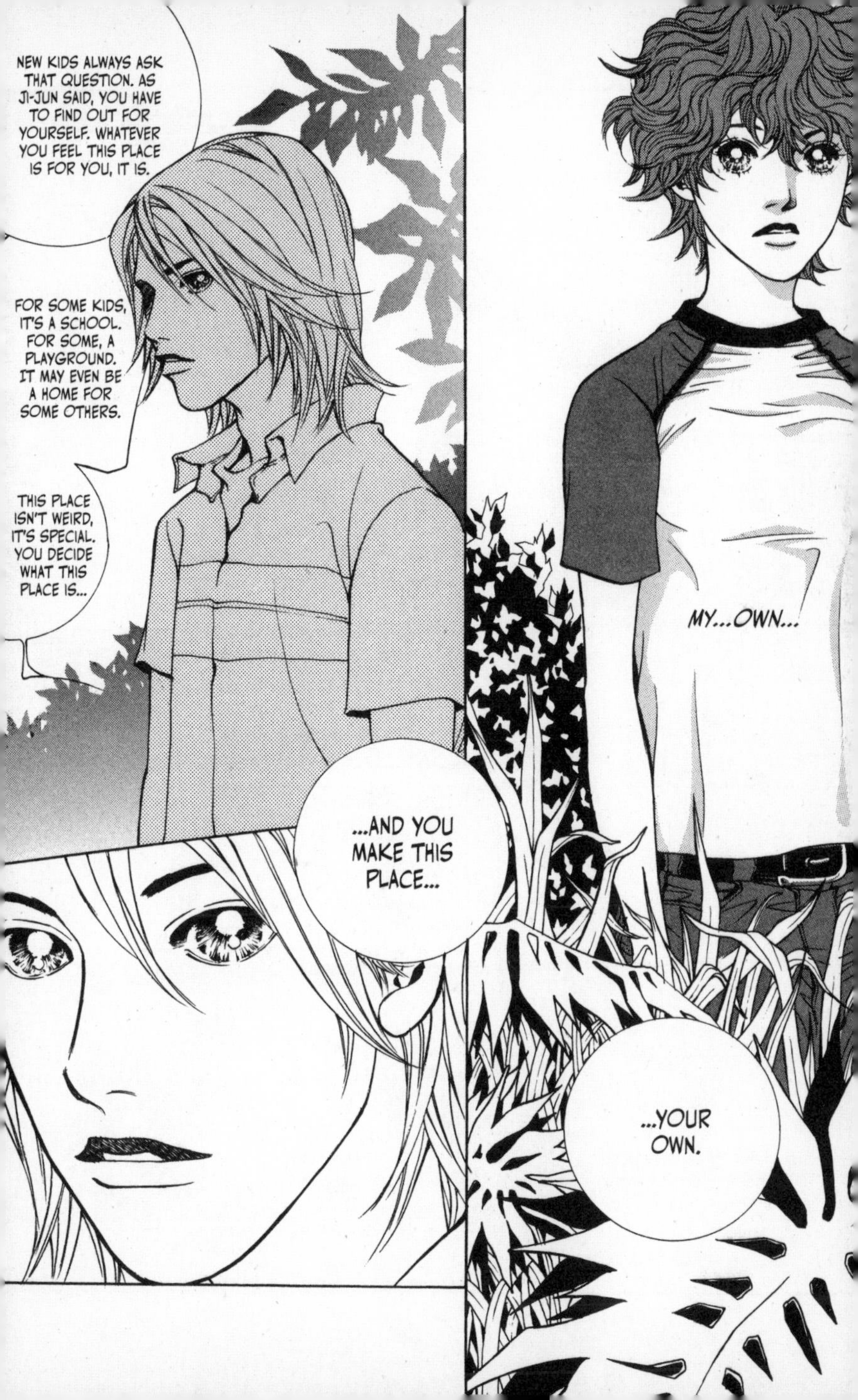
NEW KIDS ALWAYS ASK THAT QUESTION. AS JI-JUN SAID, YOU HAVE TO FIND OUT FOR YOURSELF. WHATEVER YOU FEEL THIS PLACE IS FOR YOU, IT IS.
FOR SOME KIDS, IT'S A SCHOOL. FOR SOME, A PLAYGROUND. IT MAY EVEN BE A HOME FOR SOME OTHERS.
THIS PLACE ISN'T WEIRD, IT'S SPECIAL. YOU DECIDE WHAT THIS PLACE IS...
...AND YOU MAKE THIS PLACE...
MY...OWN...
...YOUR OWN.

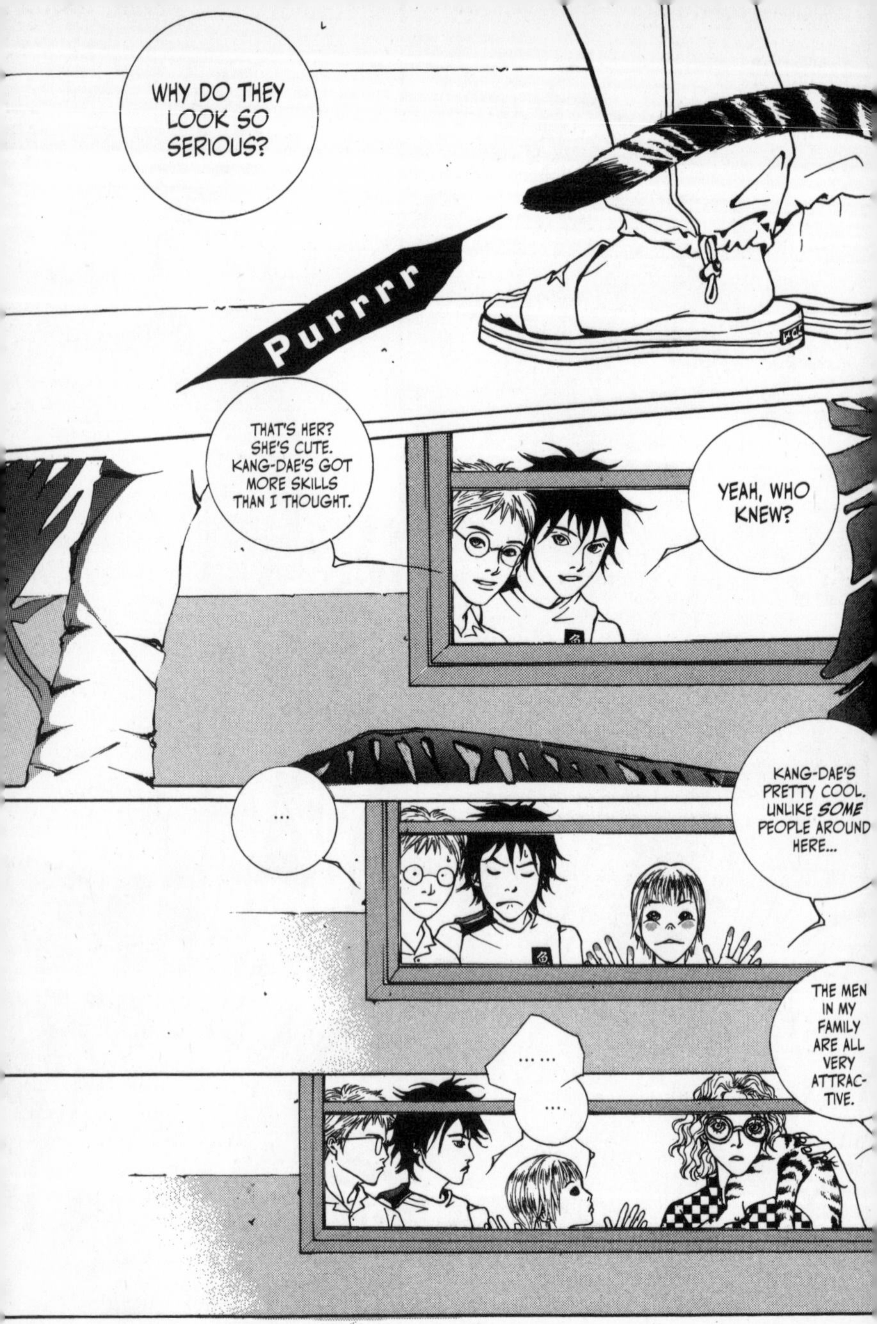
WHY DO THEY LOOK SO SERIOUS?
Purrrr
THAT'S HER? SHE'S CUTE. KANG-DAE'S GOT MORE SKILLS THAN I THOUGHT.
YEAH, WHO KNEW?
...
KANG-DAE'S PRETTY COOL. UNLIKE *SOME* PEOPLE AROUND HERE...
......
....
THE MEN IN MY FAMILY ARE ALL VERY ATTRAC-TIVE.

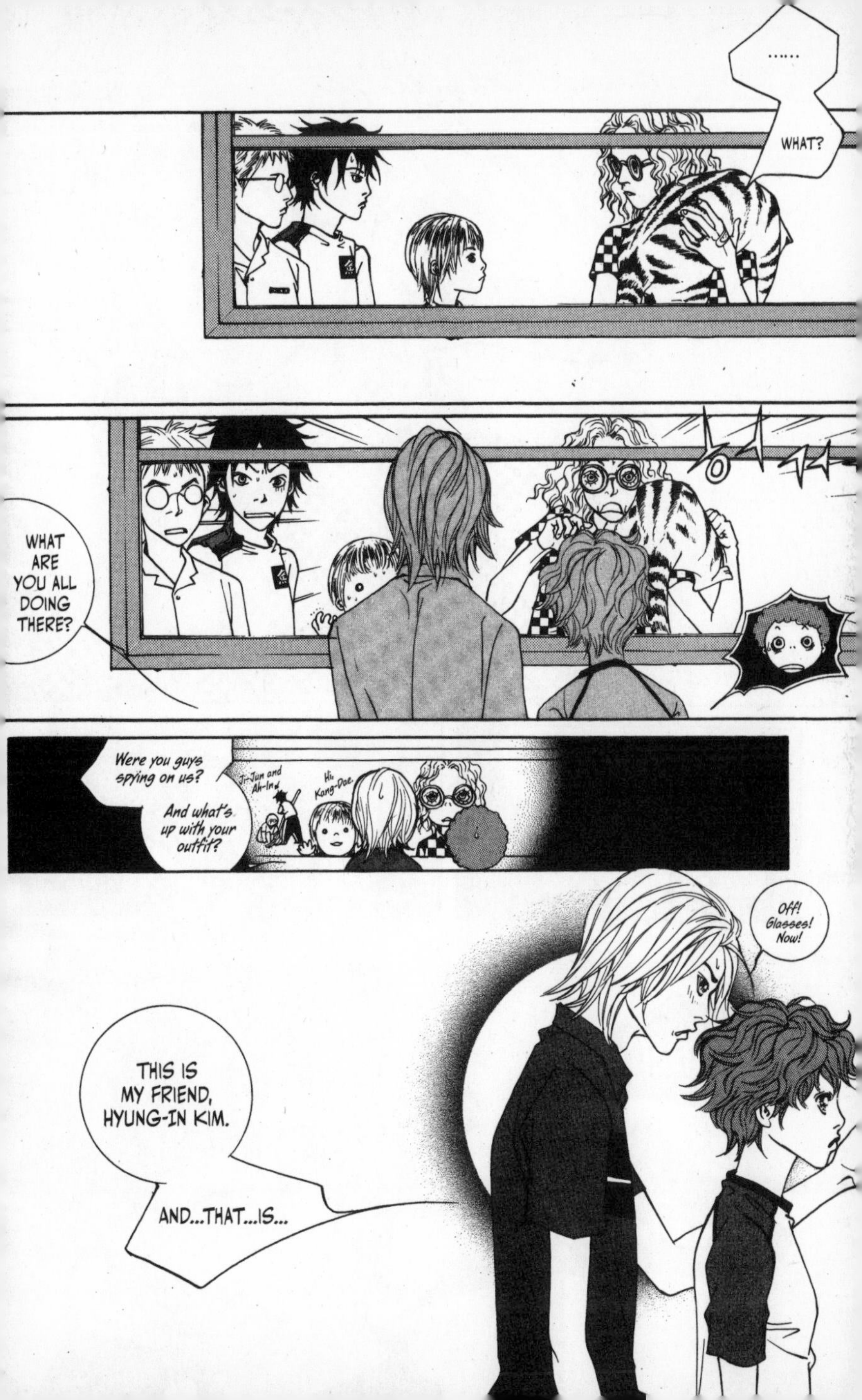
......
WHAT?
WHAT ARE YOU ALL DOING THERE?
Were you guys spying on us?
And what's up with your outfit?
Ji-Jun and Ah-In.
Hi, Kang-Dae.
Off! Glasses! Now!
THIS IS MY FRIEND, HYUNG-IN KIM.
AND...THAT...IS...

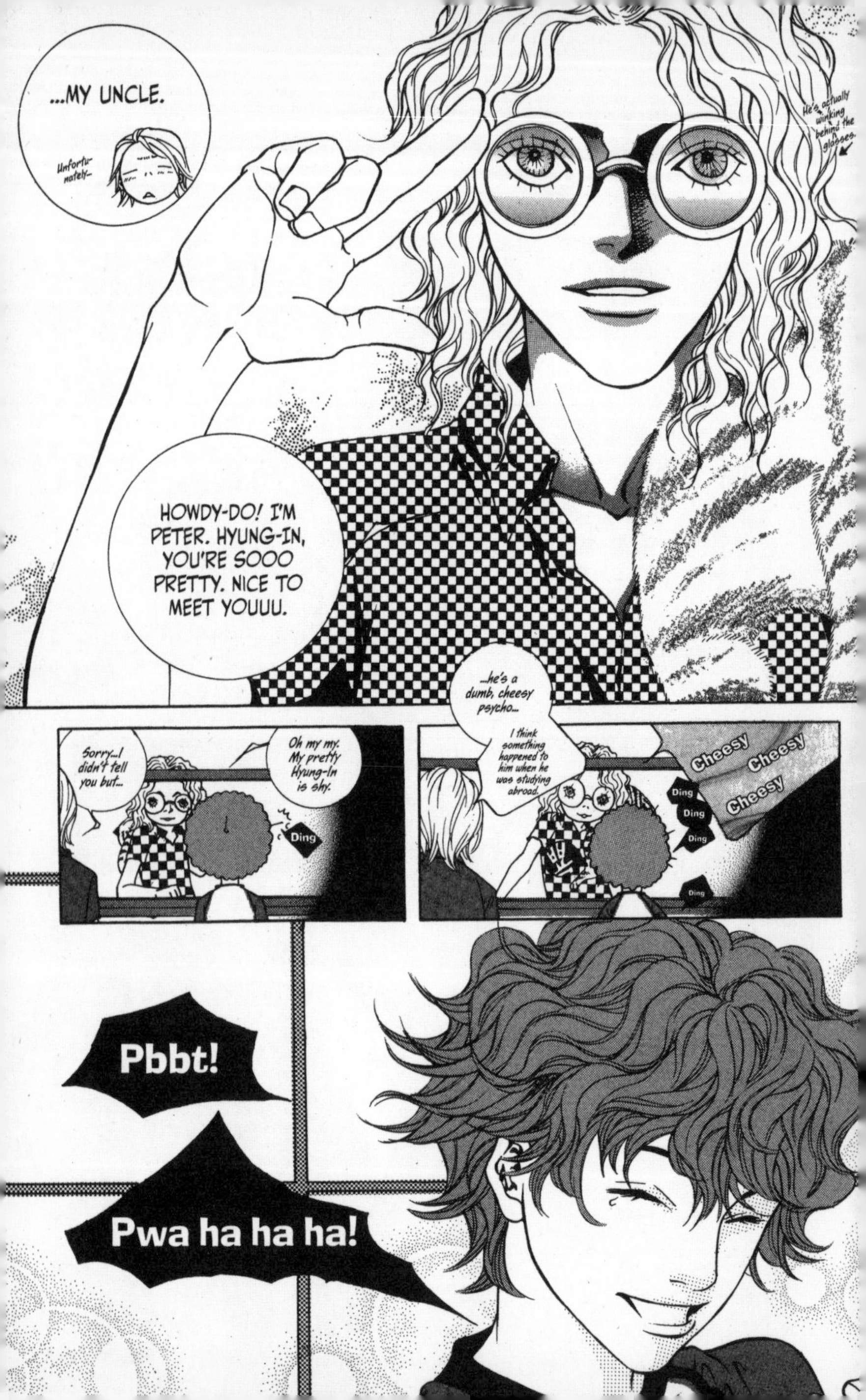
...MY UNCLE.
Unfortu-nately...
He's actually winking behind the glasses.
HOWDY-DO! I'M PETER. HYUNG-IN, YOU'RE SOOO PRETTY. NICE TO MEET YOUUU.
Sorry...I didn't tell you but...
Oh my my. My pretty Hyung-In is shy.
Ding
...he's a dumb, cheesy psycho...
I think something happened to him when he was studying abroad.
Cheesy
Cheesy
Cheesy
Ding
Ding
Ding
Ding
Pbbt!
Pwa ha ha ha!

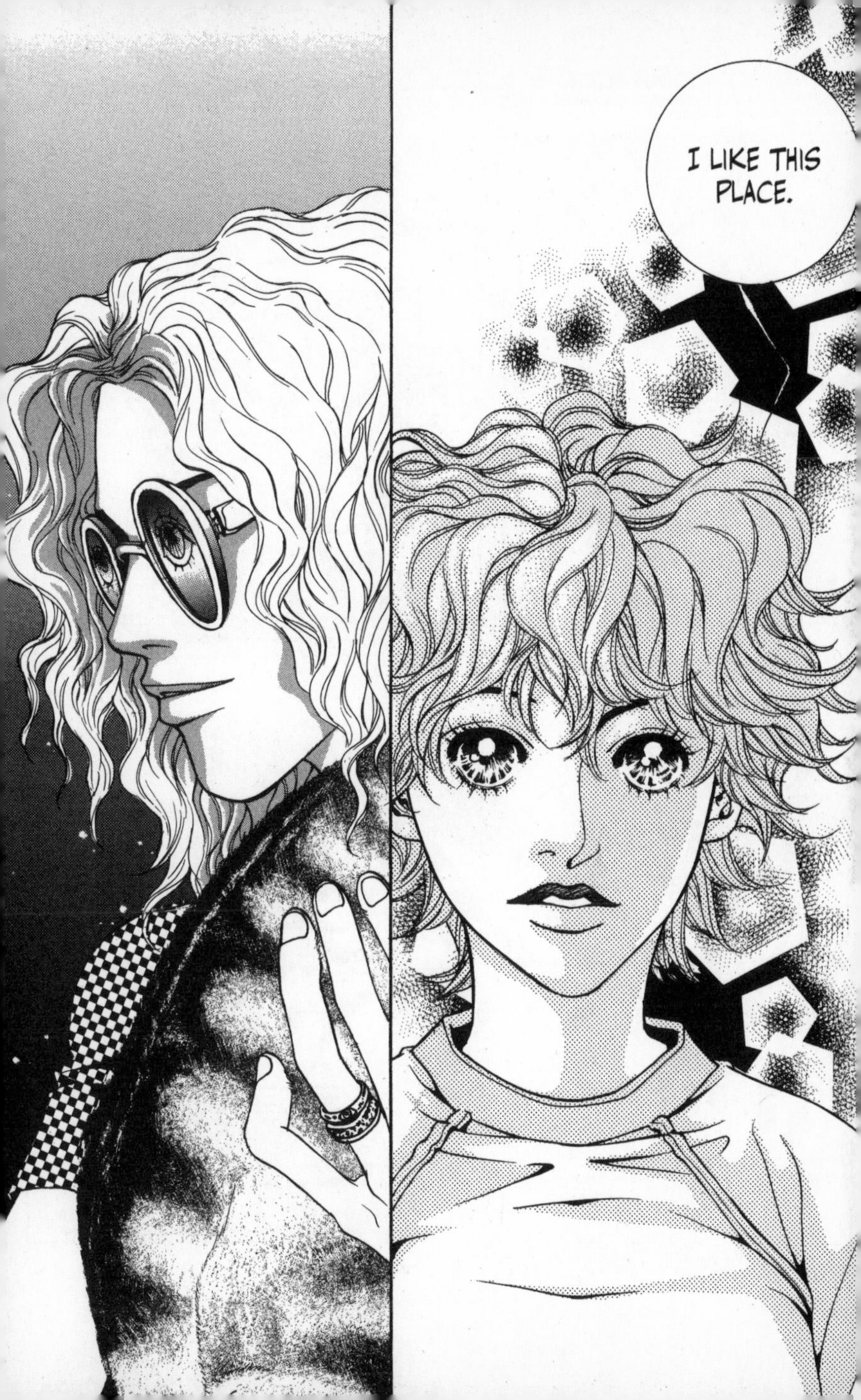
I LIKE THIS PLACE.

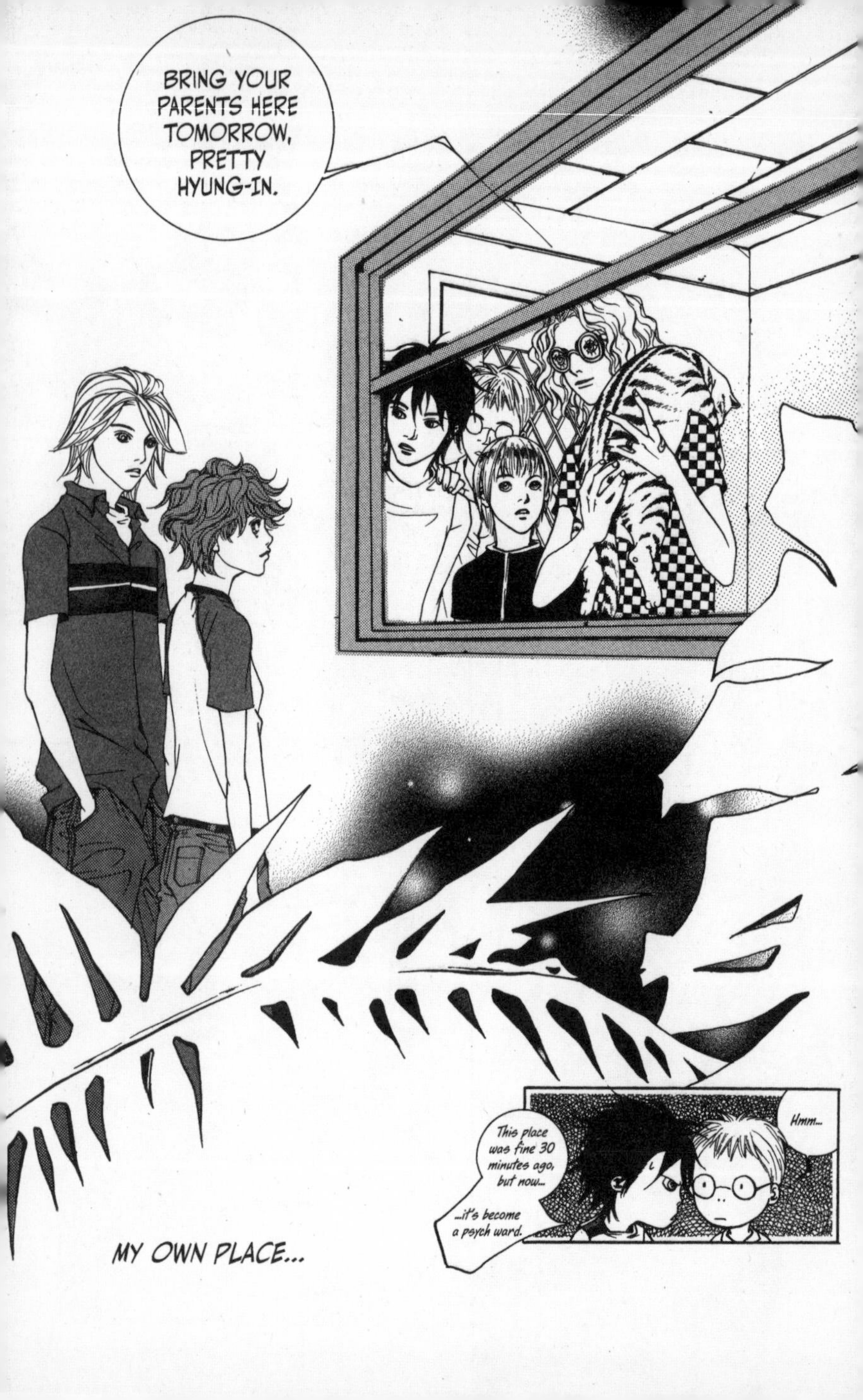
BRING YOUR PARENTS HERE TOMORROW, PRETTY HYUNG-IN.
MY OWN PLACE...
This place was fine 30 minutes ago, but now...
...it's become a psych ward.
Hmm...

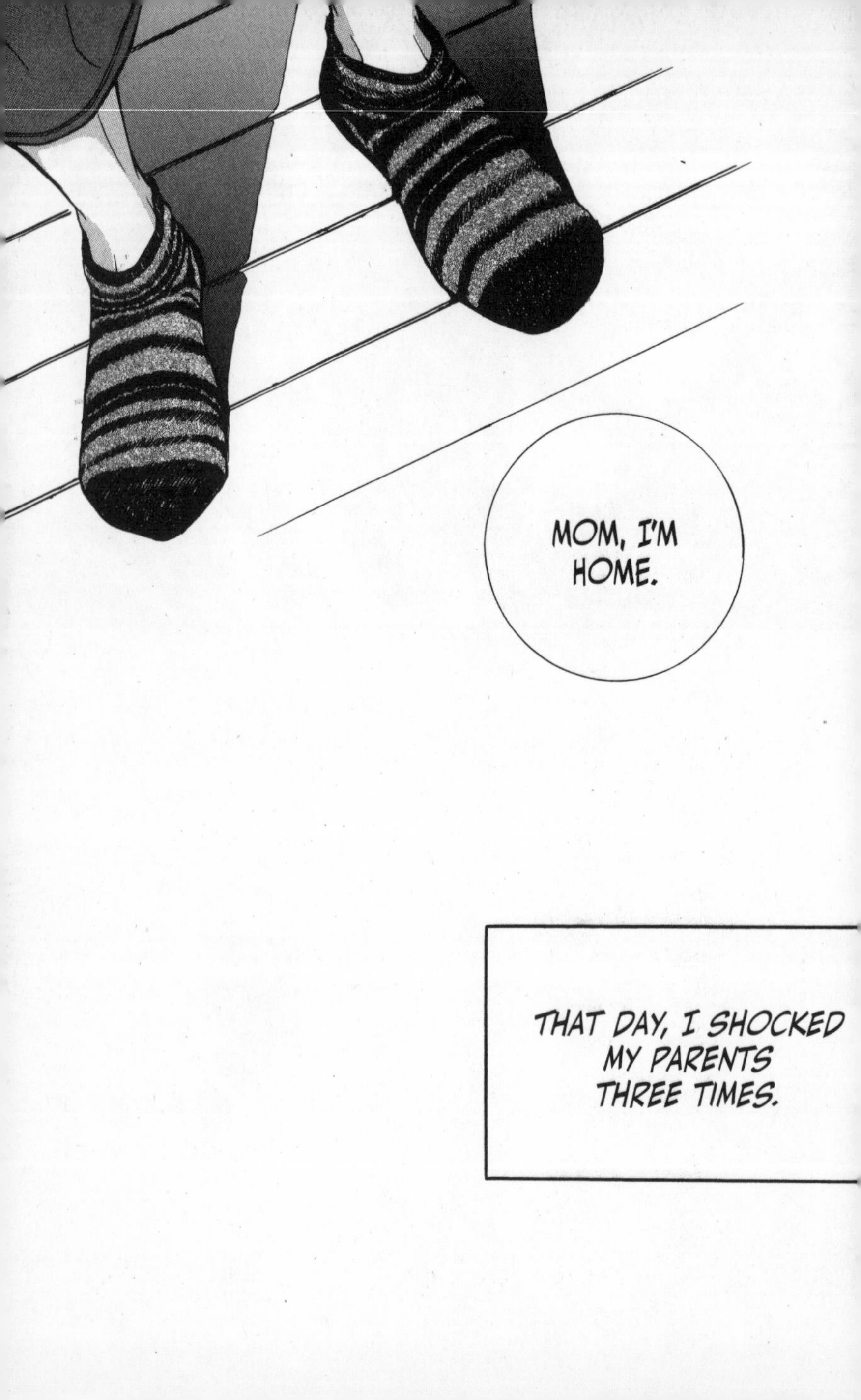
MOM, I'M HOME.
THAT DAY, I SHOCKED MY PARENTS THREE TIMES.

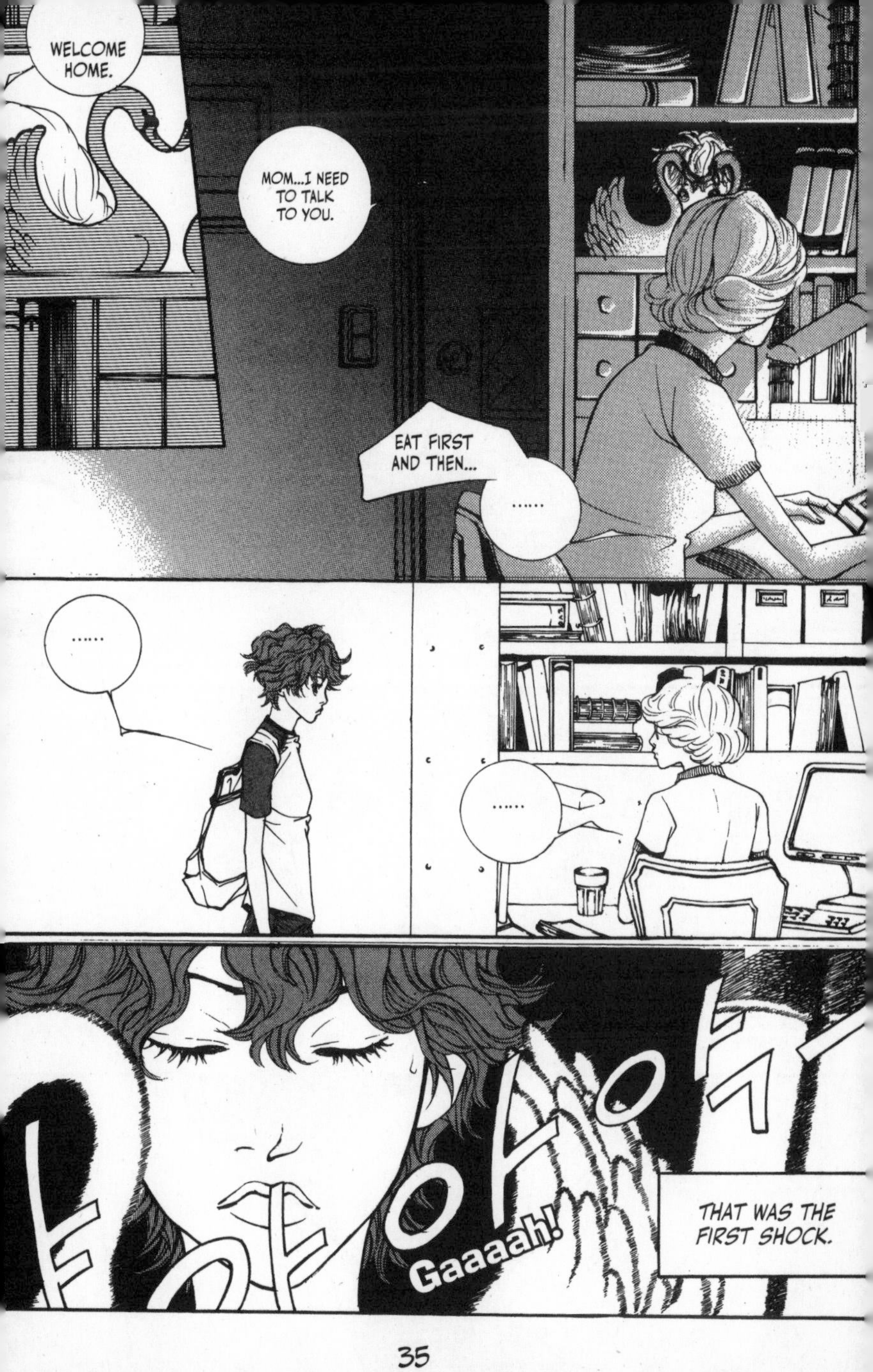
WELCOME HOME.
MOM...I NEED TO TALK TO YOU.
EAT FIRST AND THEN...
......
......
......
Gaaaah!
THAT WAS THE FIRST SHOCK.

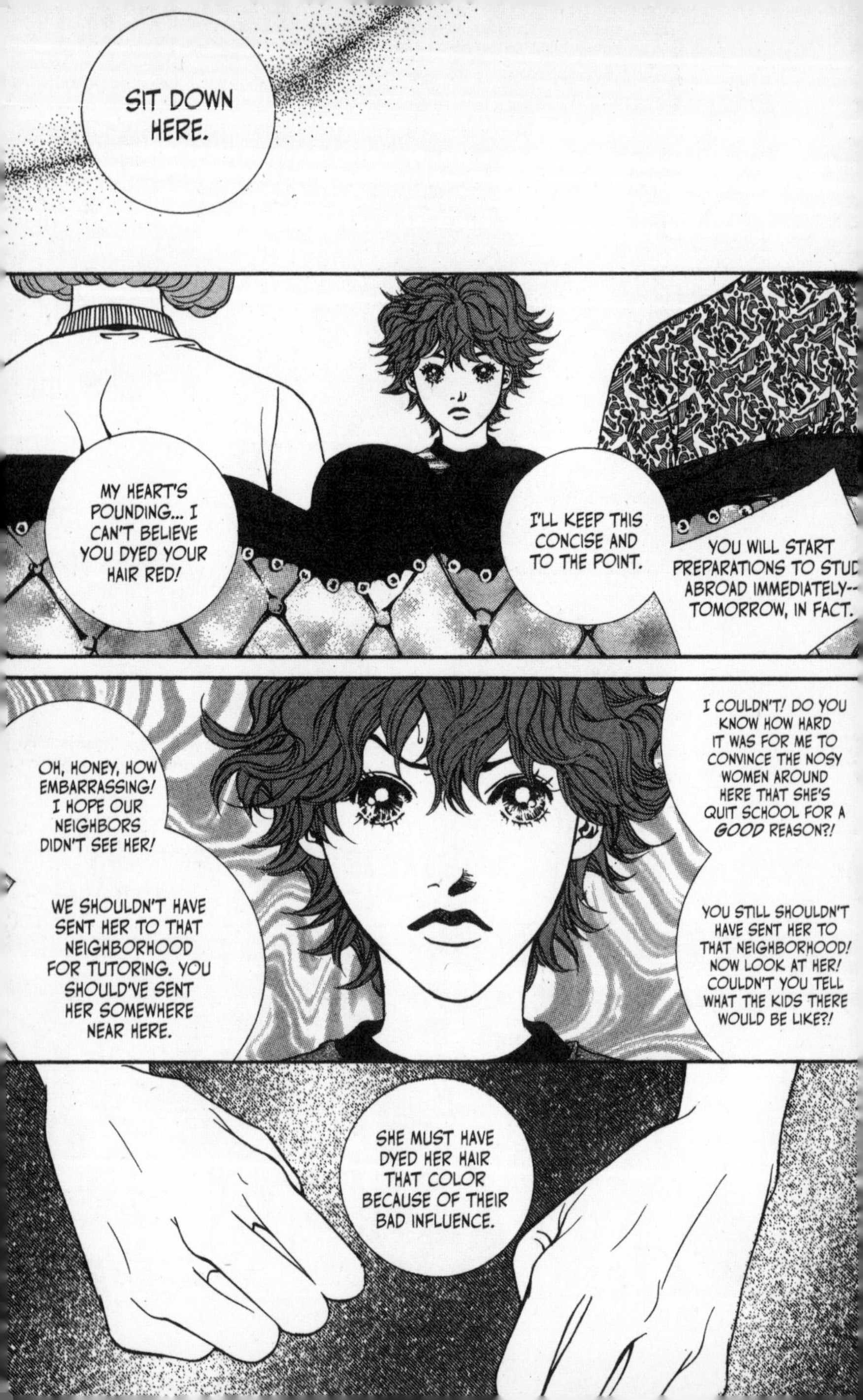
SIT DOWN HERE.
MY HEART'S POUNDING... I CAN'T BELIEVE YOU DYED YOUR HAIR RED!
I'LL KEEP THIS CONCISE AND TO THE POINT.
YOU WILL START PREPARATIONS TO STUD ABROAD IMMEDIATELY-- TOMORROW, IN FACT.
OH, HONEY, HOW EMBARRASSING! I HOPE OUR NEIGHBORS DIDN'T SEE HER!
WE SHOULDN'T HAVE SENT HER TO THAT NEIGHBORHOOD FOR TUTORING. YOU SHOULD'VE SENT HER SOMEWHERE NEAR HERE.
I COULDN'T! DO YOU KNOW HOW HARD IT WAS FOR ME TO CONVINCE THE NOSY WOMEN AROUND HERE THAT SHE'S QUIT SCHOOL FOR A *GOOD* REASON?!
YOU STILL SHOULDN'T HAVE SENT HER TO THAT NEIGHBORHOOD! NOW LOOK AT HER! COULDN'T YOU TELL WHAT THE KIDS THERE WOULD BE LIKE?!
SHE MUST HAVE DYED HER HAIR THAT COLOR BECAUSE OF THEIR BAD INFLUENCE.

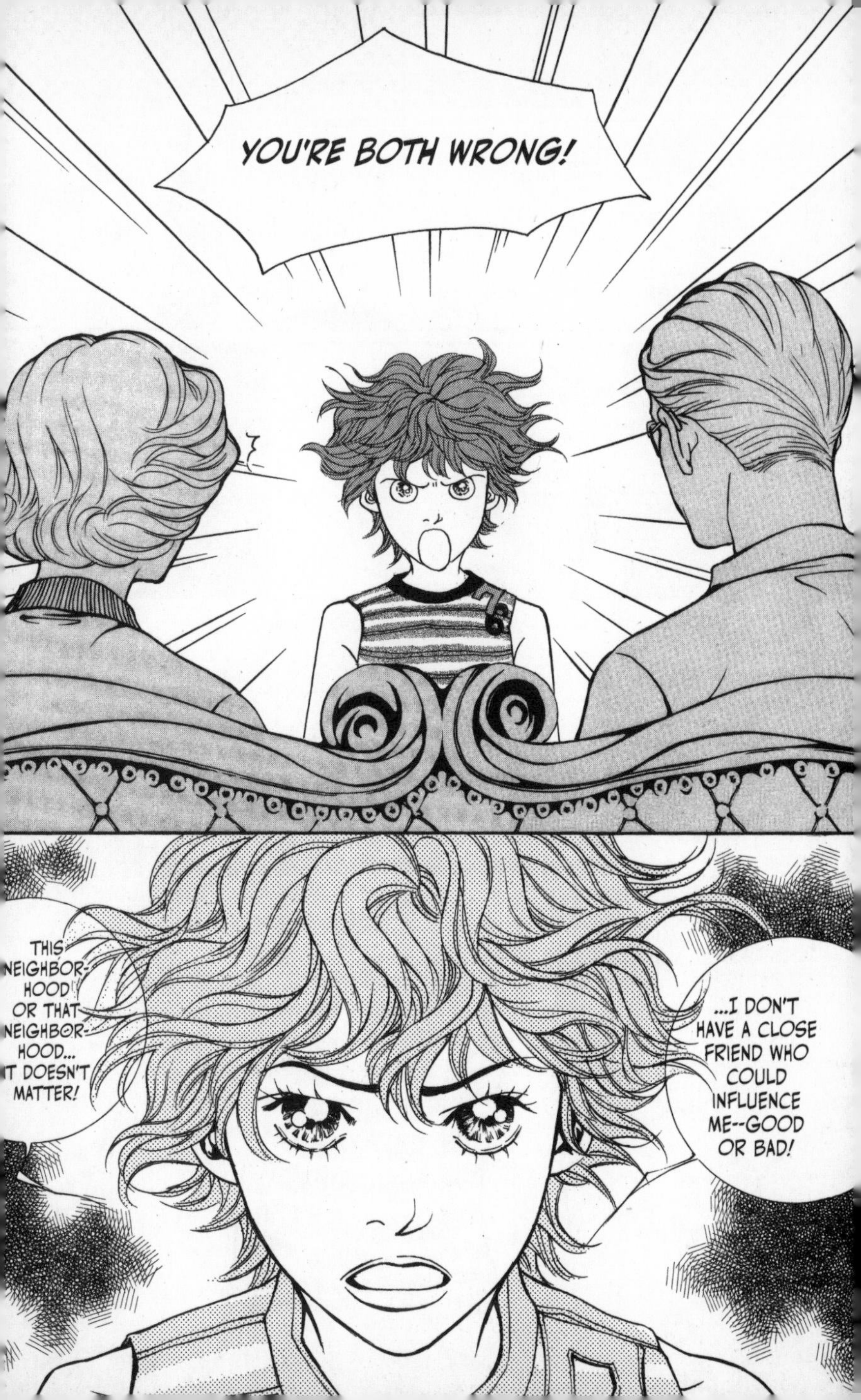
YOU'RE BOTH WRONG!
THIS NEIGHBOR-HOOD OR THAT NEIGHBOR-HOOD... IT DOESN'T MATTER!
...I DON'T HAVE A CLOSE FRIEND WHO COULD INFLUENCE ME--GOOD OR BAD!

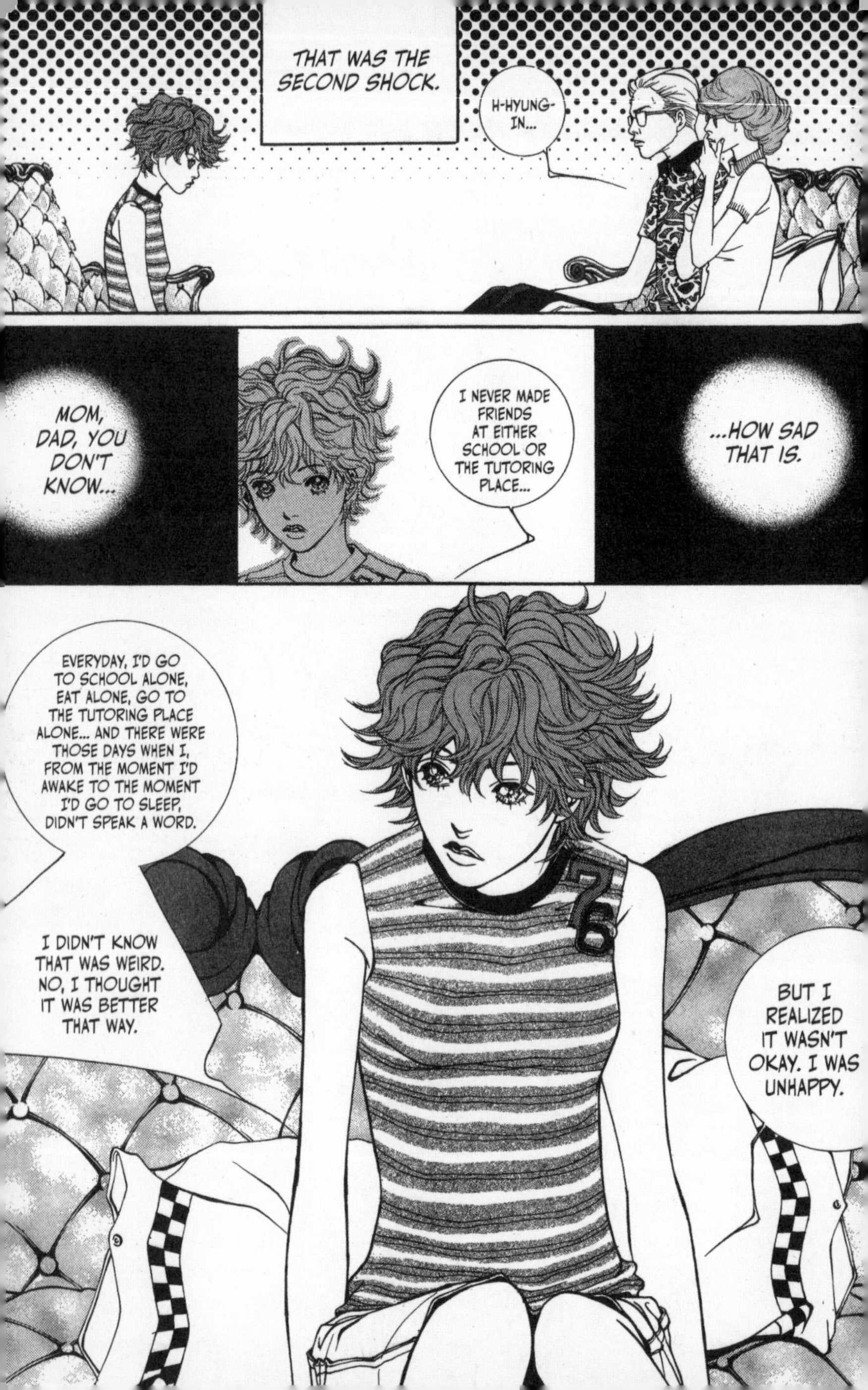
THAT WAS THE SECOND SHOCK.
H-HYUNG-IN...
MOM, DAD, YOU DON'T KNOW...
I NEVER MADE FRIENDS AT EITHER SCHOOL OR THE TUTORING PLACE...
...HOW SAD THAT IS.
EVERYDAY, I'D GO TO SCHOOL ALONE, EAT ALONE, GO TO THE TUTORING PLACE ALONE... AND THERE WERE THOSE DAYS WHEN I, FROM THE MOMENT I'D AWAKE TO THE MOMENT I'D GO TO SLEEP, DIDN'T SPEAK A WORD.
I DIDN'T KNOW THAT WAS WEIRD. NO, I THOUGHT IT WAS BETTER THAT WAY.
BUT I REALIZED IT WASN'T OKAY. I WAS UNHAPPY.

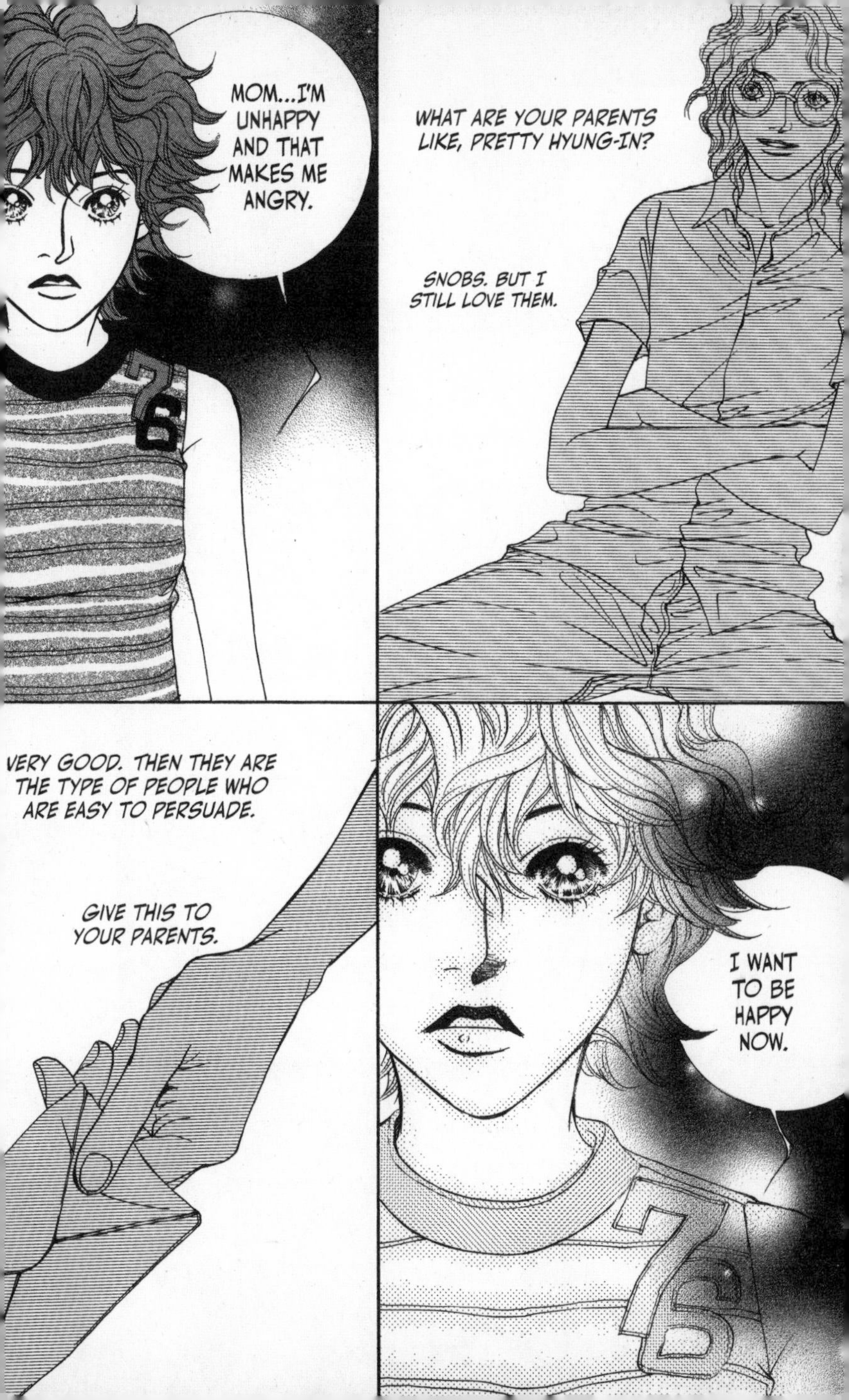
MOM...I'M UNHAPPY AND THAT MAKES ME ANGRY.
WHAT ARE YOUR PARENTS LIKE, PRETTY HYUNG-IN?
SNOBS. BUT I STILL LOVE THEM.
VERY GOOD. THEN THEY ARE THE TYPE OF PEOPLE WHO ARE EASY TO PERSUADE.
GIVE THIS TO YOUR PARENTS.
I WANT TO BE HAPPY NOW.

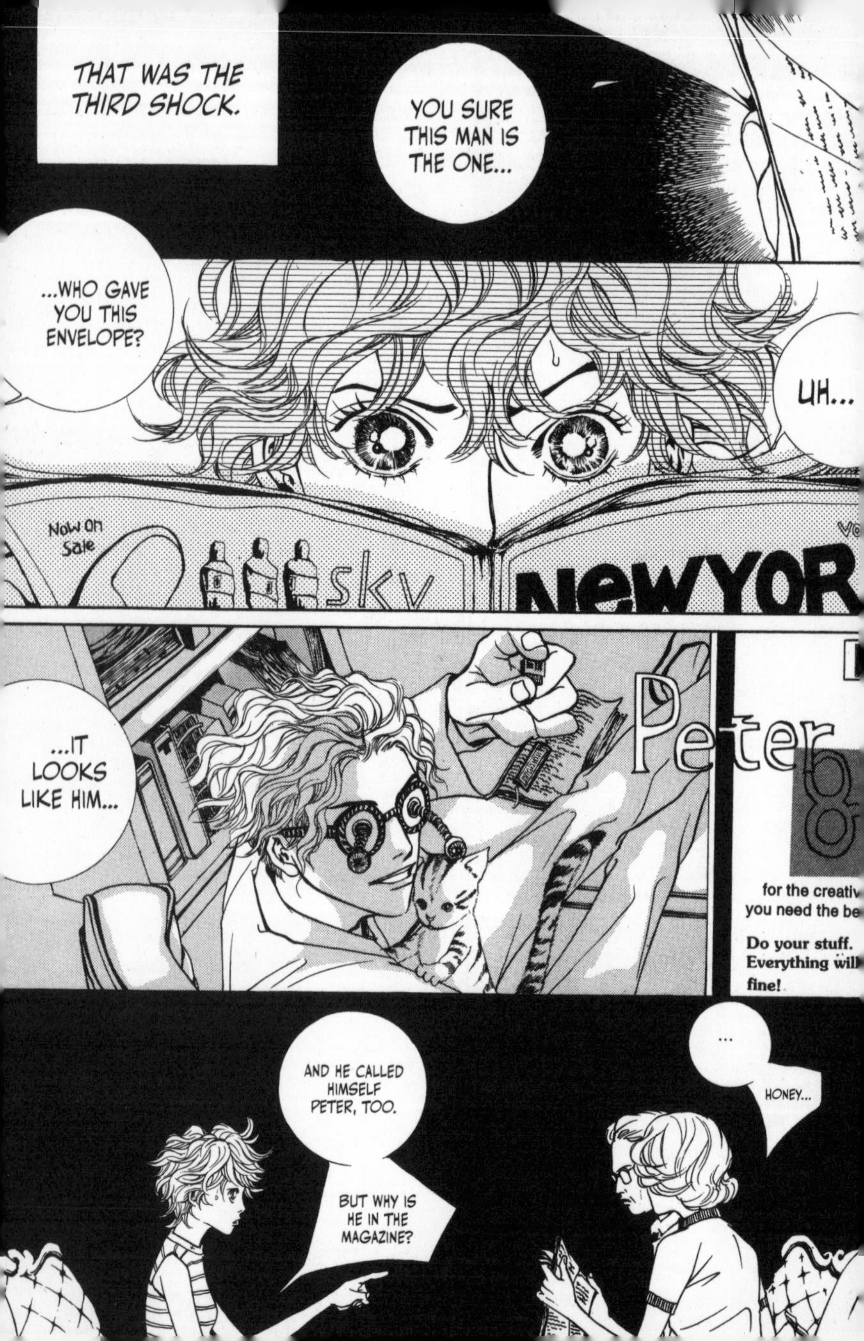
THAT WAS THE THIRD SHOCK.
YOU SURE THIS MAN IS THE ONE...
...WHO GAVE YOU THIS ENVELOPE?
UH...
Now on Sale
sky
NEWYOR
...IT LOOKS LIKE HIM...
Peter
for the creativ
you need the be
Do your stuff. Everything will
fine!
AND HE CALLED HIMSELF PETER, TOO.
BUT WHY IS HE IN THE MAGAZINE?
...
HONEY...

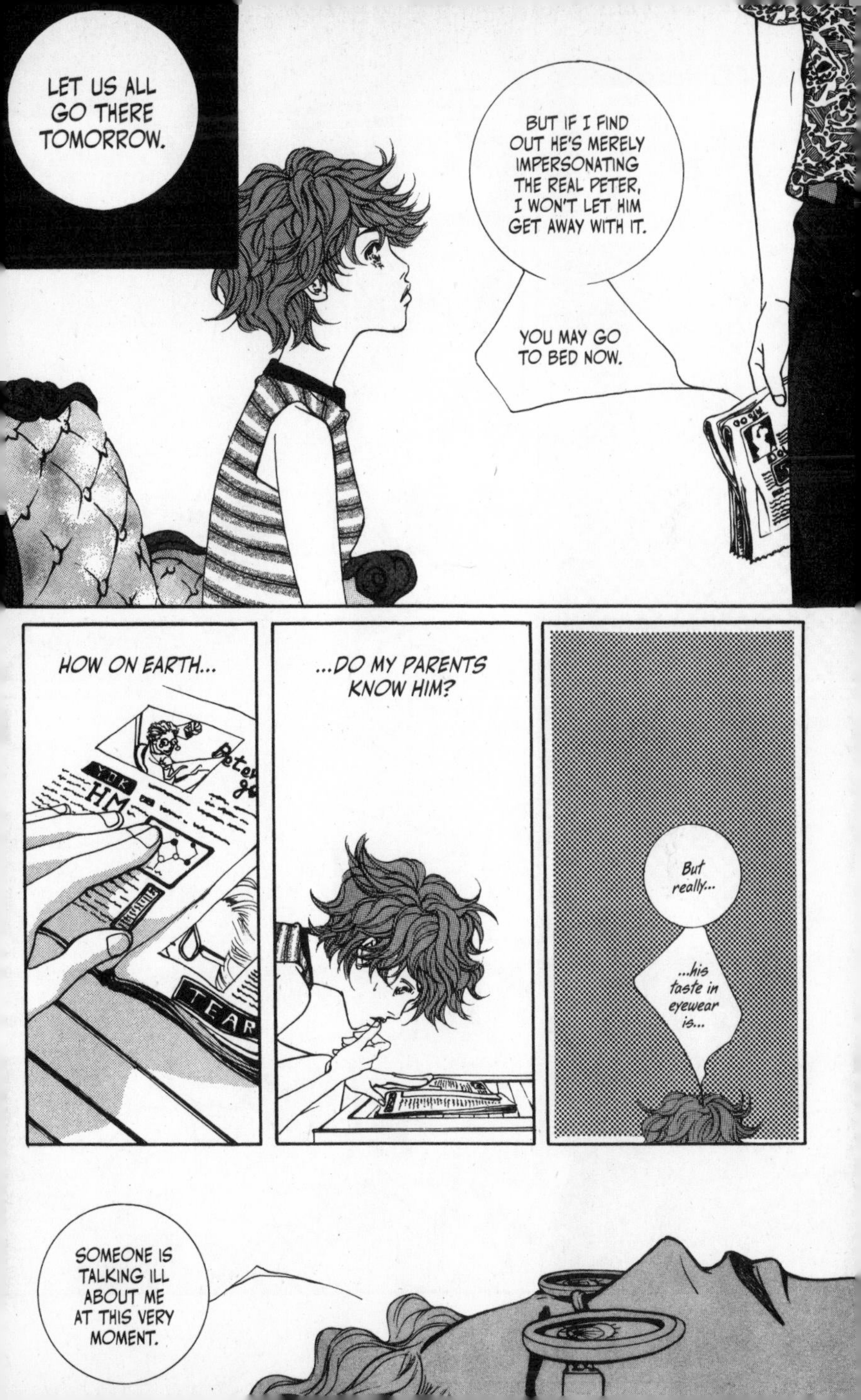
LET US ALL GO THERE TOMORROW.
BUT IF I FIND OUT HE'S MERELY IMPERSONATING THE REAL PETER, I WON'T LET HIM GET AWAY WITH IT.
YOU MAY GO TO BED NOW.
HOW ON EARTH...
...DO MY PARENTS KNOW HIM?
But really...
...his taste in eyewear is...
SOMEONE IS TALKING ILL ABOUT ME AT THIS VERY MOMENT.

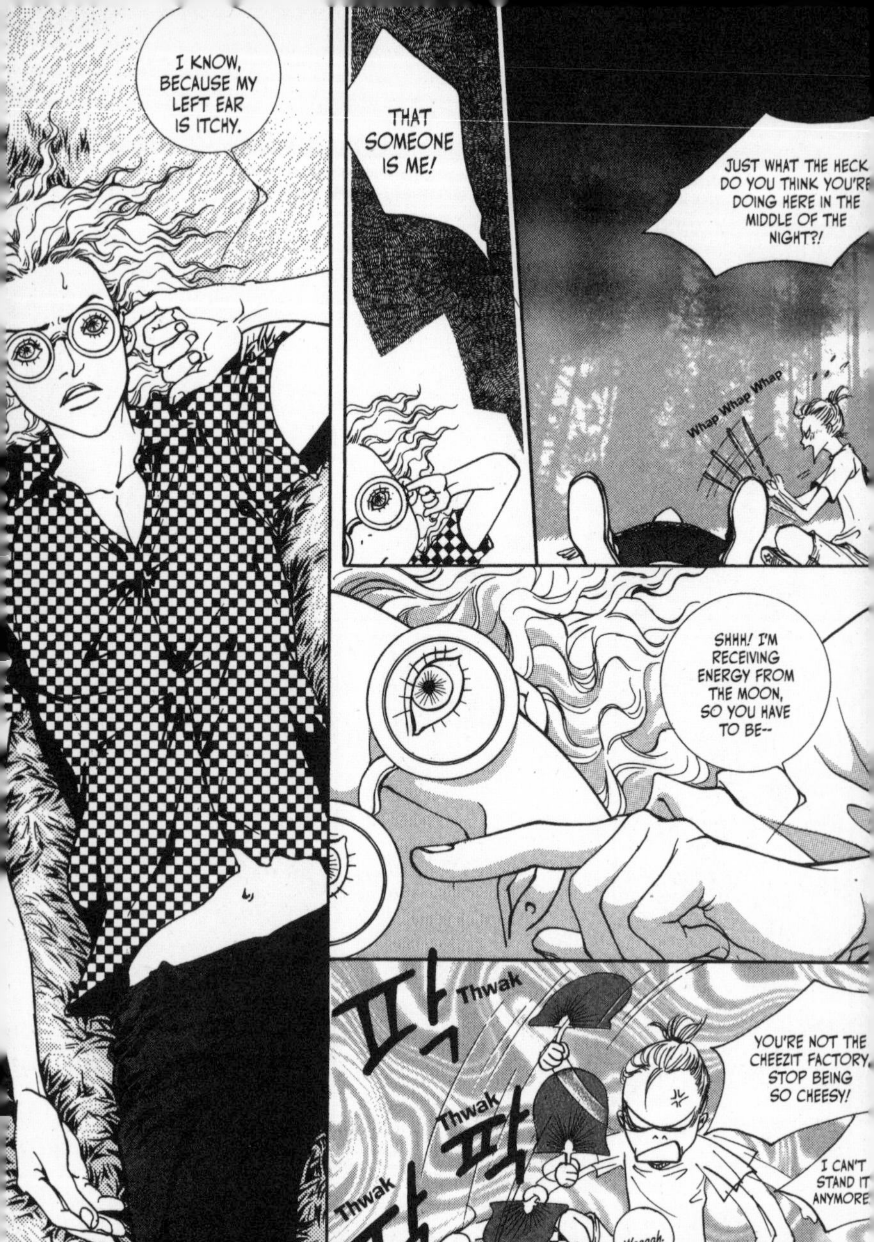
I KNOW, BECAUSE MY LEFT EAR IS ITCHY.
THAT SOMEONE IS ME!
JUST WHAT THE HECK DO YOU THINK YOU'RE DOING HERE IN THE MIDDLE OF THE NIGHT?!
Whap Whap Whap
SHHH! I'M RECEIVING ENERGY FROM THE MOON, SO YOU HAVE TO BE--
Thwak
Thwak
Thwak
YOU'RE NOT THE CHEEZIT FACTORY. STOP BEING SO CHEESY!
I CAN'T STAND IT ANYMORE
Waaaah.

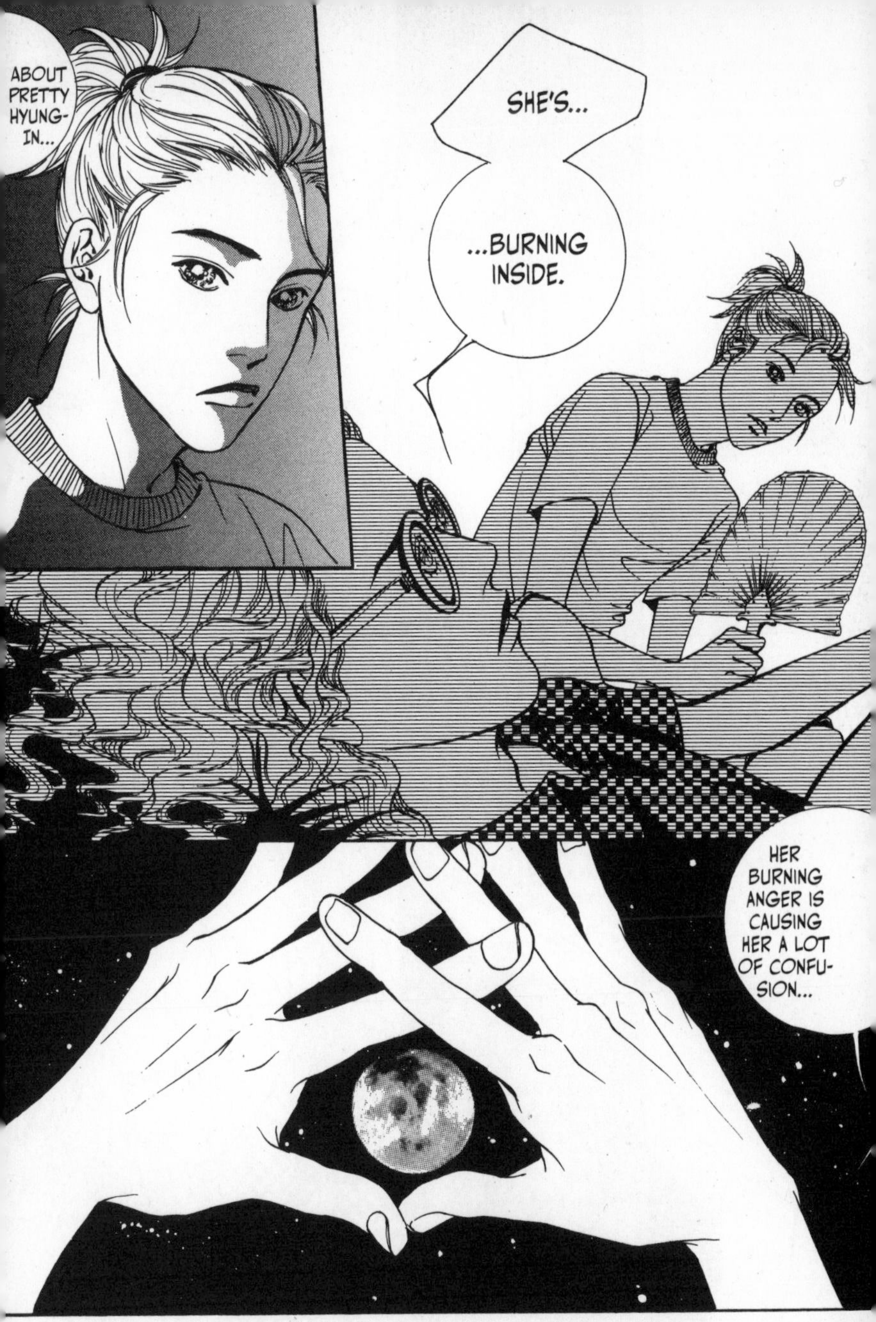
ABOUT PRETTY HYUNG-IN...
SHE'S...
...BURNING INSIDE.
HER BURNING ANGER IS CAUSING HER A LOT OF CONFU-SION...

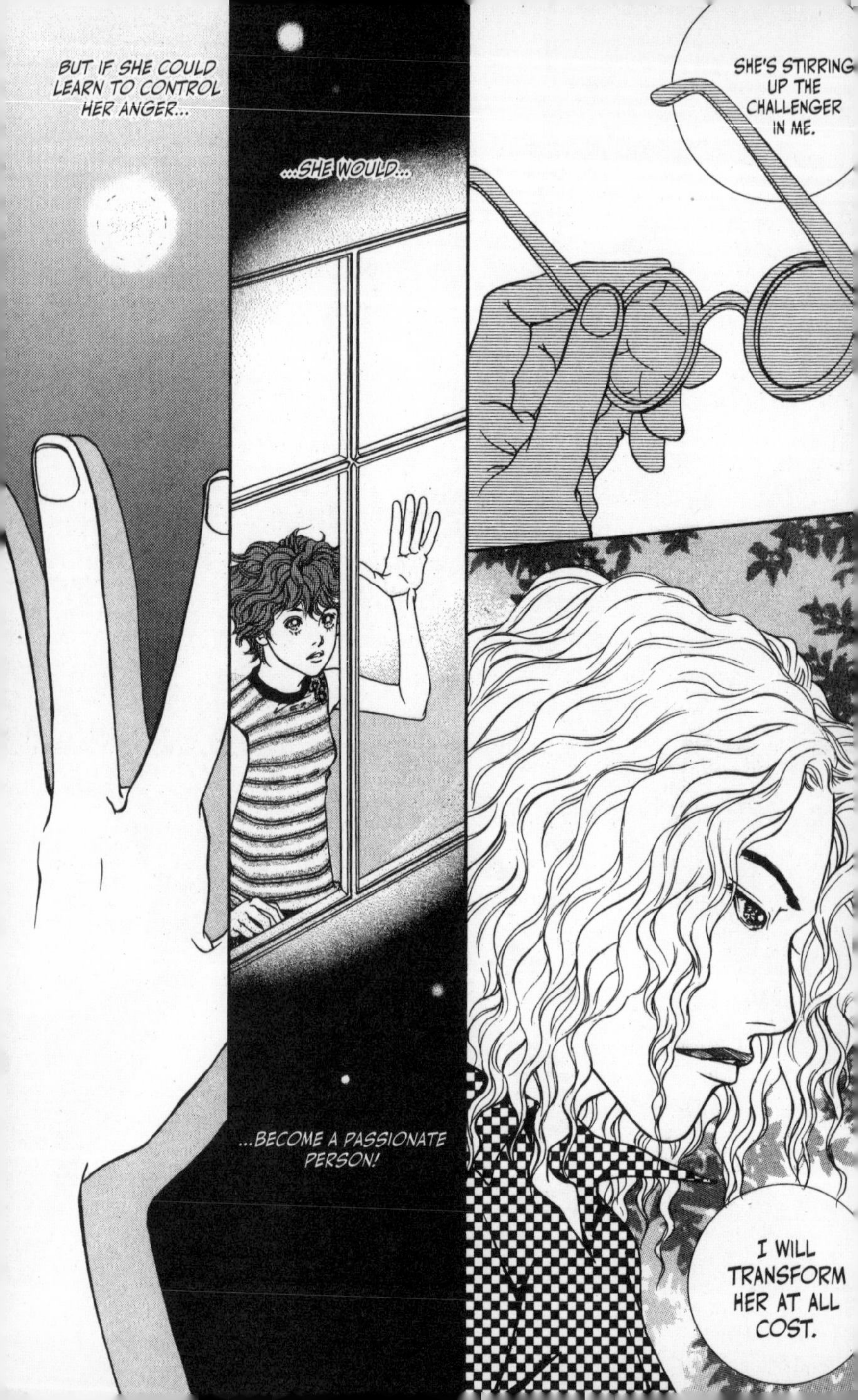
BUT IF SHE COULD LEARN TO CONTROL HER ANGER...
...SHE WOULD...
...BECOME A PASSIONATE PERSON!
SHE'S STIRRING UP THE CHALLENGER IN ME.
I WILL TRANSFORM HER AT ALL COST.

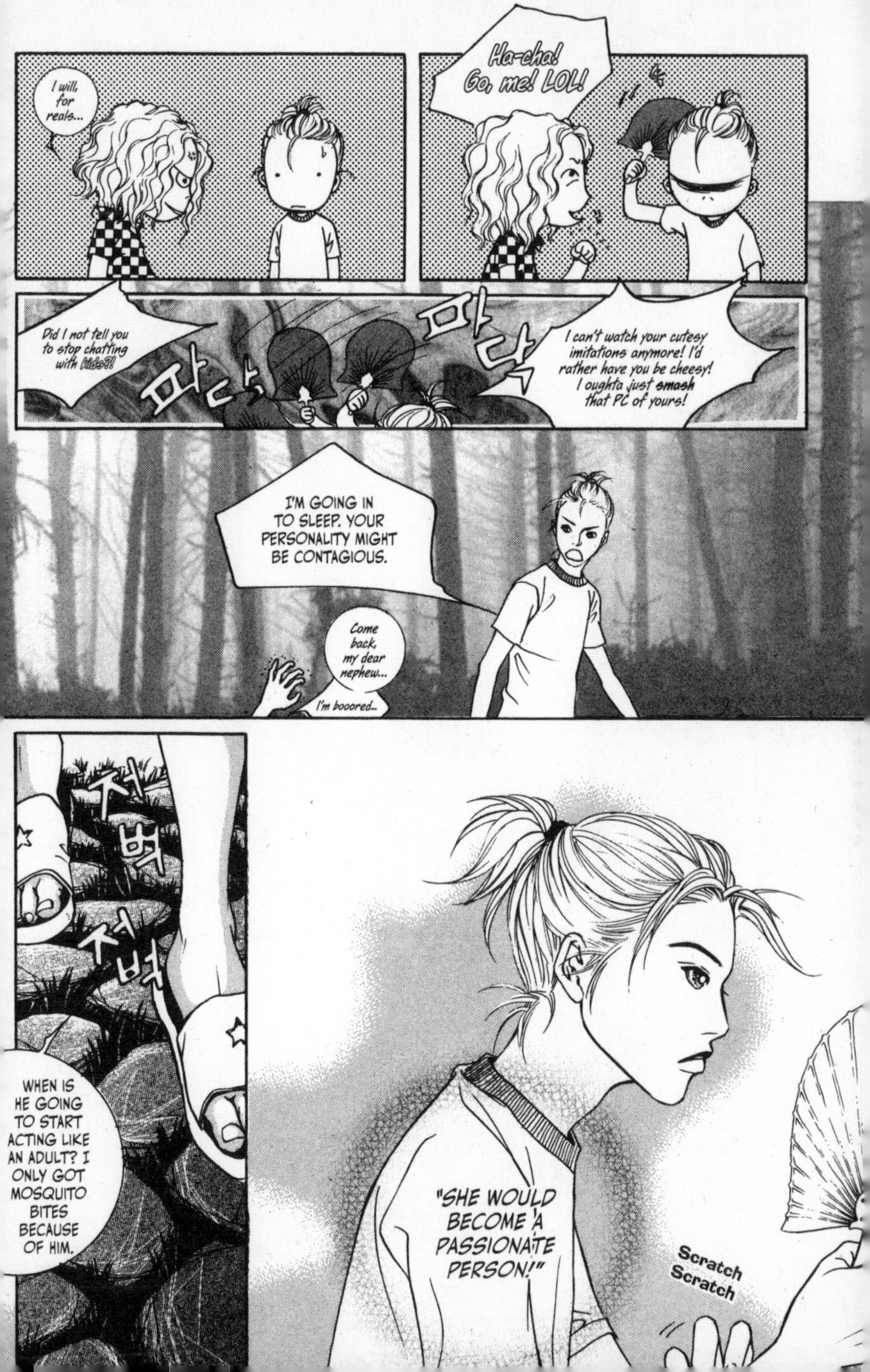

I will, for reals...
Ha-cha! Go, me! LOL!
Did I not tell you to stop chatting with kids?!
파닥,
파닥
I can't watch your cutesy imitations anymore! I'd rather have you be cheesy! I oughta just smash that PC of yours!
I'M GOING IN TO SLEEP. YOUR PERSONALITY MIGHT BE CONTAGIOUS.
Come back, my dear nephew...
I'm booored...
WHEN IS HE GOING TO START ACTING LIKE AN ADULT? I ONLY GOT MOSQUITO BITES BECAUSE OF HIM.
"SHE WOULD BECOME A PASSIONATE PERSON!"
Scratch Scratch

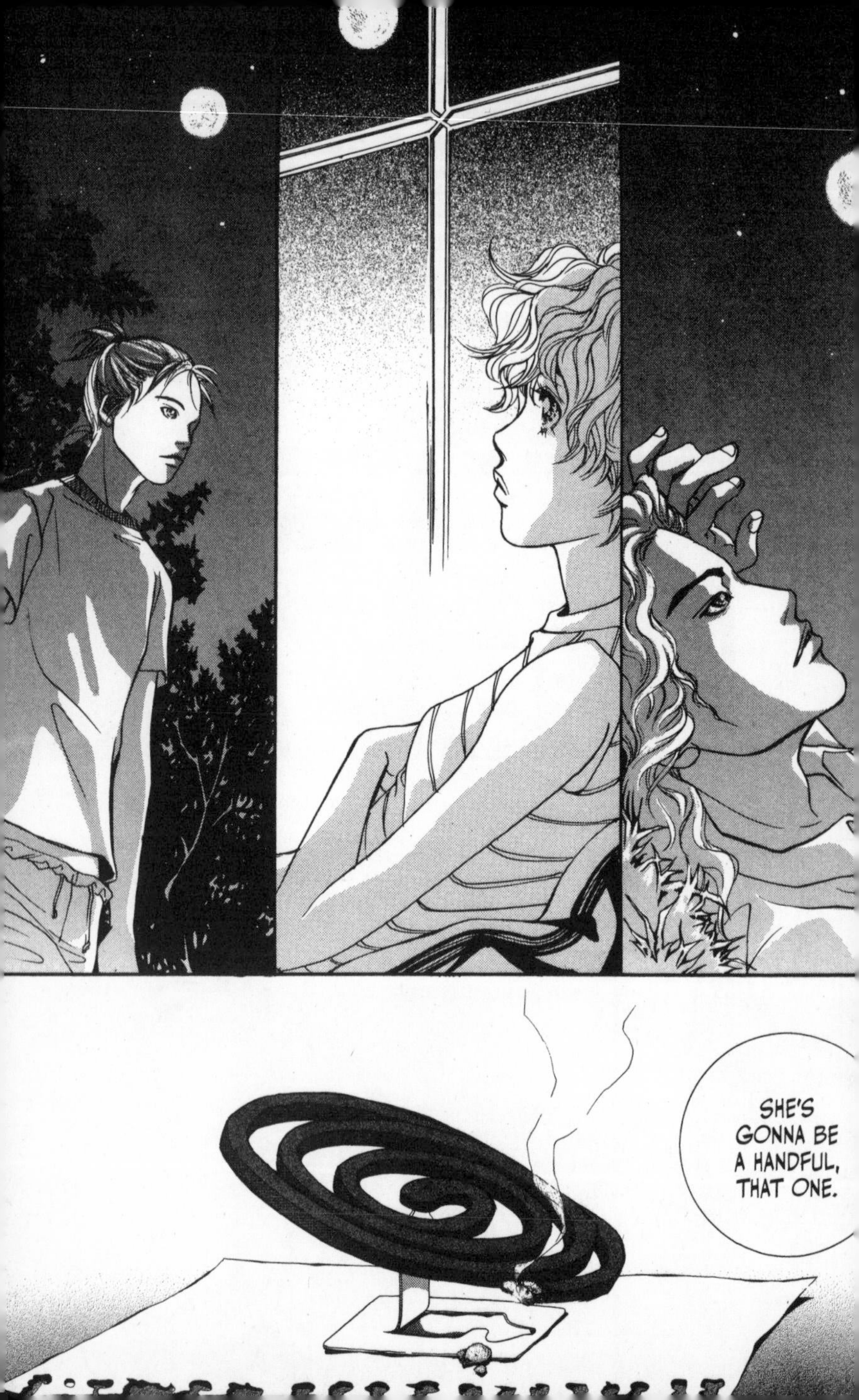
SHE'S GONNA BE A HANDFUL, THAT ONE.

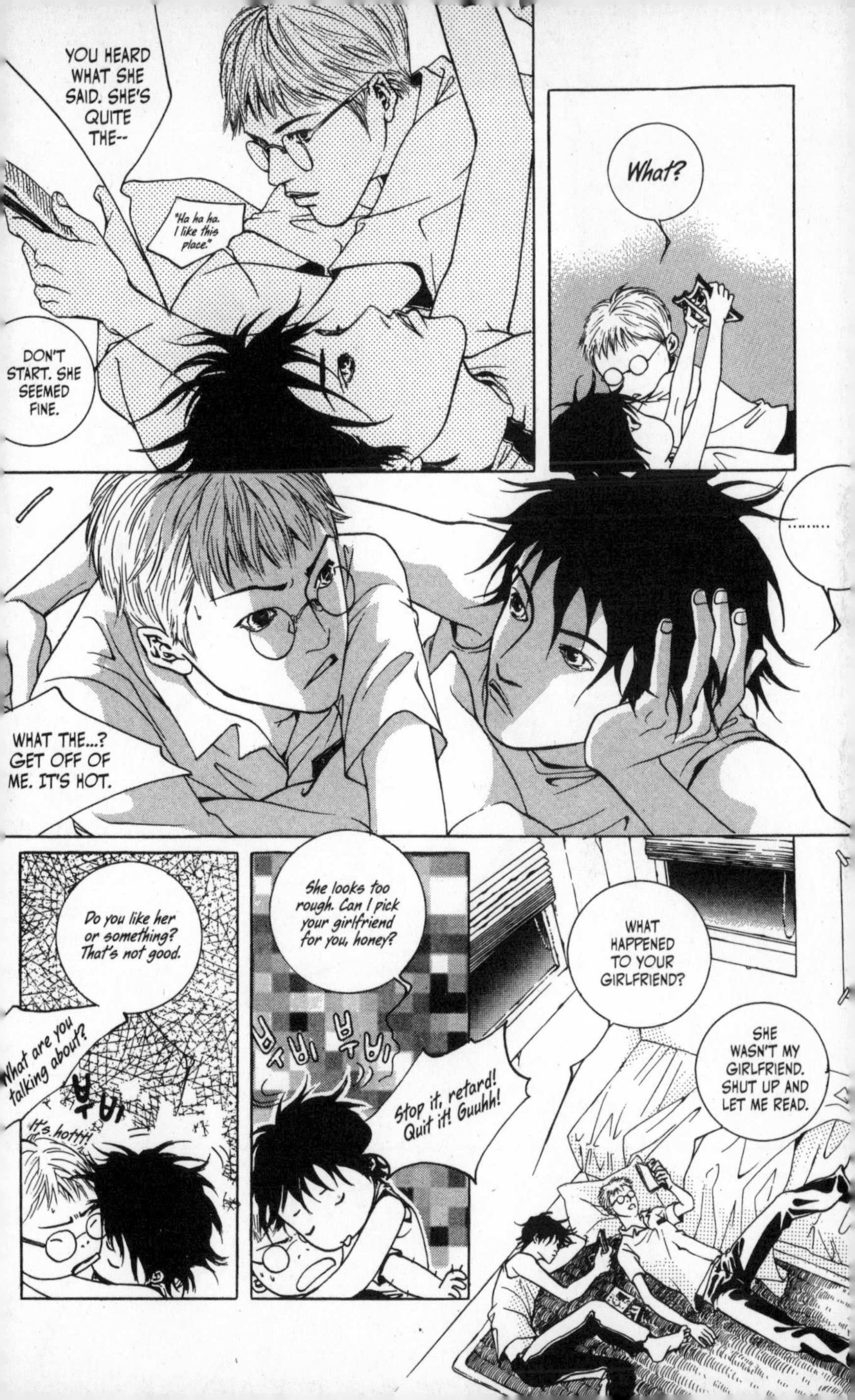
YOU HEARD WHAT SHE SAID. SHE'S QUITE THE--
"Ha ha ha. I like this place."
DON'T START. SHE SEEMED FINE.
What?
WHAT THE...? GET OFF OF ME. IT'S HOT.
....
Do you like her or something? That's not good.
What are you talking about?
It's hottt!
She looks too rough. Can I pick your girlfriend for you, honey?
Stop it, retard! Quit it! Guuhh!
WHAT HAPPENED TO YOUR GIRLFRIEND?
SHE WASN'T MY GIRLFRIEND. SHUT UP AND LET ME READ.

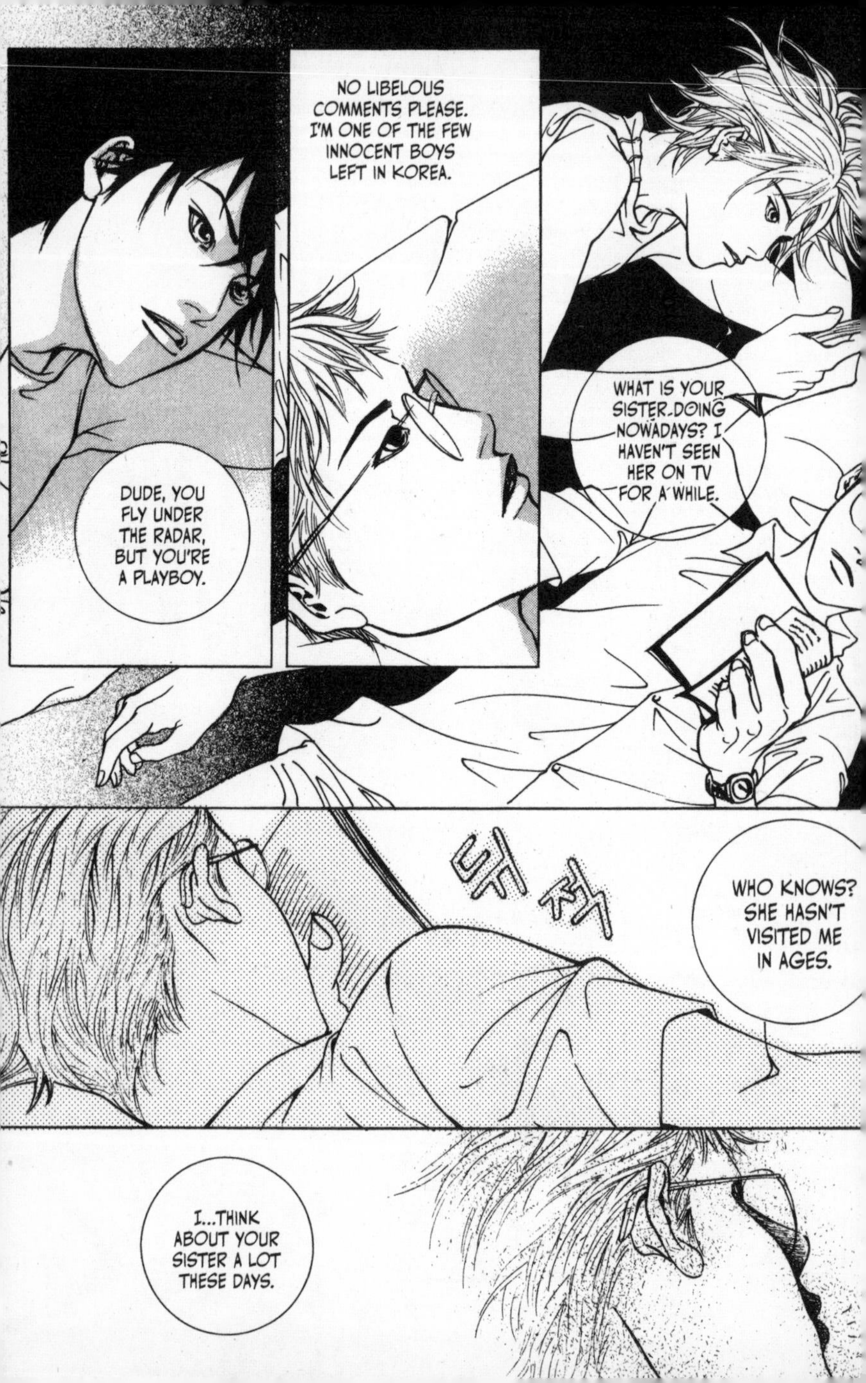
DUDE, YOU FLY UNDER THE RADAR, BUT YOU'RE A PLAYBOY.
NO LIBELOUS COMMENTS PLEASE. I'M ONE OF THE FEW INNOCENT BOYS LEFT IN KOREA.
WHAT IS YOUR SISTER DOING NOWADAYS? I HAVEN'T SEEN HER ON TV FOR A WHILE.
WHO KNOWS? SHE HASN'T VISITED ME IN AGES.
I...THINK ABOUT YOUR SISTER A LOT THESE DAYS.

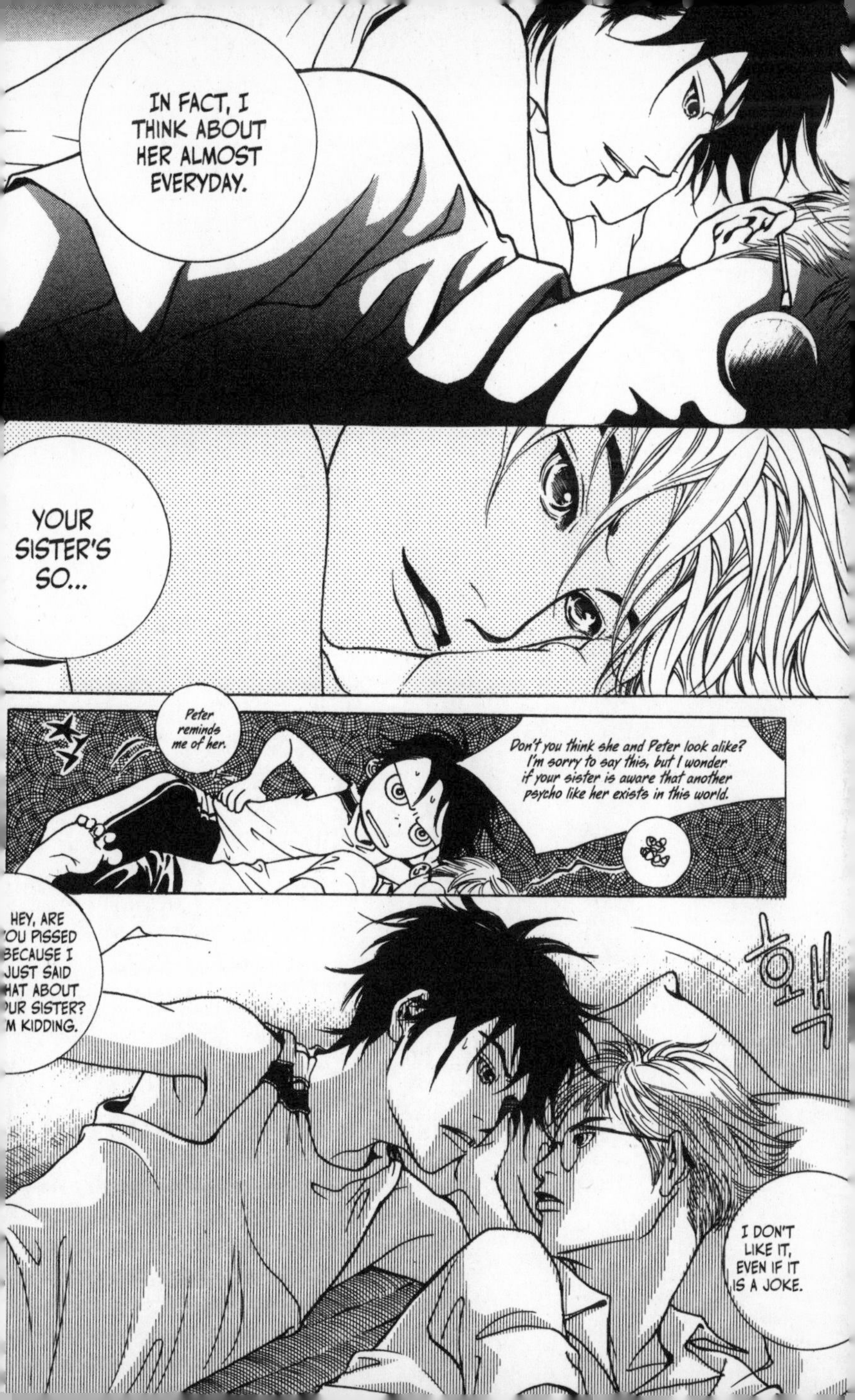
IN FACT, I THINK ABOUT HER ALMOST EVERYDAY.
YOUR SISTER'S SO...
Peter reminds me of her.
Don't you think she and Peter look alike? I'm sorry to say this, but I wonder if your sister is aware that another psycho like her exists in this world.
HEY, ARE OU PISSED BECAUSE I JUST SAID HAT ABOUT UR SISTER? M KIDDING.
I DON'T LIKE IT, EVEN IF IT IS A JOKE.

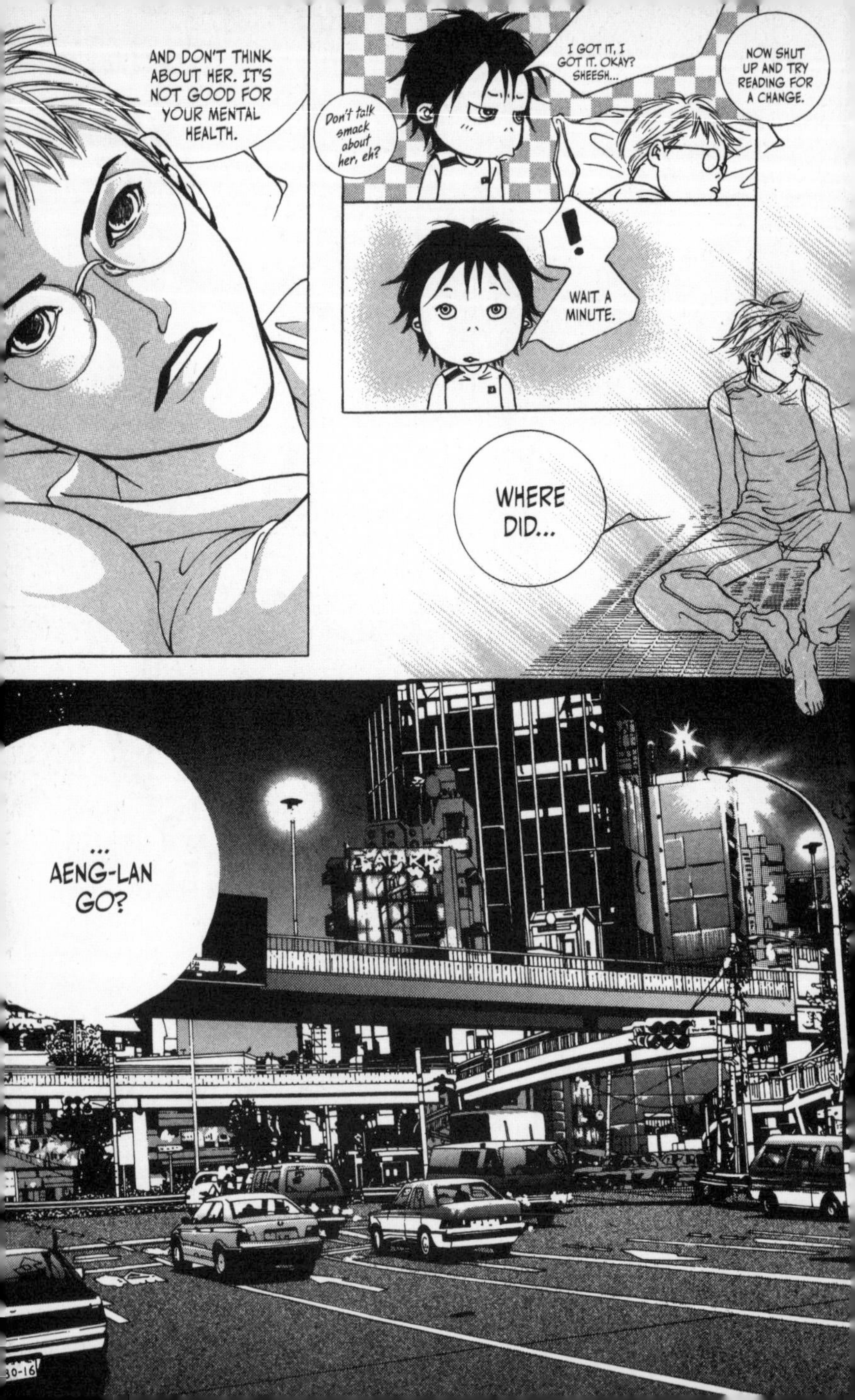
AND DON'T THINK ABOUT HER. IT'S NOT GOOD FOR YOUR MENTAL HEALTH.
Don't talk smack about her, eh?
I GOT IT, I GOT IT. OKAY? SHEESH...
NOW SHUT UP AND TRY READING FOR A CHANGE.
!
WAIT A MINUTE.
WHERE DID...
... AENG-LAN GO?

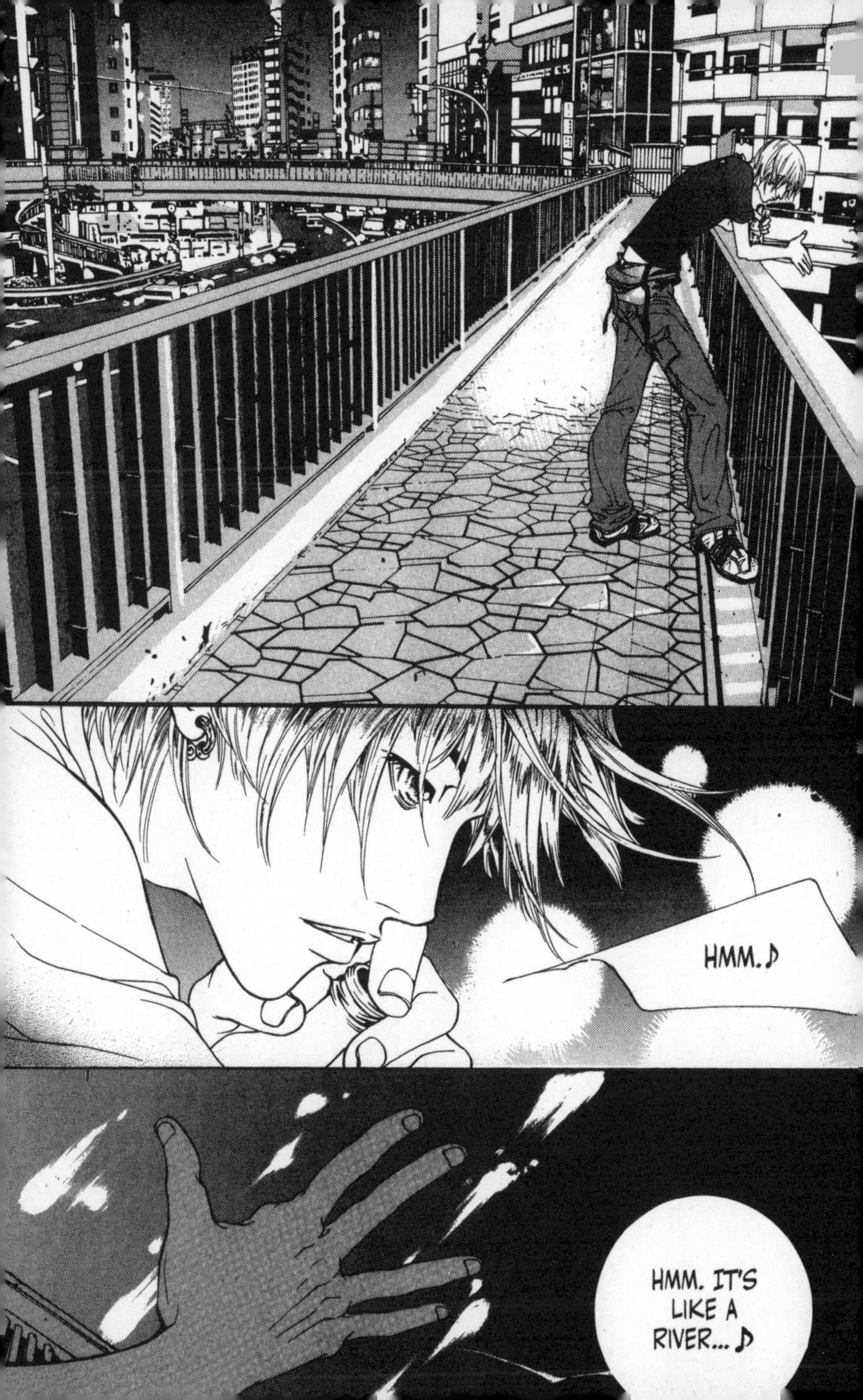
HMM.♪
HMM. IT'S LIKE A RIVER...♪

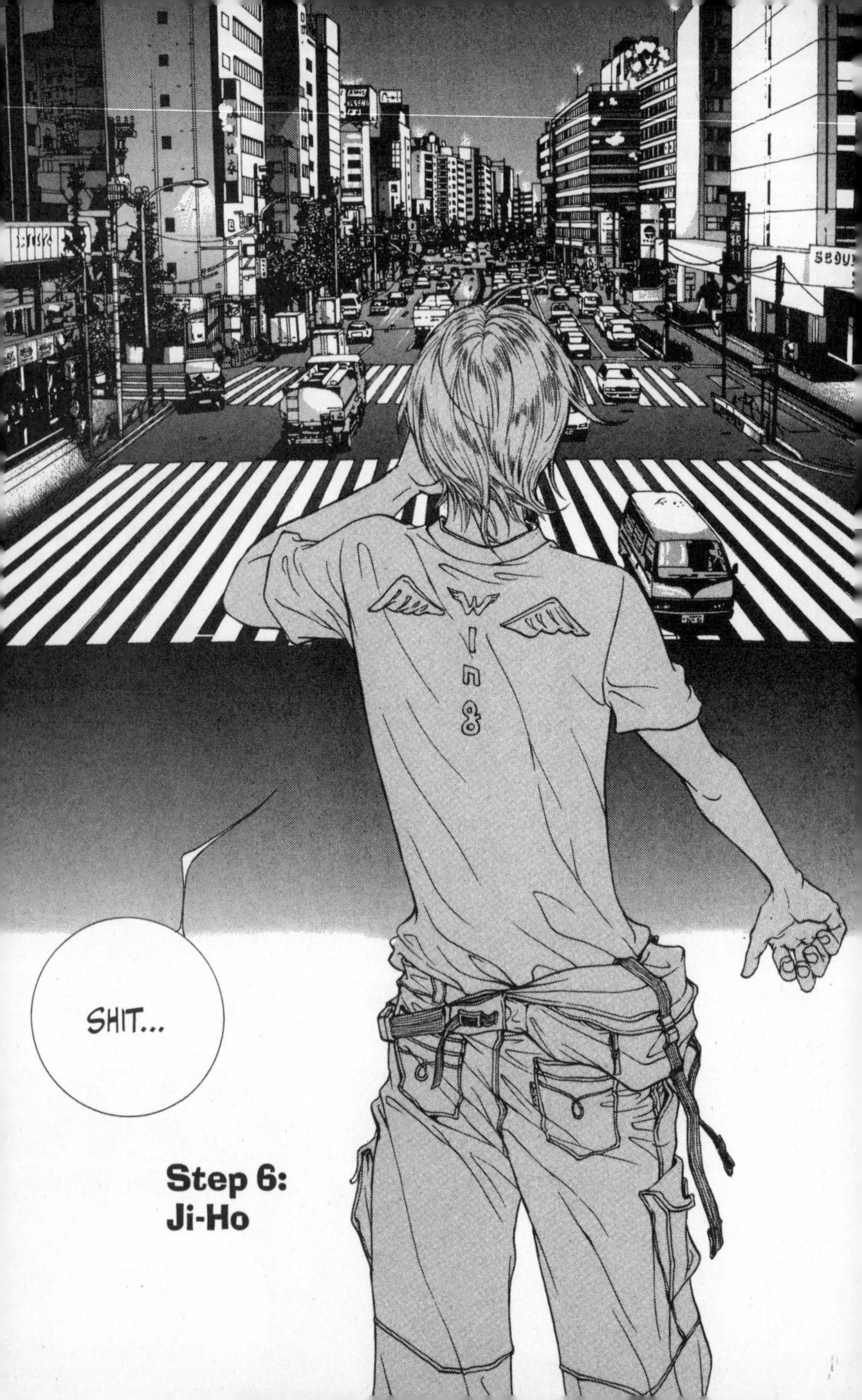
SHIT...

Step 6: Ji-Ho

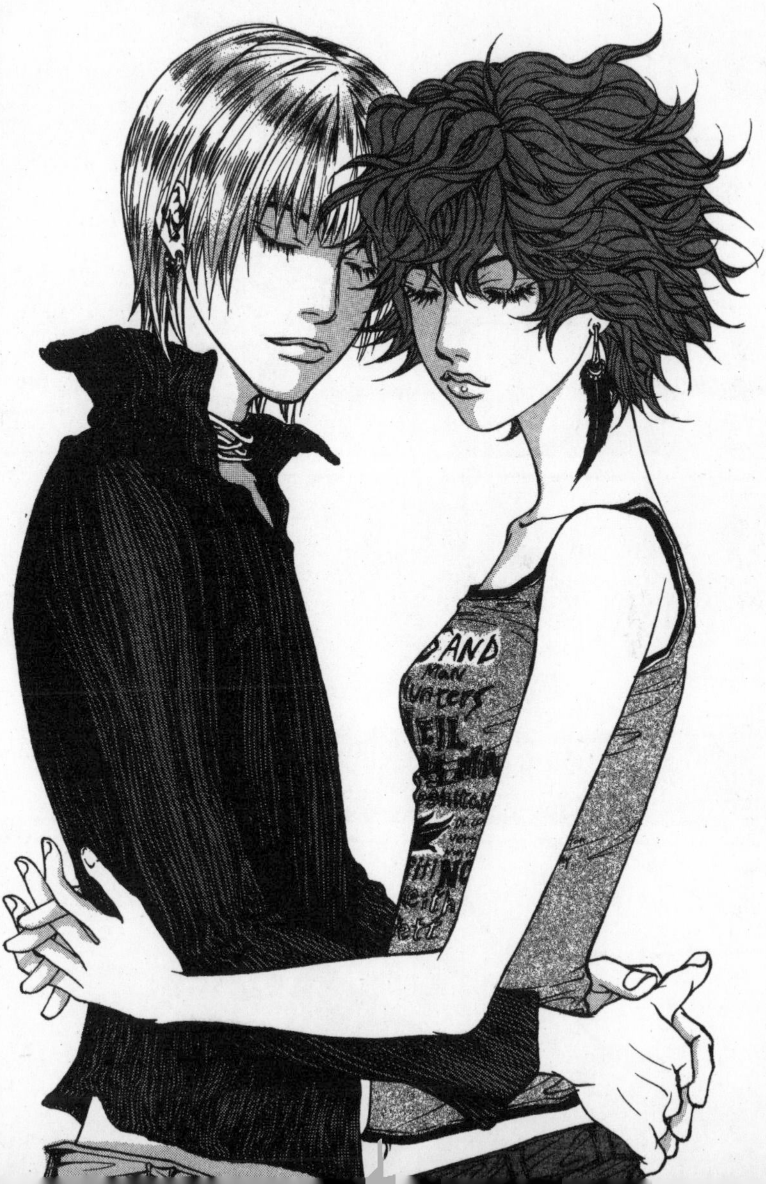

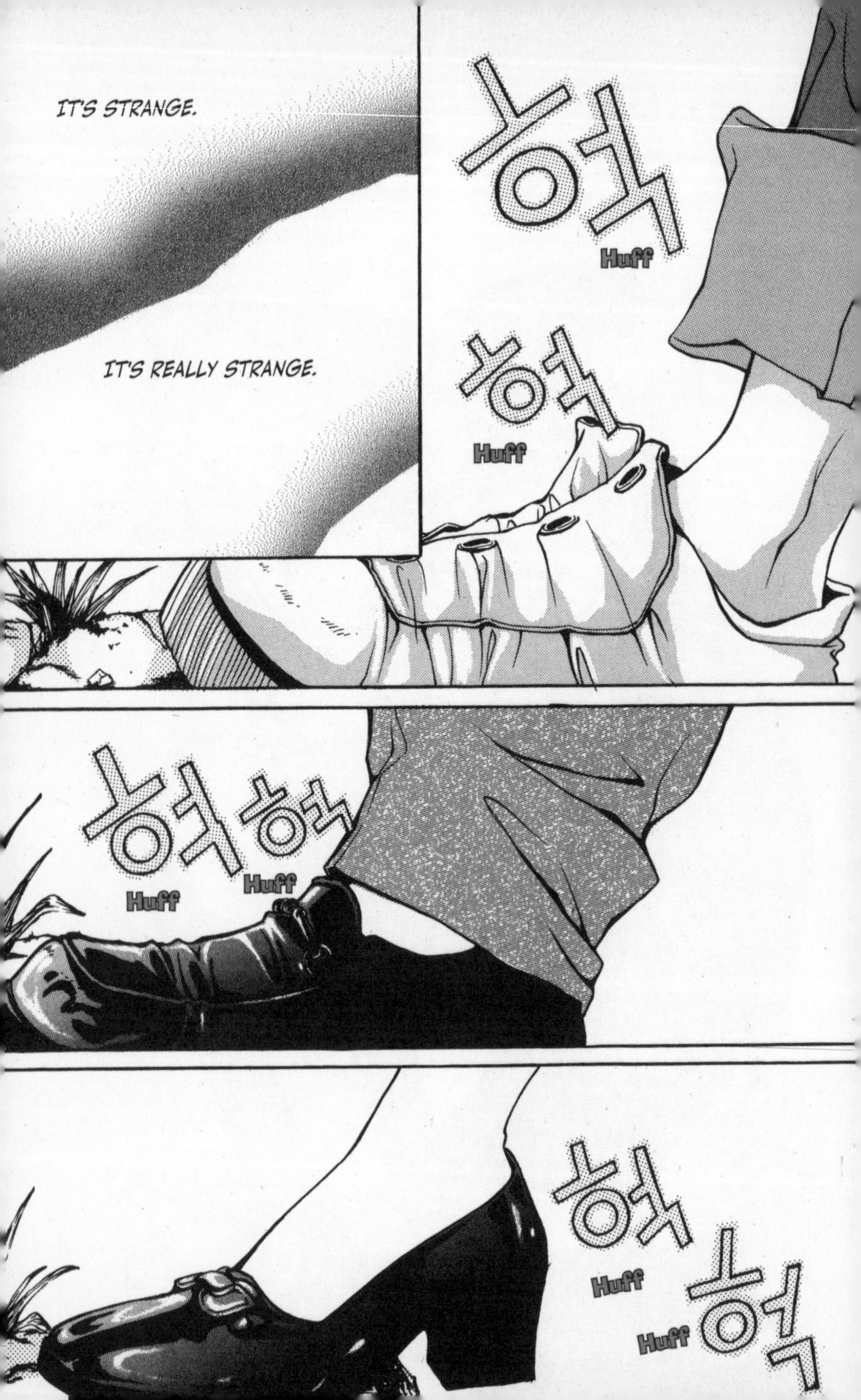
IT'S STRANGE.
IT'S REALLY STRANGE.
헉
Huff
헉
Huff
헉
Huff
헉
Huff
헉
Huff
헉
Huff

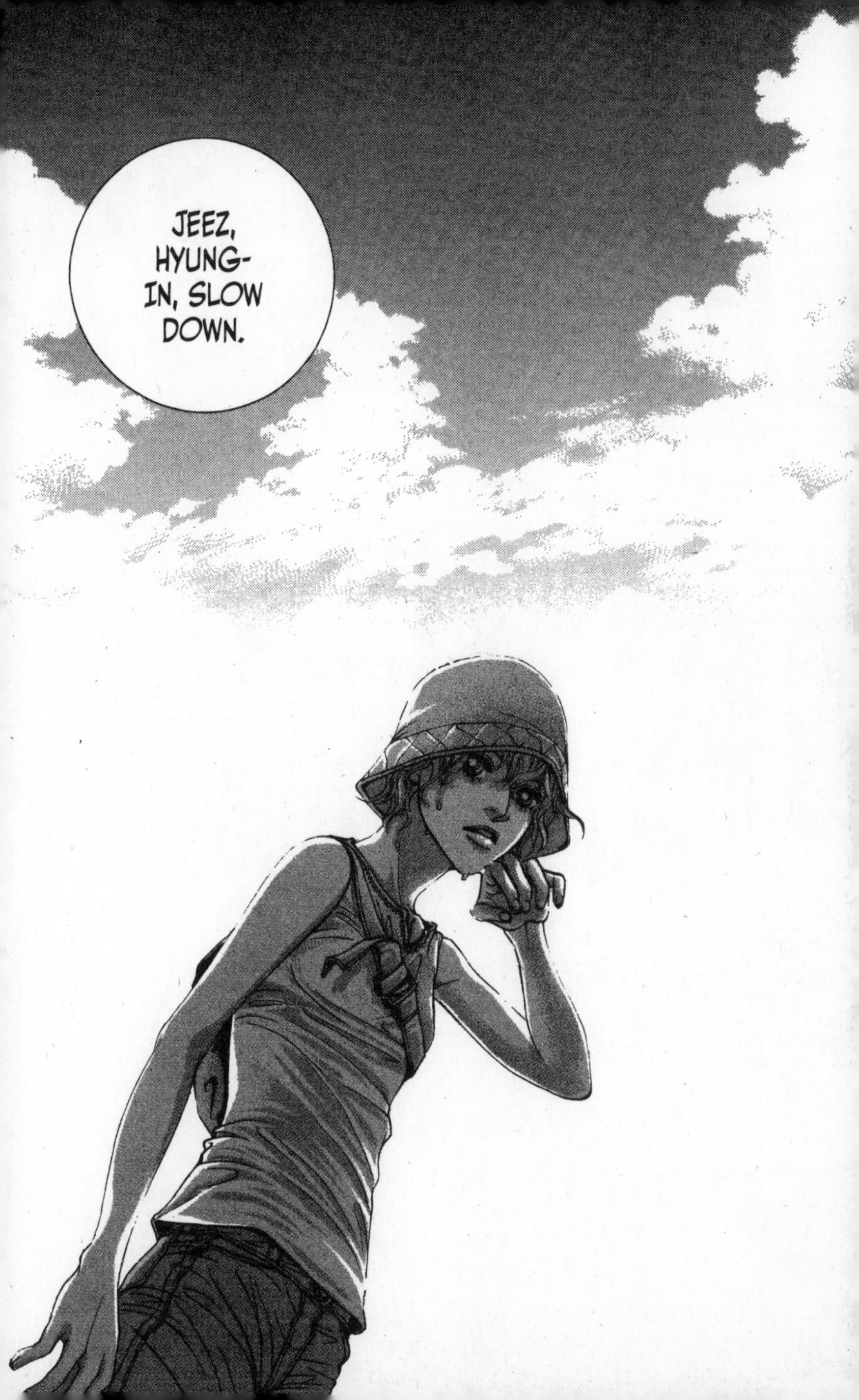
JEEZ, HYUNG-IN, SLOW DOWN.

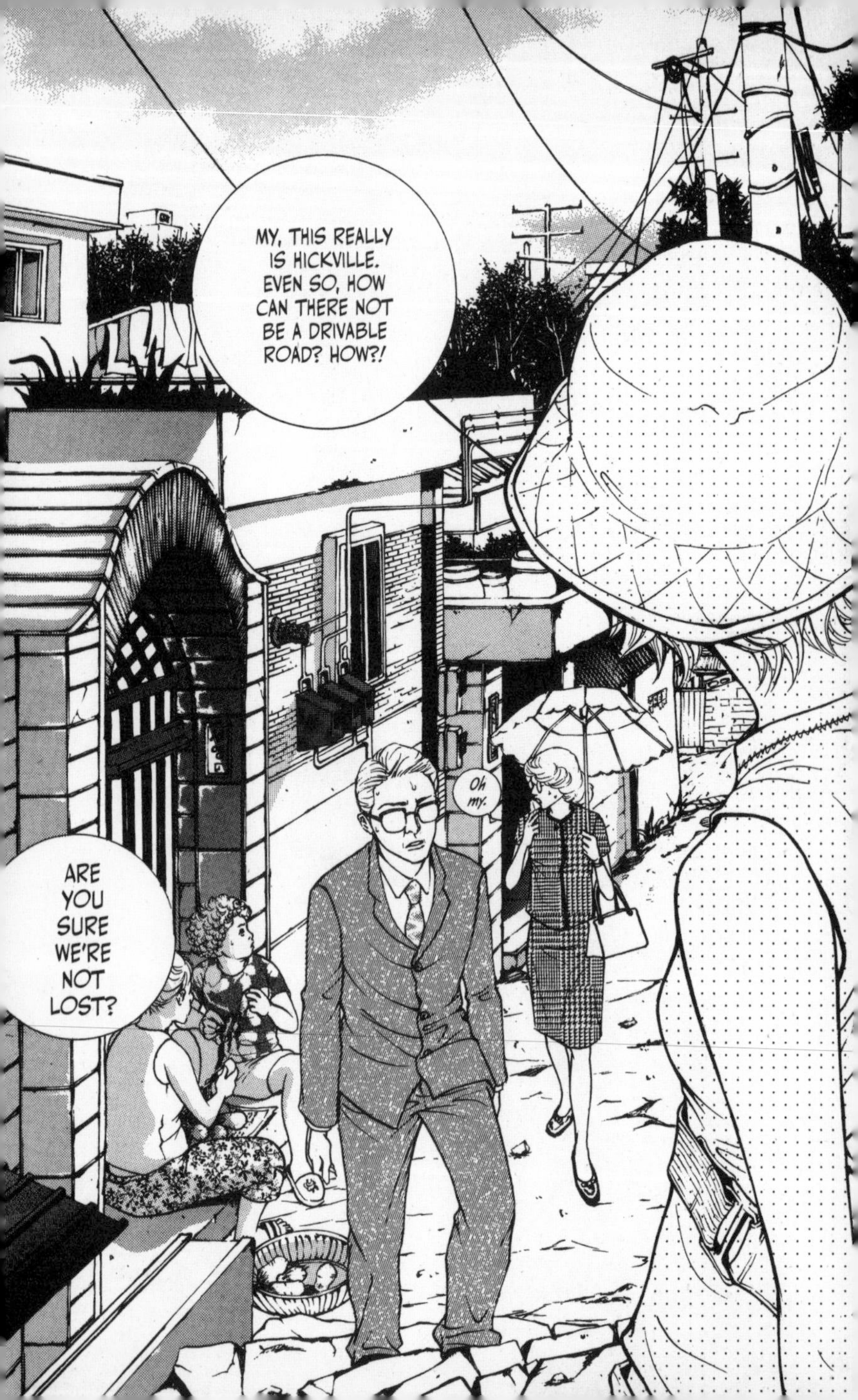
MY, THIS REALLY IS HICKVILLE. EVEN SO, HOW CAN THERE NOT BE A DRIVABLE ROAD? HOW?!
Oh my.
ARE YOU SURE WE'RE NOT LOST?

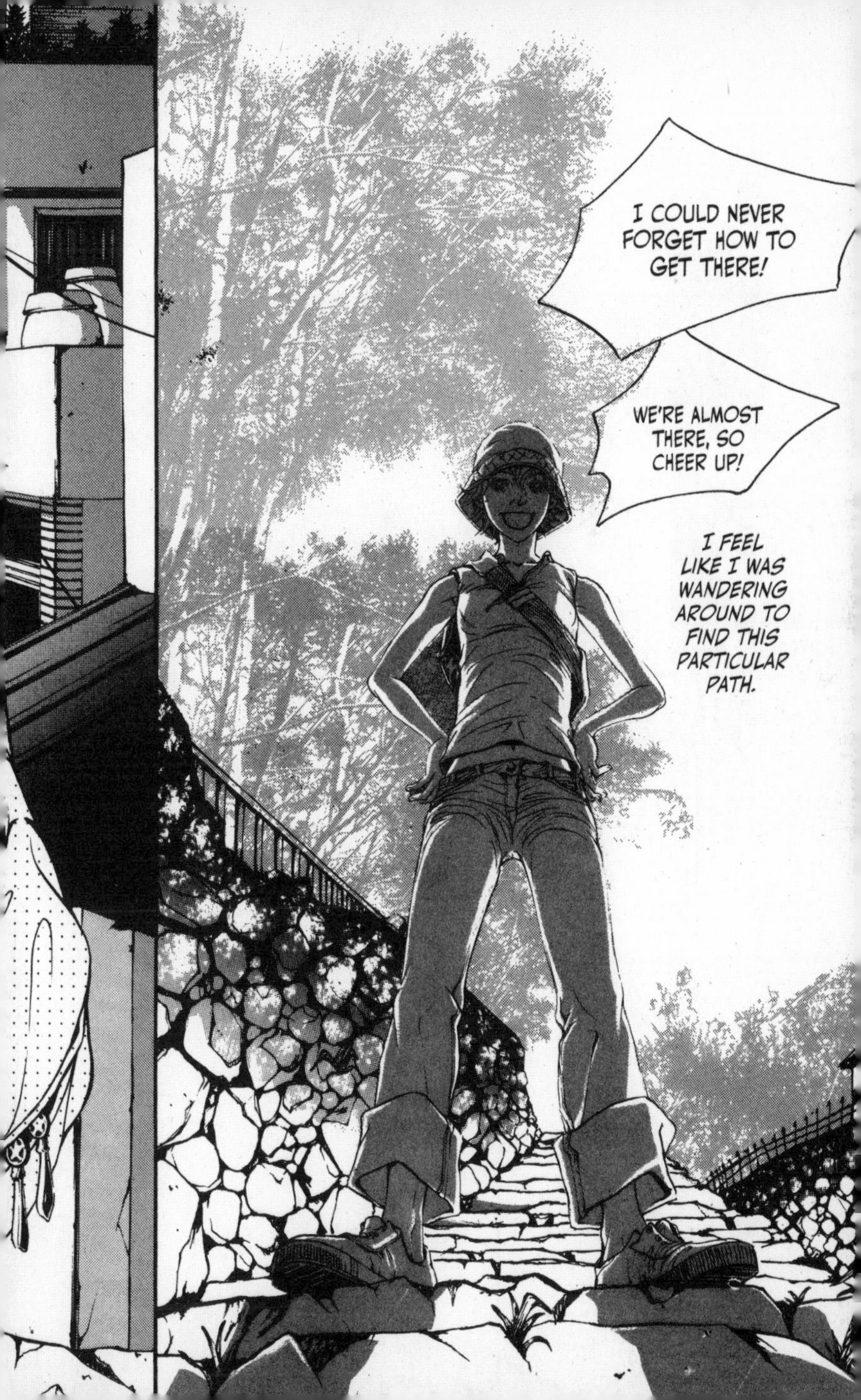
I COULD NEVER FORGET HOW TO GET THERE!
WE'RE ALMOST THERE, SO CHEER UP!
I FEEL LIKE I WAS WANDERING AROUND TO FIND THIS PARTICULAR PATH.

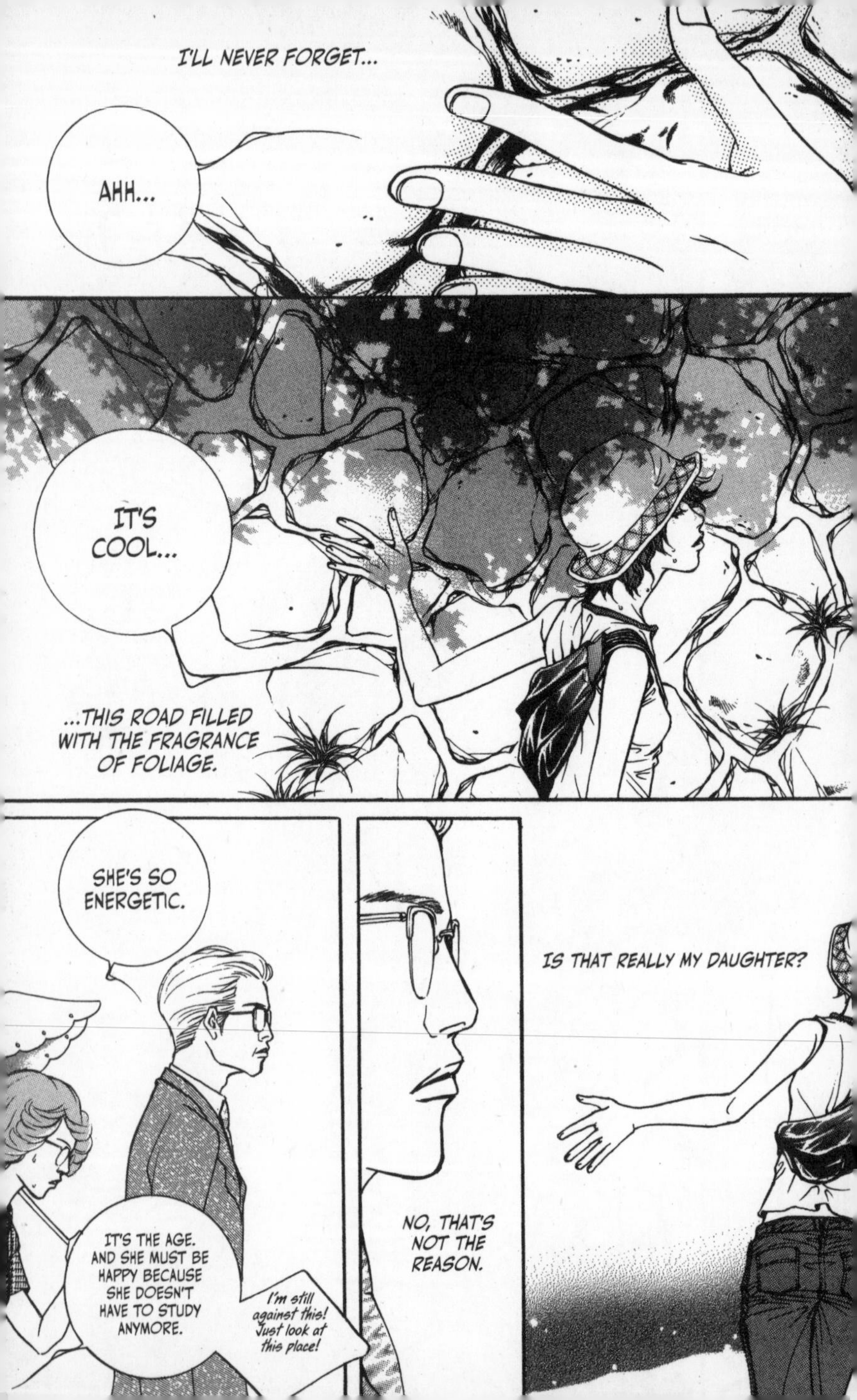
I'LL NEVER FORGET...
AHH...
IT'S COOL...
...THIS ROAD FILLED WITH THE FRAGRANCE OF FOLIAGE.
SHE'S SO ENERGETIC.
IT'S THE AGE. AND SHE MUST BE HAPPY BECAUSE SHE DOESN'T HAVE TO STUDY ANYMORE.
I'm still against this! Just look at this place!
NO, THAT'S NOT THE REASON.
IS THAT REALLY MY DAUGHTER?

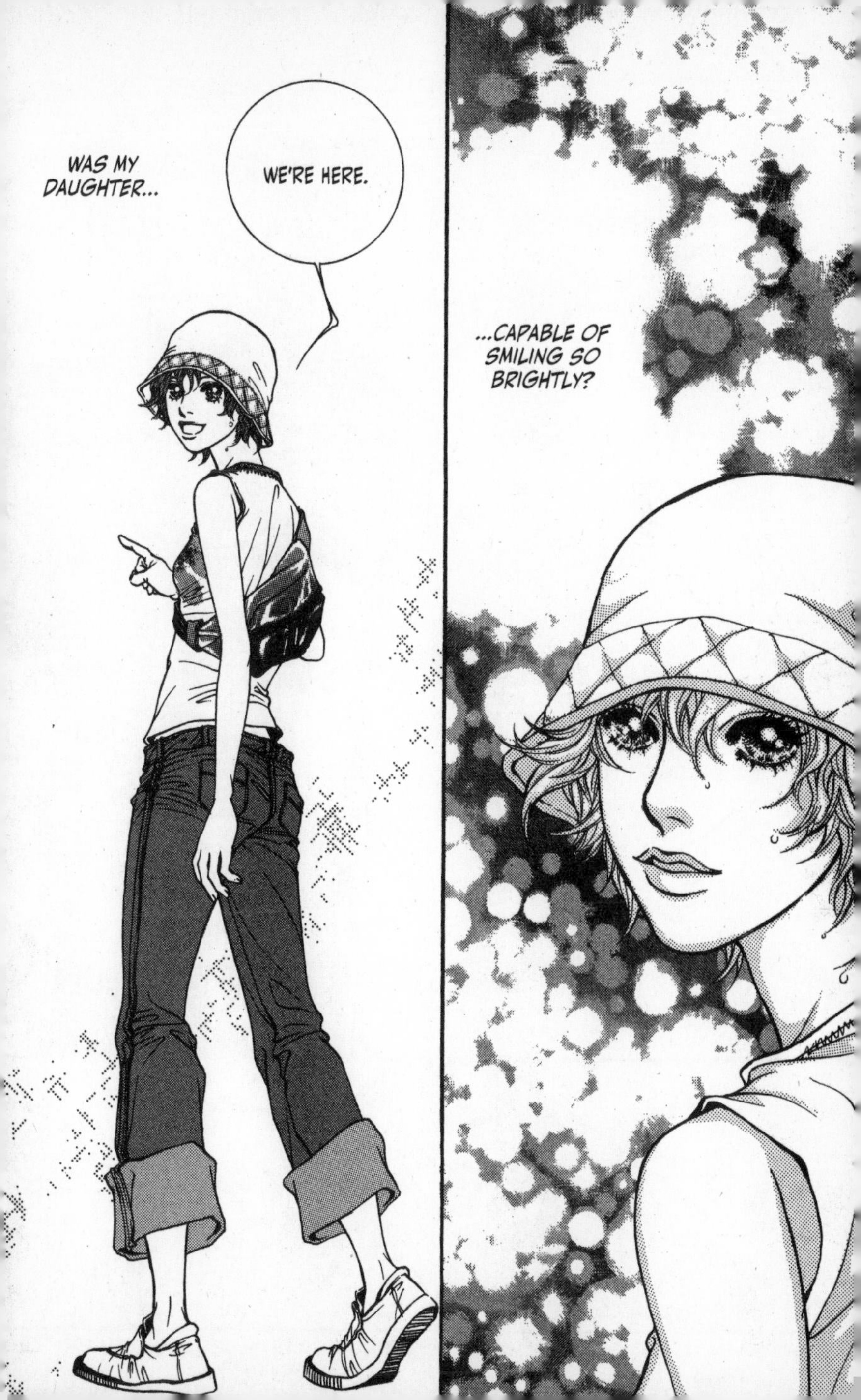
WAS MY DAUGHTER...
WE'RE HERE.
...CAPABLE OF SMILING SO BRIGHTLY?

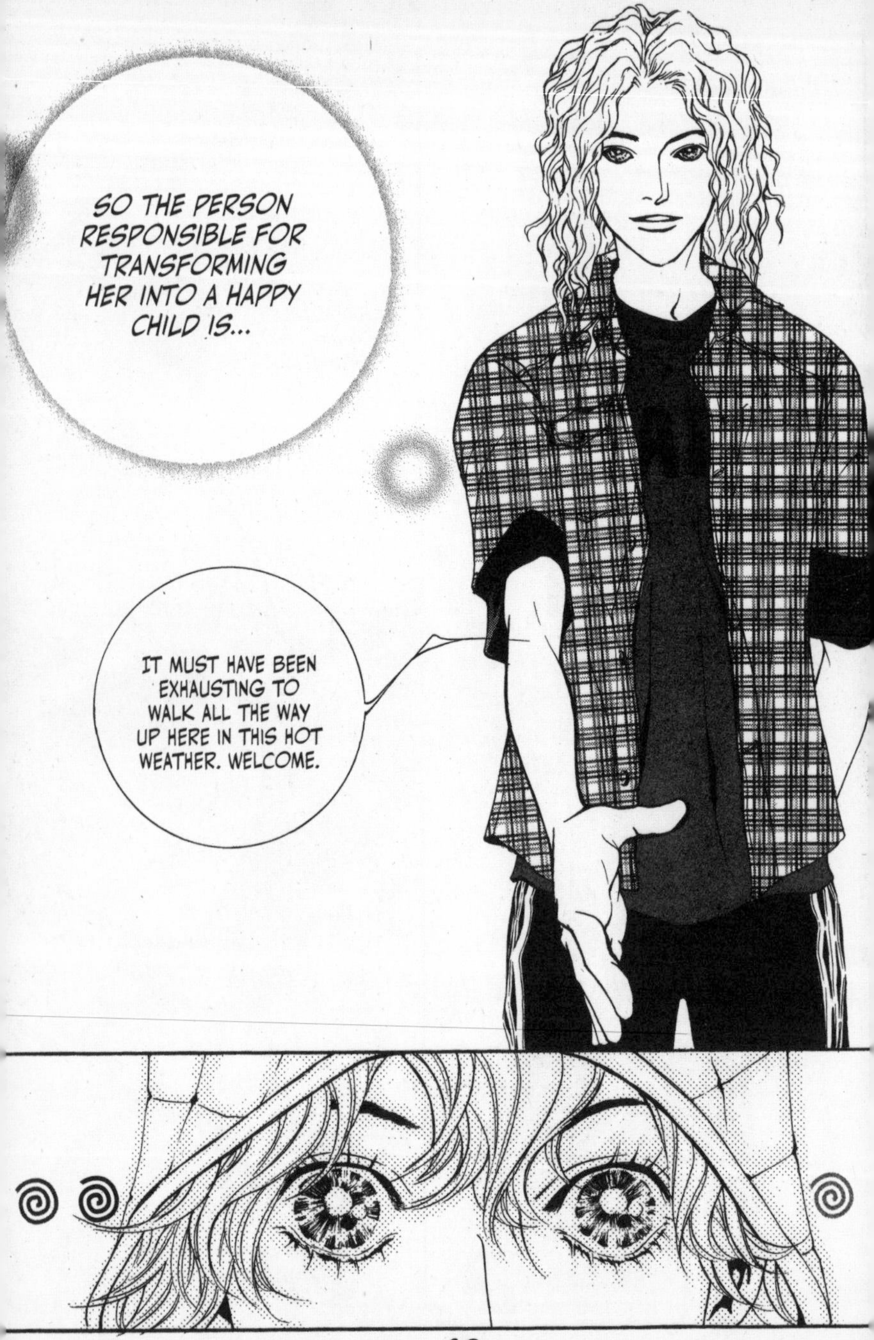
SO THE PERSON RESPONSIBLE FOR TRANSFORMING HER INTO A HAPPY CHILD IS...
IT MUST HAVE BEEN EXHAUSTING TO WALK ALL THE WAY UP HERE IN THIS HOT WEATHER. WELCOME.

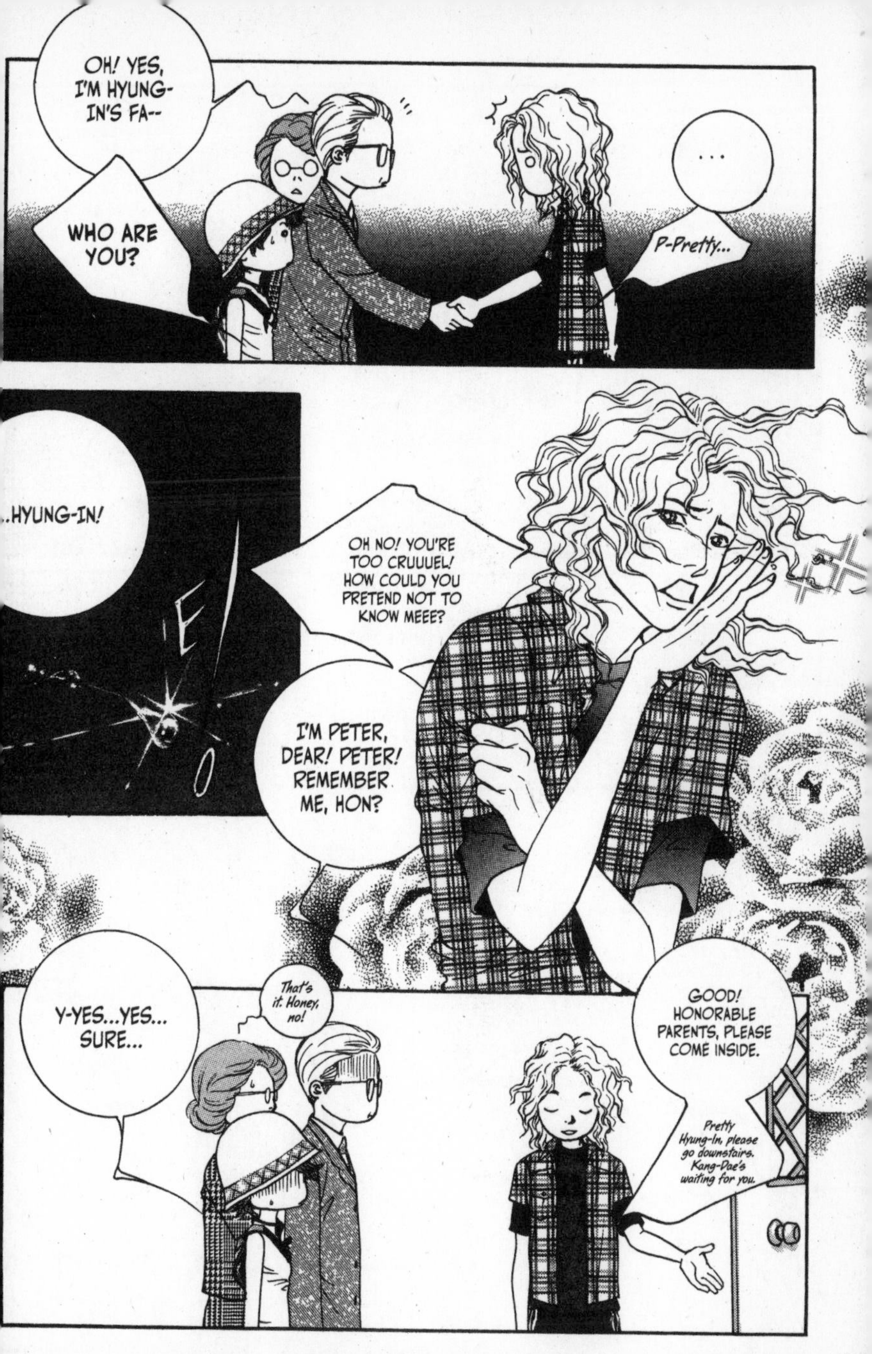
OH! YES, I'M HYUNG-IN'S FA--
WHO ARE YOU?
...
P-Pretty...
.HYUNG-IN!
OH NO! YOU'RE TOO CRUUUEL! HOW COULD YOU PRETEND NOT TO KNOW MEEE?
I'M PETER, DEAR! PETER! REMEMBER ME, HON?
Y-YES...YES... SURE...
That's it. Honey, no!
GOOD! HONORABLE PARENTS, PLEASE COME INSIDE.
Pretty Hyung-In, please go downstairs. Kang-Dae's waiting for you.

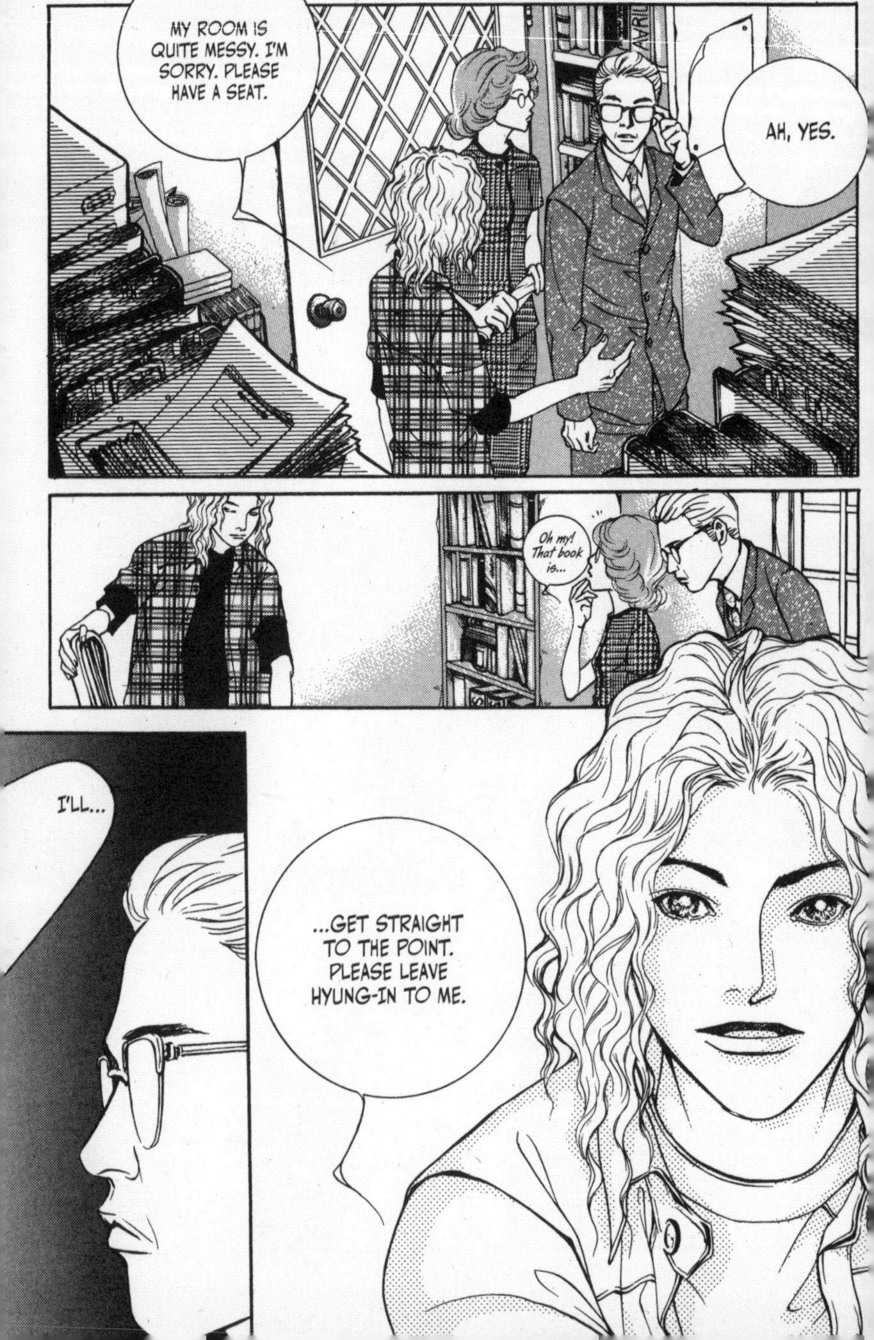
MY ROOM IS QUITE MESSY. I'M SORRY. PLEASE HAVE A SEAT.
AH, YES.
Oh my! That book is...
I'LL...
...GET STRAIGHT TO THE POINT. PLEASE LEAVE HYUNG-IN TO ME.

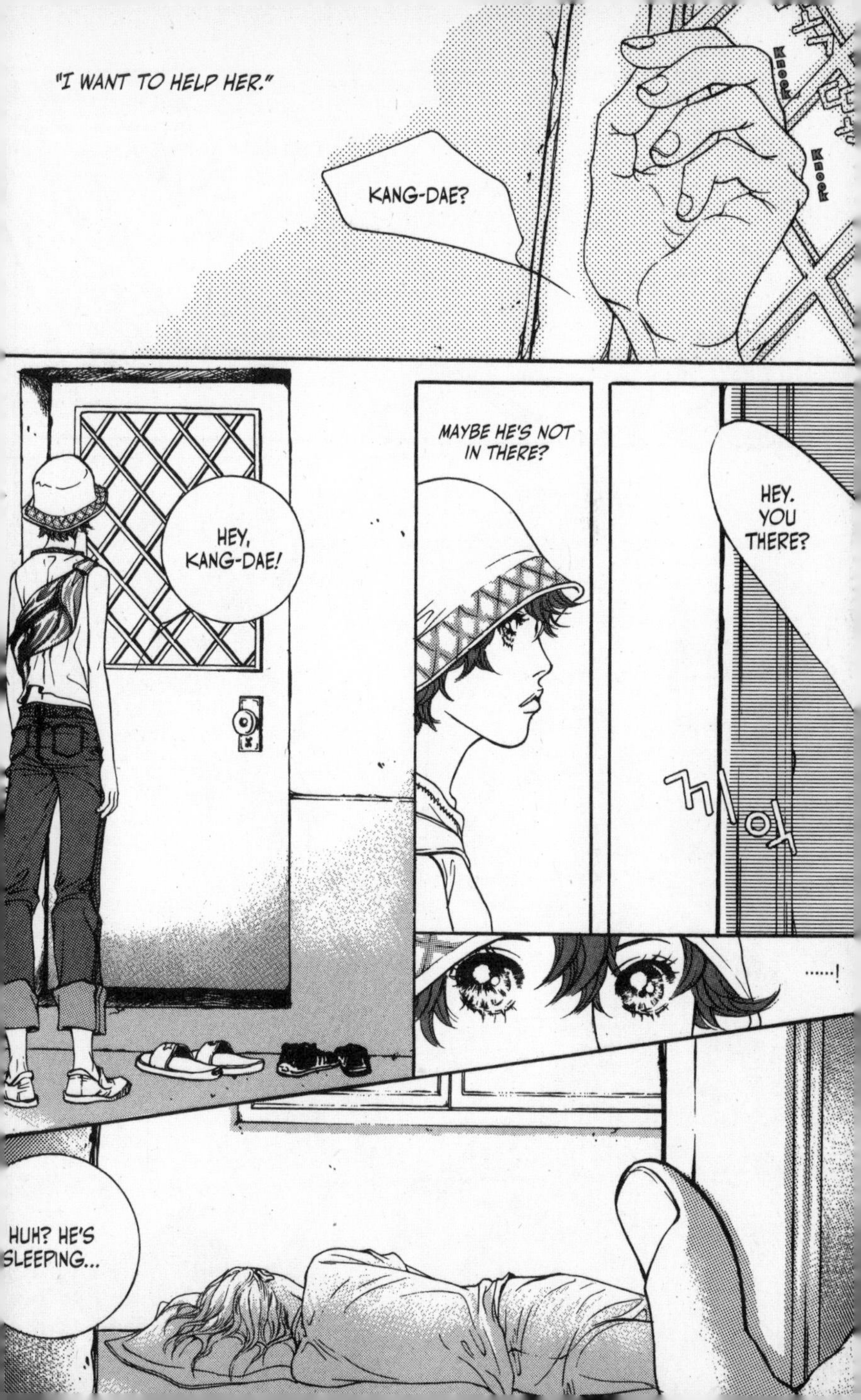
"I WANT TO HELP HER."
KANG-DAE?
Knock
Knock
HEY, KANG-DAE!
MAYBE HE'S NOT IN THERE?
HEY. YOU THERE?
......!
HUH? HE'S SLEEPING...

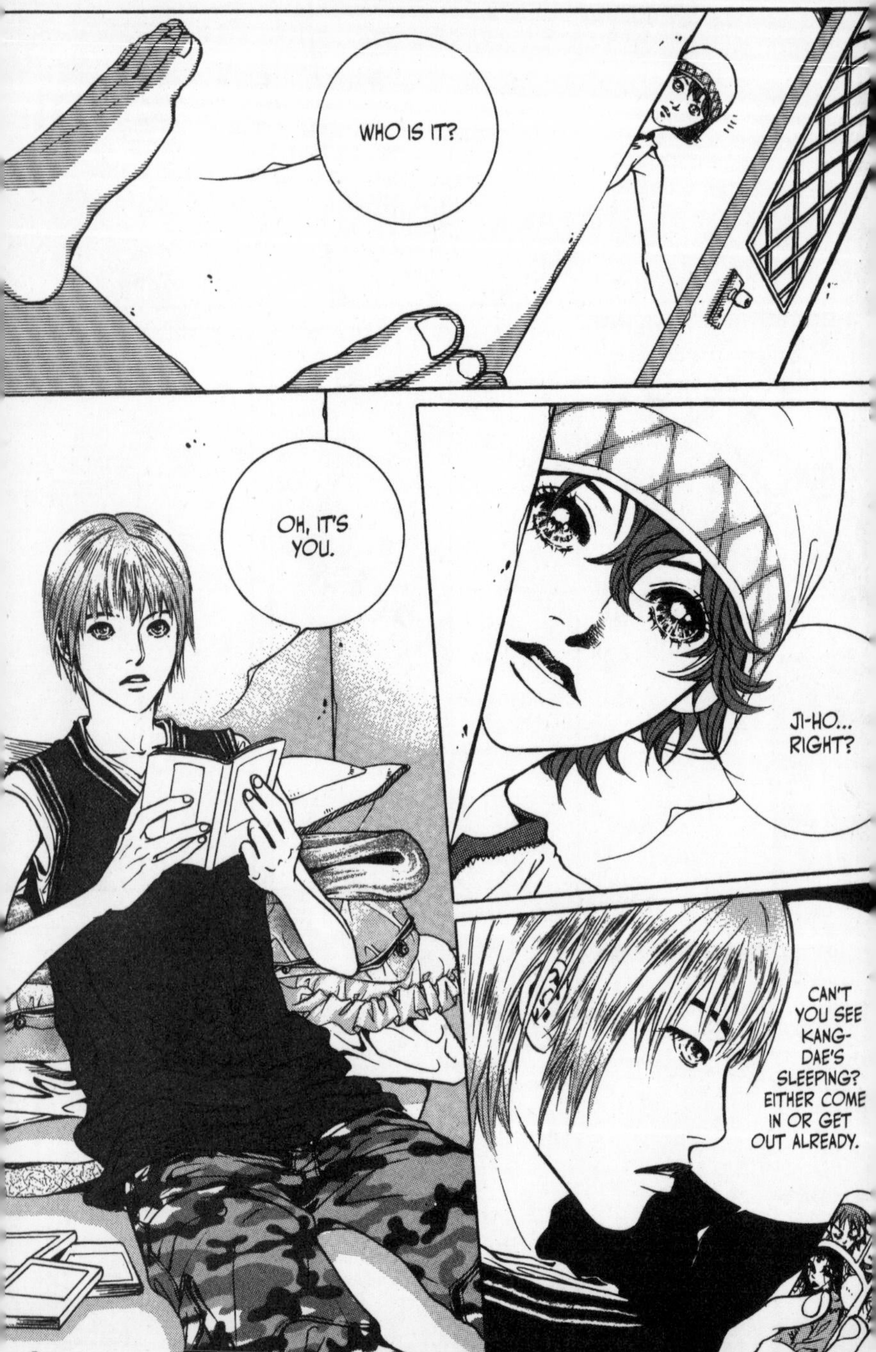
WHO IS IT?
OH, IT'S YOU.
JI-HO... RIGHT?
CAN'T YOU SEE KANG-DAE'S SLEEPING? EITHER COME IN OR GET OUT ALREADY.

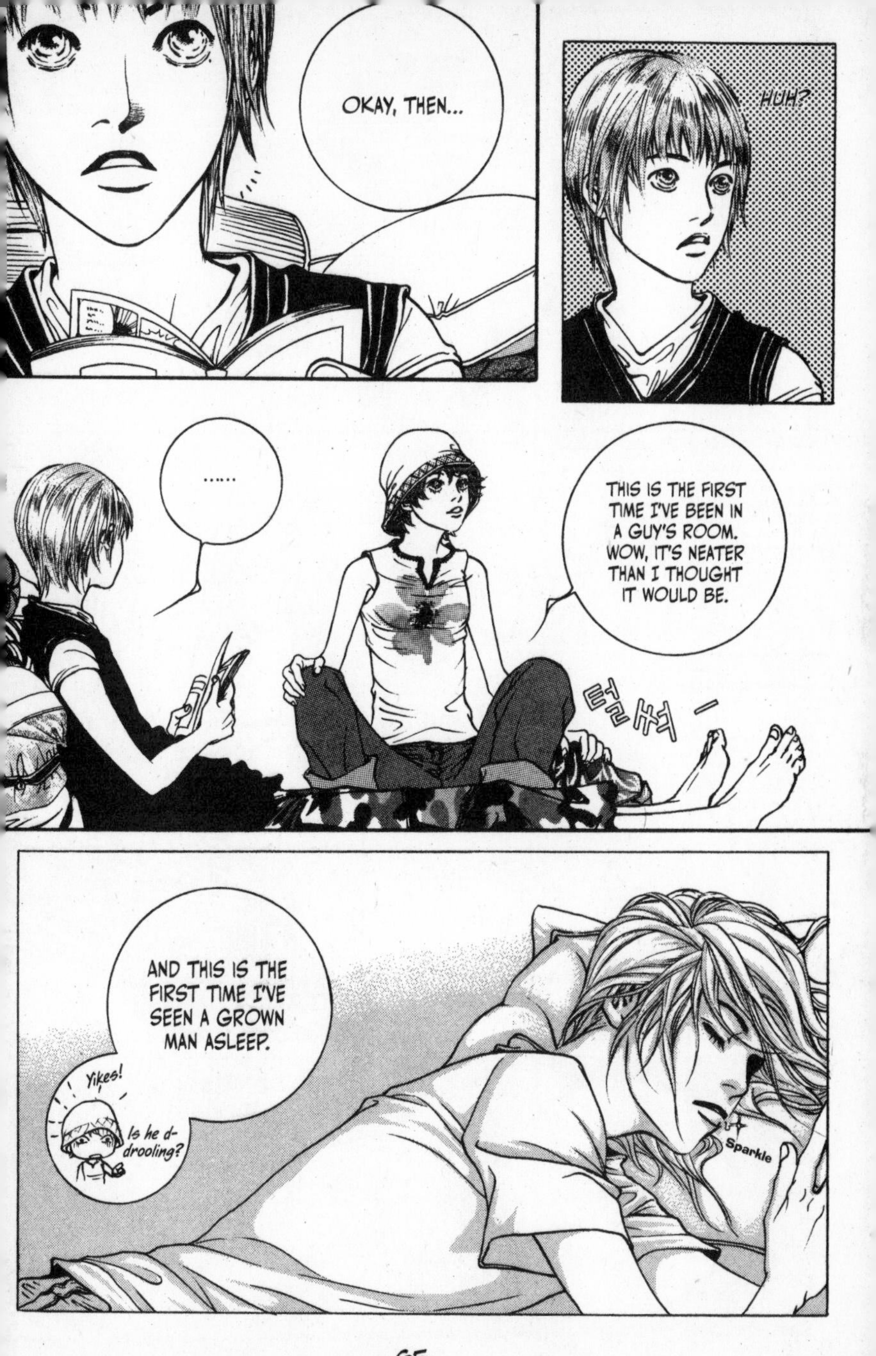
OKAY, THEN...
HUH?
......
THIS IS THE FIRST TIME I'VE BEEN IN A GUY'S ROOM. WOW, IT'S NEATER THAN I THOUGHT IT WOULD BE.
털썩 -
AND THIS IS THE FIRST TIME I'VE SEEN A GROWN MAN ASLEEP.
Yikes!
Is he d-drooling?
Sparkle

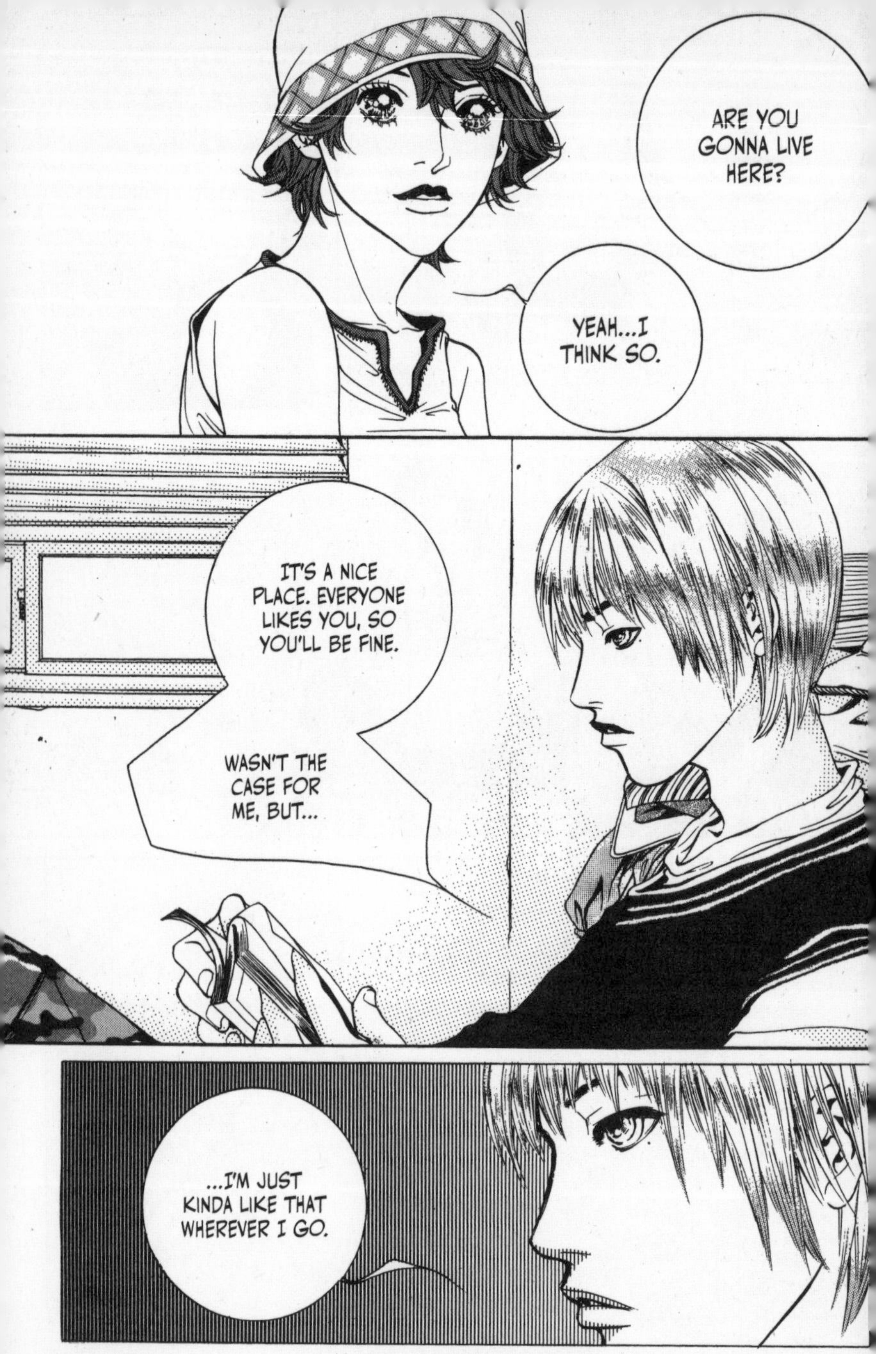
ARE YOU GONNA LIVE HERE?
YEAH...I THINK SO.
IT'S A NICE PLACE. EVERYONE LIKES YOU, SO YOU'LL BE FINE.
WASN'T THE CASE FOR ME, BUT...
...I'M JUST KINDA LIKE THAT WHEREVER I GO.

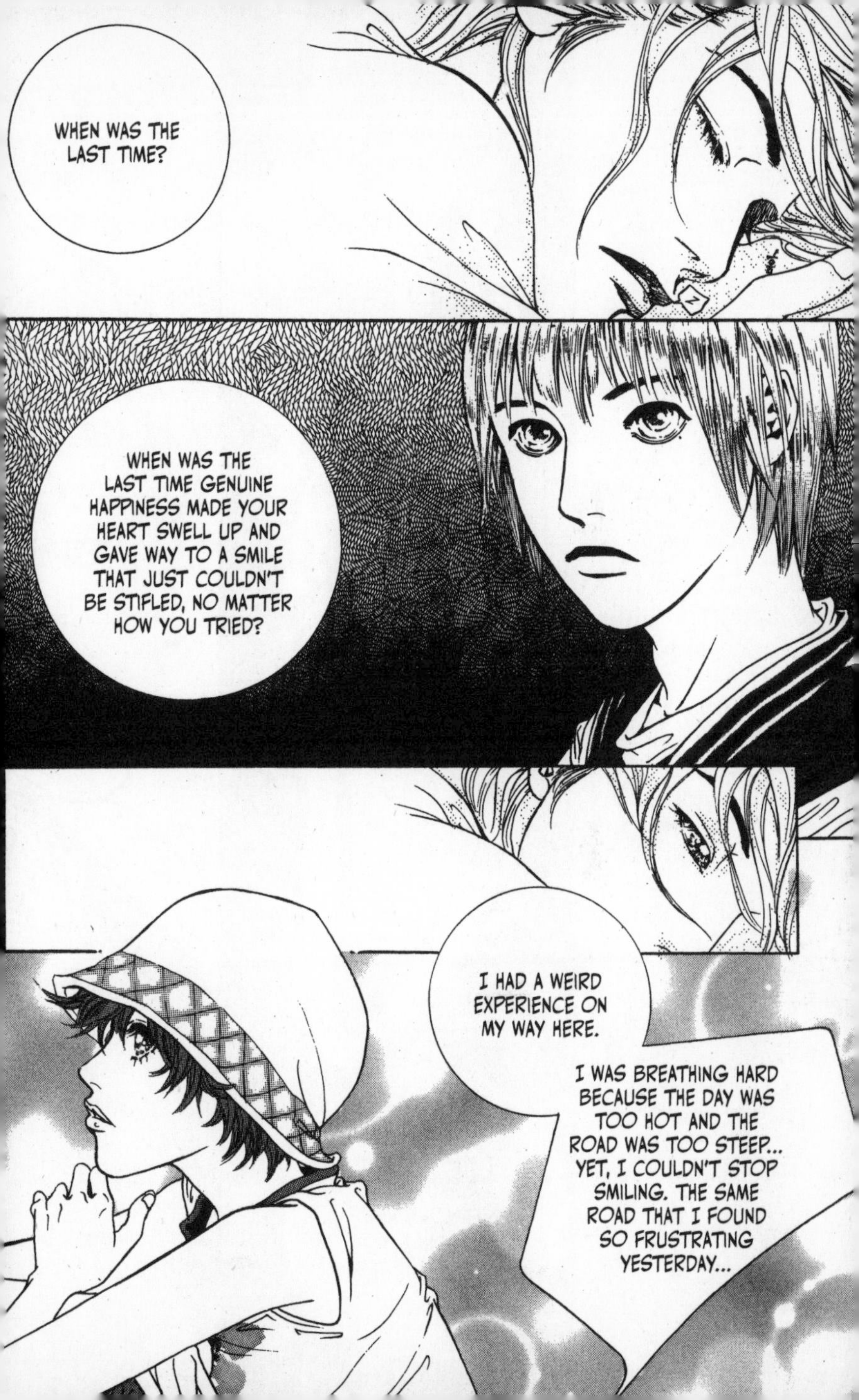
WHEN WAS THE LAST TIME?
WHEN WAS THE LAST TIME GENUINE HAPPINESS MADE YOUR HEART SWELL UP AND GAVE WAY TO A SMILE THAT JUST COULDN'T BE STIFLED, NO MATTER HOW YOU TRIED?
I HAD A WEIRD EXPERIENCE ON MY WAY HERE.
I WAS BREATHING HARD BECAUSE THE DAY WAS TOO HOT AND THE ROAD WAS TOO STEEP... YET, I COULDN'T STOP SMILING. THE SAME ROAD THAT I FOUND SO FRUSTRATING YESTERDAY...

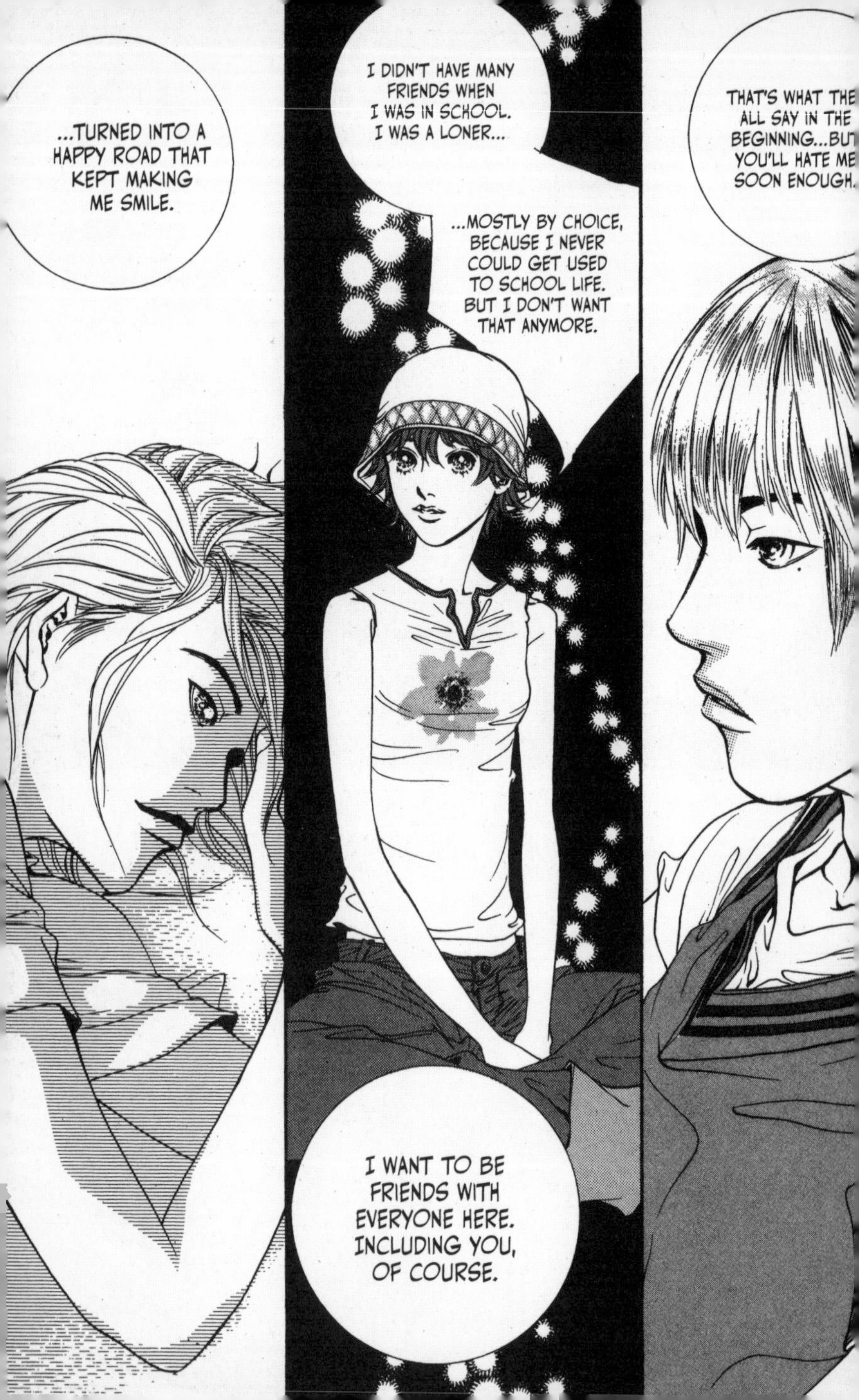
...TURNED INTO A HAPPY ROAD THAT KEPT MAKING ME SMILE.
I DIDN'T HAVE MANY FRIENDS WHEN I WAS IN SCHOOL. I WAS A LONER...
...MOSTLY BY CHOICE, BECAUSE I NEVER COULD GET USED TO SCHOOL LIFE. BUT I DON'T WANT THAT ANYMORE.
I WANT TO BE FRIENDS WITH EVERYONE HERE. INCLUDING YOU, OF COURSE.
THAT'S WHAT THE ALL SAY IN THE BEGINNING...BUT YOU'LL HATE ME SOON ENOUGH.

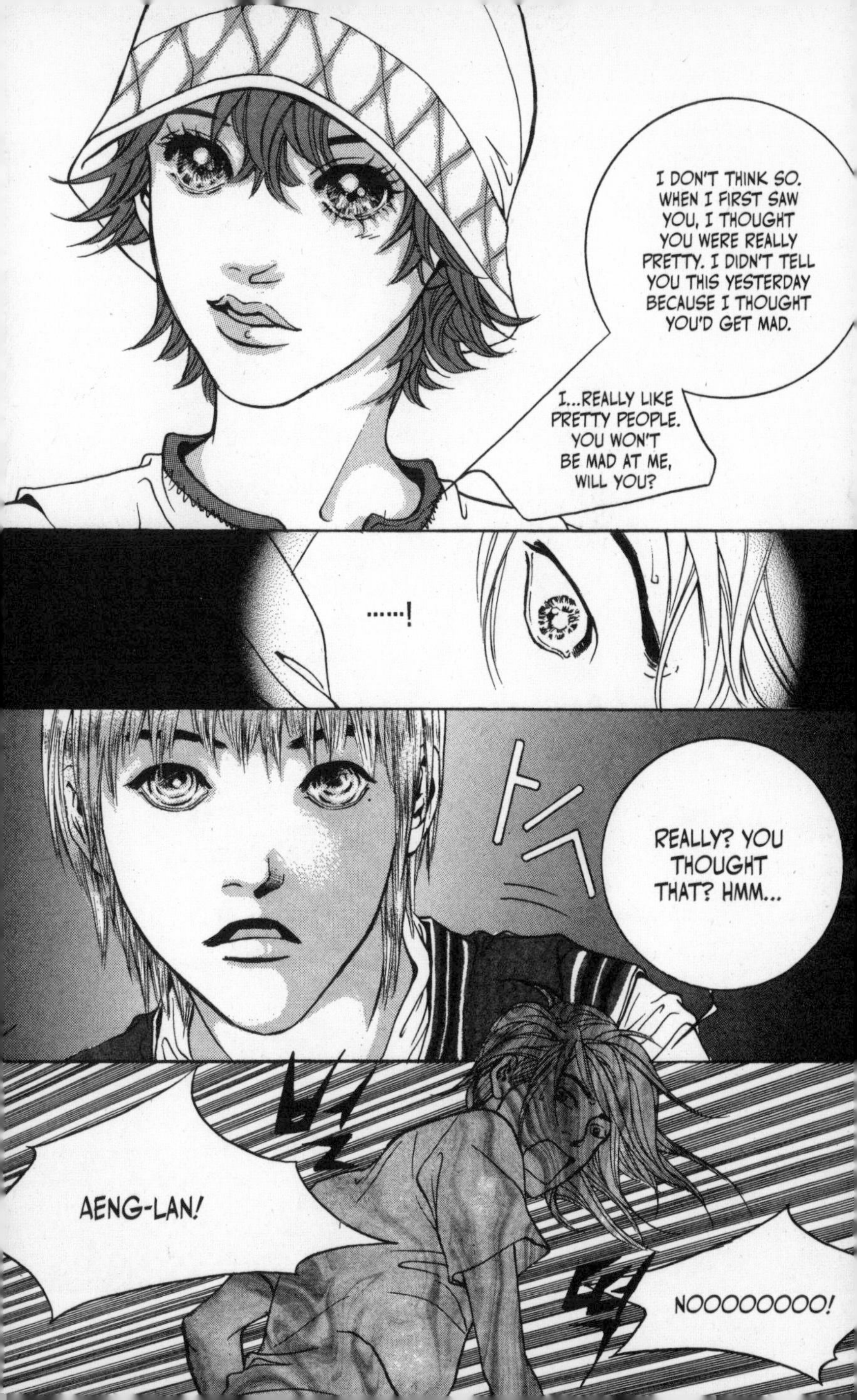
I DON'T THINK SO. WHEN I FIRST SAW YOU, I THOUGHT YOU WERE REALLY PRETTY. I DIDN'T TELL YOU THIS YESTERDAY BECAUSE I THOUGHT YOU'D GET MAD.
I...REALLY LIKE PRETTY PEOPLE. YOU WON'T BE MAD AT ME, WILL YOU?
......!
REALLY? YOU THOUGHT THAT? HMM...
AENG-LAN!
NOOOOOOOO!

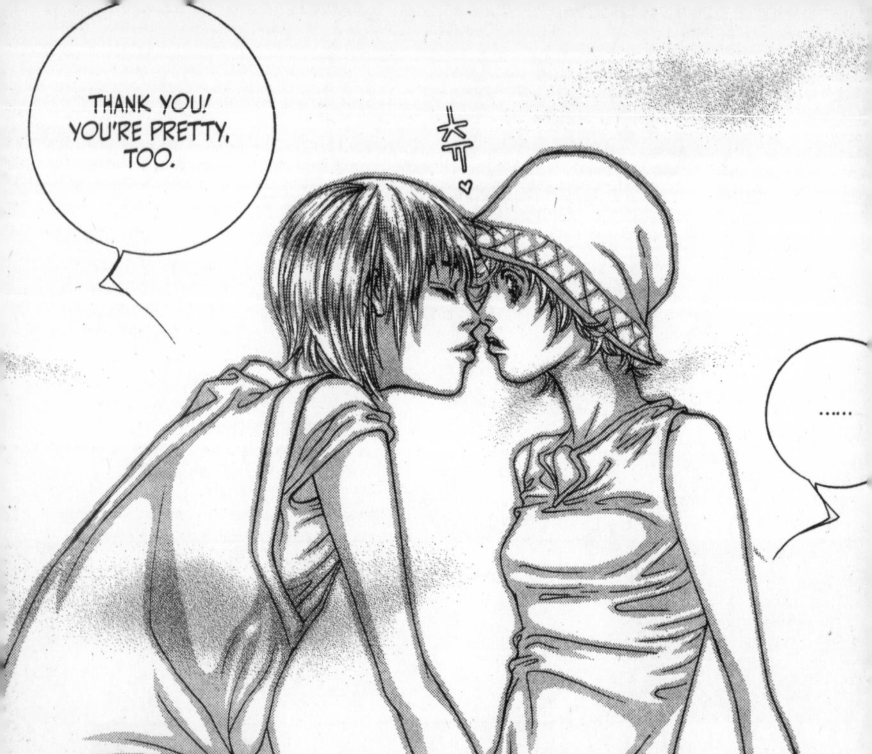
THANK YOU! YOU'RE PRETTY, TOO.
츄♡
......
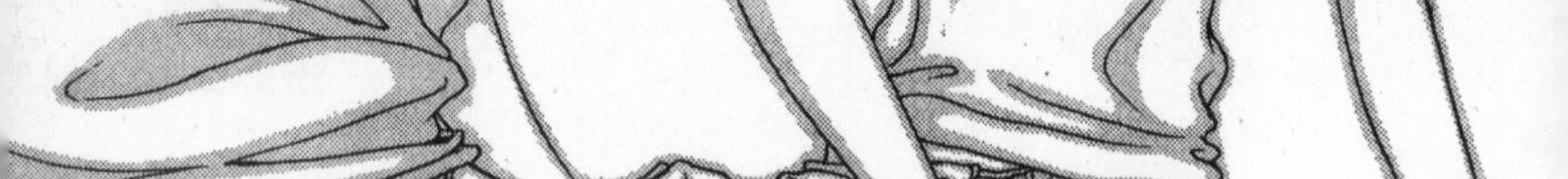
NO...AENG-LAN...

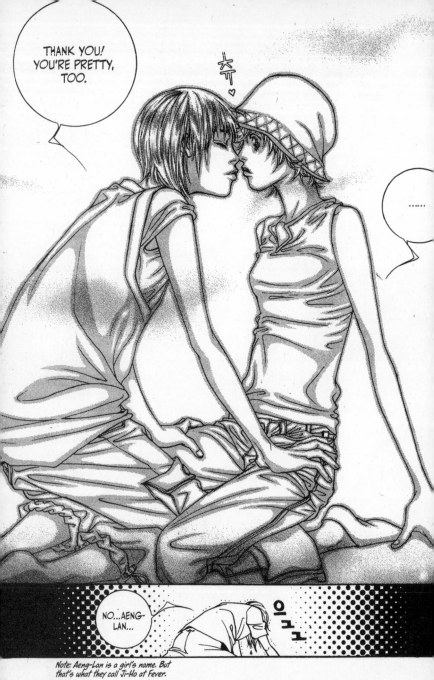

Note: Aeng-Lan is a girl's name. But that's what they call Ji-Ho at Fever.

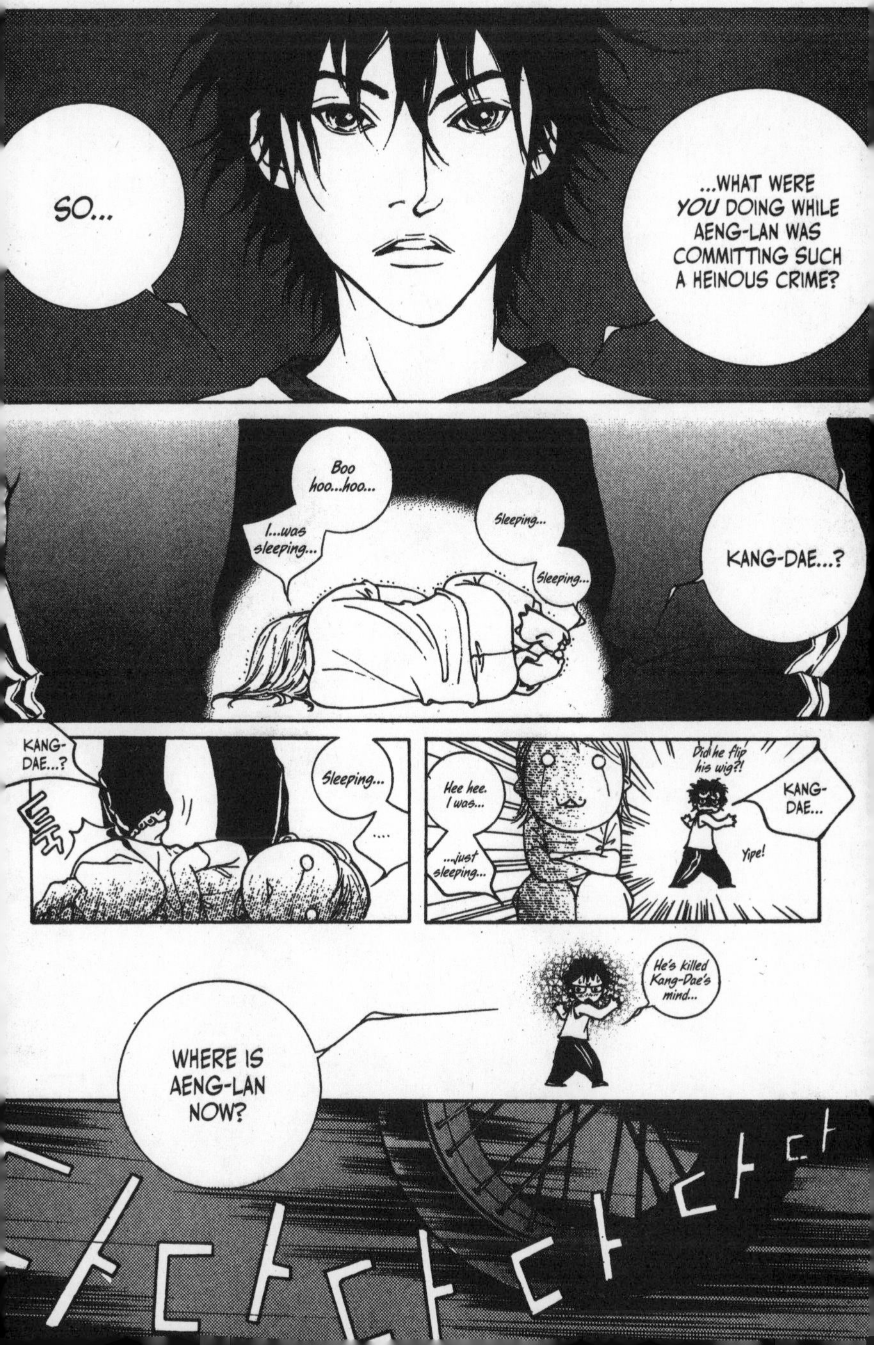
SO...
...WHAT WERE *YOU* DOING WHILE AENG-LAN WAS COMMITTING SUCH A HEINOUS CRIME?
Boo hoo...hoo...
I...was sleeping...
Sleeping...
Sleeping...
KANG-DAE...?
KANG-DAE...?
Sleeping...
...
Hee hee. I was...
...just sleeping...
Did he flip his wig?!
KANG-DAE...
Yipe!
WHERE IS AENG-LAN NOW?
He's killed Kang-Dae's mind...

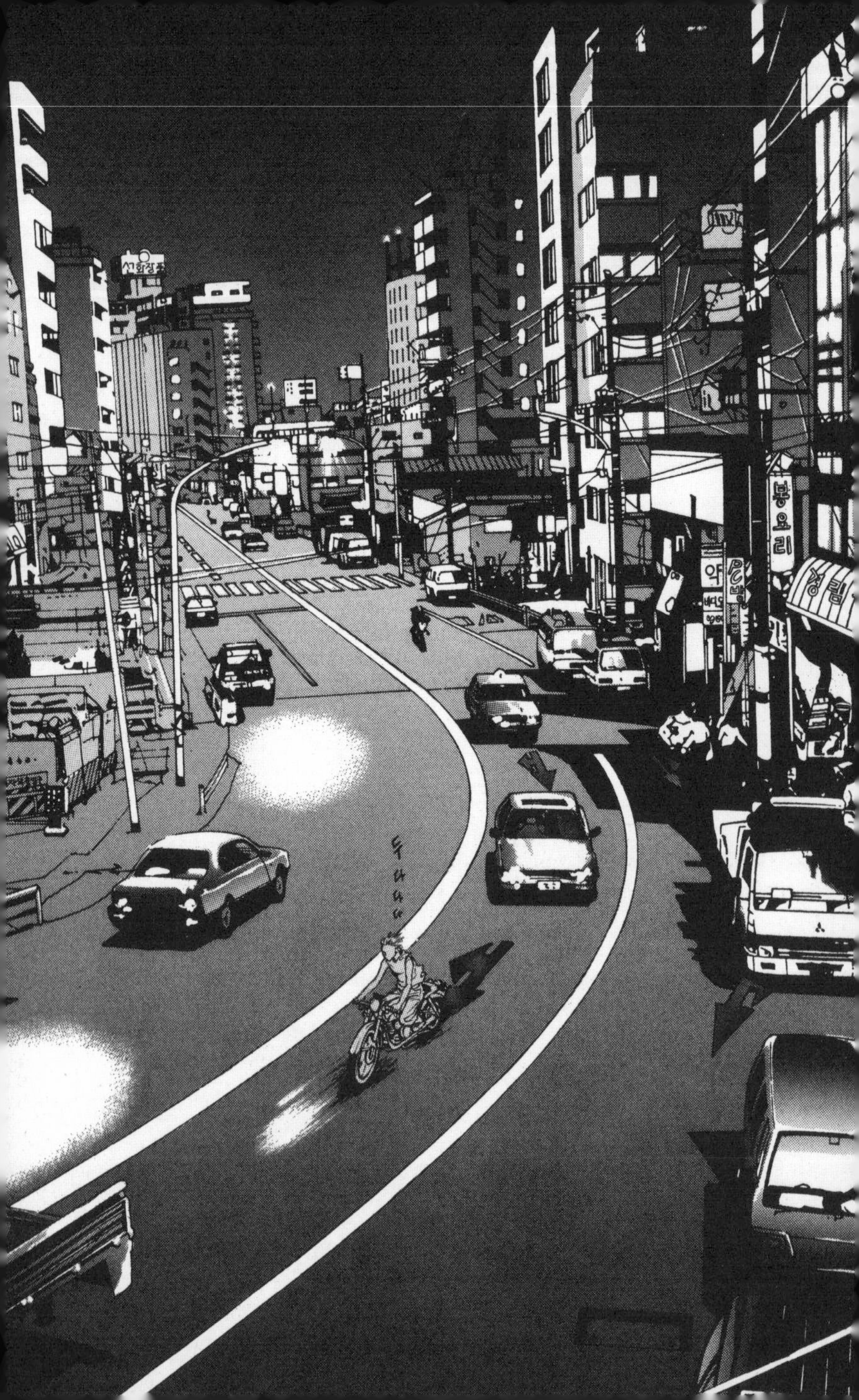
두다다다
봉요리
약
경림

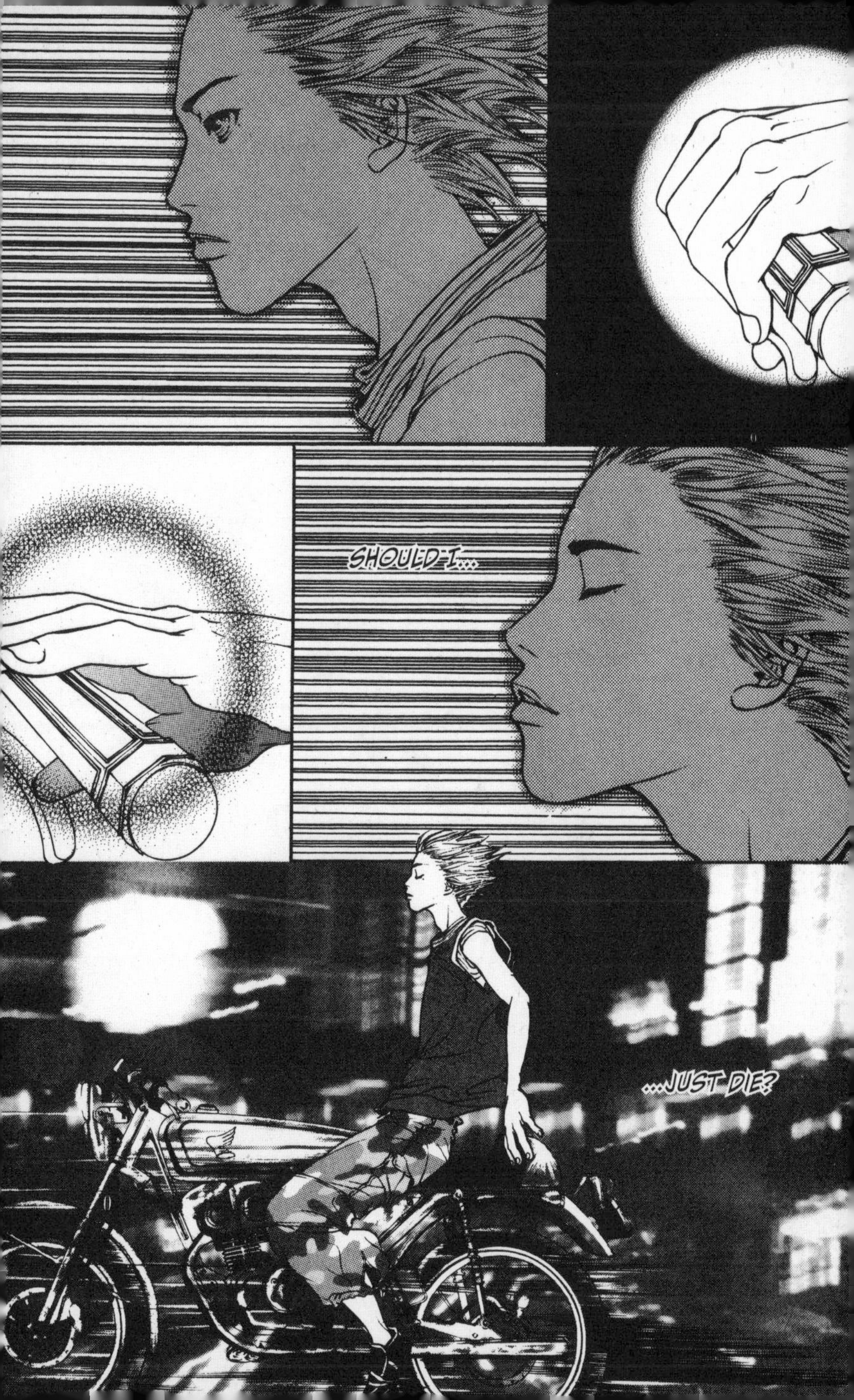
SHOULD I...
...JUST DIE?

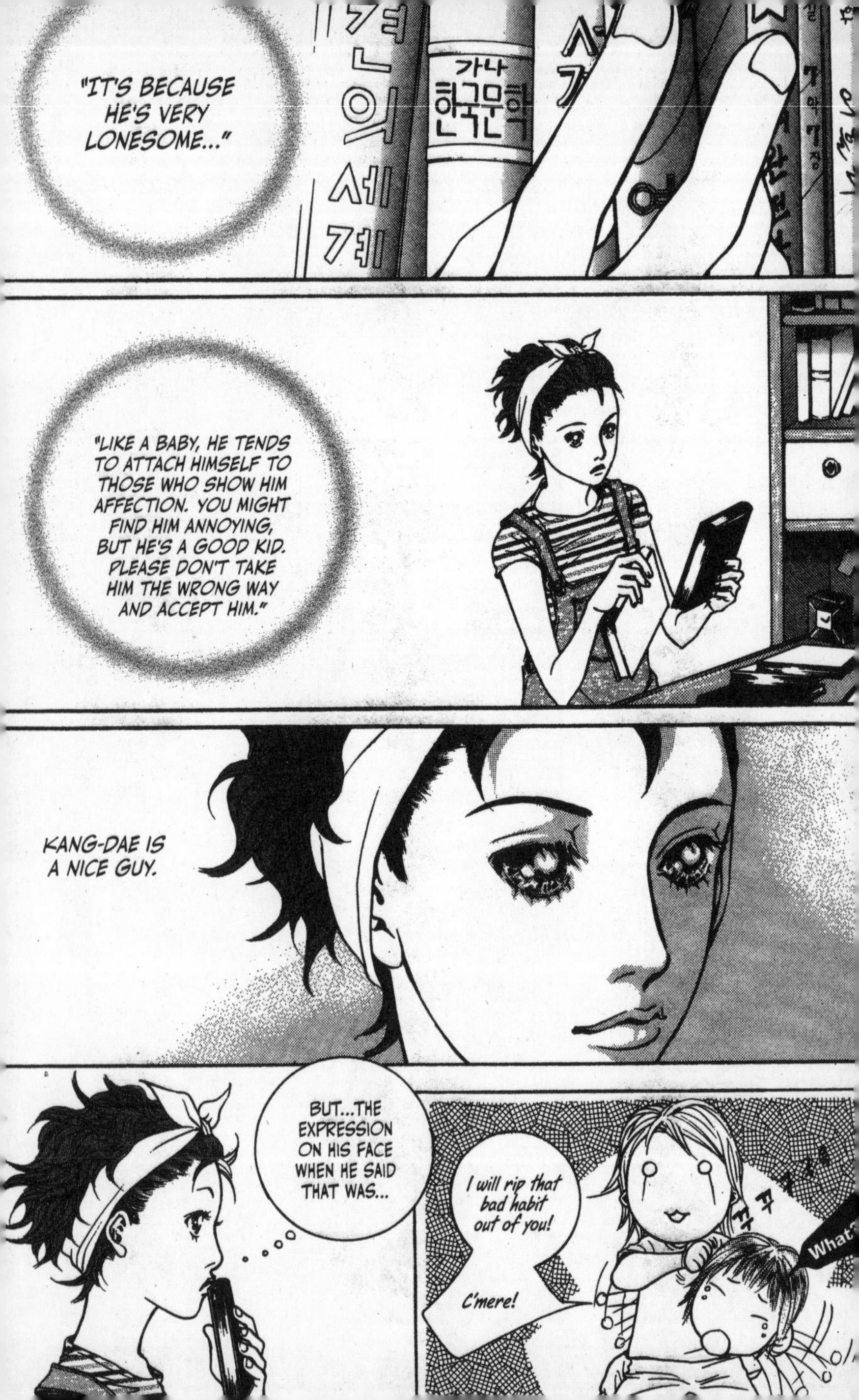
"IT'S BECAUSE HE'S VERY LONESOME..."
가나
한국문학
"LIKE A BABY, HE TENDS TO ATTACH HIMSELF TO THOSE WHO SHOW HIM AFFECTION. YOU MIGHT FIND HIM ANNOYING, BUT HE'S A GOOD KID. PLEASE DON'T TAKE HIM THE WRONG WAY AND ACCEPT HIM."
KANG-DAE IS A NICE GUY.
BUT...THE EXPRESSION ON HIS FACE WHEN HE SAID THAT WAS...
I will rip that bad habit out of you!
C'mere!

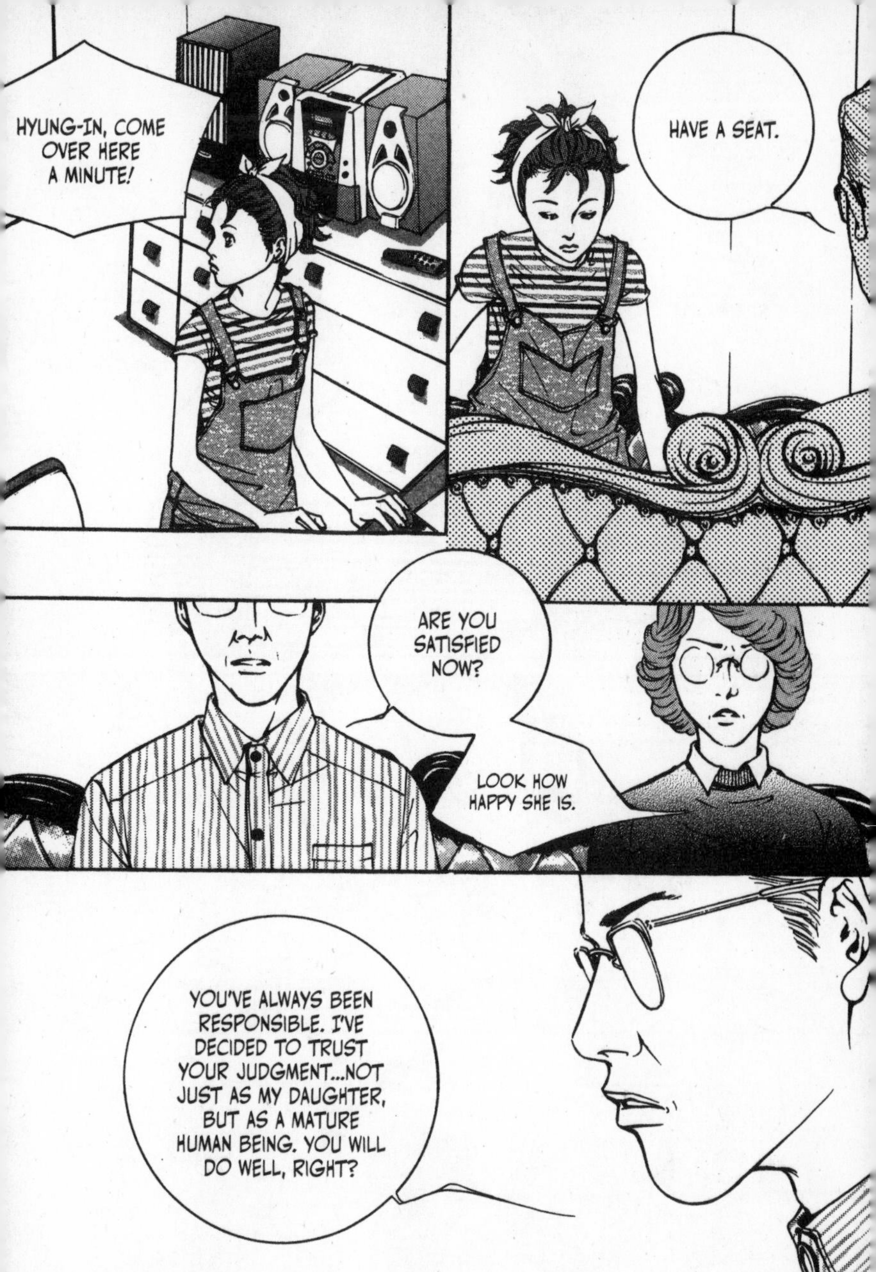

HYUNG-IN, COME OVER HERE A MINUTE!
HAVE A SEAT.
ARE YOU SATISFIED NOW?
LOOK HOW HAPPY SHE IS.
YOU'VE ALWAYS BEEN RESPONSIBLE. I'VE DECIDED TO TRUST YOUR JUDGMENT...NOT JUST AS MY DAUGHTER, BUT AS A MATURE HUMAN BEING. YOU WILL DO WELL, RIGHT?

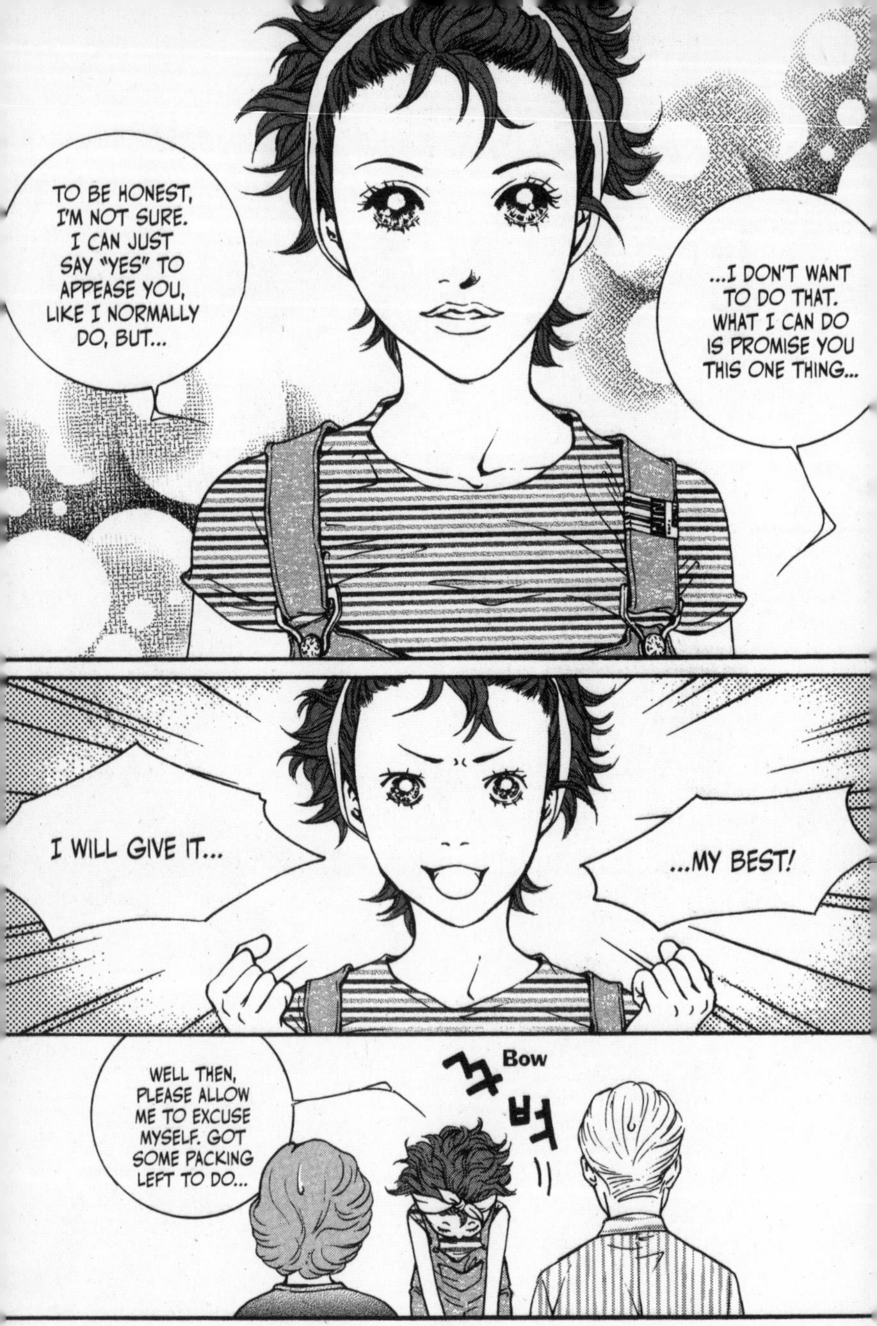
TO BE HONEST, I'M NOT SURE. I CAN JUST SAY "YES" TO APPEASE YOU, LIKE I NORMALLY DO, BUT...
...I DON'T WANT TO DO THAT. WHAT I CAN DO IS PROMISE YOU THIS ONE THING...
I WILL GIVE IT...
...MY BEST!
WELL THEN, PLEASE ALLOW ME TO EXCUSE MYSELF. GOT SOME PACKING LEFT TO DO...
Bow

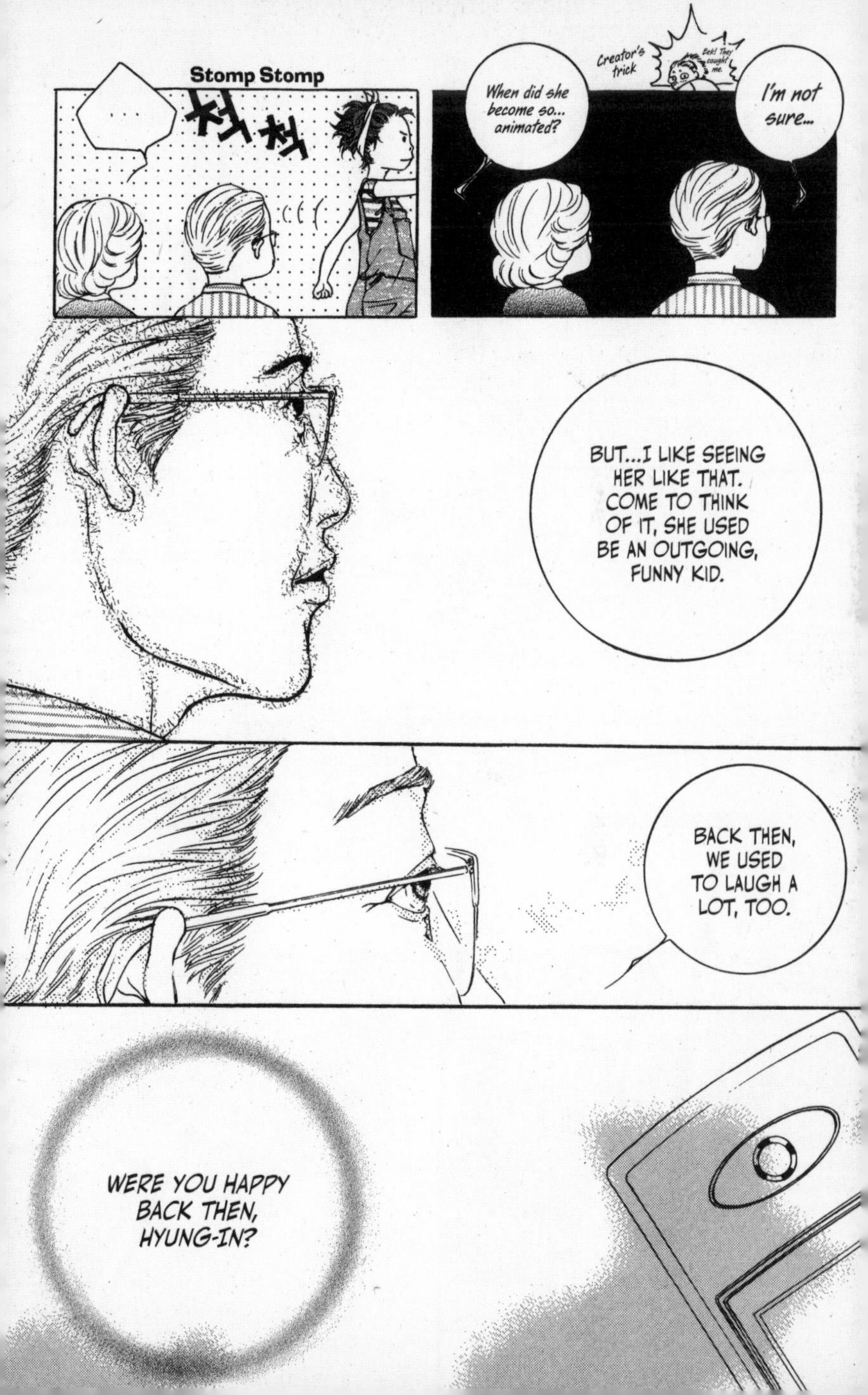
Stomp Stomp
척 척
...
When did she become so... animated?
Creator's trick
Eek! They caught me.
I'm not sure...
BUT...I LIKE SEEING HER LIKE THAT. COME TO THINK OF IT, SHE USED BE AN OUTGOING, FUNNY KID.
BACK THEN, WE USED TO LAUGH A LOT, TOO.
WERE YOU HAPPY BACK THEN, HYUNG-IN?

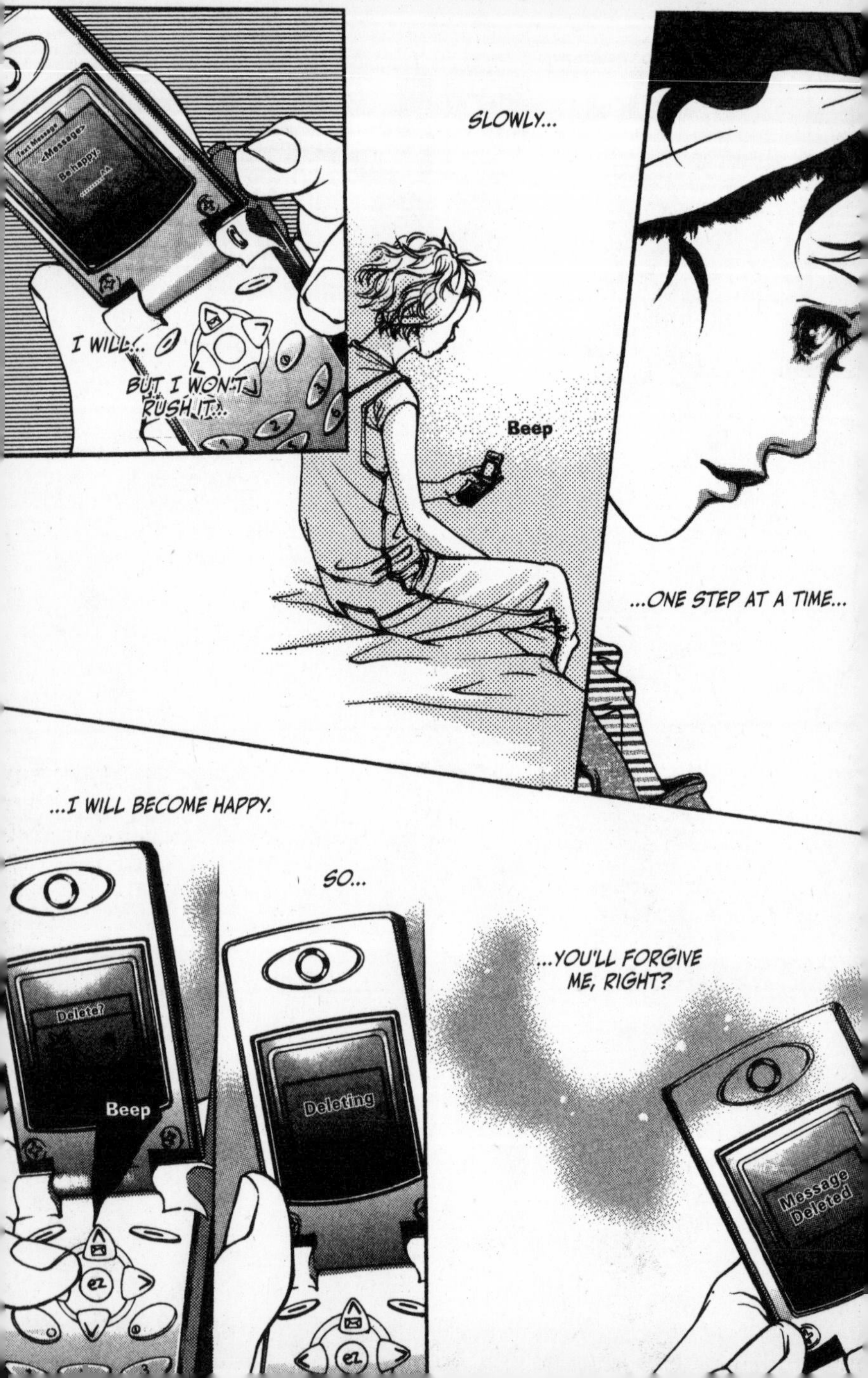
Text Message
<Message>
Be happy.
I WILL...
BUT I WON'T RUSH IT...
SLOWLY...
Beep
...ONE STEP AT A TIME...
...I WILL BECOME HAPPY.
Delete?
Beep
SO...
Deleting
...YOU'LL FORGIVE ME, RIGHT?
Message Deleted

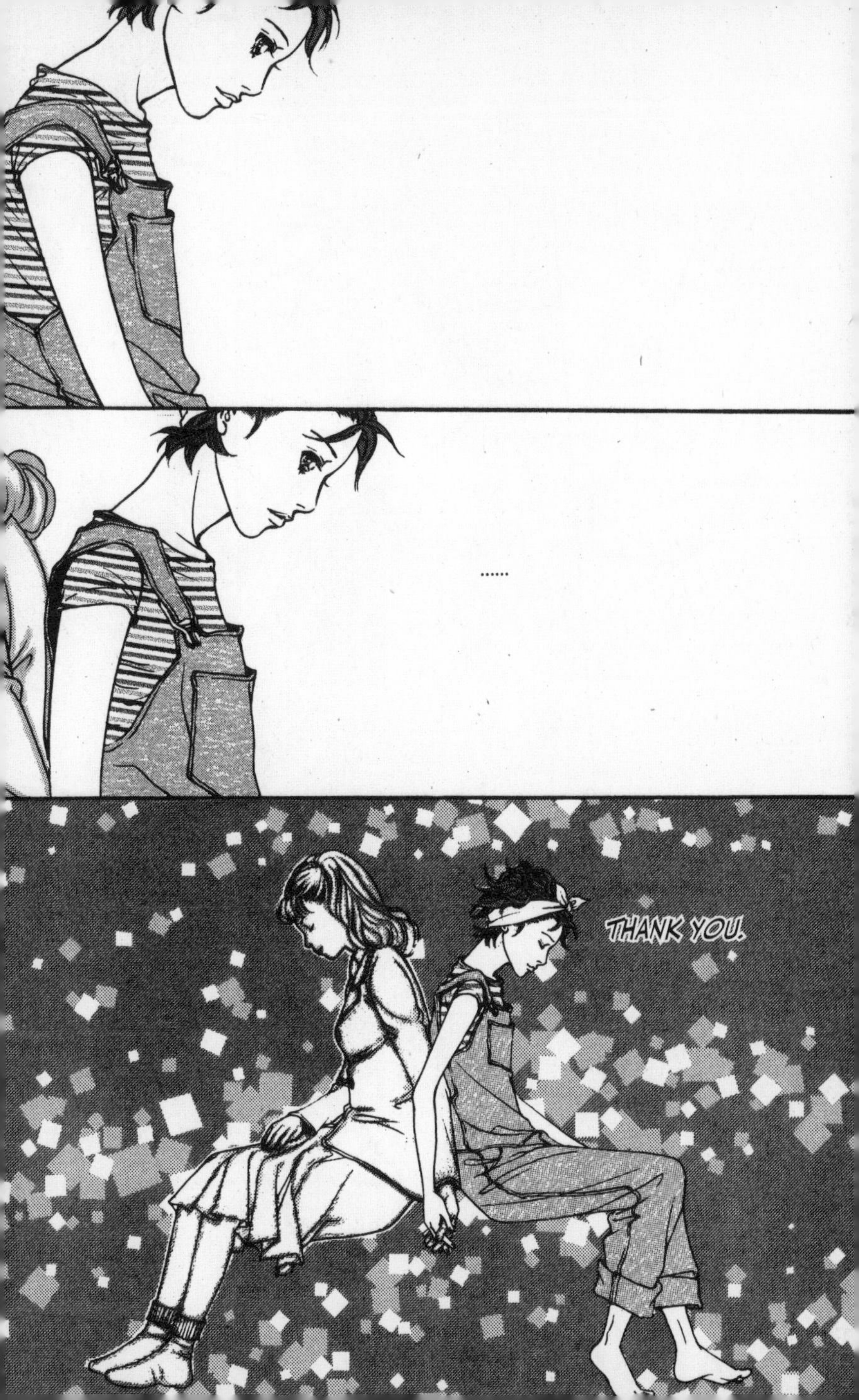
......
THANK YOU.

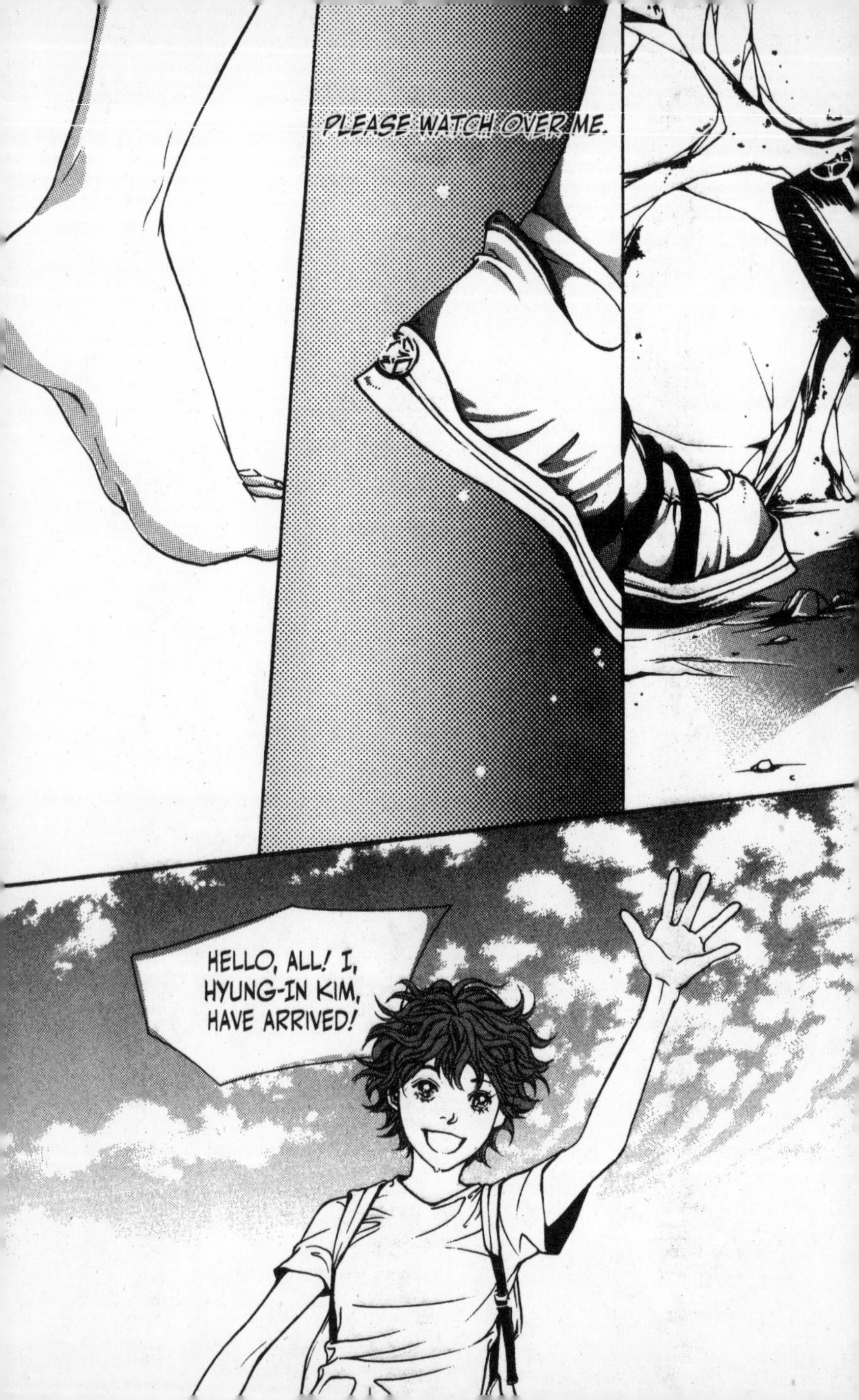
PLEASE WATCH OVER ME.
HELLO, ALL! I, HYUNG-IN KIM, HAVE ARRIVED!

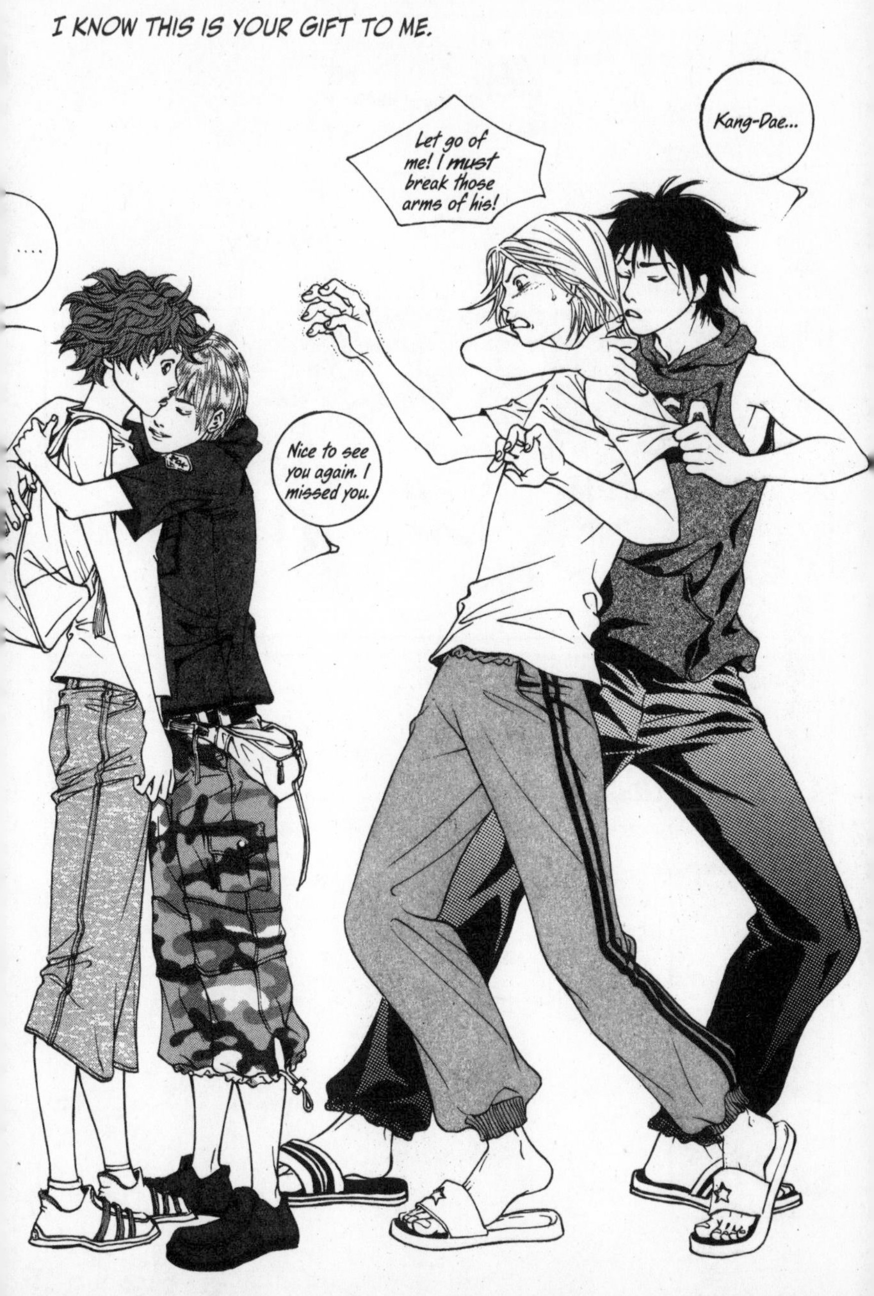
I KNOW THIS IS YOUR GIFT TO ME.
....
Let go of me! I must break those arms of his!
Kang-Dae...
Nice to see you again. I missed you.

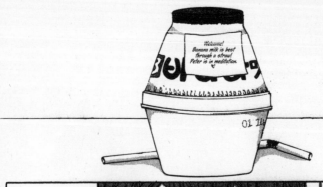

Welcome!
Banana milk is best
through a straw!
Peter is in meditation.

01 1

......

I GUESS HE REALLY
LIKES BANANA MILK.

씨ㅡ익

이익

IT'S HOT, SO MILK
ISN'T THE BEST
THING TO DRINK
RIGHT NOW, BUT...

...IT REALLY
IS SWEET.

나나맛우유

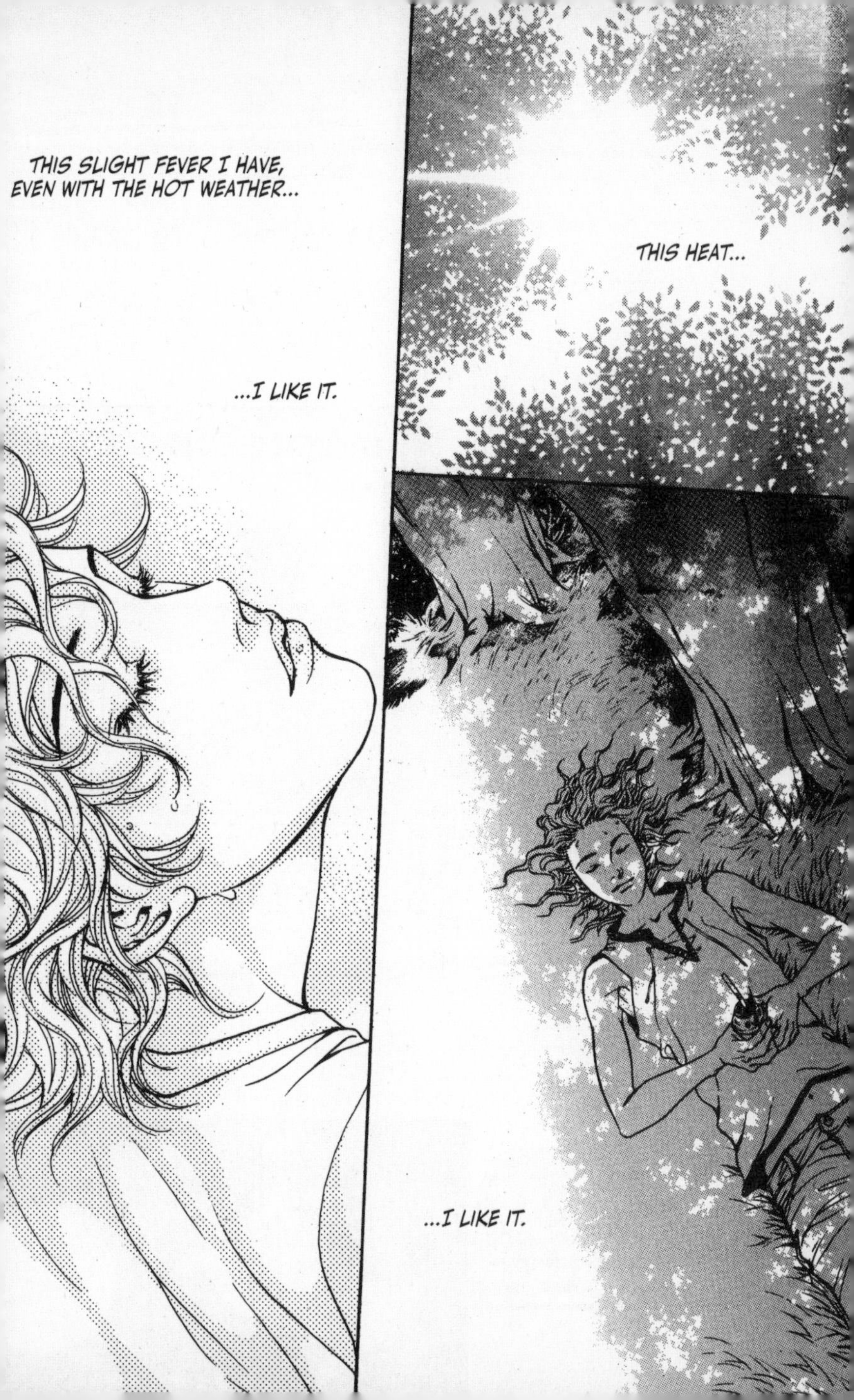
THIS SLIGHT FEVER I HAVE, EVEN WITH THE HOT WEATHER...
...I LIKE IT.
THIS HEAT...
...I LIKE IT.

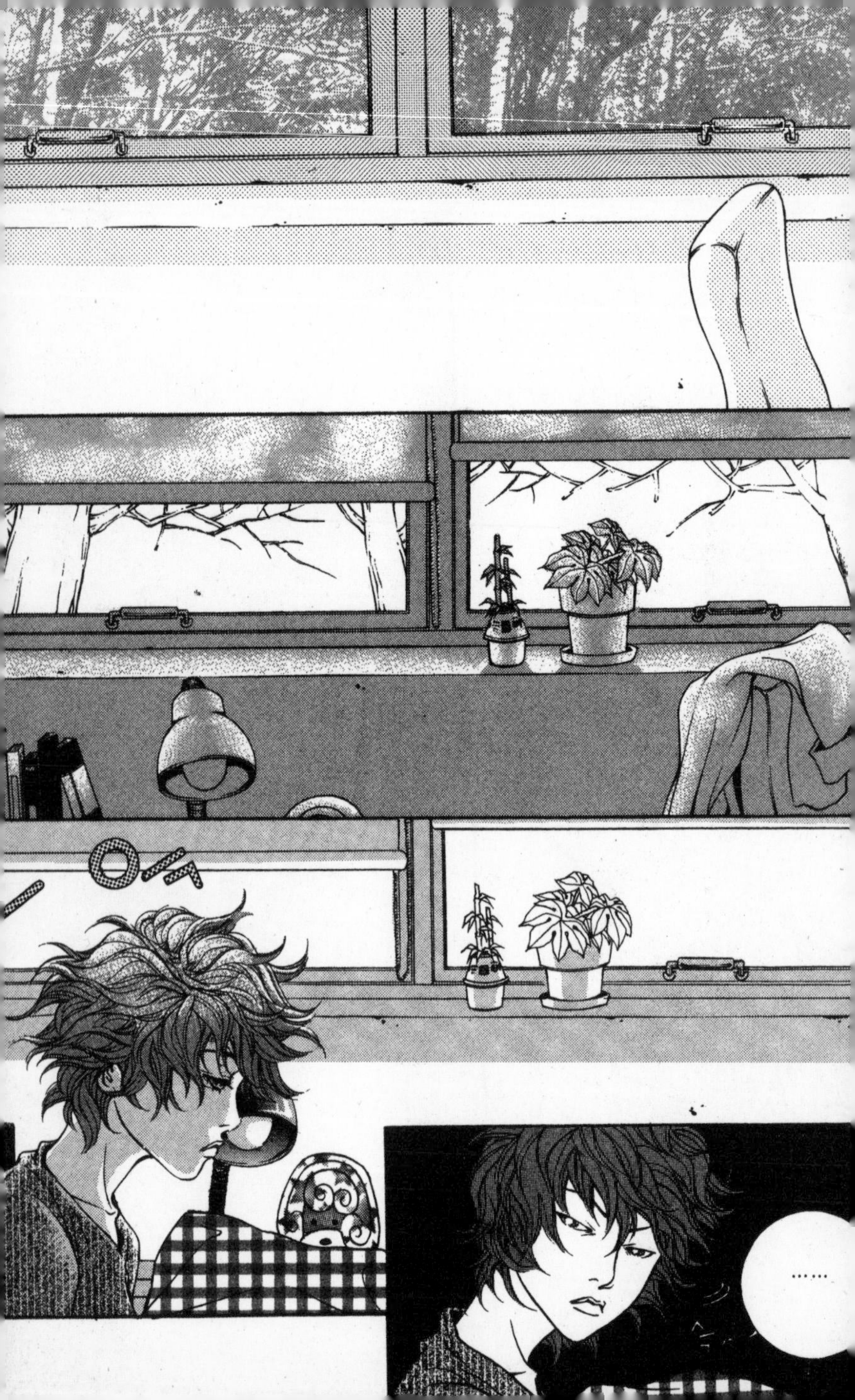
……

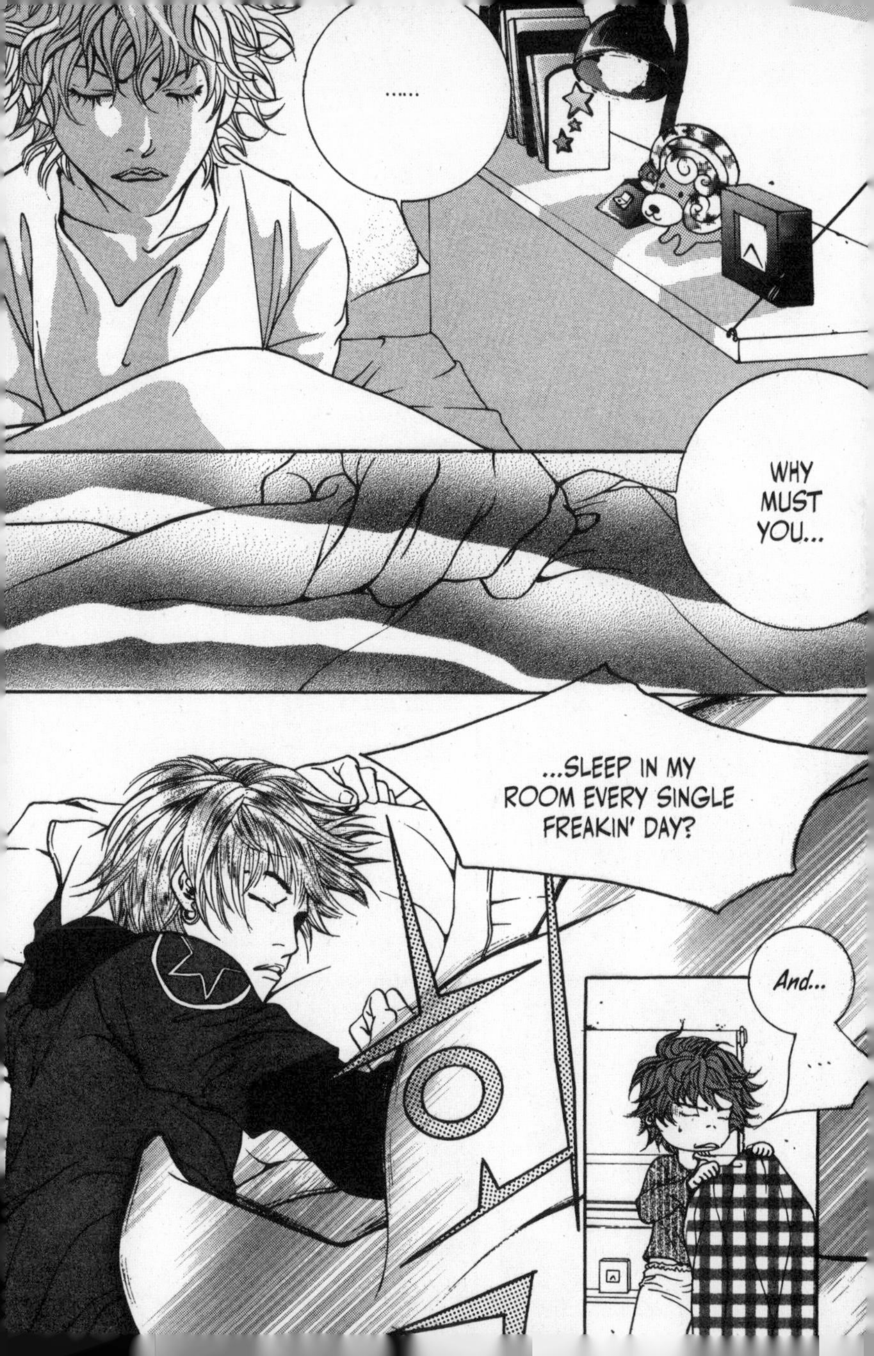
......
WHY MUST YOU...
...SLEEP IN MY ROOM EVERY SINGLE FREAKIN' DAY?
And...
...

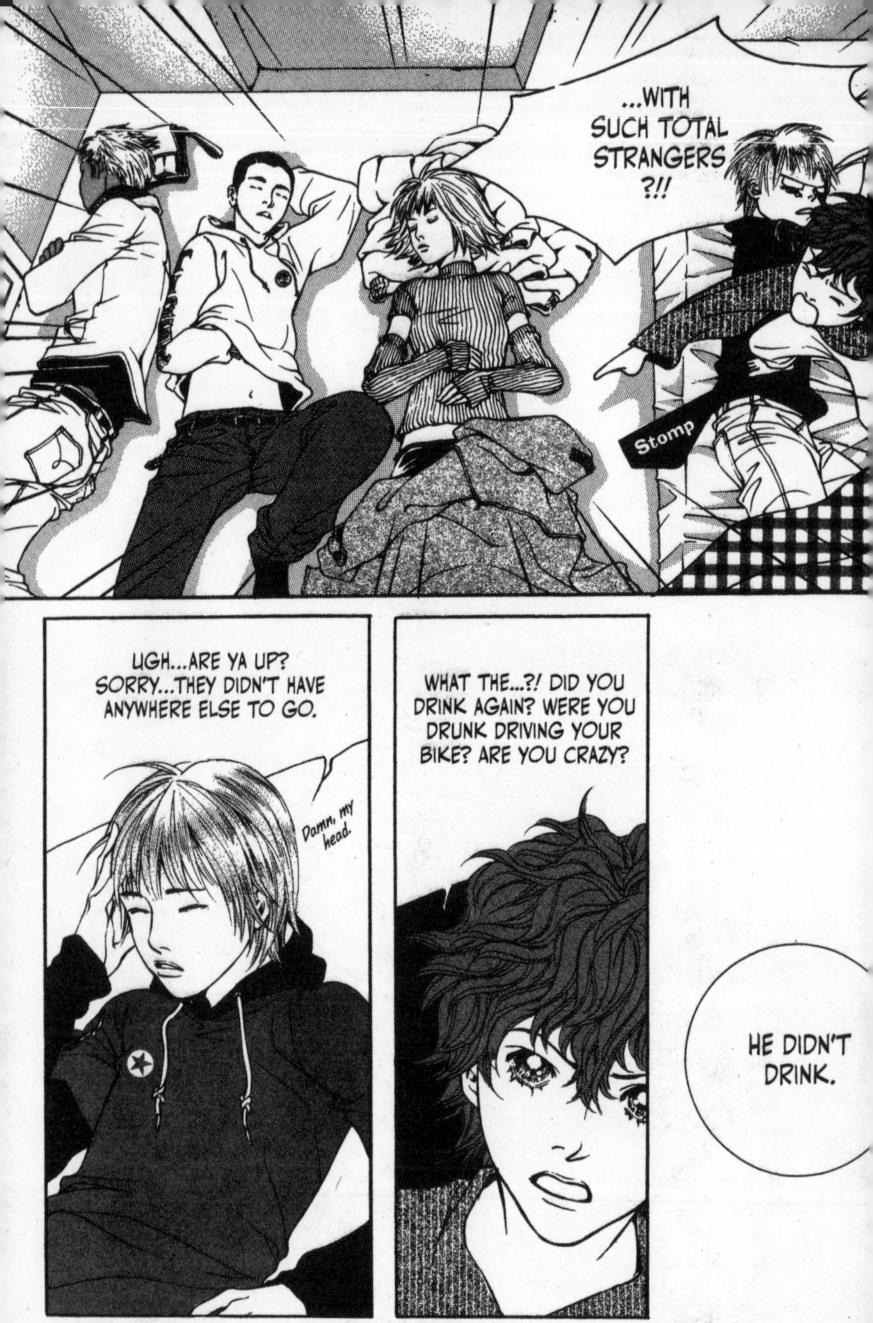
...WITH SUCH TOTAL STRANGERS ?!!
Stomp
UGH...ARE YA UP? SORRY...THEY DIDN'T HAVE ANYWHERE ELSE TO GO.
Damn, my head.
WHAT THE...?! DID YOU DRINK AGAIN? WERE YOU DRUNK DRIVING YOUR BIKE? ARE YOU CRAZY?
HE DIDN'T DRINK.

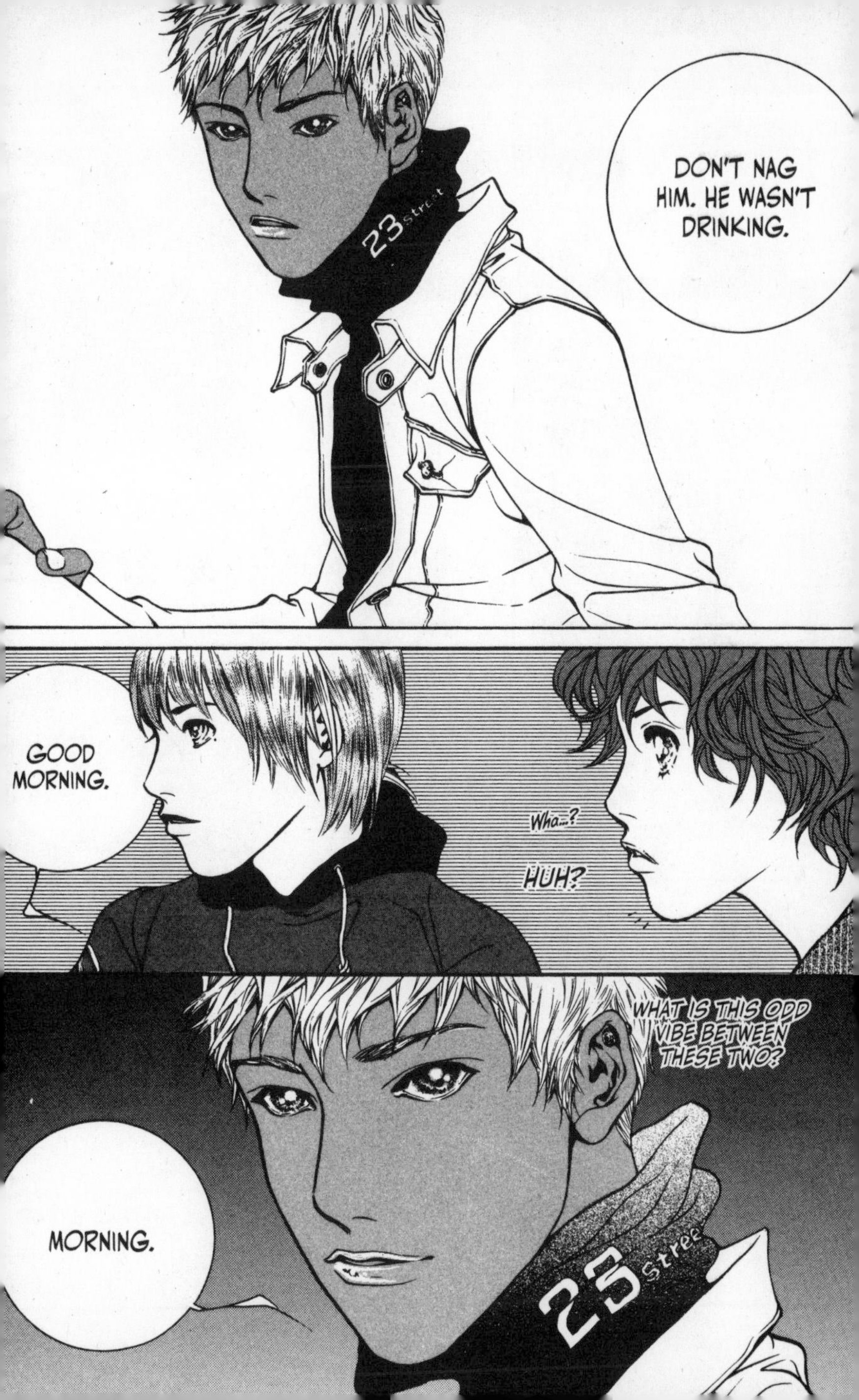
DON'T NAG HIM. HE WASN'T DRINKING.
HUH?
Wha...?
GOOD MORNING.
WHAT IS THIS ODD VIBE BETWEEN THESE TWO?
MORNING.

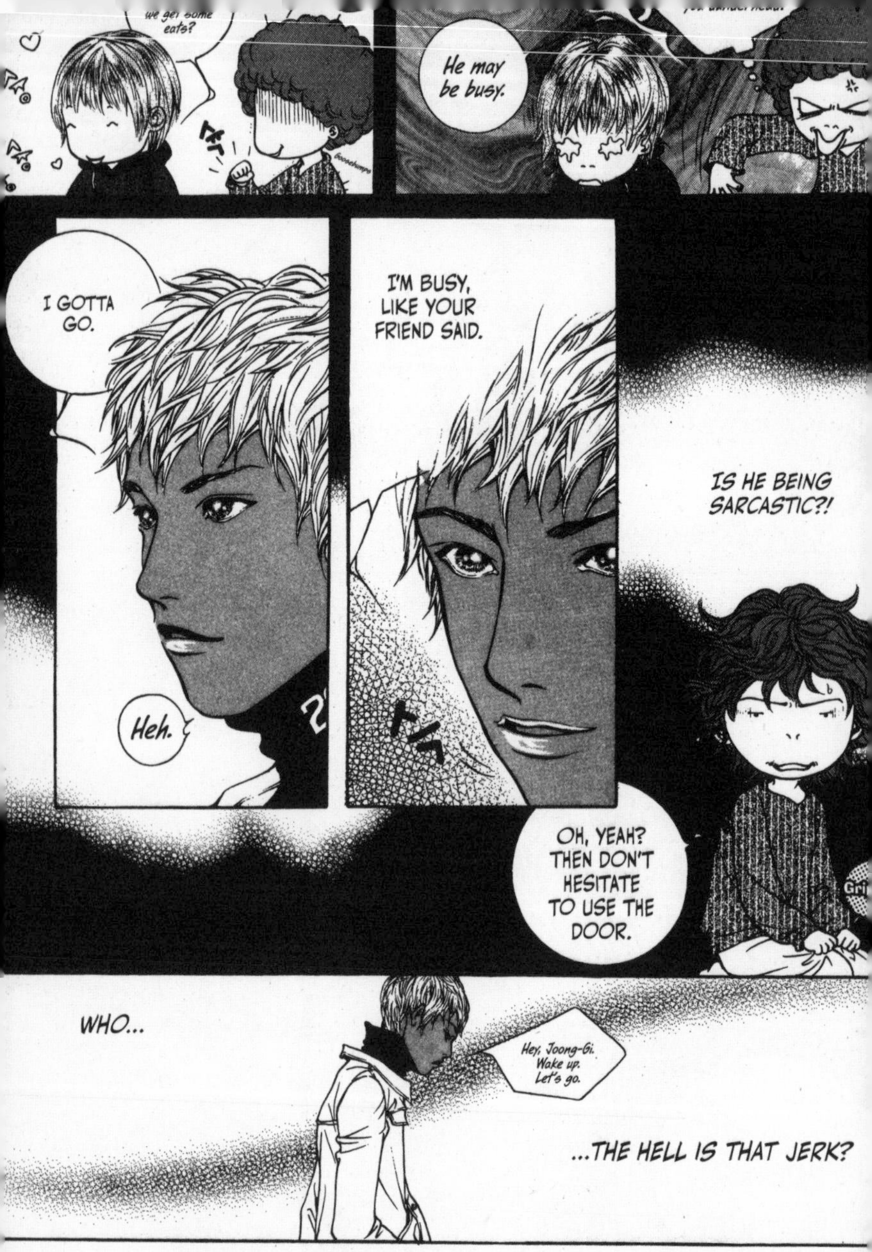
we get some
eats?
Goosebumps
He may be busy.
I GOTTA GO.
Heh.
I'M BUSY, LIKE YOUR FRIEND SAID.
IS HE BEING SARCASTIC?!
OH, YEAH? THEN DON'T HESITATE TO USE THE DOOR.
WHO...
Hey, Joong-Gi. Wake up. Let's go.
...THE HELL IS THAT JERK?

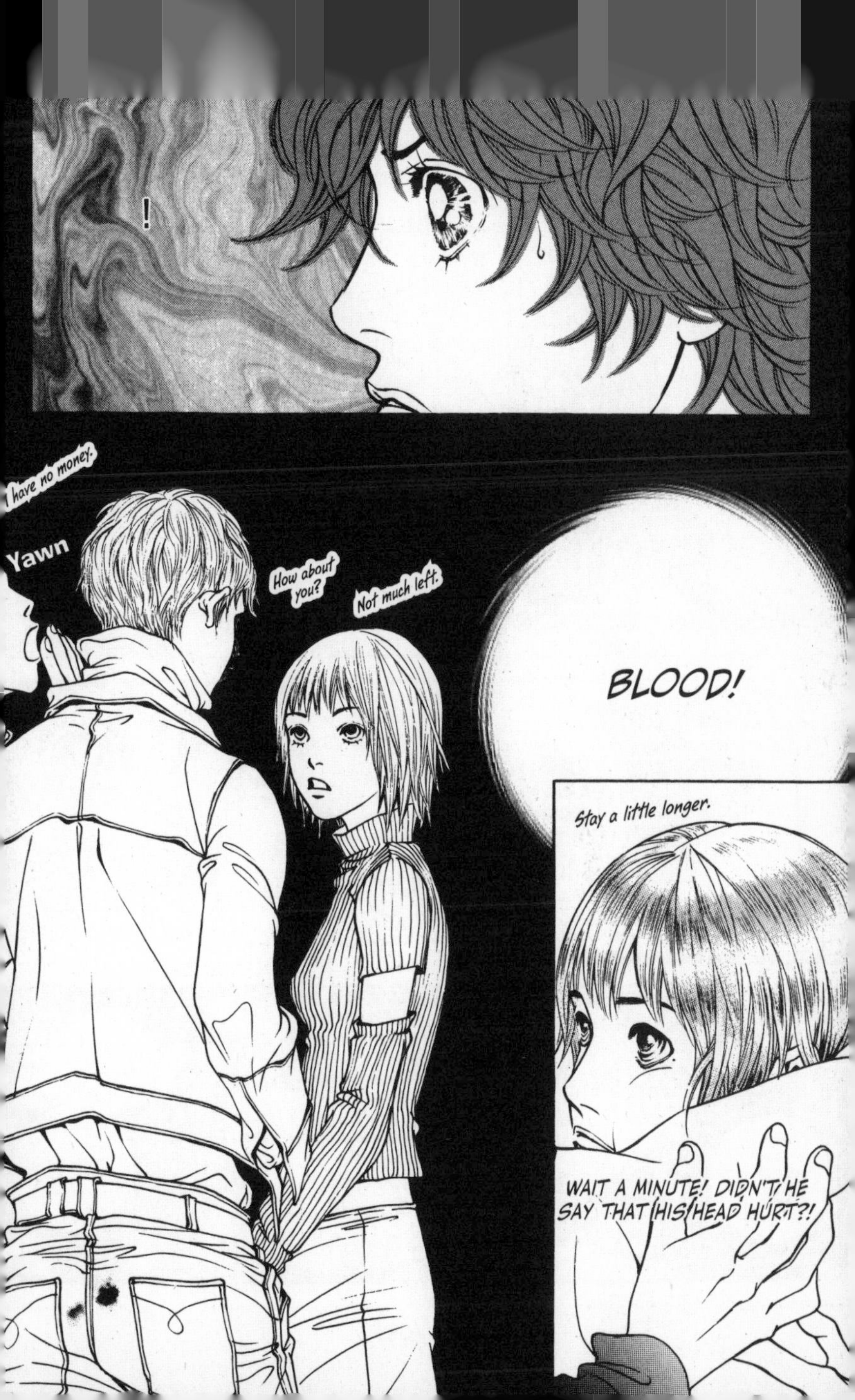
!
I have no money.
Yawn
How about you?
Not much left.
BLOOD!
Stay a little longer.
WAIT A MINUTE! DIDN'T HE SAY THAT HIS HEAD HURT?!

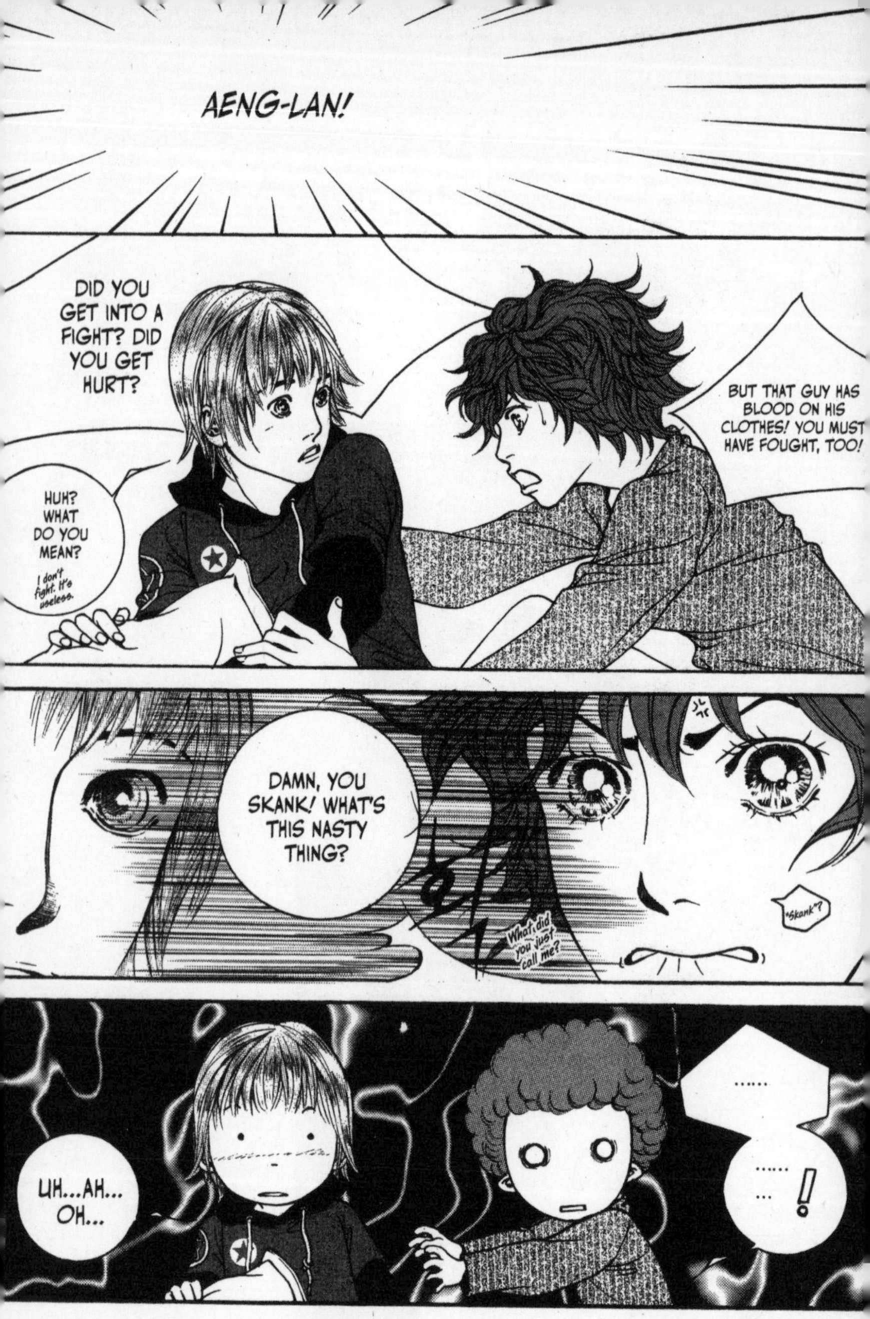
AENG-LAN!
DID YOU GET INTO A FIGHT? DID YOU GET HURT?
HUH? WHAT DO YOU MEAN?
I don't fight. It's useless.
BUT THAT GUY HAS BLOOD ON HIS CLOTHES! YOU MUST HAVE FOUGHT, TOO!
DAMN, YOU SKANK! WHAT'S THIS NASTY THING?
What did you just call me?
"Skank"?
UH...AH... OH...
......
......
... !

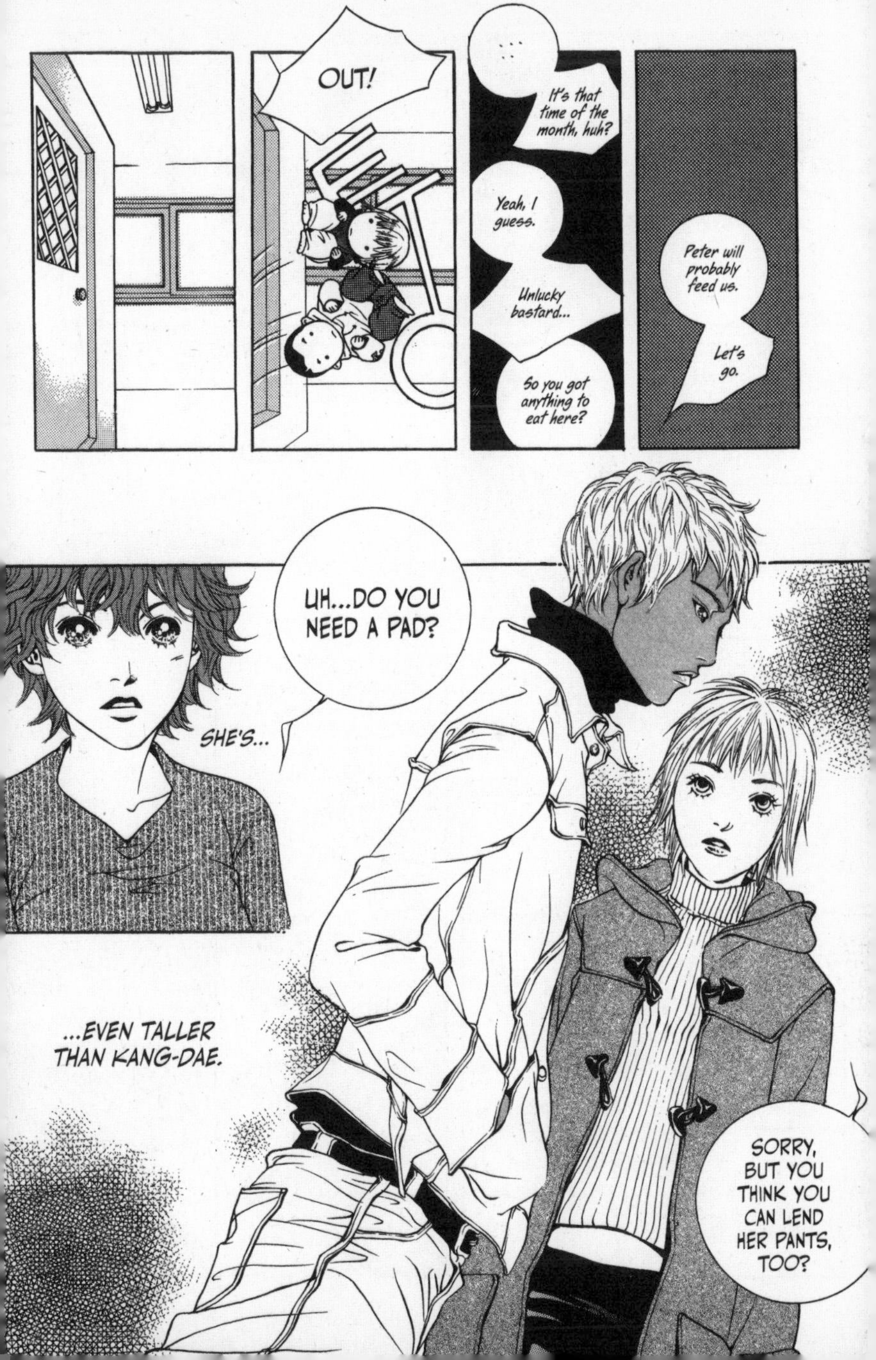
OUT!
. . .
It's that time of the month, huh?
Yeah, I guess.
Unlucky bastard...
So you got anything to eat here?
Peter will probably feed us.
Let's go.
SHE'S...
UH...DO YOU NEED A PAD?
...EVEN TALLER THAN KANG-DAE.
SORRY, BUT YOU THINK YOU CAN LEND HER PANTS, TOO?

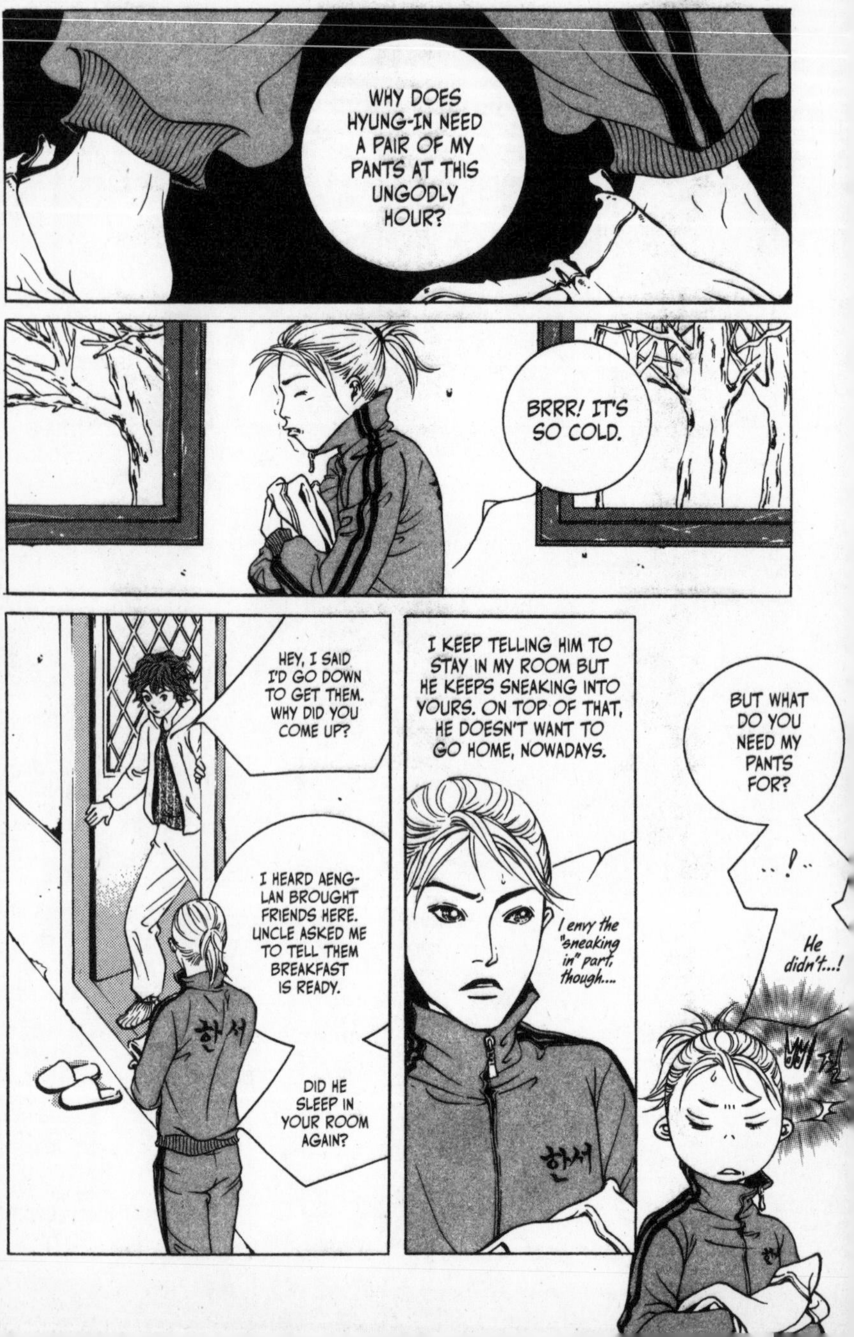
WHY DOES HYUNG-IN NEED A PAIR OF MY PANTS AT THIS UNGODLY HOUR?
BRRR! IT'S SO COLD.
HEY, I SAID I'D GO DOWN TO GET THEM. WHY DID YOU COME UP?
I HEARD AENG-LAN BROUGHT FRIENDS HERE. UNCLE ASKED ME TO TELL THEM BREAKFAST IS READY.
DID HE SLEEP IN YOUR ROOM AGAIN?
I KEEP TELLING HIM TO STAY IN MY ROOM BUT HE KEEPS SNEAKING INTO YOURS. ON TOP OF THAT, HE DOESN'T WANT TO GO HOME, NOWADAYS.
I envy the "sneaking in" part, though....
BUT WHAT DO YOU NEED MY PANTS FOR?
..!..
He didn't...!

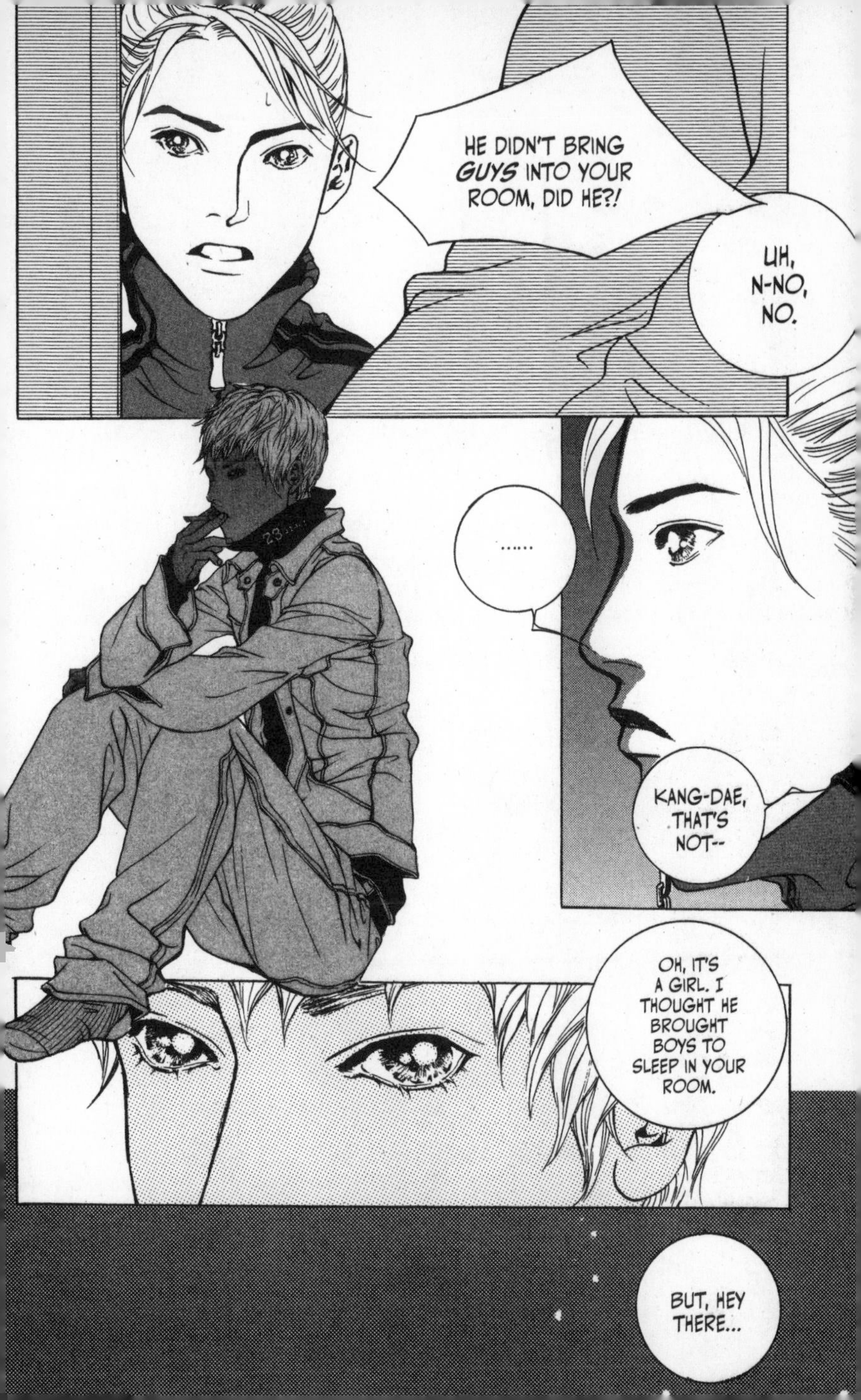
HE DIDN'T BRING *GUYS* INTO YOUR ROOM, DID HE?!
UH, N-NO, NO.
......
KANG-DAE, THAT'S NOT--
OH, IT'S A GIRL. I THOUGHT HE BROUGHT BOYS TO SLEEP IN YOUR ROOM.
BUT, HEY THERE...

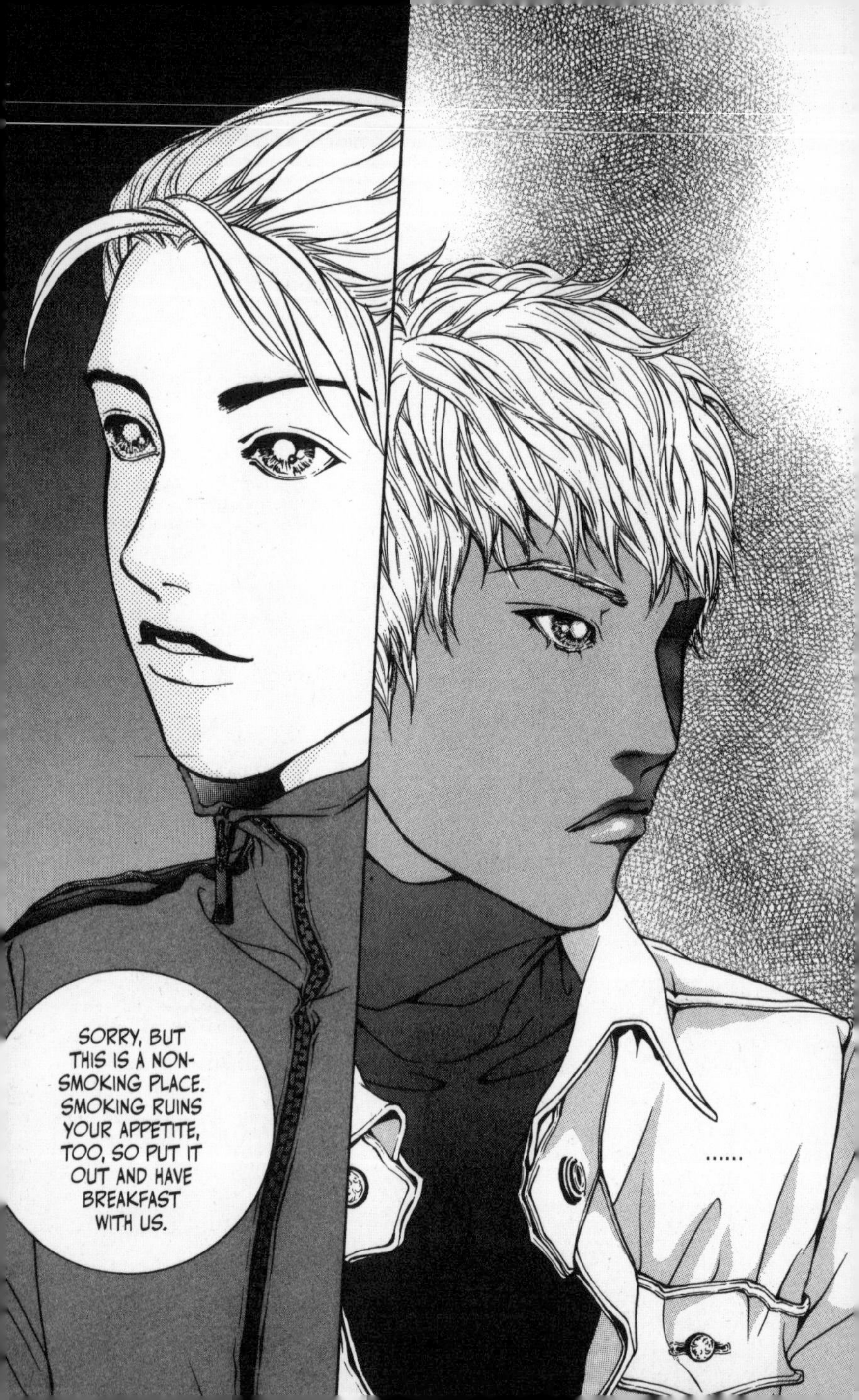
SORRY, BUT THIS IS A NON-SMOKING PLACE. SMOKING RUINS YOUR APPETITE, TOO, SO PUT IT OUT AND HAVE BREAKFAST WITH US.
......

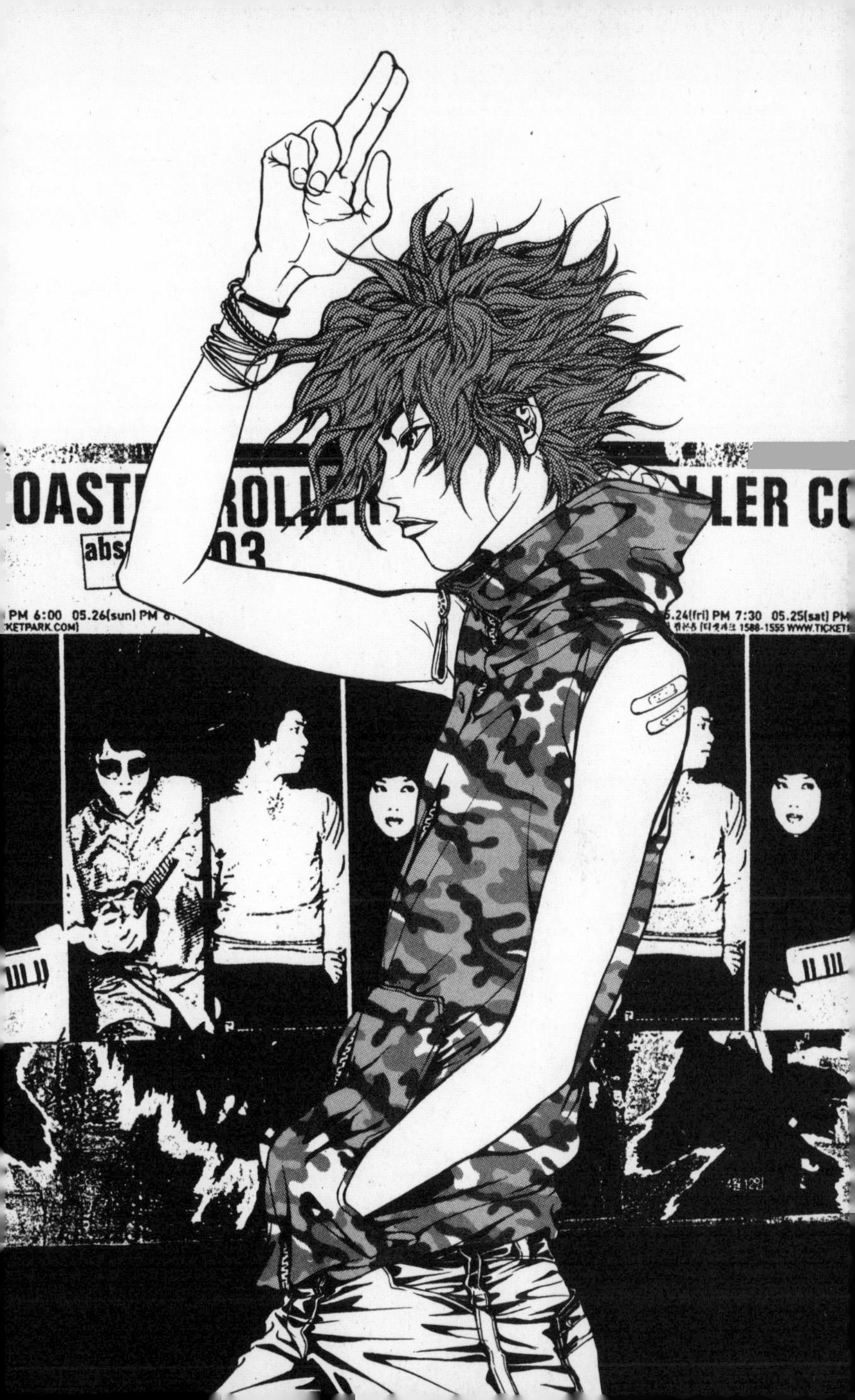
OASTE ROLLER
LLER CO
abs
03
PM 6:00 05.26(sun) PM
KETPARK.COM)
5.24(fri) PM 7:30 05.25(sat) PM
1588-1555 WWW.TICKET

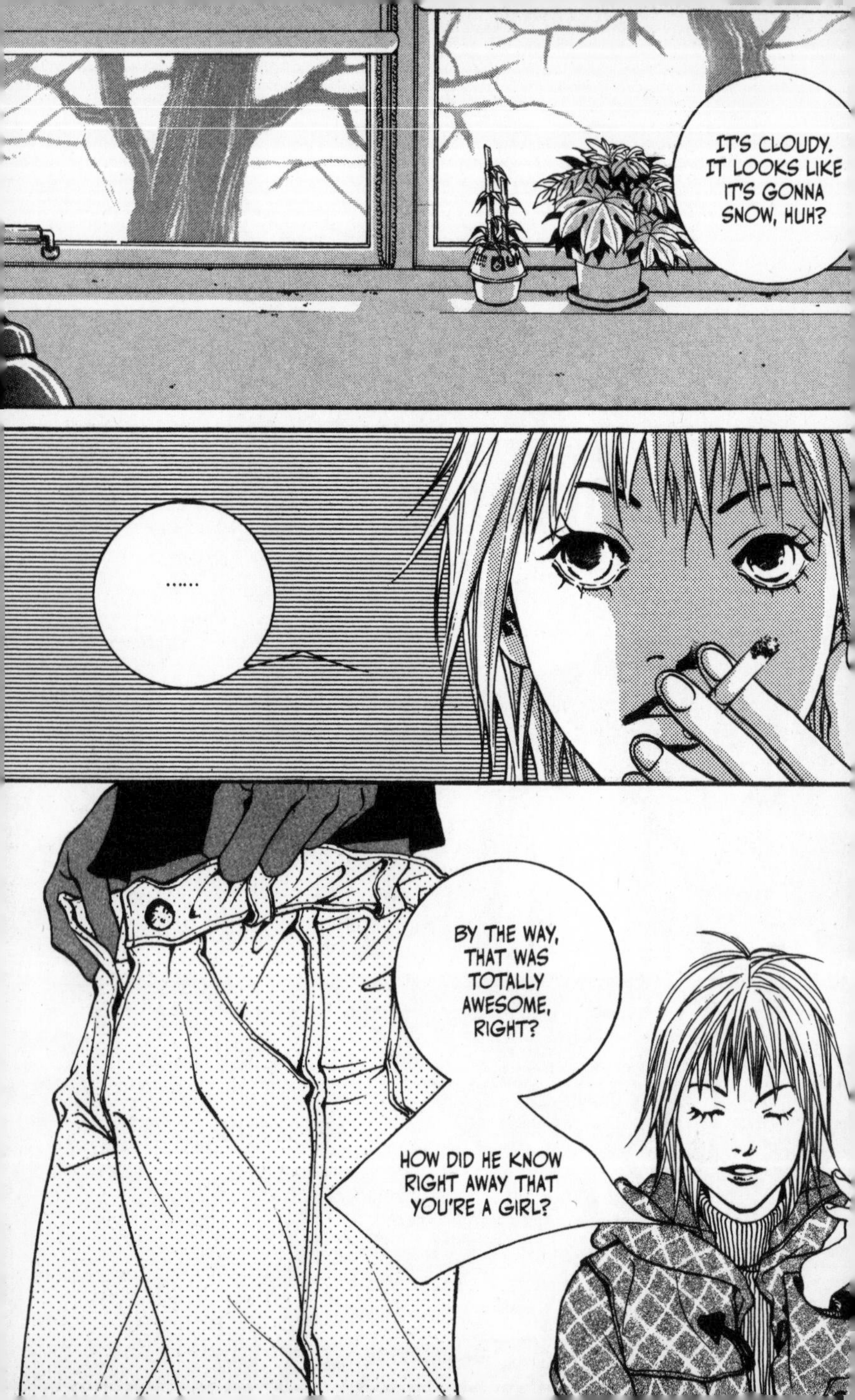
IT'S CLOUDY. IT LOOKS LIKE IT'S GONNA SNOW, HUH?
......
BY THE WAY, THAT WAS TOTALLY AWESOME, RIGHT?
HOW DID HE KNOW RIGHT AWAY THAT YOU'RE A GIRL?

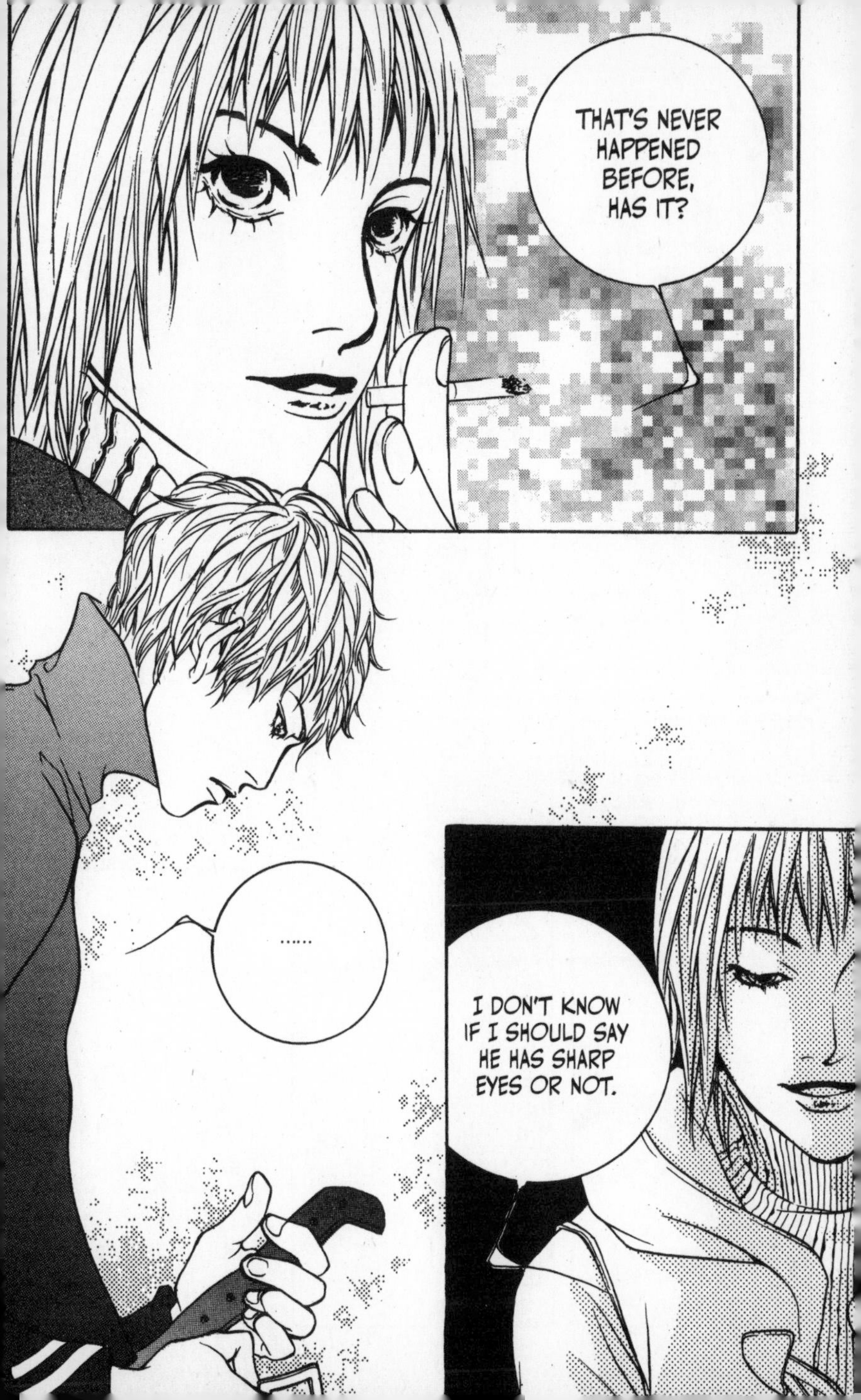
THAT'S NEVER HAPPENED BEFORE, HAS IT?
......
I DON'T KNOW IF I SHOULD SAY HE HAS SHARP EYES OR NOT.

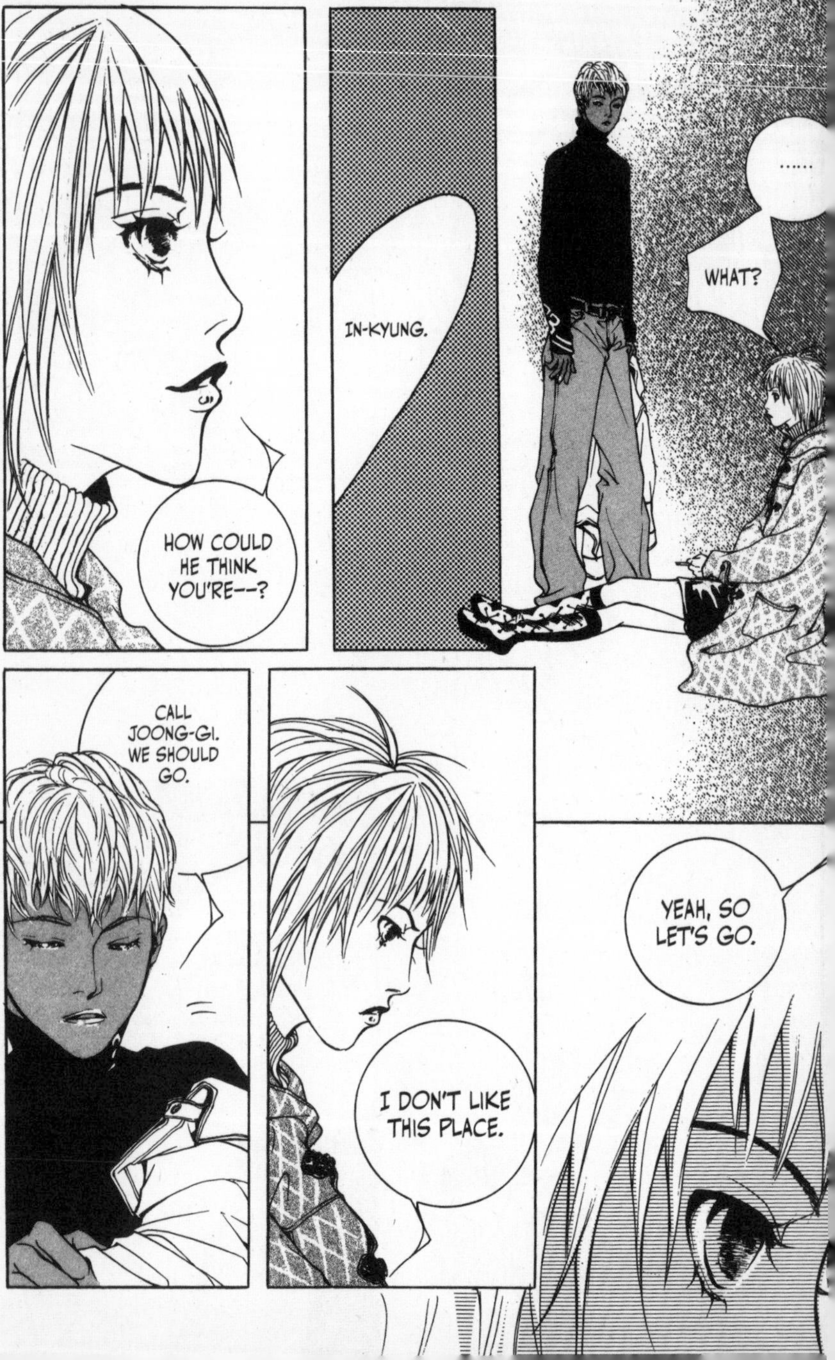
HOW COULD HE THINK YOU'RE--?
IN-KYUNG.
......
WHAT?
CALL JOONG-GI. WE SHOULD GO.
I DON'T LIKE THIS PLACE.
YEAH, SO LET'S GO.

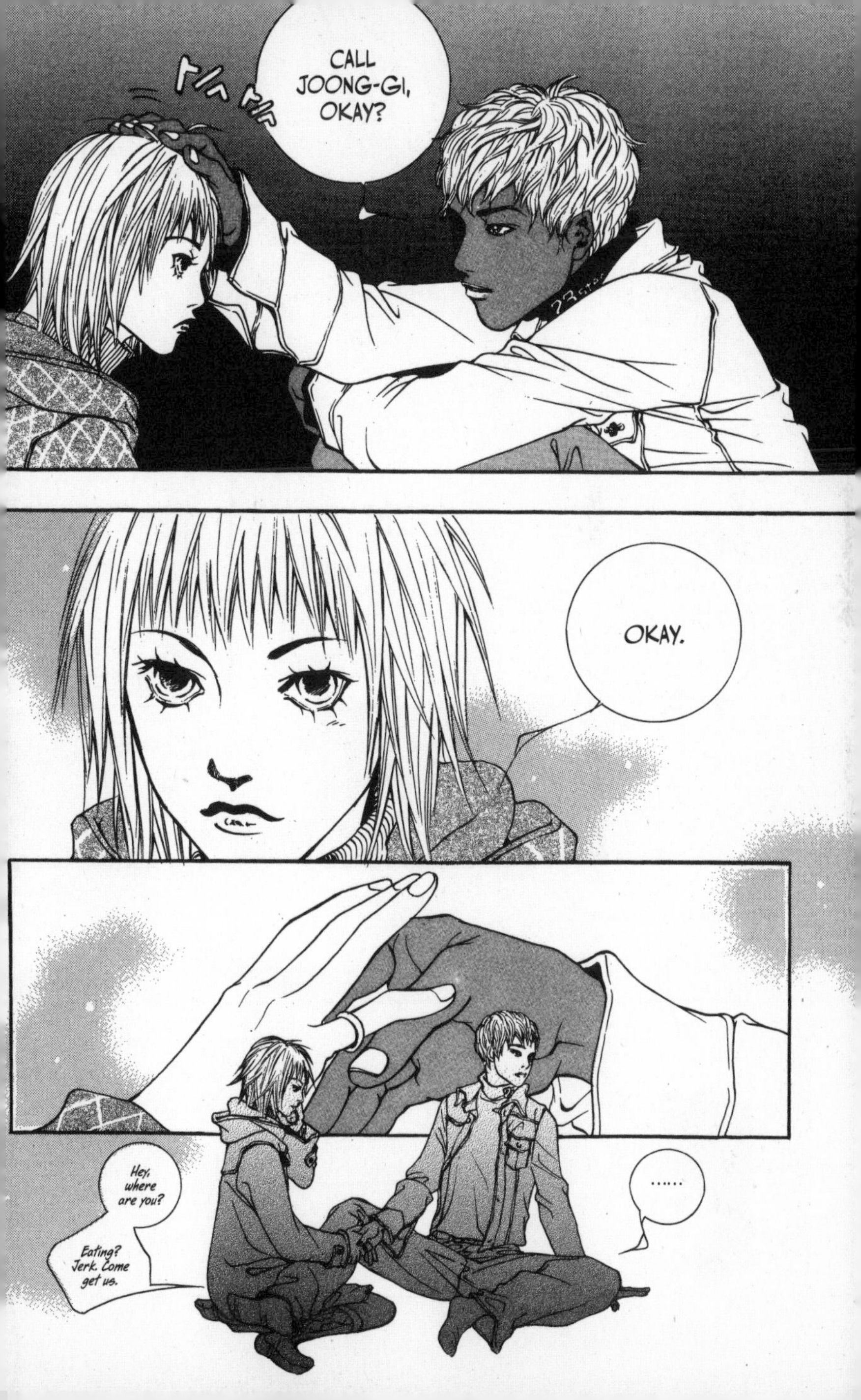
CALL JOONG-GI, OKAY?
OKAY.
Hey, where are you?
Eating? Jerk. Come get us.
......

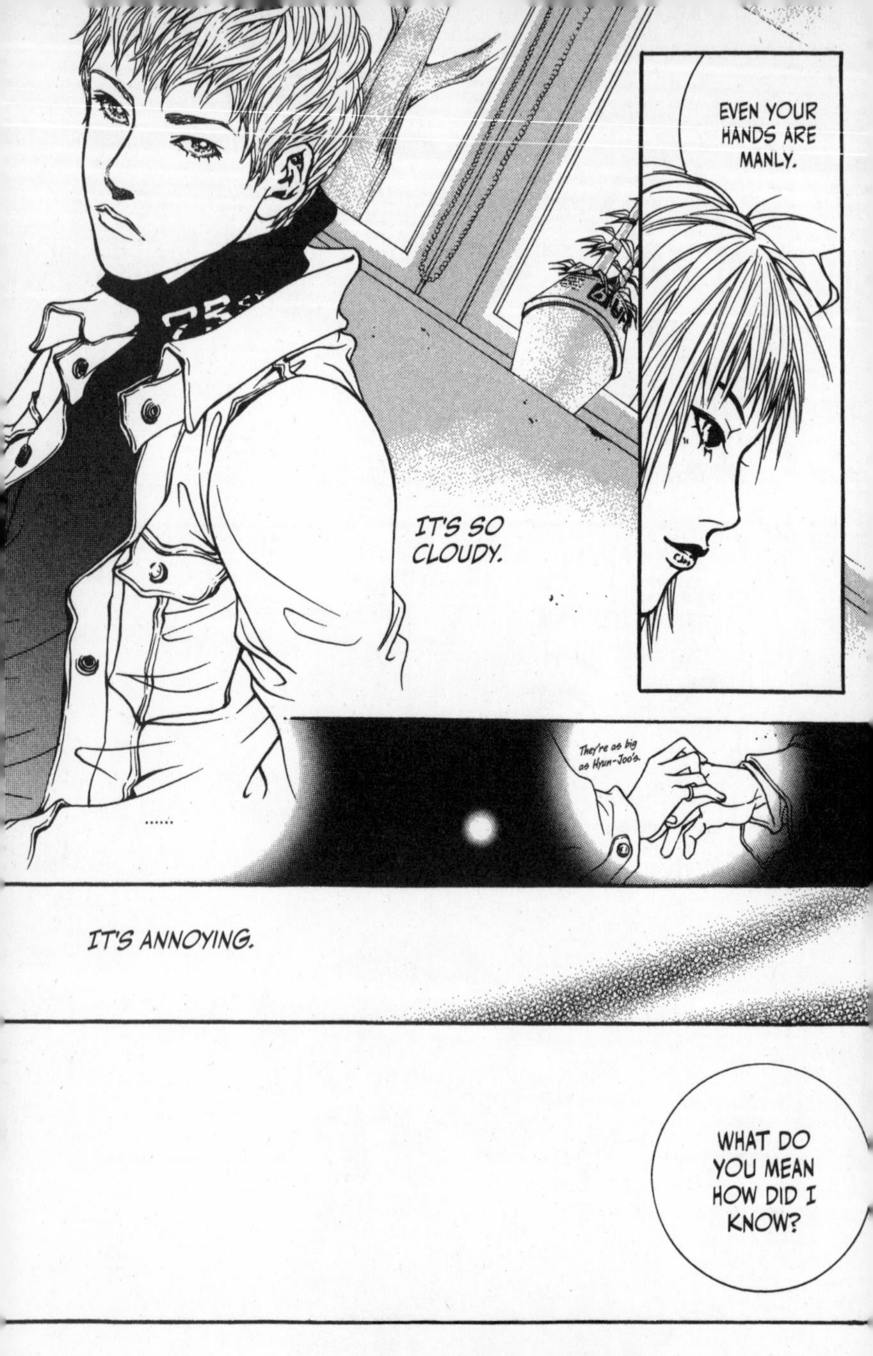
IT'S SO CLOUDY.
......
EVEN YOUR HANDS ARE MANLY.
They're as big as Hyun-Joo's.
IT'S ANNOYING.
WHAT DO YOU MEAN HOW DID I KNOW?

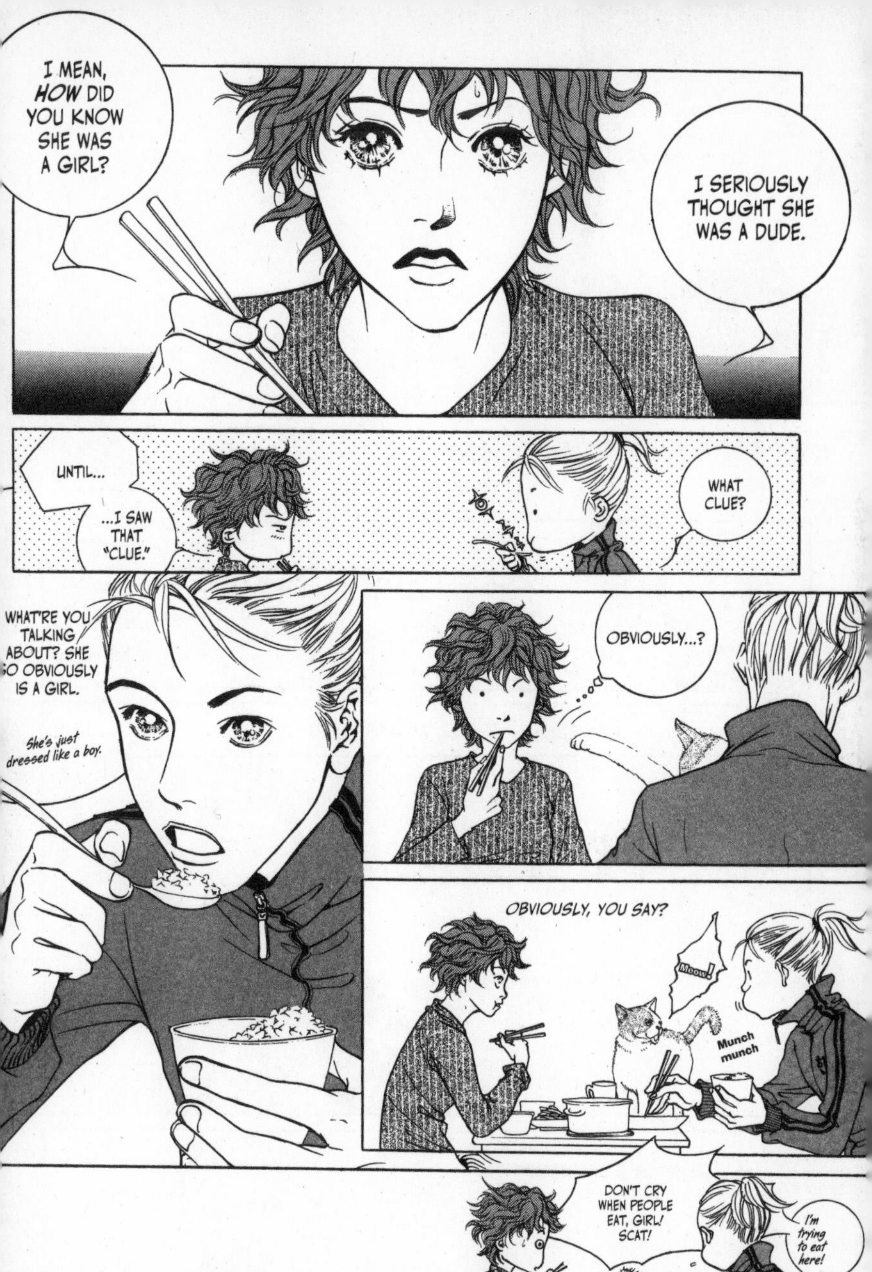
I MEAN, HOW DID YOU KNOW SHE WAS A GIRL?
I SERIOUSLY THOUGHT SHE WAS A DUDE.
UNTIL...
...I SAW THAT "CLUE."
WHAT CLUE?
WHAT'RE YOU TALKING ABOUT? SHE SO OBVIOUSLY IS A GIRL.
She's just dressed like a boy.
OBVIOUSLY...?
OBVIOUSLY, YOU SAY?
Meow!
Munch munch
DON'T CRY WHEN PEOPLE EAT, GIRL! SCAT!
I'm trying to eat here!
Girl?
Keow!

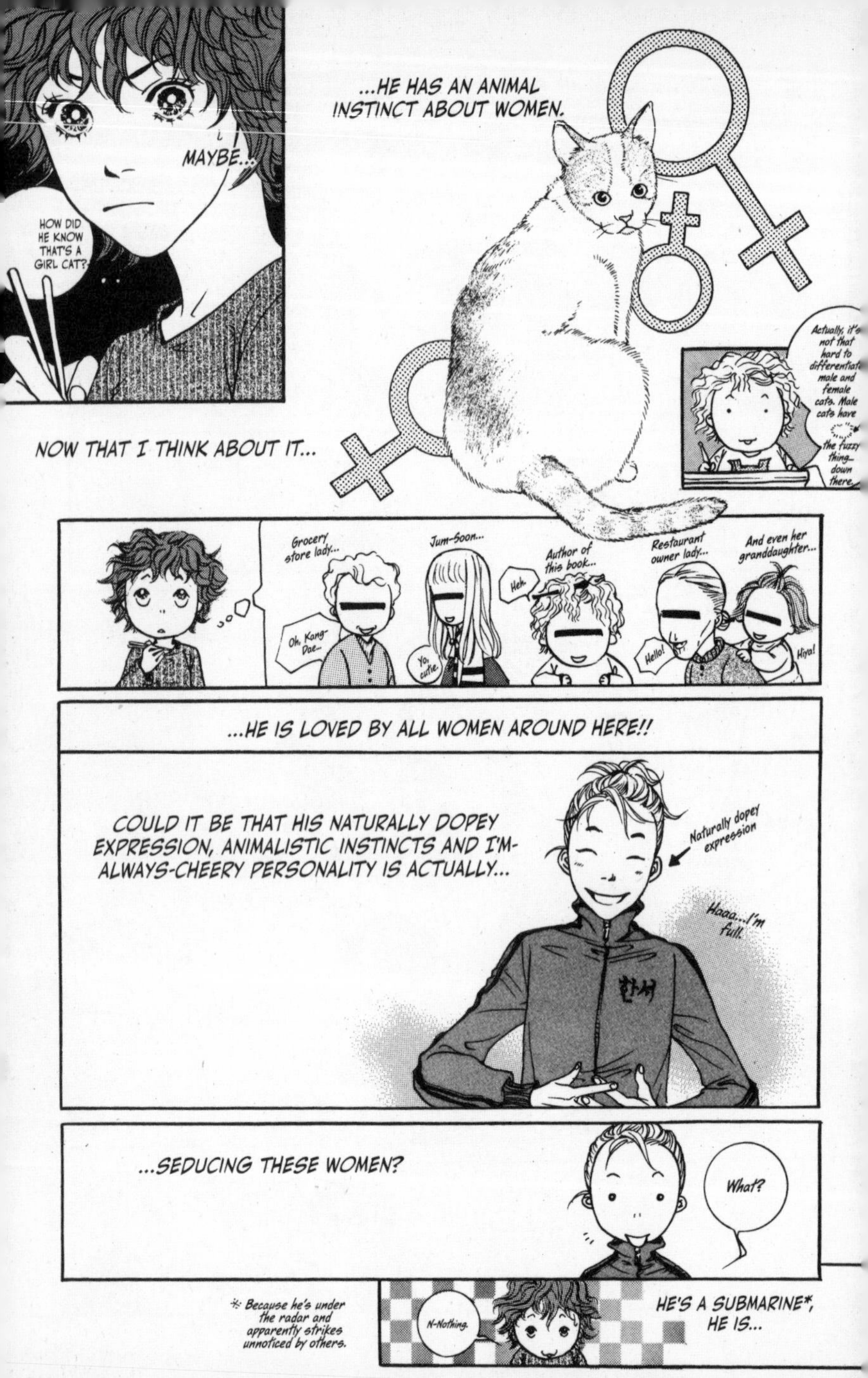

MAYBE...
HOW DID HE KNOW THAT'S A GIRL CAT?
...HE HAS AN ANIMAL INSTINCT ABOUT WOMEN.
NOW THAT I THINK ABOUT IT...
Actually, it's not that hard to differentiate male and female cats. Male cats have the fuzzy thing down there.
Grocery store lady...
Oh, Kang-Dae...
Jum-Soon...
Yo, cutie.
Author of this book...
Heh.
Restaurant owner lady...
Hello!
And even her granddaughter...
Hiya!
...HE IS LOVED BY ALL WOMEN AROUND HERE!!
COULD IT BE THAT HIS NATURALLY DOPEY EXPRESSION, ANIMALISTIC INSTINCTS AND I'M-ALWAYS-CHEERY PERSONALITY IS ACTUALLY...
Naturally dopey expression
Haaa...I'm full.
...SEDUCING THESE WOMEN?
What?
*: Because he's under the radar and apparently strikes unnoticed by others.
N-Nothing.
HE'S A SUBMARINE*, HE IS...

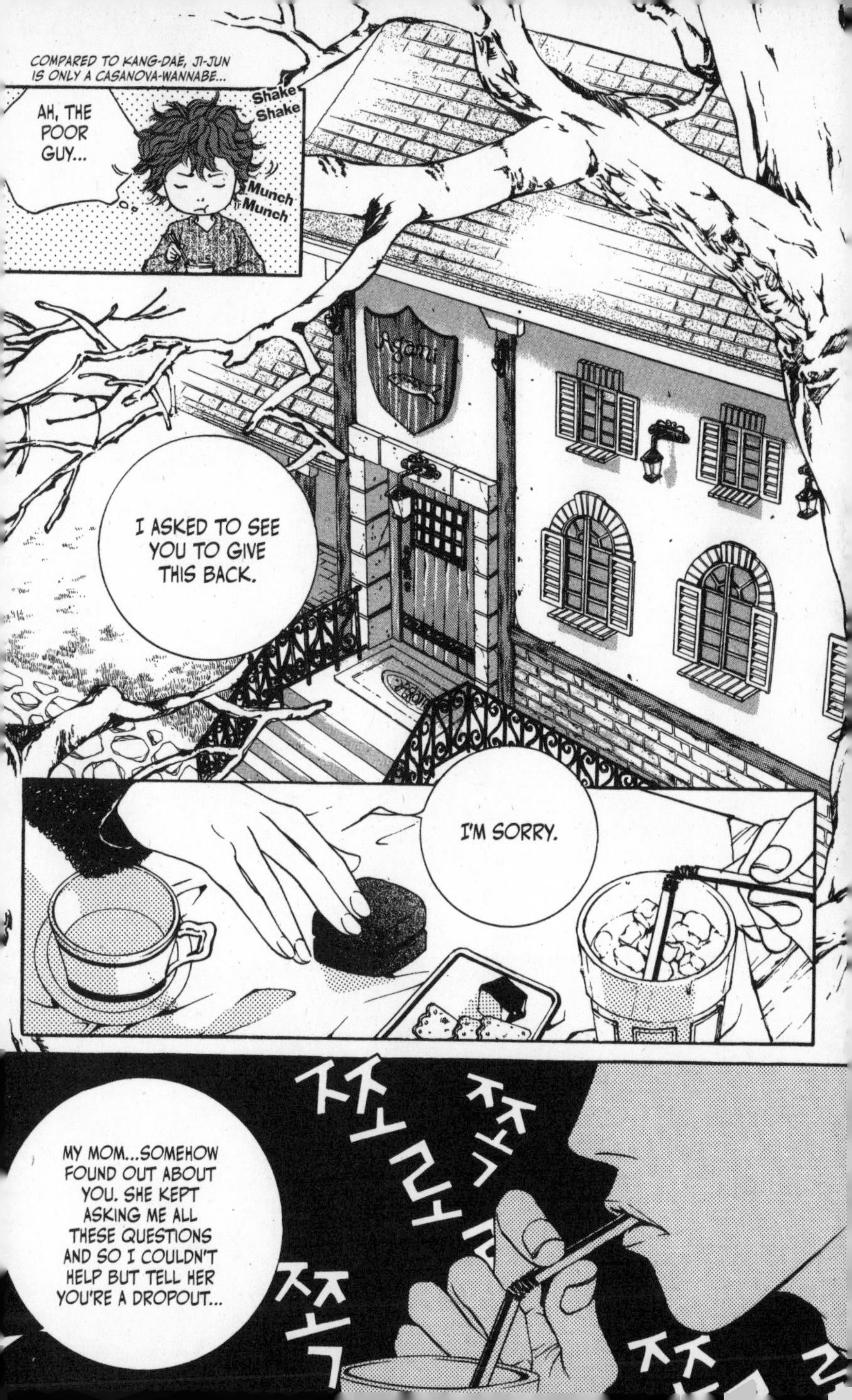
COMPARED TO KANG-DAE, JI-JUN IS ONLY A CASANOVA-WANNABE...
AH, THE POOR GUY...
Shake Shake
Munch Munch
I ASKED TO SEE YOU TO GIVE THIS BACK.
I'M SORRY.
MY MOM...SOMEHOW FOUND OUT ABOUT YOU. SHE KEPT ASKING ME ALL THESE QUESTIONS AND SO I COULDN'T HELP BUT TELL HER YOU'RE A DROPOUT...

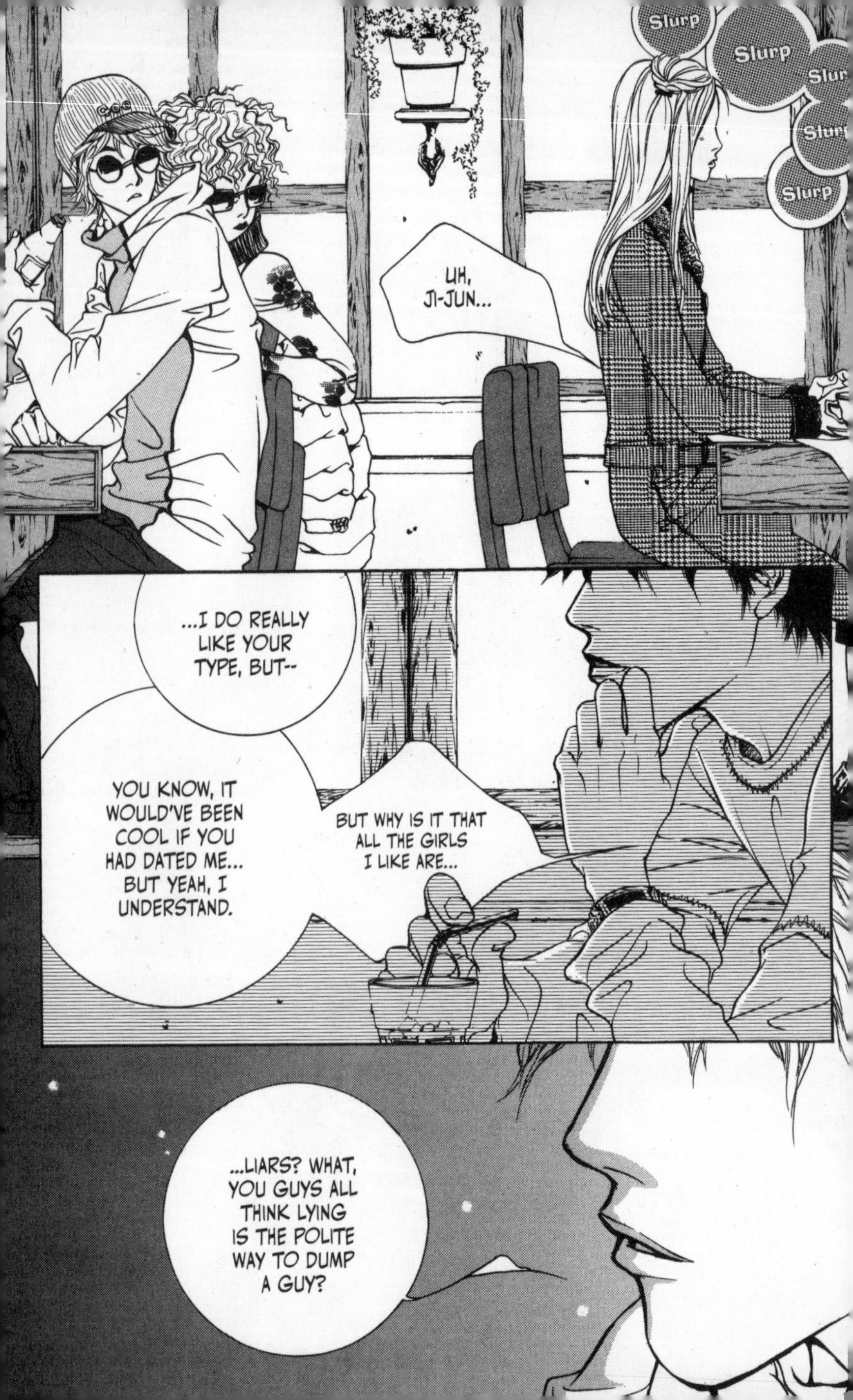
Slurp
Slurp
Slurp
Slurp
Slurp
UH, JI-JUN...
...I DO REALLY LIKE YOUR TYPE, BUT--
YOU KNOW, IT WOULD'VE BEEN COOL IF YOU HAD DATED ME... BUT YEAH, I UNDERSTAND.
BUT WHY IS IT THAT ALL THE GIRLS I LIKE ARE...
...LIARS? WHAT, YOU GUYS ALL THINK LYING IS THE POLITE WAY TO DUMP A GUY?

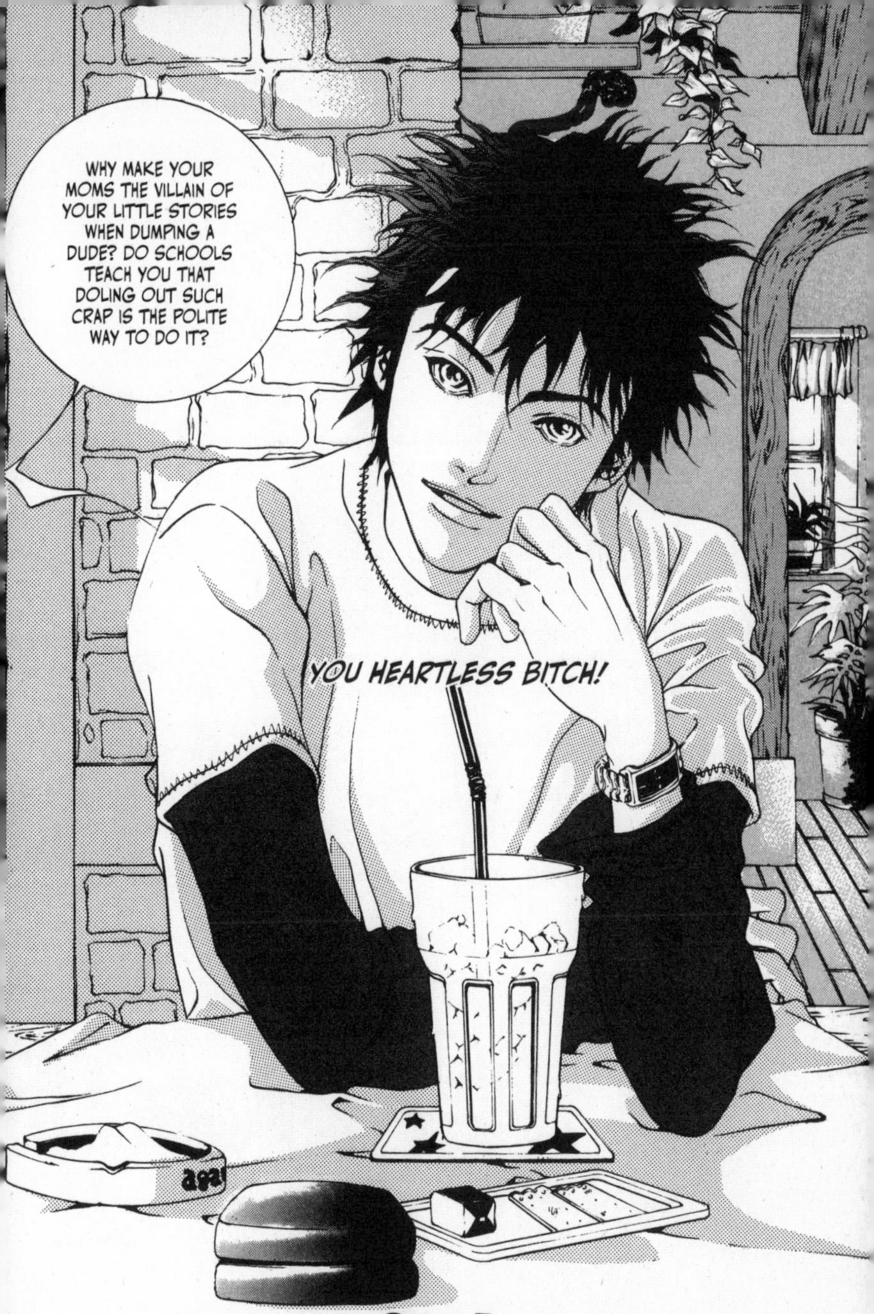
WHY MAKE YOUR MOMS THE VILLAIN OF YOUR LITTLE STORIES WHEN DUMPING A DUDE? DO SCHOOLS TEACH YOU THAT DOLING OUT SUCH CRAP IS THE POLITE WAY TO DO IT?
YOU HEARTLESS BITCH!

Step 7:
24 Years Old, That Woman!

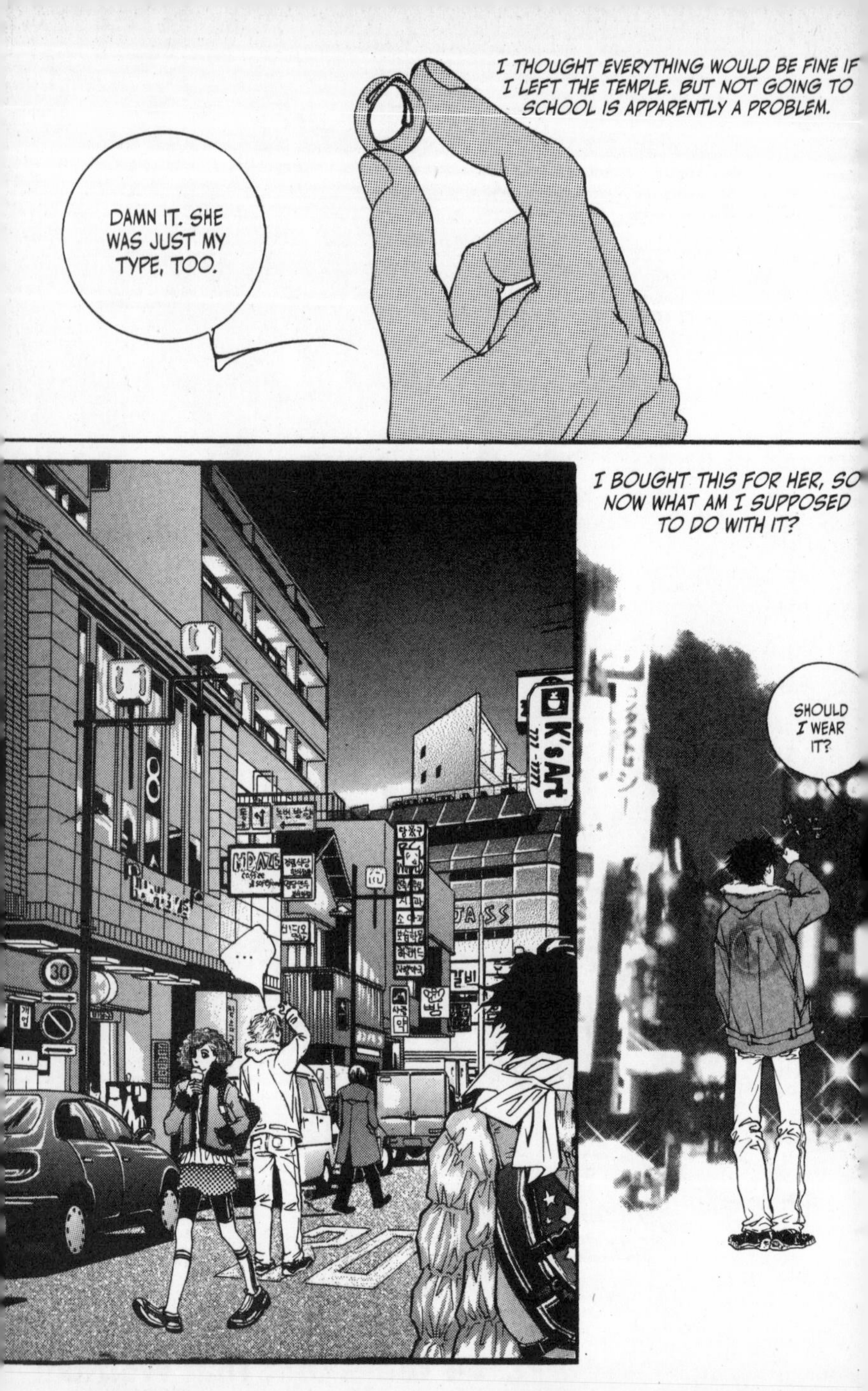
I THOUGHT EVERYTHING WOULD BE FINE IF I LEFT THE TEMPLE. BUT NOT GOING TO SCHOOL IS APPARENTLY A PROBLEM.
DAMN IT. SHE WAS JUST MY TYPE, TOO.
K's Art
...
I BOUGHT THIS FOR HER, SO NOW WHAT AM I SUPPOSED TO DO WITH IT?
SHOULD I WEAR IT?

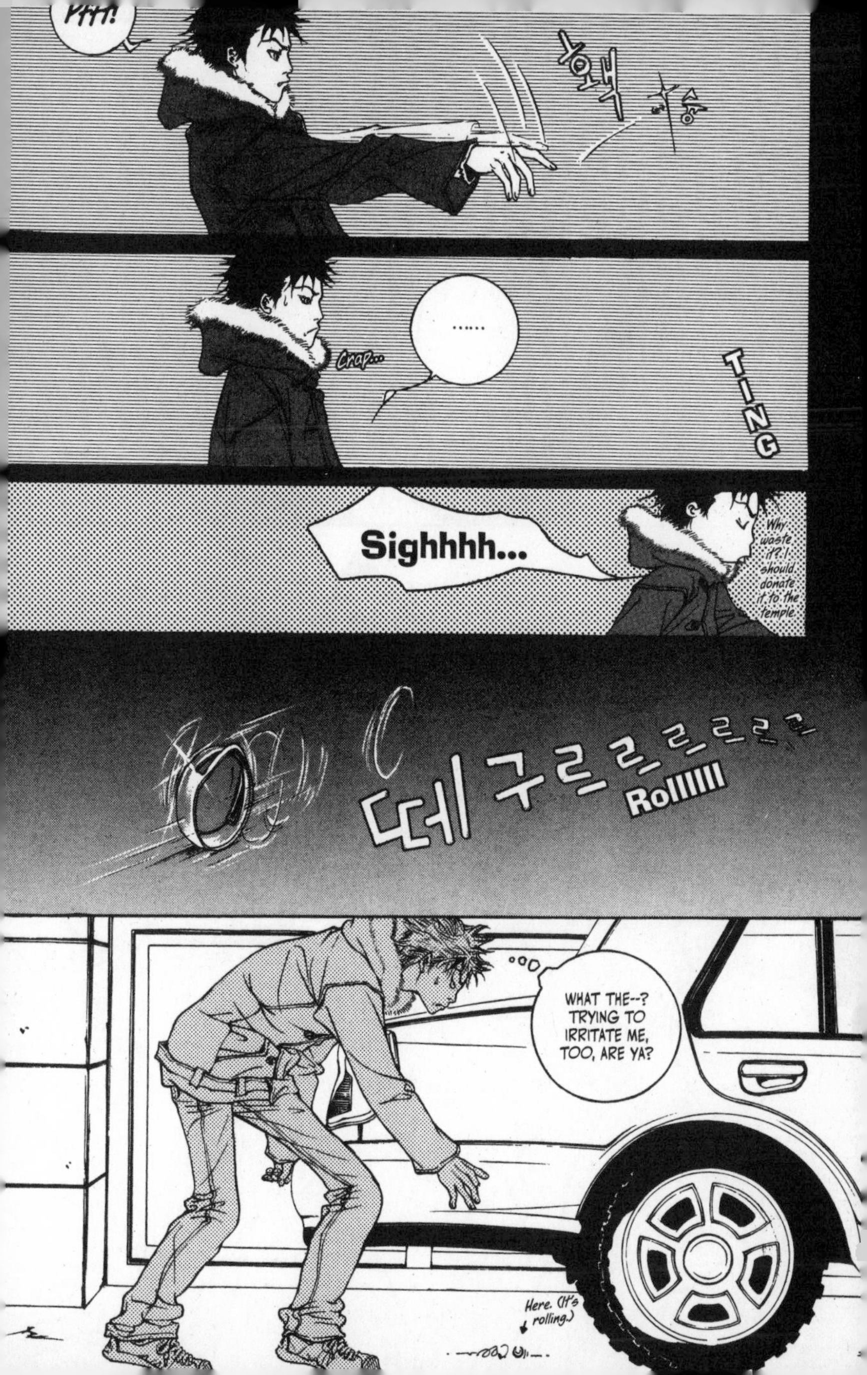

Pfft!
홱
......
Crap...
TING
Sighhhh...
Why waste it?! I should donate it to the temple
떼구르르르르르
Rolllllll
WHAT THE--? TRYING TO IRRITATE ME, TOO, ARE YA?
Here. (It's rolling.)

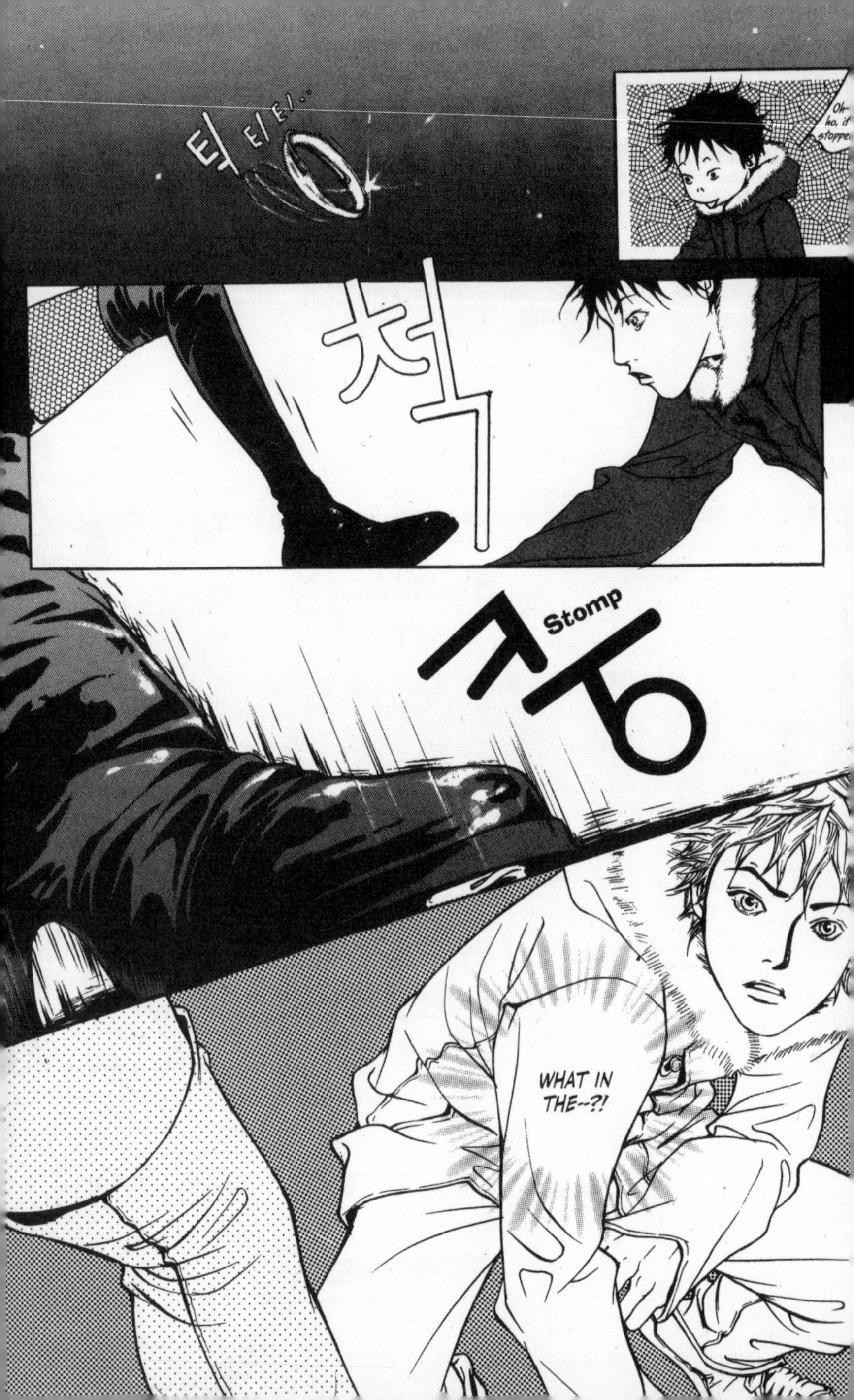
Oh-ho, it stoppe
척
Stomp
WHAT IN THE--?!

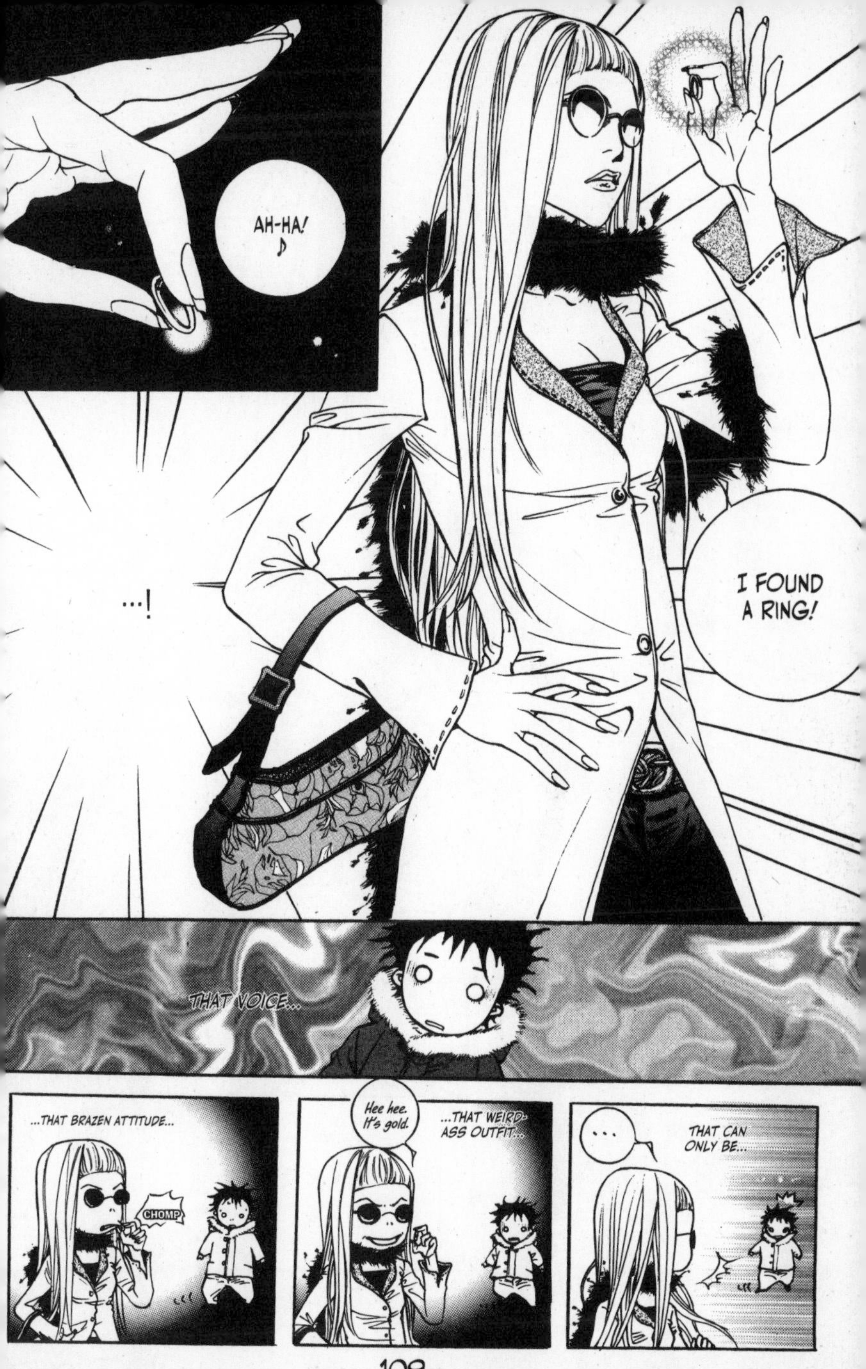

AH-HA! ♪
...!
I FOUND A RING!
THAT VOICE...
...THAT BRAZEN ATTITUDE...
CHOMP
Hee hee. It's gold.
...THAT WEIRD-ASS OUTFIT...
...
THAT CAN ONLY BE...

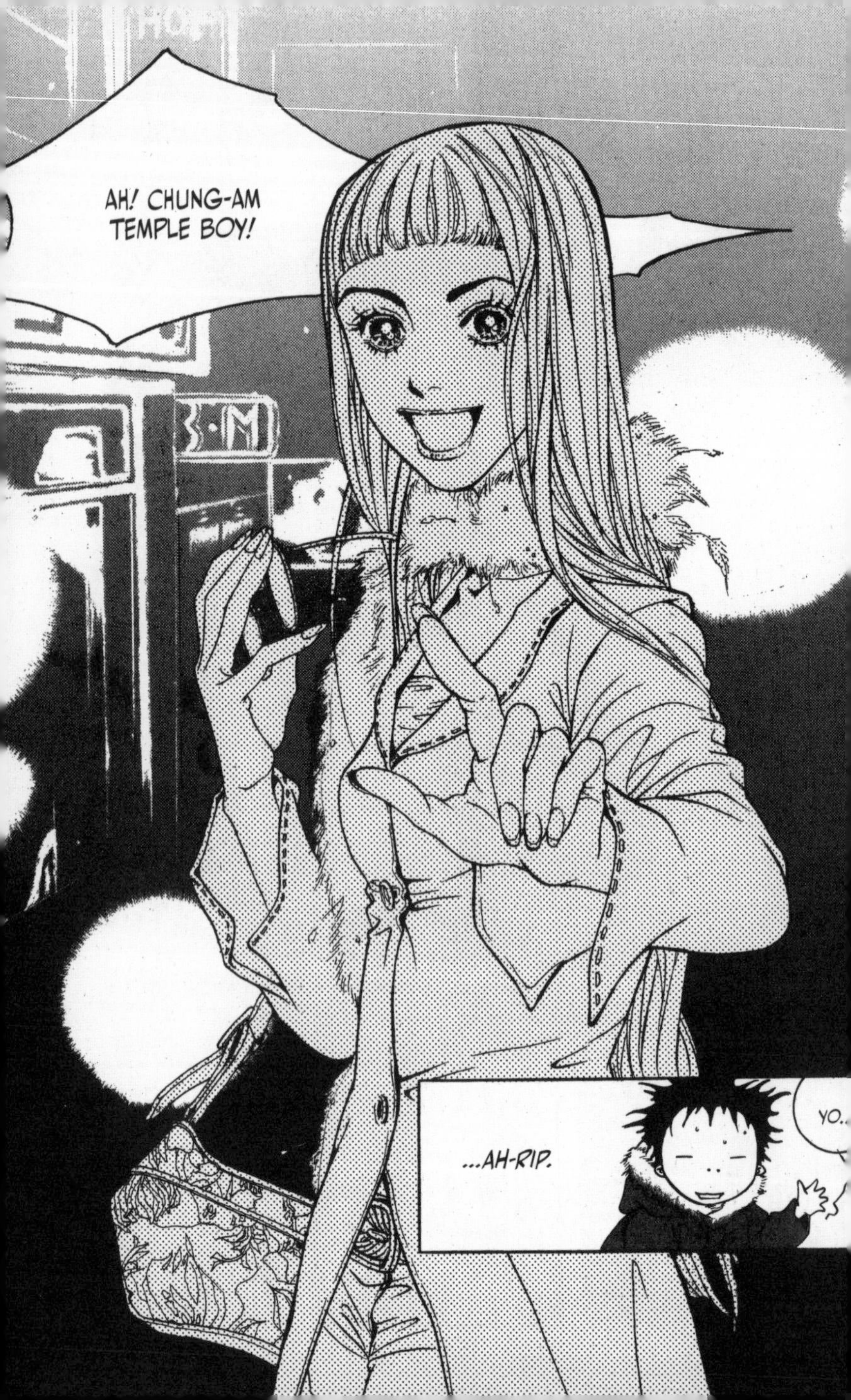
AH! CHUNG-AM TEMPLE BOY!
...AH-RIP.
YO..

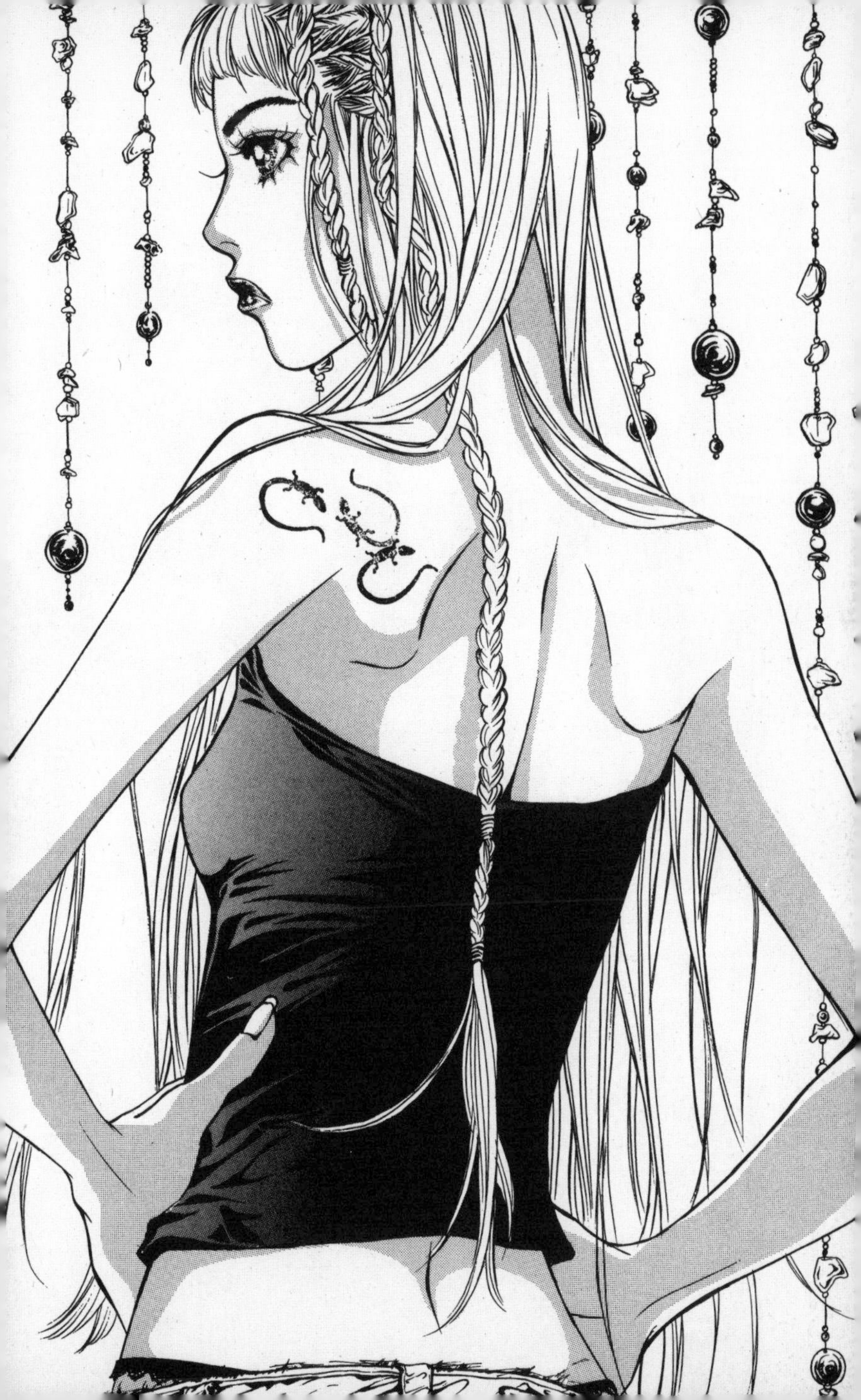

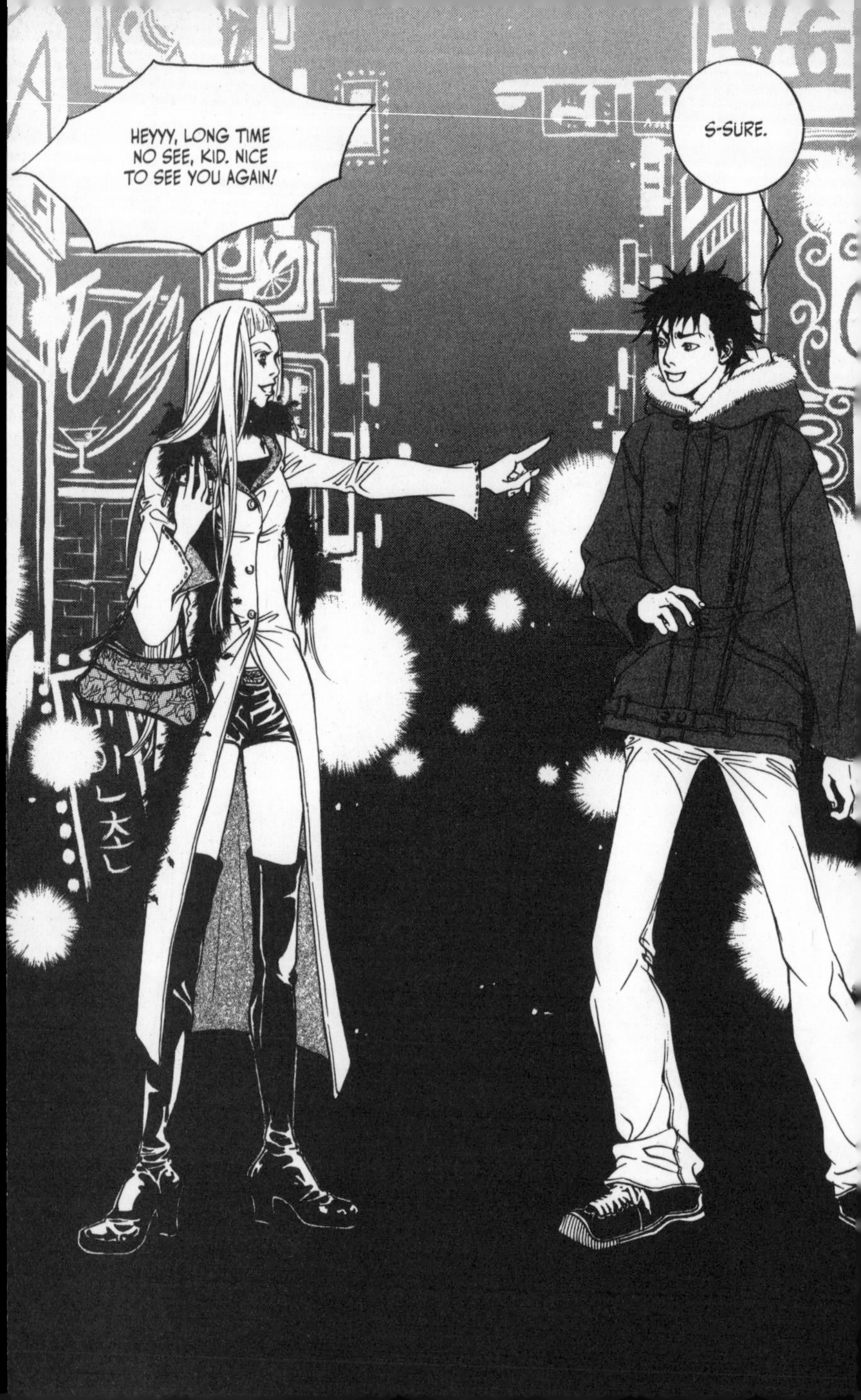
HEYYY, LONG TIME NO SEE, KID. NICE TO SEE YOU AGAIN!
S-SURE.

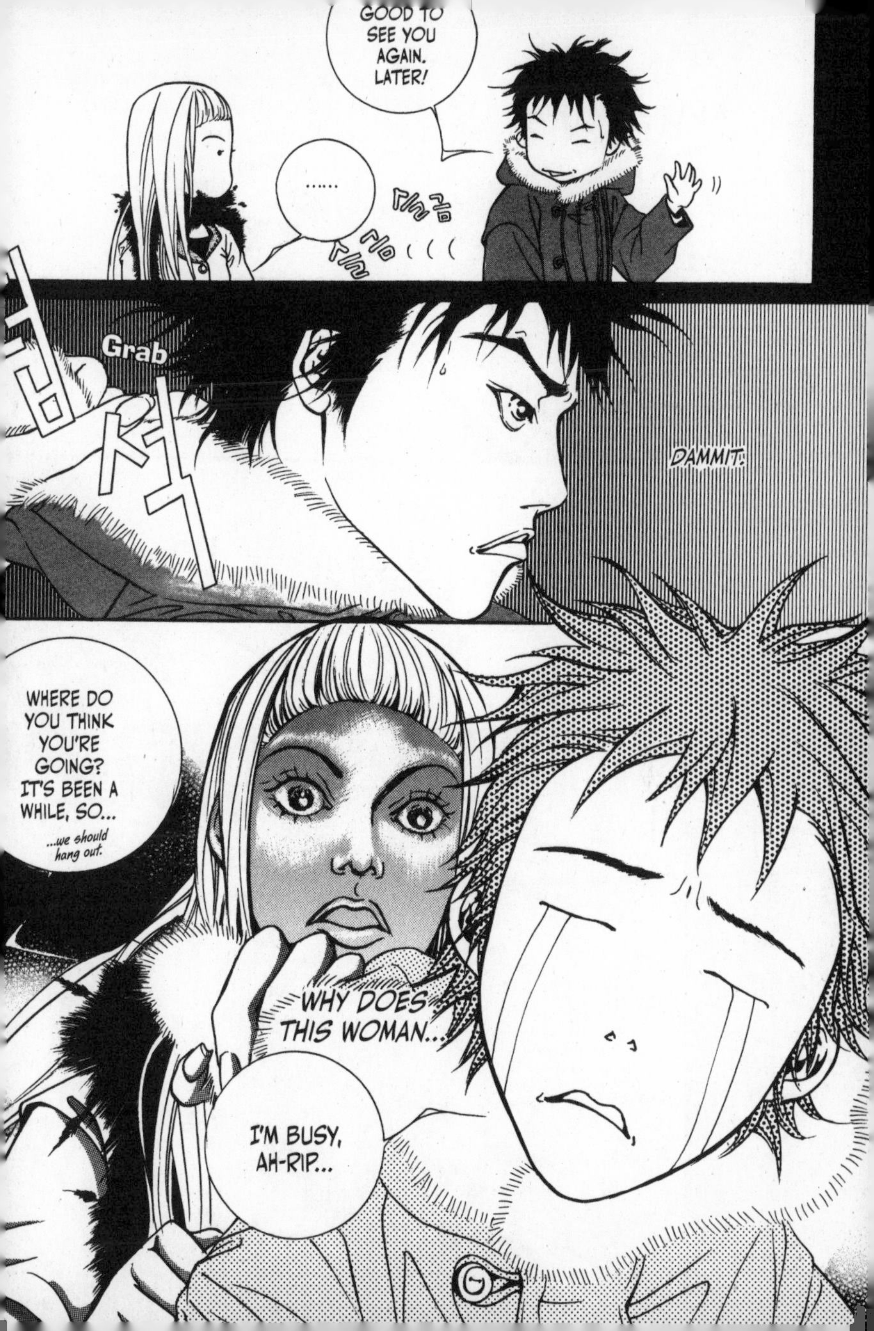
GOOD TO SEE YOU AGAIN. LATER!
......
Grab
DAMMIT.
WHERE DO YOU THINK YOU'RE GOING? IT'S BEEN A WHILE, SO...
...we should hang out.
WHY DOES THIS WOMAN...
I'M BUSY, AH-RIP...

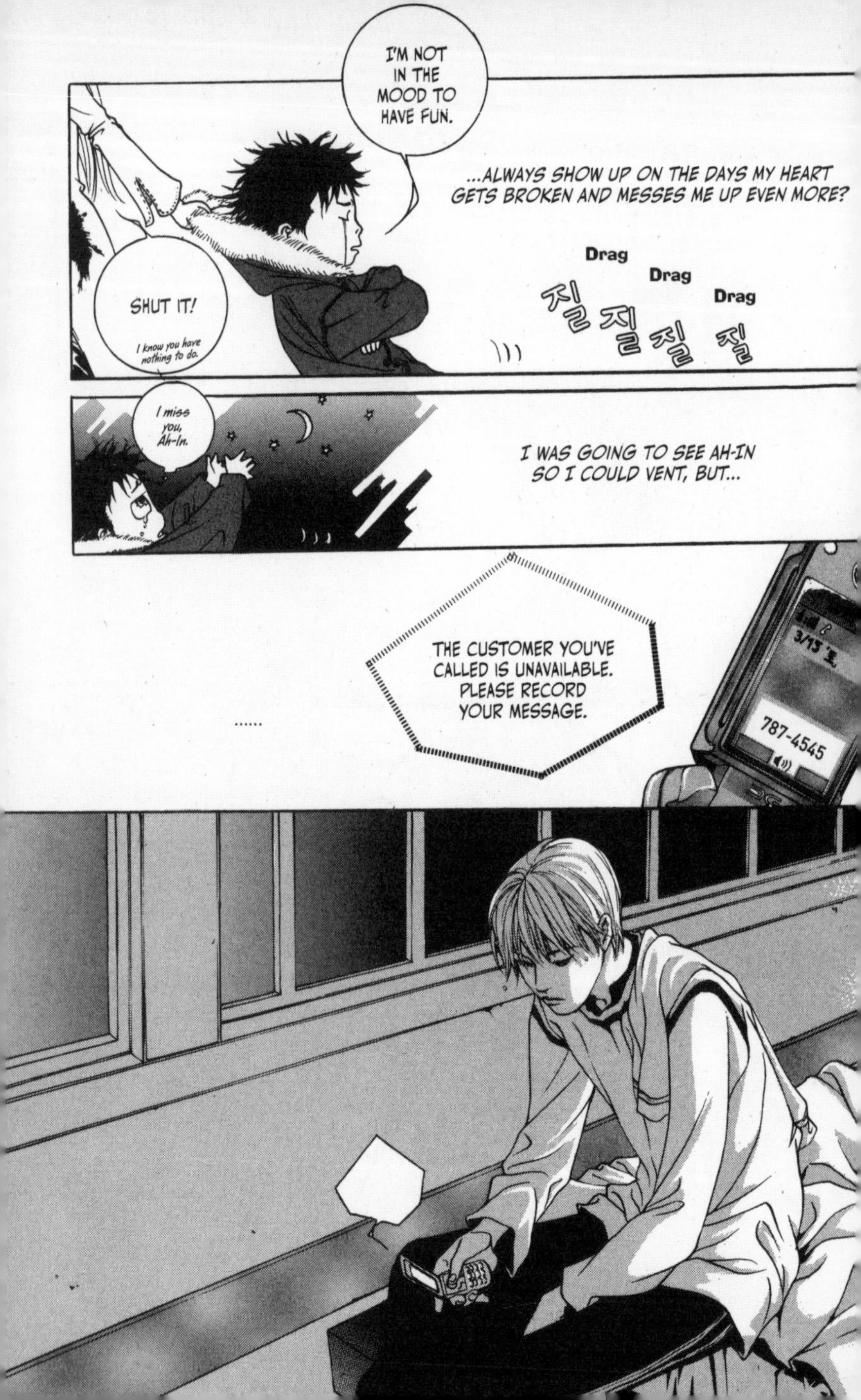
I'M NOT IN THE MOOD TO HAVE FUN.
SHUT IT!
I know you have nothing to do.
...ALWAYS SHOW UP ON THE DAYS MY HEART GETS BROKEN AND MESSES ME UP EVEN MORE?
Drag
Drag
Drag
질질질질
I miss you, Ah-In.
I WAS GOING TO SEE AH-IN SO I COULD VENT, BUT...
......
THE CUSTOMER YOU'VE CALLED IS UNAVAILABLE. PLEASE RECORD YOUR MESSAGE.
787-4545

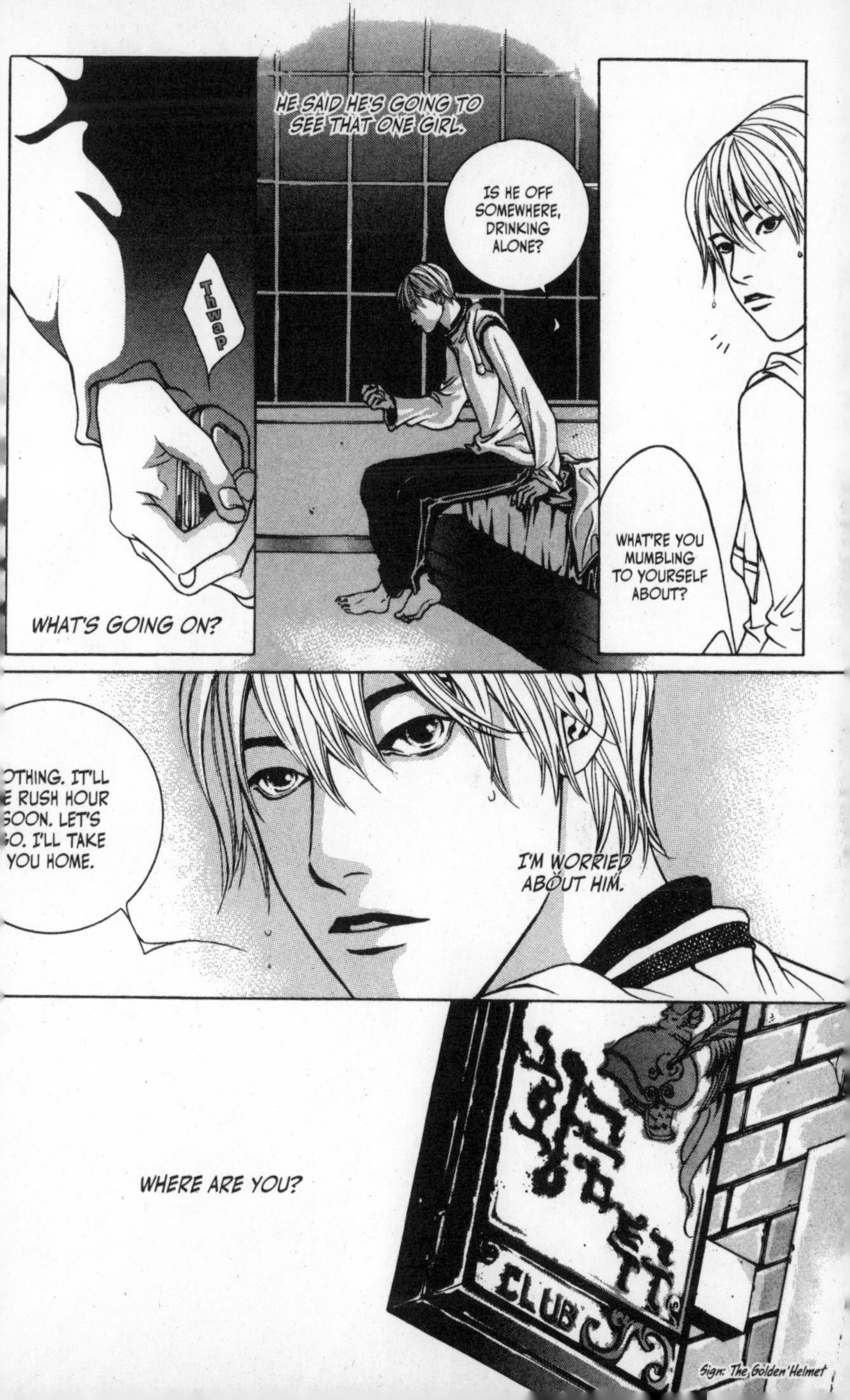
Thwap
WHAT'S GOING ON?
HE SAID HE'S GOING TO SEE THAT ONE GIRL.
IS HE OFF SOMEWHERE, DRINKING ALONE?
WHAT'RE YOU MUMBLING TO YOURSELF ABOUT?
OTHING. IT'LL E RUSH HOUR SOON. LET'S GO. I'LL TAKE YOU HOME.
I'M WORRIED ABOUT HIM.
WHERE ARE YOU?
CLUB
Sign: The Golden Helmet

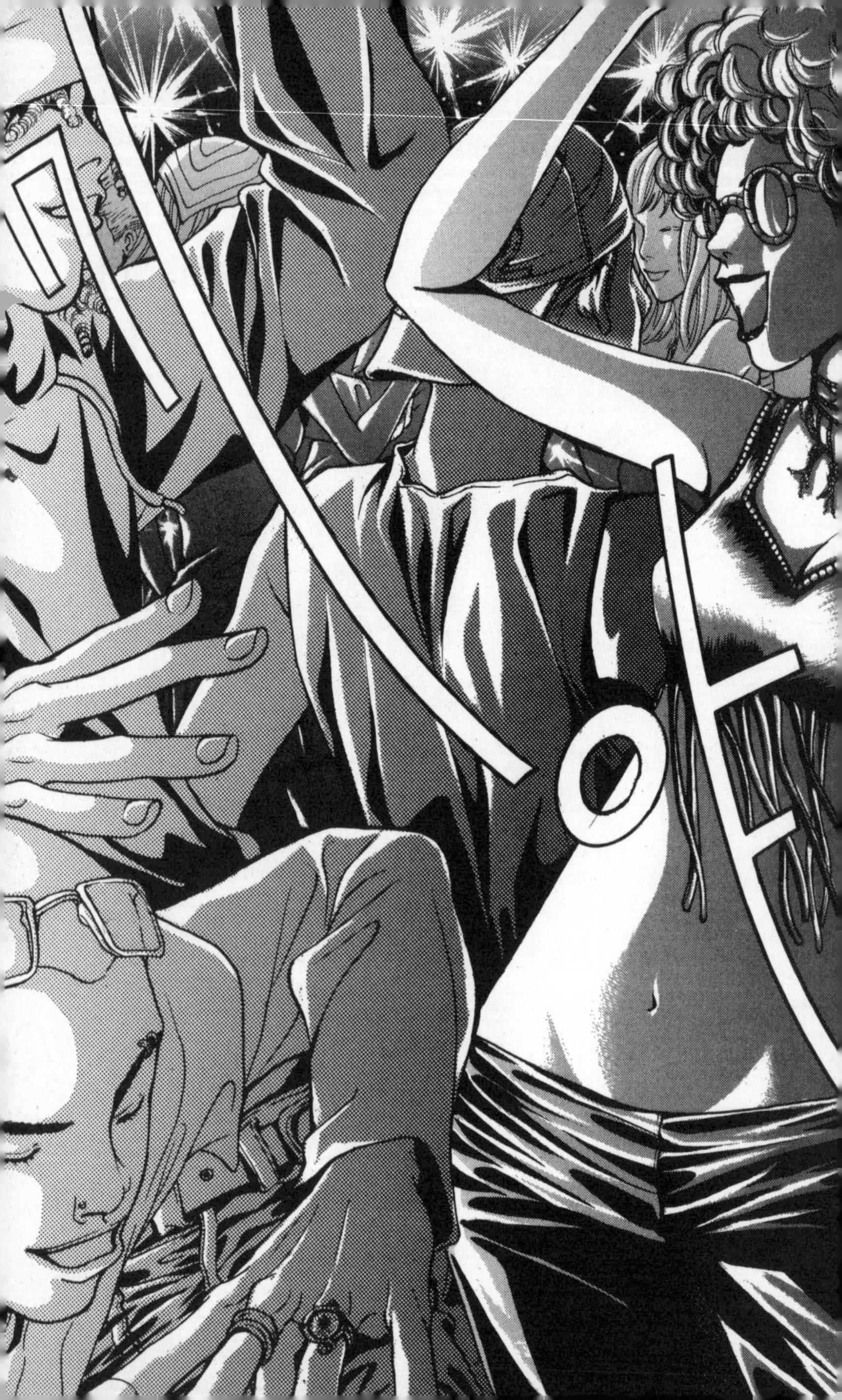

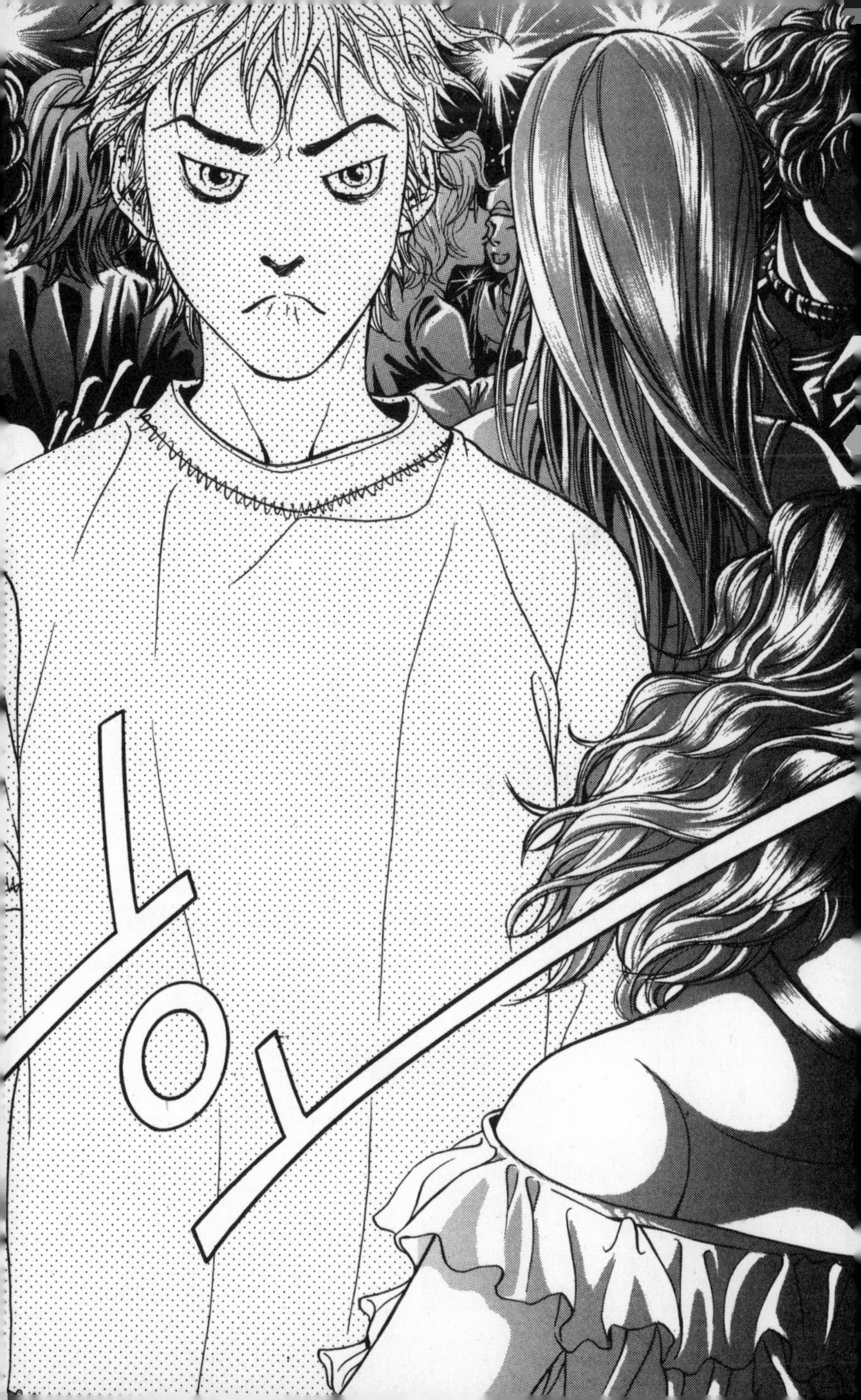

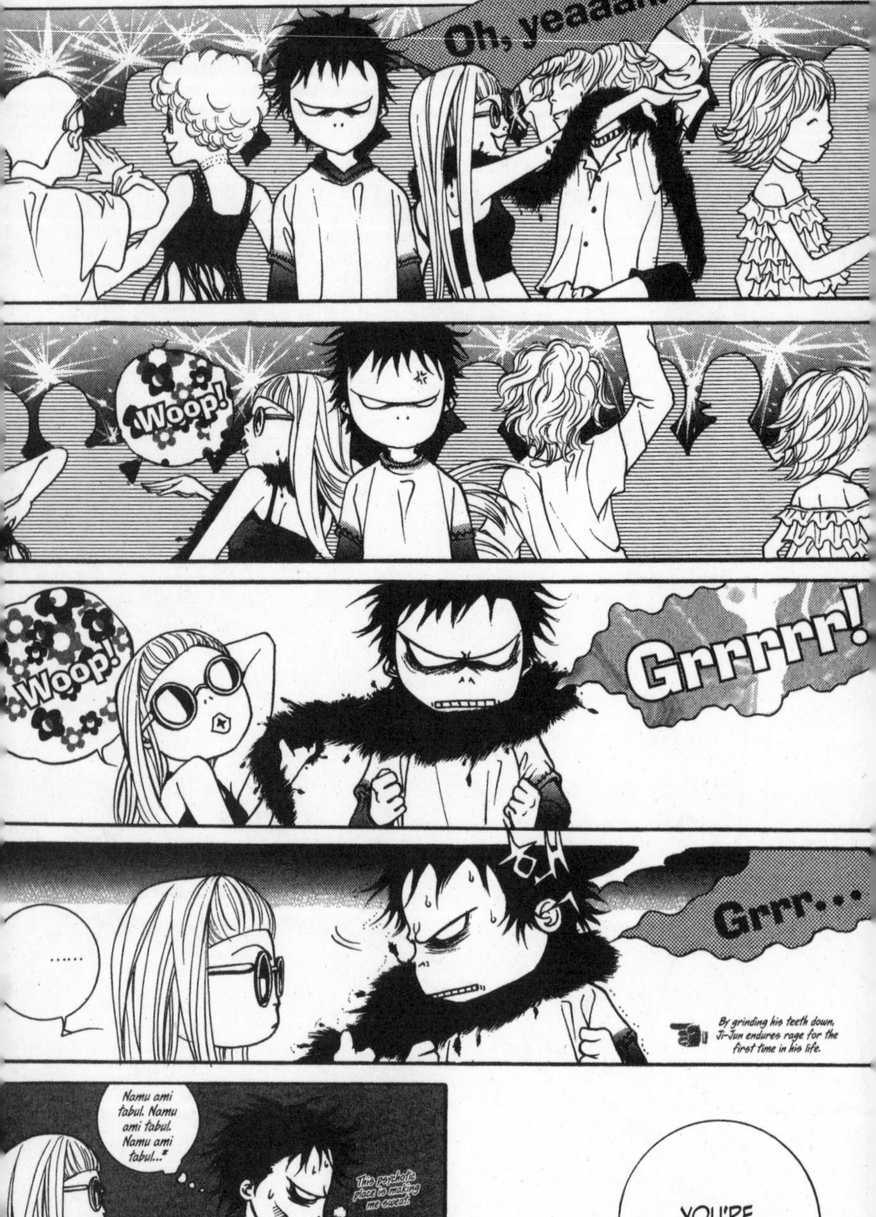
Oh, yeaaaah!
Woop!
Woop!
Grrrrrr!
......
Grrr...
By grinding his teeth down, Ji-Jun endures rage for the first time in his life.
Namu ami tabul. Namu ami tabul. Namu ami tabul...*
This psychotic place is making me sweat.
Huff Huff
YOU'RE BORING.

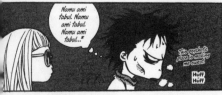

* Buddhist chant

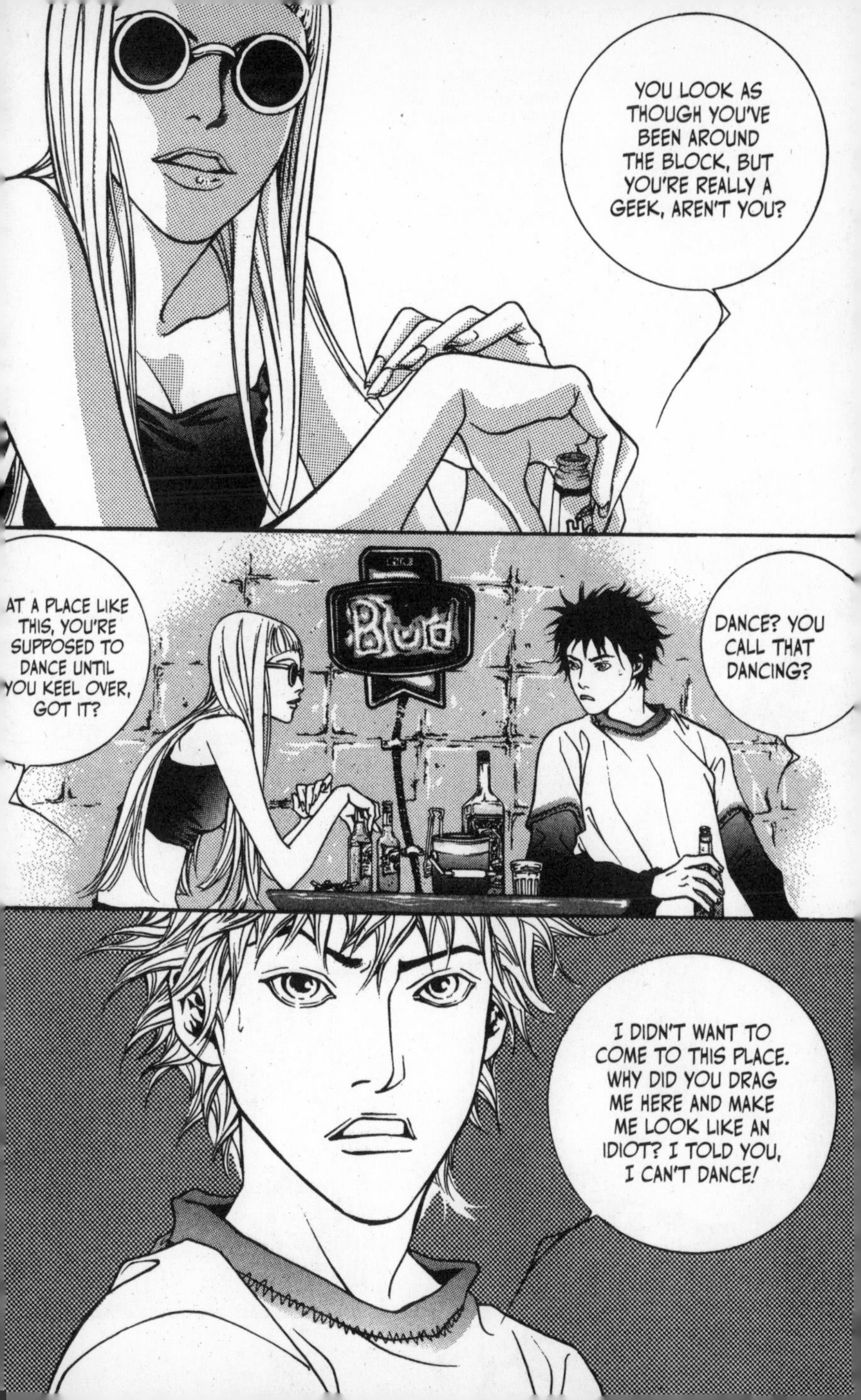

YOU LOOK AS THOUGH YOU'VE BEEN AROUND THE BLOCK, BUT YOU'RE REALLY A GEEK, AREN'T YOU?
AT A PLACE LIKE THIS, YOU'RE SUPPOSED TO DANCE UNTIL YOU KEEL OVER, GOT IT?
Blud
DANCE? YOU CALL THAT DANCING?
I DIDN'T WANT TO COME TO THIS PLACE. WHY DID YOU DRAG ME HERE AND MAKE ME LOOK LIKE AN IDIOT? I TOLD YOU, I CAN'T DANCE!

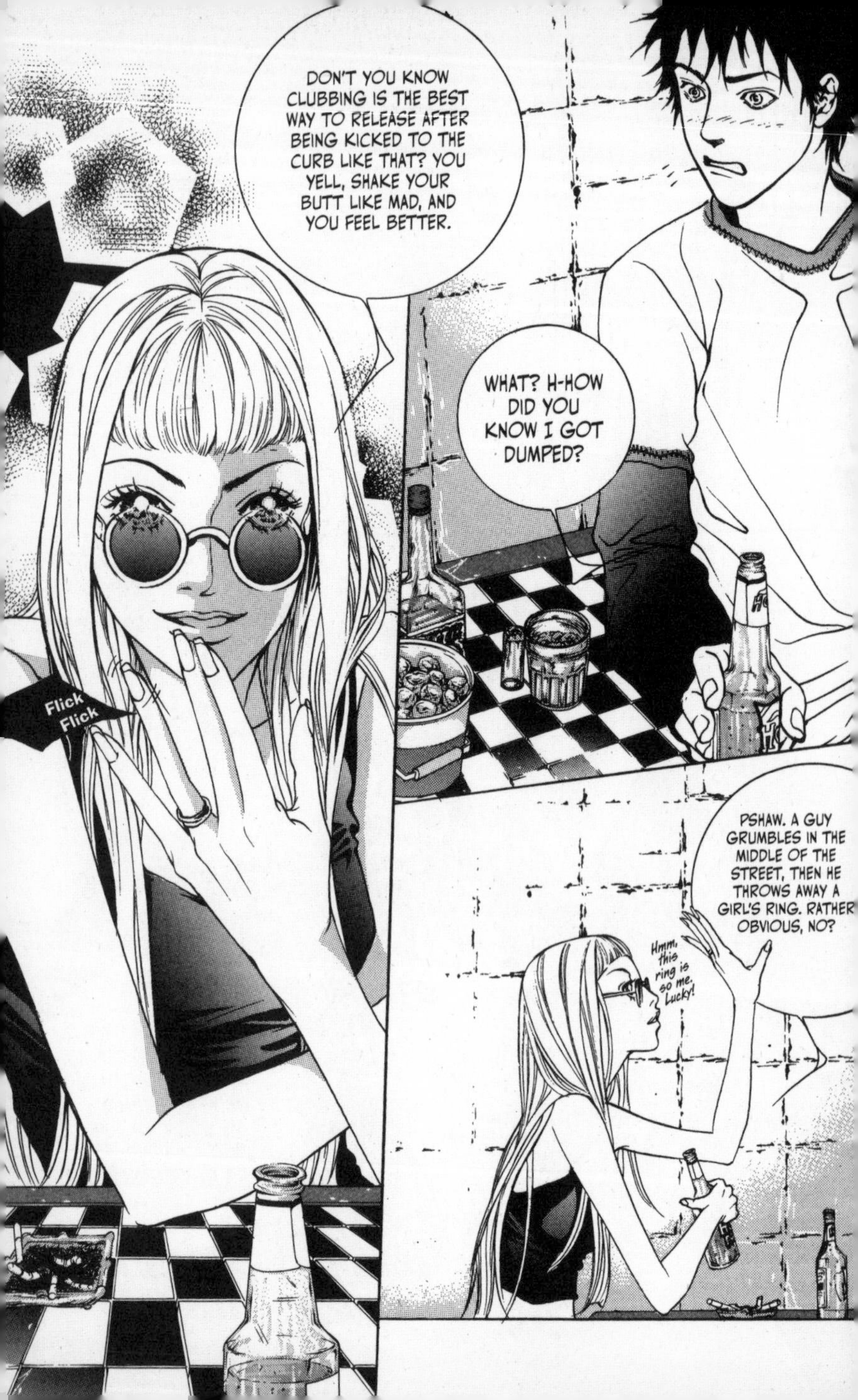
DON'T YOU KNOW CLUBBING IS THE BEST WAY TO RELEASE AFTER BEING KICKED TO THE CURB LIKE THAT? YOU YELL, SHAKE YOUR BUTT LIKE MAD, AND YOU FEEL BETTER.
Flick Flick
WHAT? H-HOW DID YOU KNOW I GOT DUMPED?
PSHAW. A GUY GRUMBLES IN THE MIDDLE OF THE STREET, THEN HE THROWS AWAY A GIRL'S RING. RATHER OBVIOUS, NO?
Hmm, this ring is so me. Lucky!

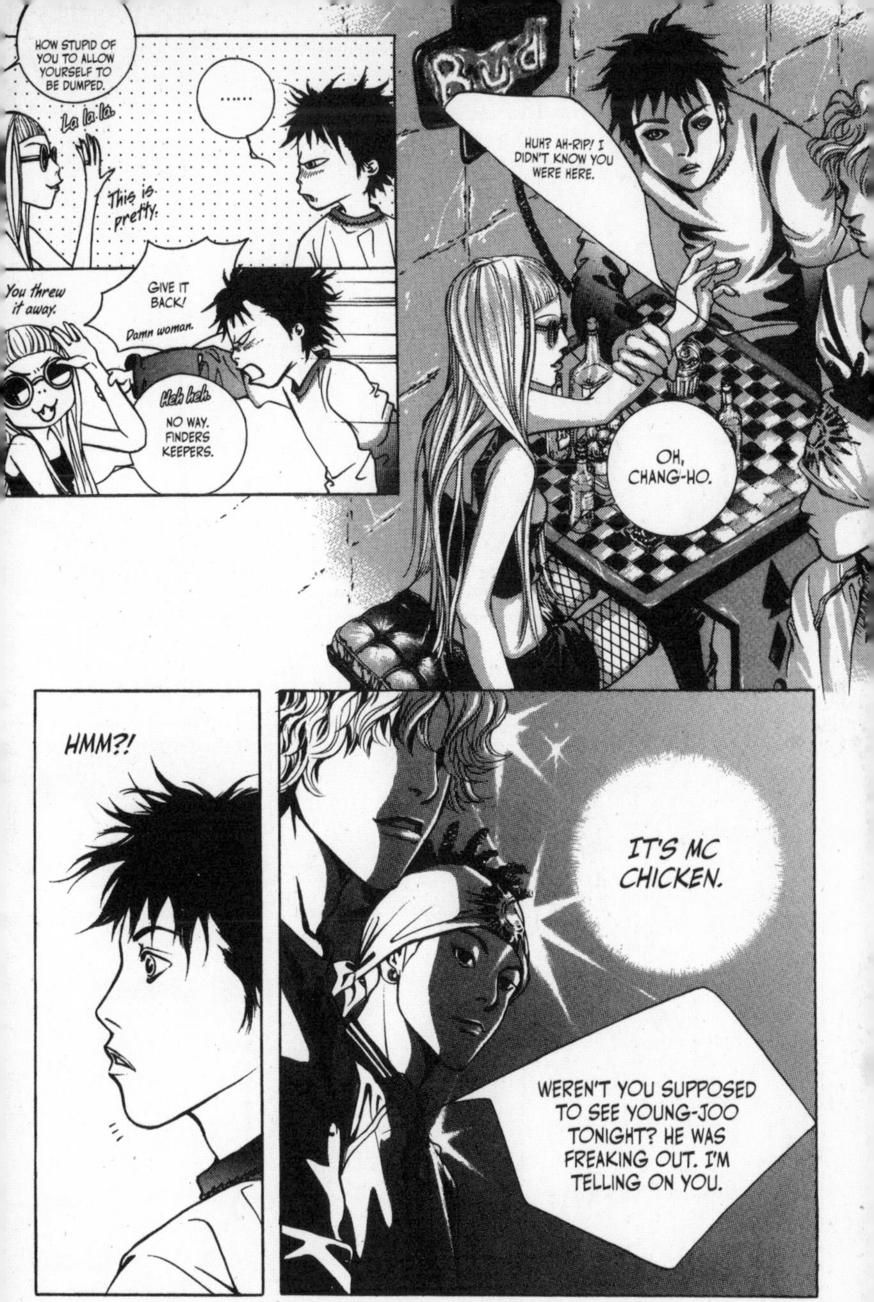
HOW STUPID OF YOU TO ALLOW YOURSELF TO BE DUMPED.
La la la.
......
This is pretty.
You threw it away.
GIVE IT BACK!
Damn woman.
Heh heh.
NO WAY. FINDERS KEEPERS.
Bud
HUH? AH-RIP! I DIDN'T KNOW YOU WERE HERE.
OH, CHANG-HO.
HMM?!
IT'S MC CHICKEN.
WEREN'T YOU SUPPOSED TO SEE YOUNG-JOO TONIGHT? HE WAS FREAKING OUT. I'M TELLING ON YOU.

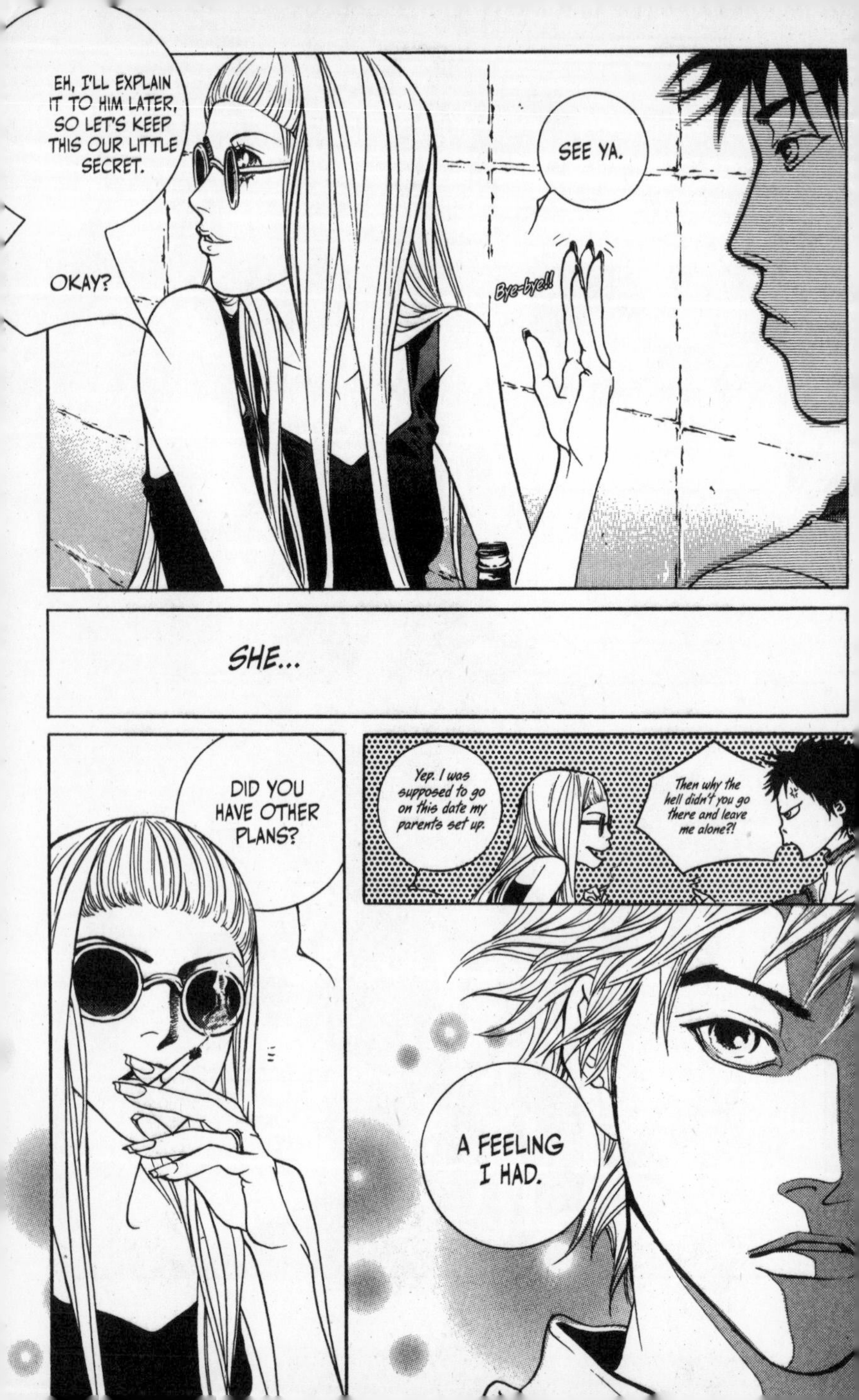
EH, I'LL EXPLAIN IT TO HIM LATER, SO LET'S KEEP THIS OUR LITTLE SECRET.
OKAY?
SEE YA.
Bye-bye!!
SHE...
DID YOU HAVE OTHER PLANS?
Yep. I was supposed to go on this date my parents set up.
Then why the hell didn't you go there and leave me alone?!
A FEELING I HAD.

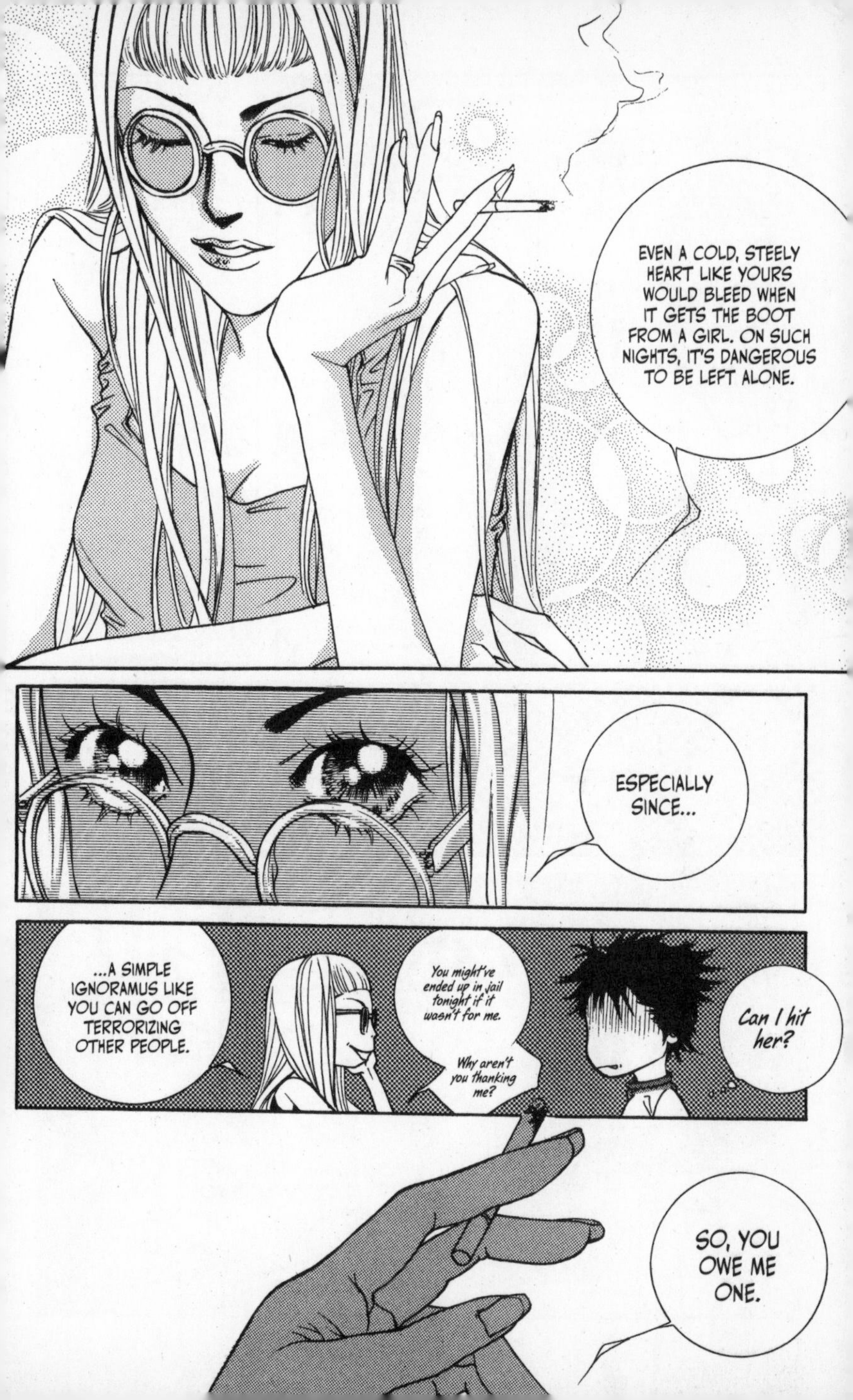
EVEN A COLD, STEELY HEART LIKE YOURS WOULD BLEED WHEN IT GETS THE BOOT FROM A GIRL. ON SUCH NIGHTS, IT'S DANGEROUS TO BE LEFT ALONE.
ESPECIALLY SINCE...
...A SIMPLE IGNORAMUS LIKE YOU CAN GO OFF TERRORIZING OTHER PEOPLE.
You might've ended up in jail tonight if it wasn't for me.
Why aren't you thanking me?
Can I hit her?
SO, YOU OWE ME ONE.

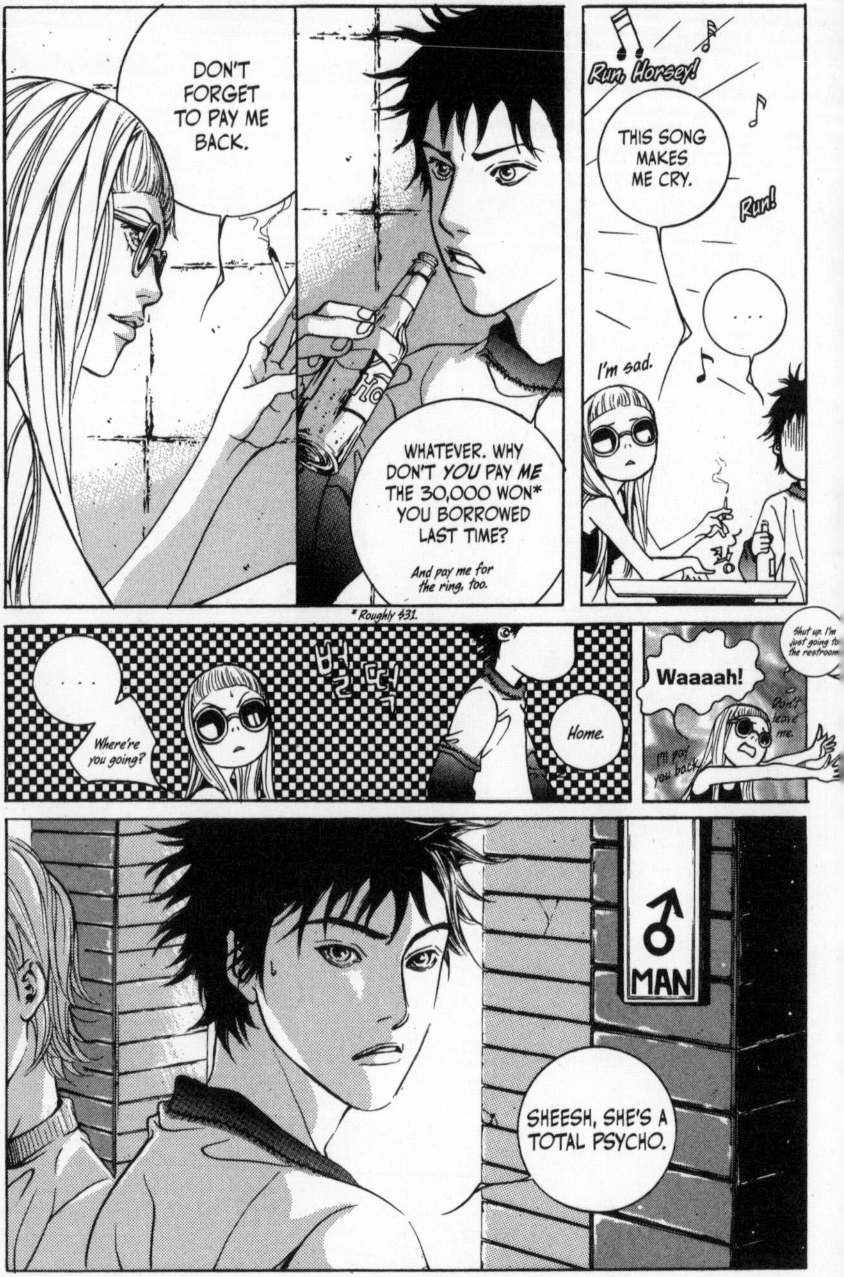
DON'T FORGET TO PAY ME BACK.
WHATEVER. WHY DON'T *YOU* PAY *ME* THE 30,000 WON* YOU BORROWED LAST TIME?
And pay me for the ring, too.
Run, Horsey!
THIS SONG MAKES ME CRY.
Run!
. . .
I'm sad.
. . .
Where're you going?
Home.
Waaaah!
Shut up. I'm just going to the restroom.
Don't leave me.
I'll pay you back.
MAN
SHEESH, SHE'S A TOTAL PSYCHO.

* Roughly $31.

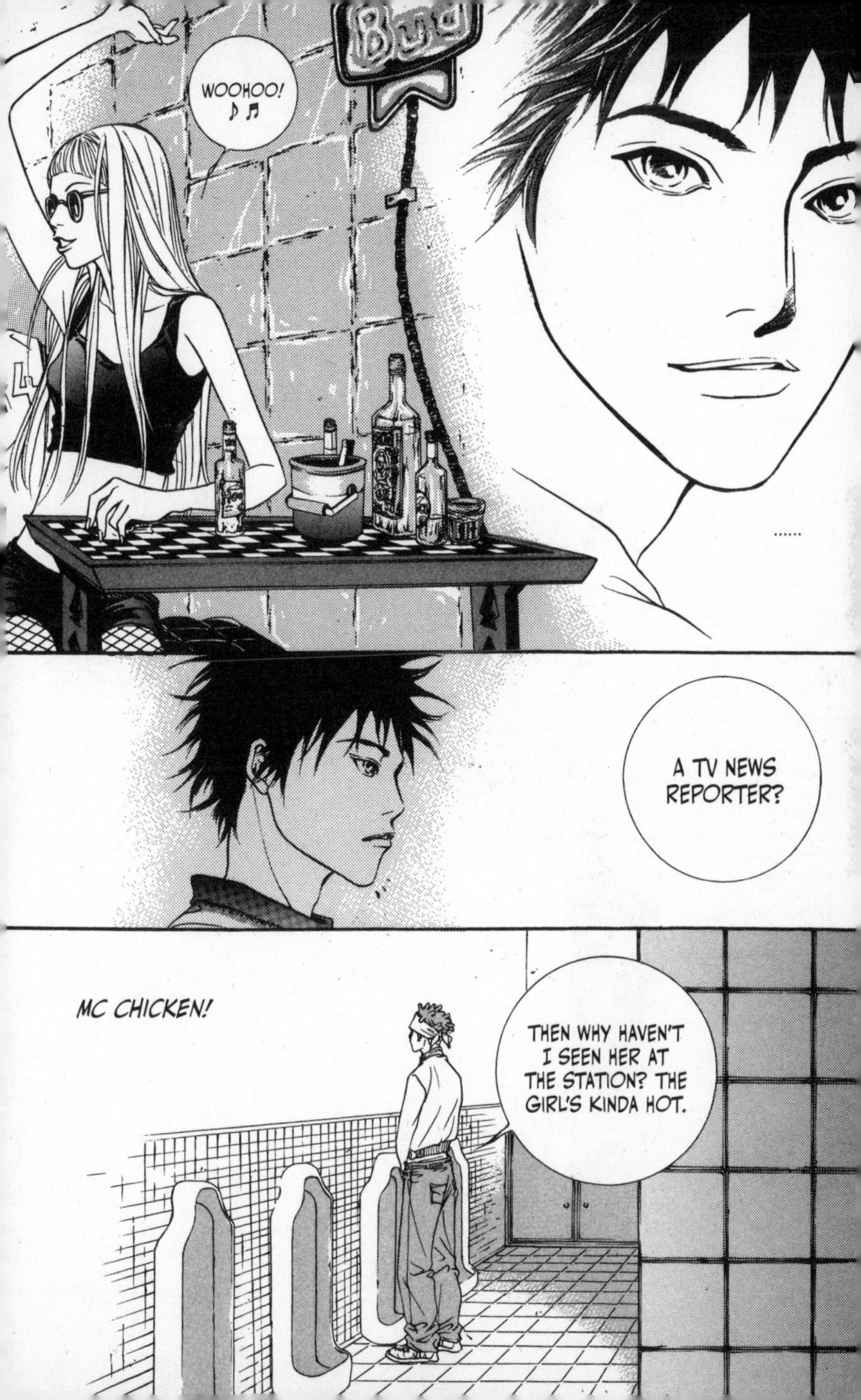
WOOHOO! ♪ ♬
......
A TV NEWS REPORTER?
MC CHICKEN!
THEN WHY HAVEN'T I SEEN HER AT THE STATION? THE GIRL'S KINDA HOT.

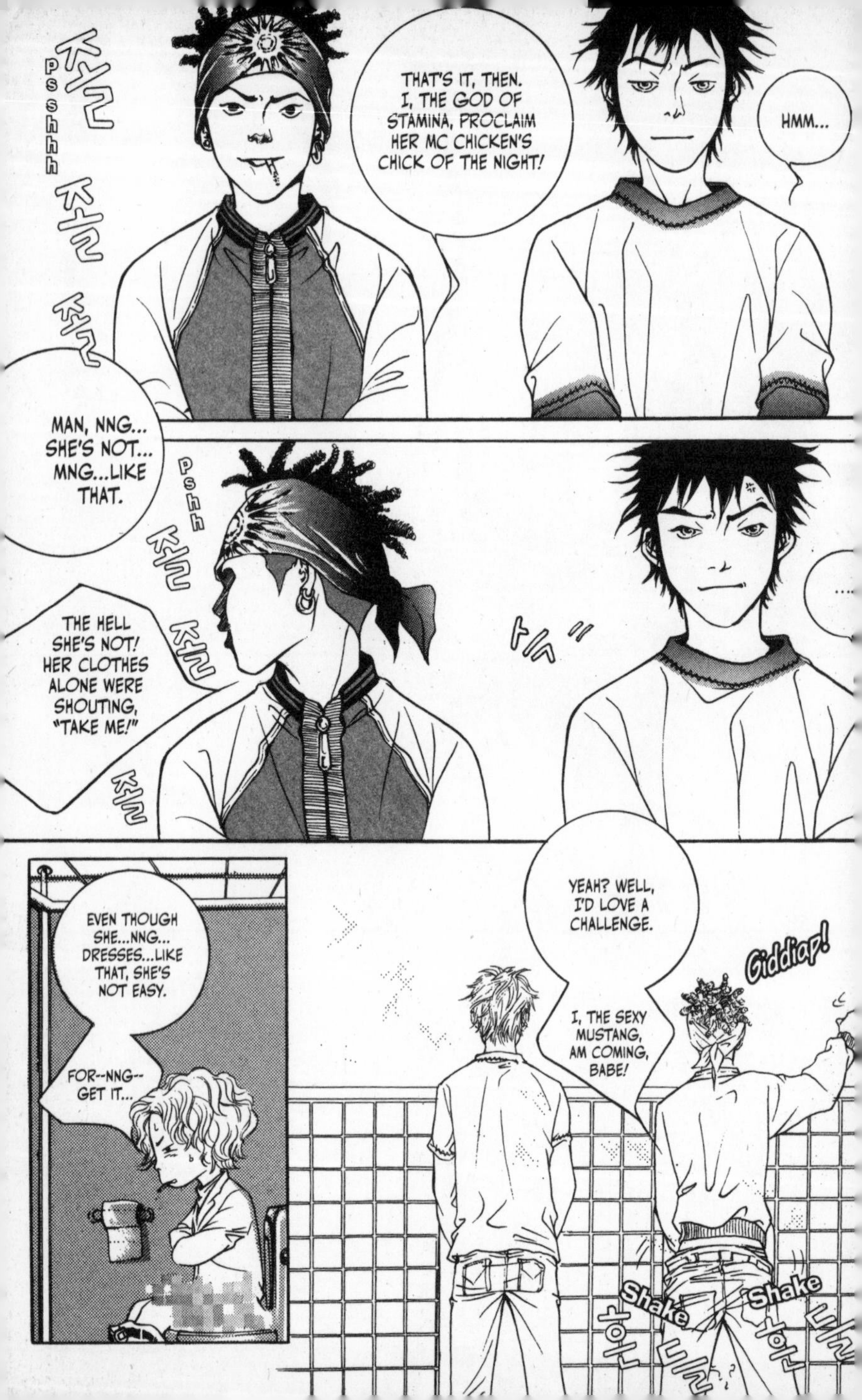

pssshhh
THAT'S IT, THEN. I, THE GOD OF STAMINA, PROCLAIM HER MC CHICKEN'S CHICK OF THE NIGHT!
HMM...
MAN, NNG... SHE'S NOT... MNG...LIKE THAT.
pshh
THE HELL SHE'S NOT! HER CLOTHES ALONE WERE SHOUTING, "TAKE ME!"
....
EVEN THOUGH SHE...NNG... DRESSES...LIKE THAT, SHE'S NOT EASY.
FOR--NNG-- GET IT...
YEAH? WELL, I'D LOVE A CHALLENGE.
I, THE SEXY MUSTANG, AM COMING, BABE!
Giddiap!
Shake
Shake

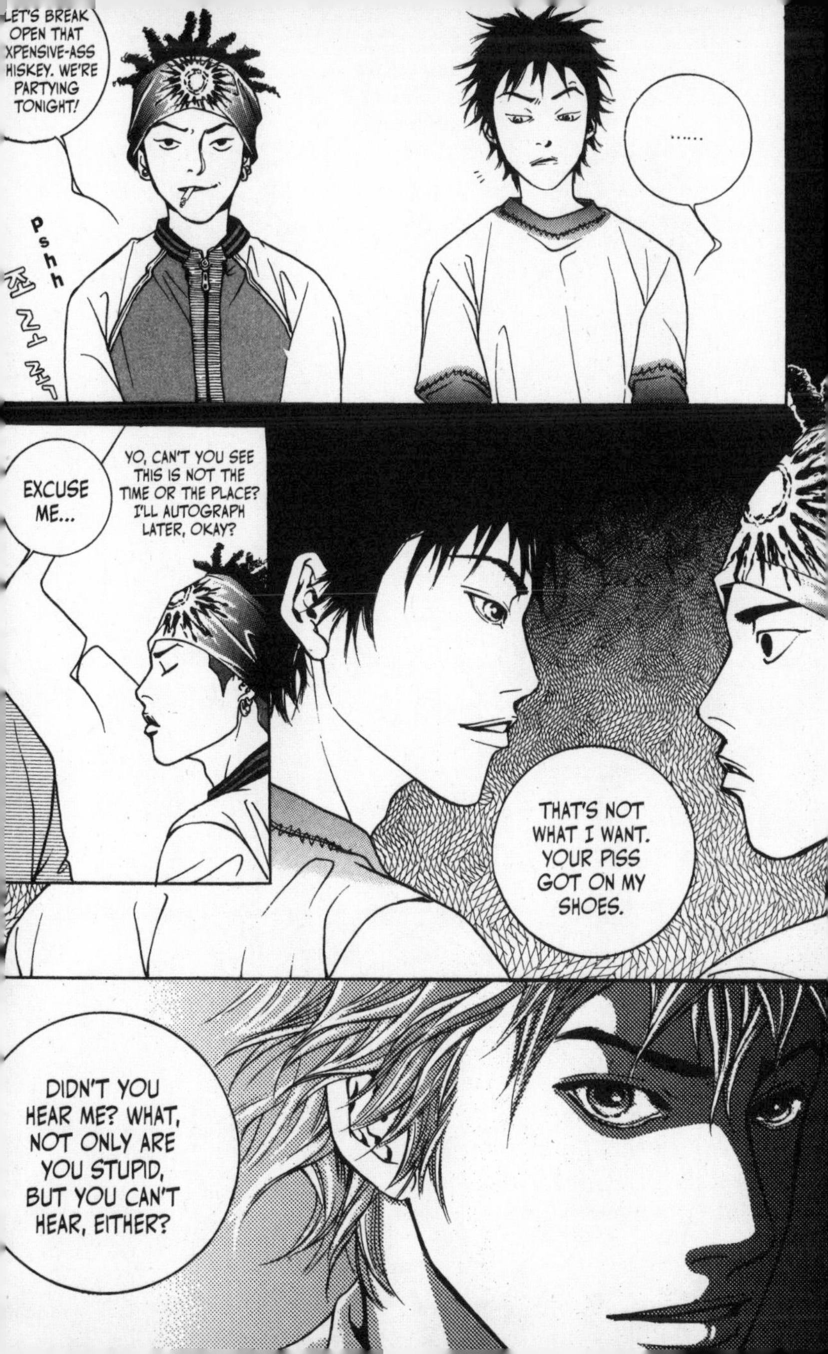
LET'S BREAK OPEN THAT XPENSIVE-ASS HISKEY. WE'RE PARTYING TONIGHT!
Pshh
......
EXCUSE ME...
YO, CAN'T YOU SEE THIS IS NOT THE TIME OR THE PLACE? I'LL AUTOGRAPH LATER, OKAY?
THAT'S NOT WHAT I WANT. YOUR PISS GOT ON MY SHOES.
DIDN'T YOU HEAR ME? WHAT, NOT ONLY ARE YOU STUPID, BUT YOU CAN'T HEAR, EITHER?

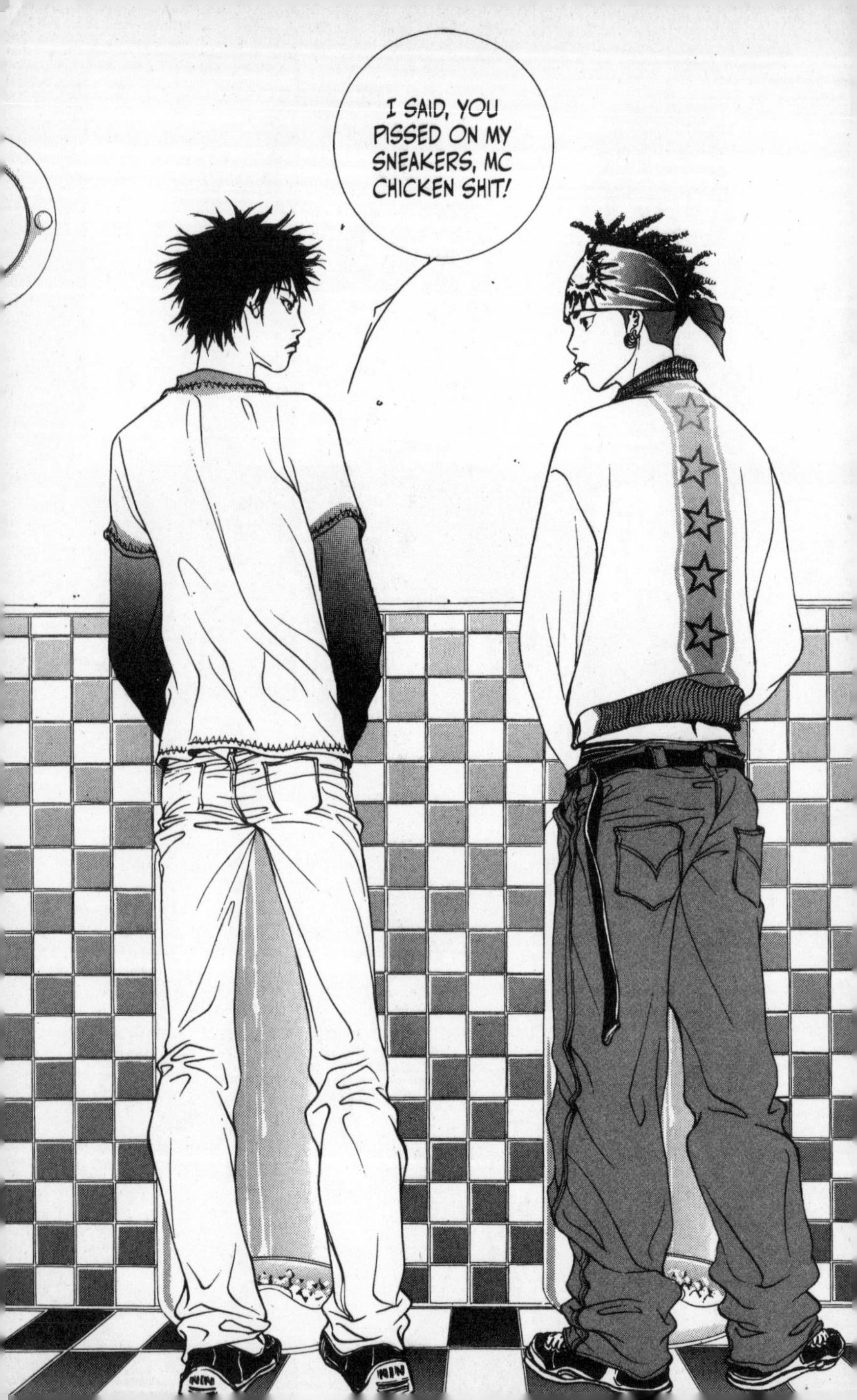
I SAID, YOU PISSED ON MY SNEAKERS, MC CHICKEN SHIT!

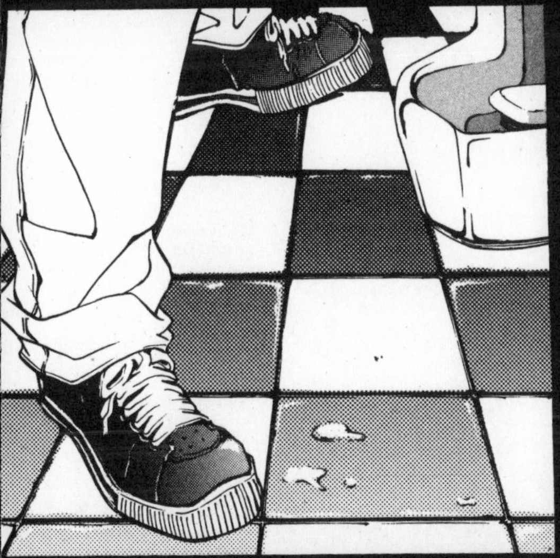

"COW MILK IS THE PROBLEM, I TELL YOU."

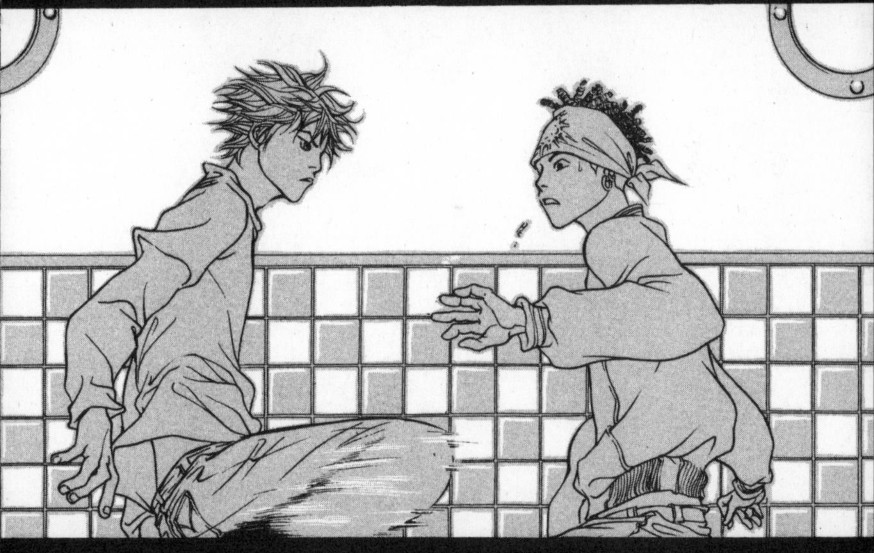

"YOU'RE NOT MENTALLY STABLE BECAUSE YOU WERE RAISED ON COW MILK INSTEAD OF MOTHER'S MILK..."

...IS WHAT AH-RIP TOLD ME LATER.

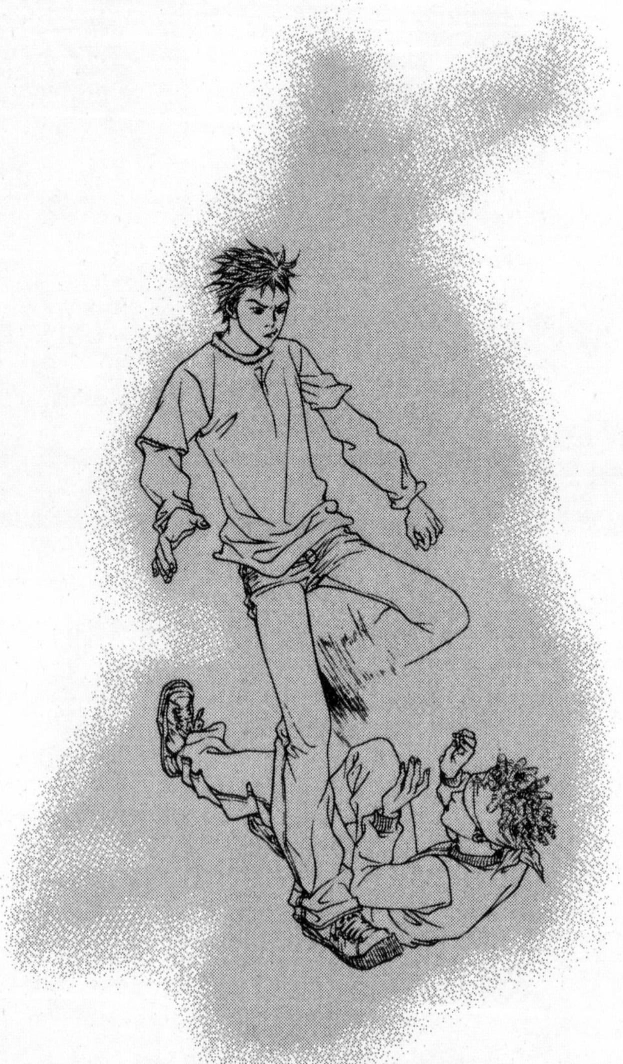

SO MY NASTY TEMPER REALLY ISN'T MY FAULT.

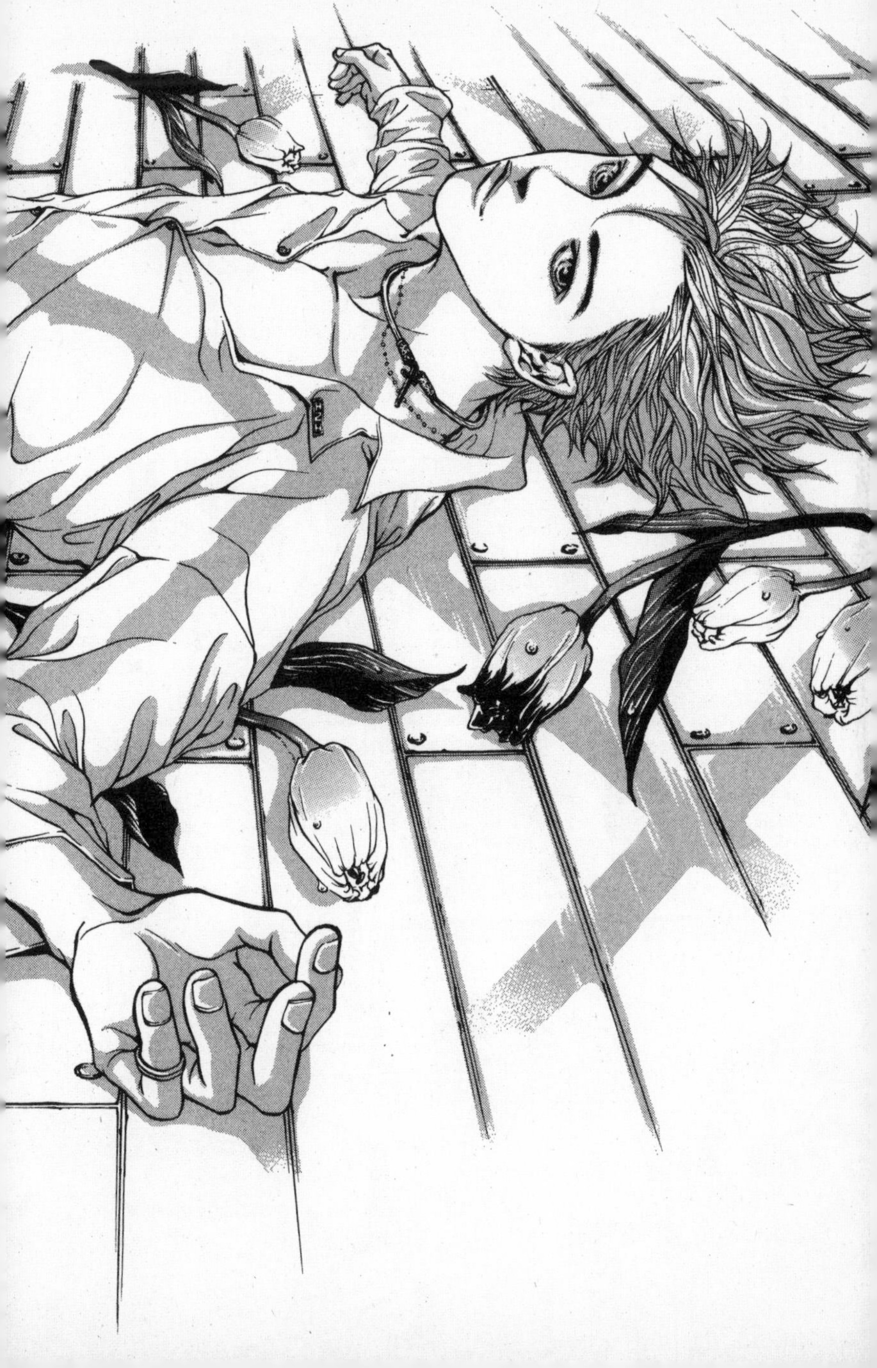

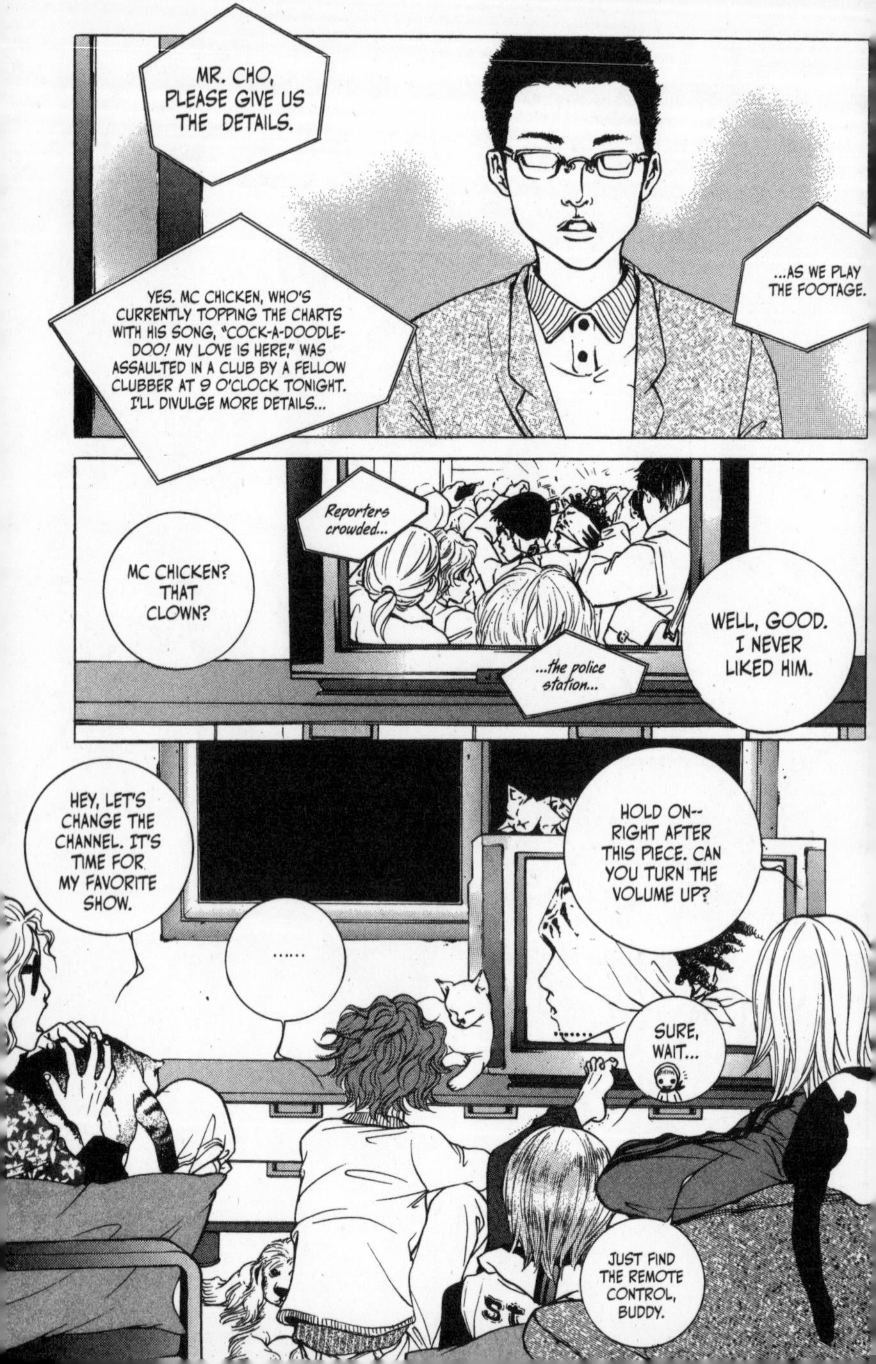
MR. CHO, PLEASE GIVE US THE DETAILS.
YES. MC CHICKEN, WHO'S CURRENTLY TOPPING THE CHARTS WITH HIS SONG, "COCK-A-DOODLE-DOO! MY LOVE IS HERE," WAS ASSAULTED IN A CLUB BY A FELLOW CLUBBER AT 9 O'CLOCK TONIGHT. I'LL DIVULGE MORE DETAILS...
...AS WE PLAY THE FOOTAGE.
MC CHICKEN? THAT CLOWN?
Reporters crowded...
...the police station...
WELL, GOOD. I NEVER LIKED HIM.
HEY, LET'S CHANGE THE CHANNEL. IT'S TIME FOR MY FAVORITE SHOW.
......
HOLD ON-- RIGHT AFTER THIS PIECE. CAN YOU TURN THE VOLUME UP?
......
SURE, WAIT...
JUST FIND THE REMOTE CONTROL, BUDDY.

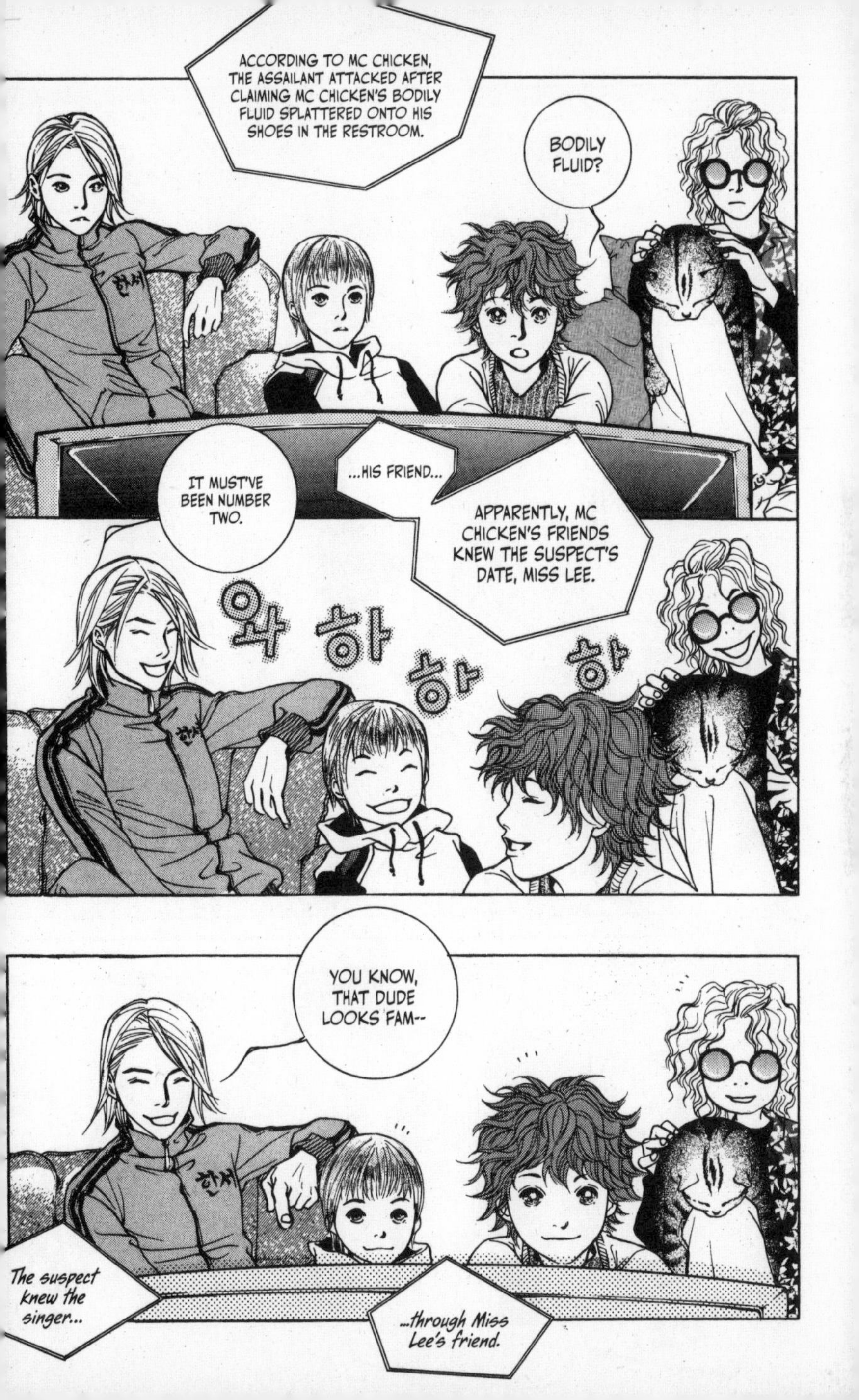
ACCORDING TO MC CHICKEN, THE ASSAILANT ATTACKED AFTER CLAIMING MC CHICKEN'S BODILY FLUID SPLATTERED ONTO HIS SHOES IN THE RESTROOM.
BODILY FLUID?
IT MUST'VE BEEN NUMBER TWO.
...HIS FRIEND...
APPARENTLY, MC CHICKEN'S FRIENDS KNEW THE SUSPECT'S DATE, MISS LEE.
와 하 하 하
YOU KNOW, THAT DUDE LOOKS FAM--
The suspect knew the singer...
...through Miss Lee's friend.

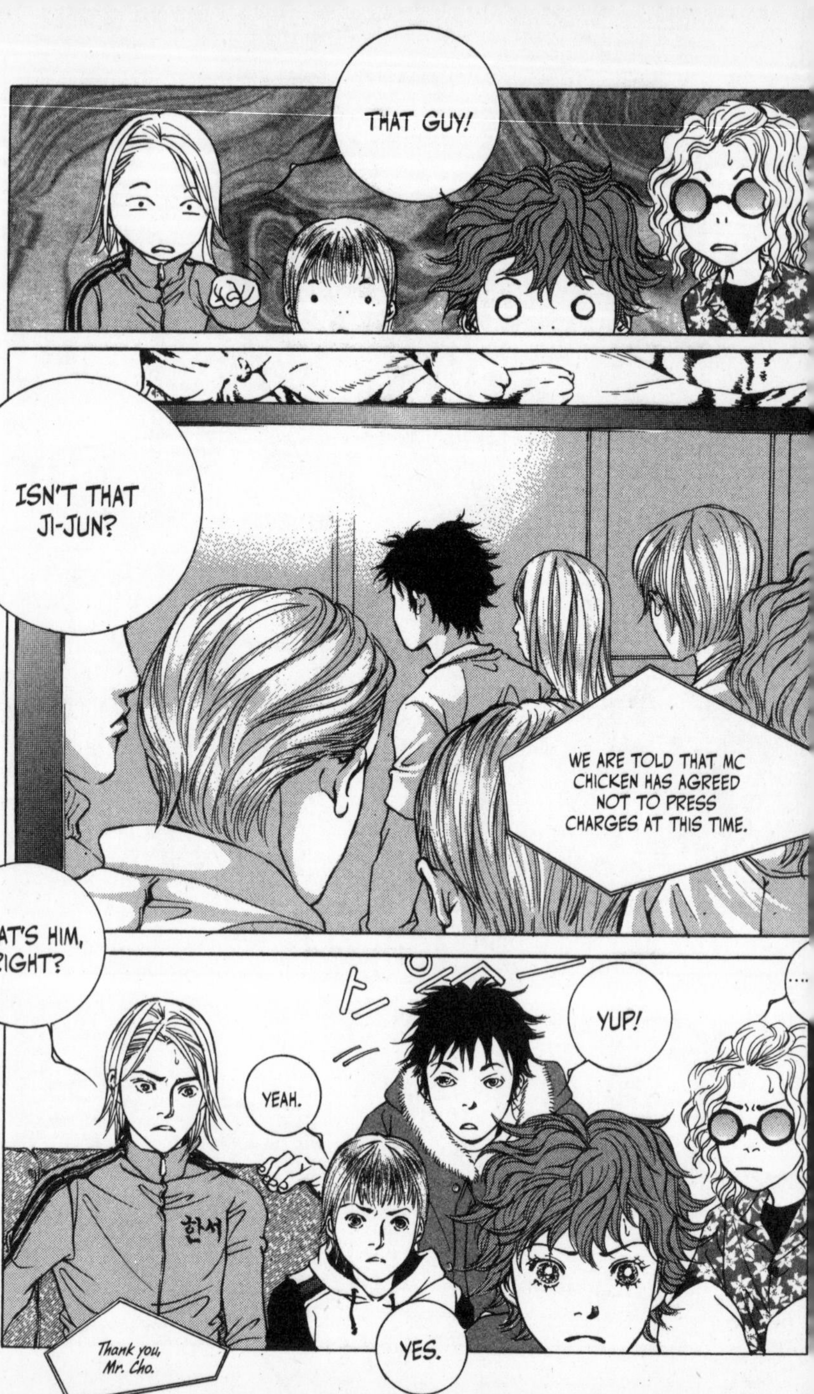
THAT GUY!
ISN'T THAT JI-JUN?
WE ARE TOLD THAT MC CHICKEN HAS AGREED NOT TO PRESS CHARGES AT THIS TIME.
THAT'S HIM, RIGHT?
YEAH.
YUP!
....
한서
Thank you, Mr. Cho.
YES.

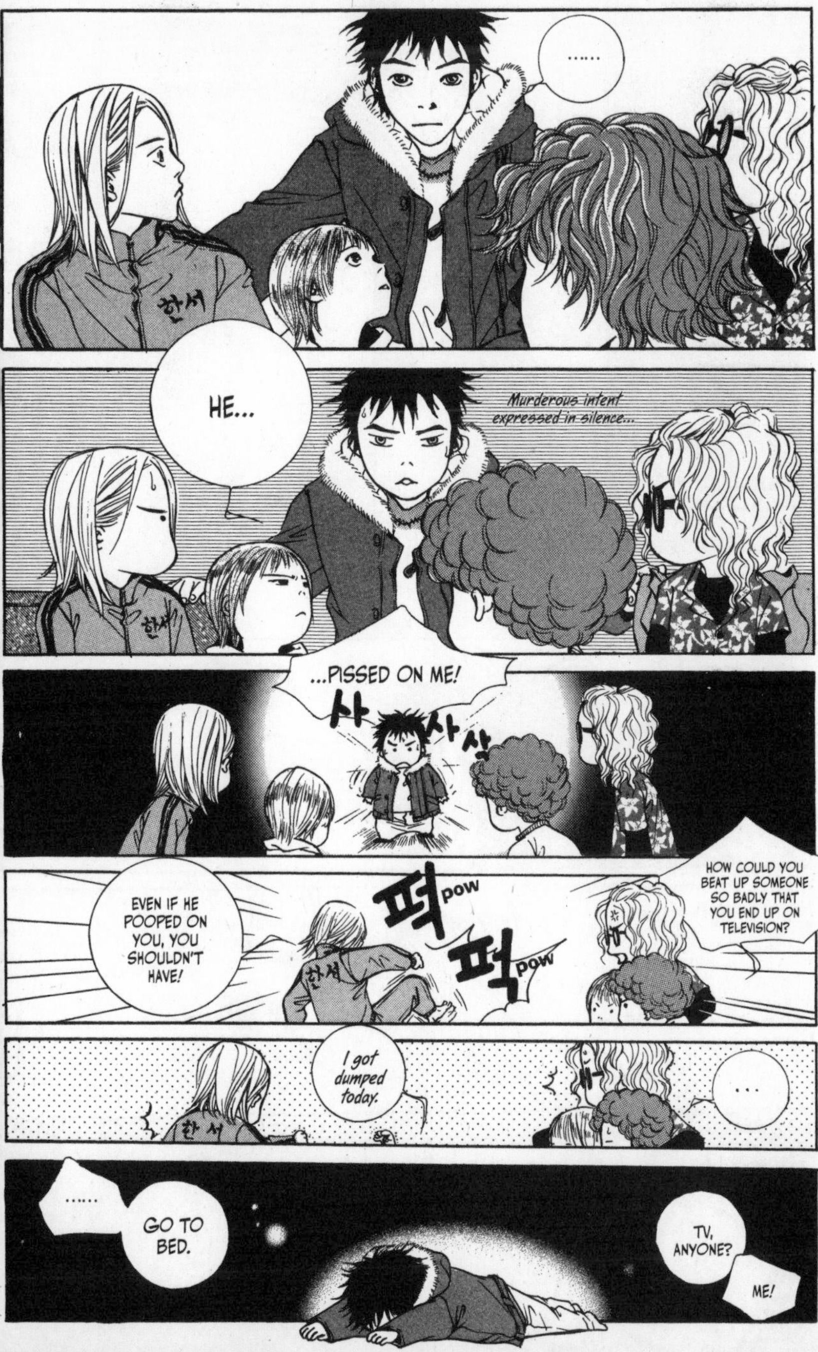
......
HE...
Murderous intent expressed in silence...
...PISSED ON ME!
사 사 삭
EVEN IF HE POOPED ON YOU, YOU SHOULDN'T HAVE!
퍽 POW
퍽 POW
HOW COULD YOU BEAT UP SOMEONE SO BADLY THAT YOU END UP ON TELEVISION?
I got dumped today.
...
......
GO TO BED.
TV, ANYONE?
ME!

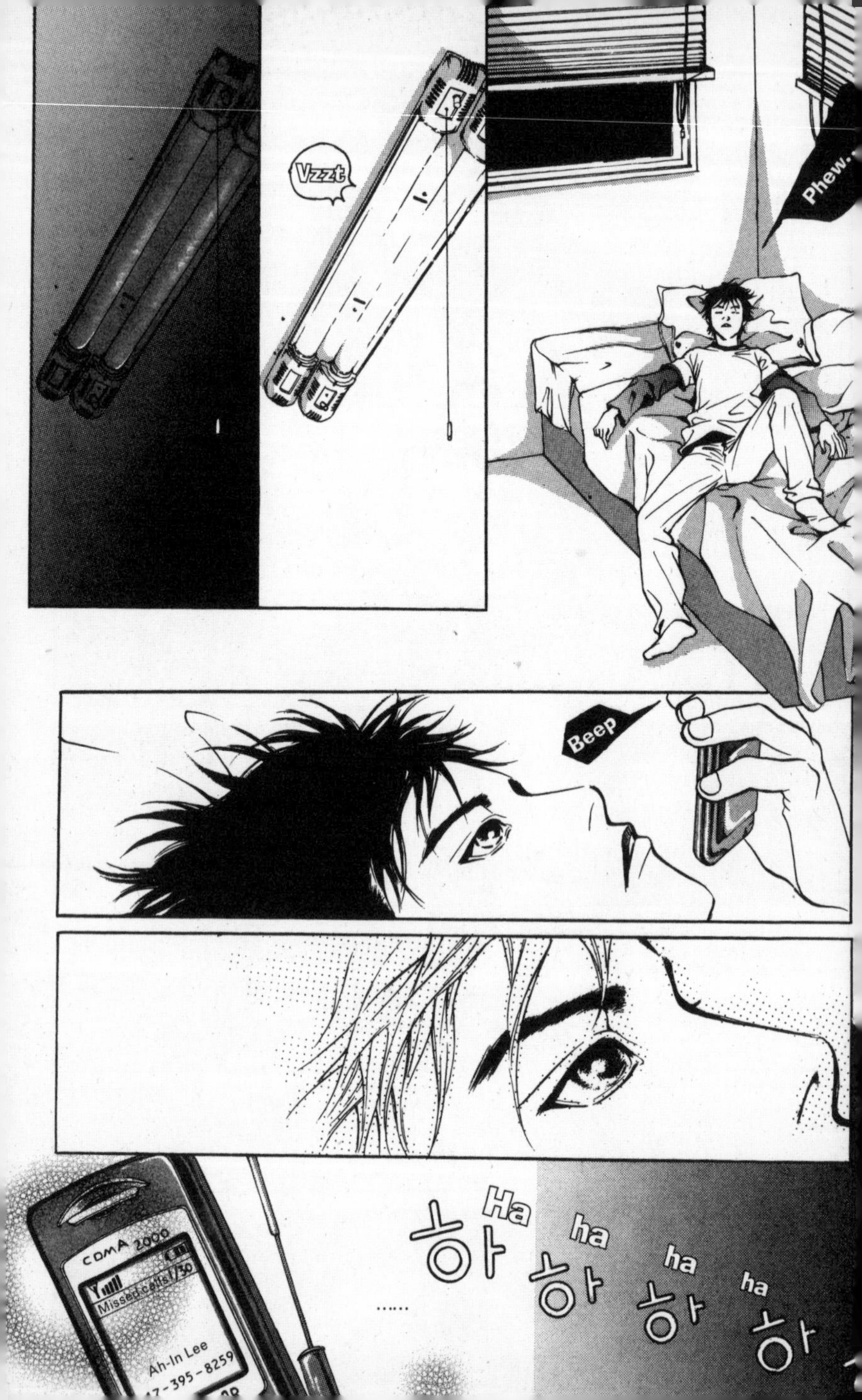
Vzzt
Phew...
Beep
CDMA 2000
Missed calls 1/30
Ah-In Lee
Ha ha ha ha
하하하하
......

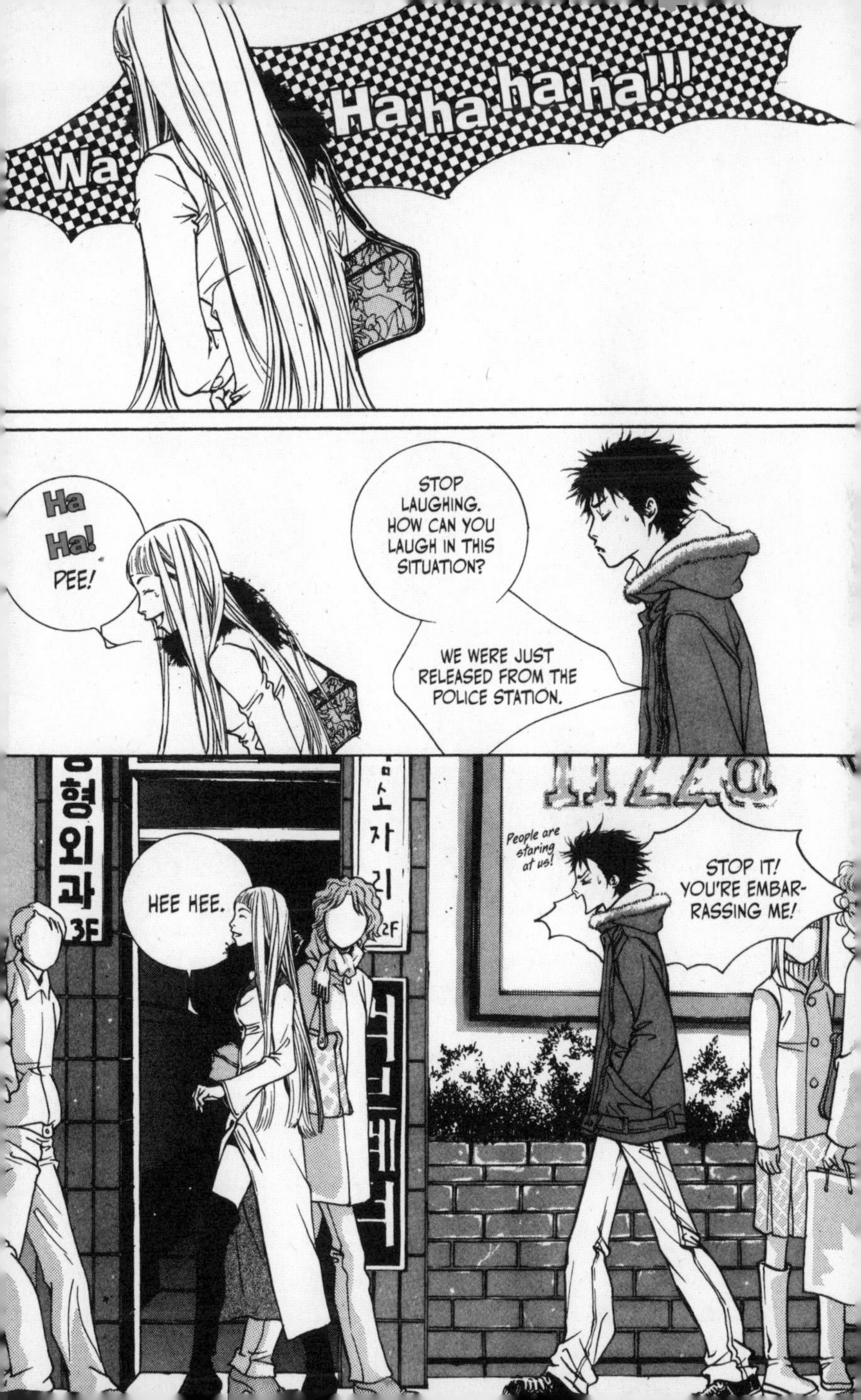

Wa
Ha ha ha ha!!!
Ha Ha! PEE!
STOP LAUGHING. HOW CAN YOU LAUGH IN THIS SITUATION?
WE WERE JUST RELEASED FROM THE POLICE STATION.
HEE HEE.
People are staring at us!
STOP IT! YOU'RE EMBARRASSING ME!

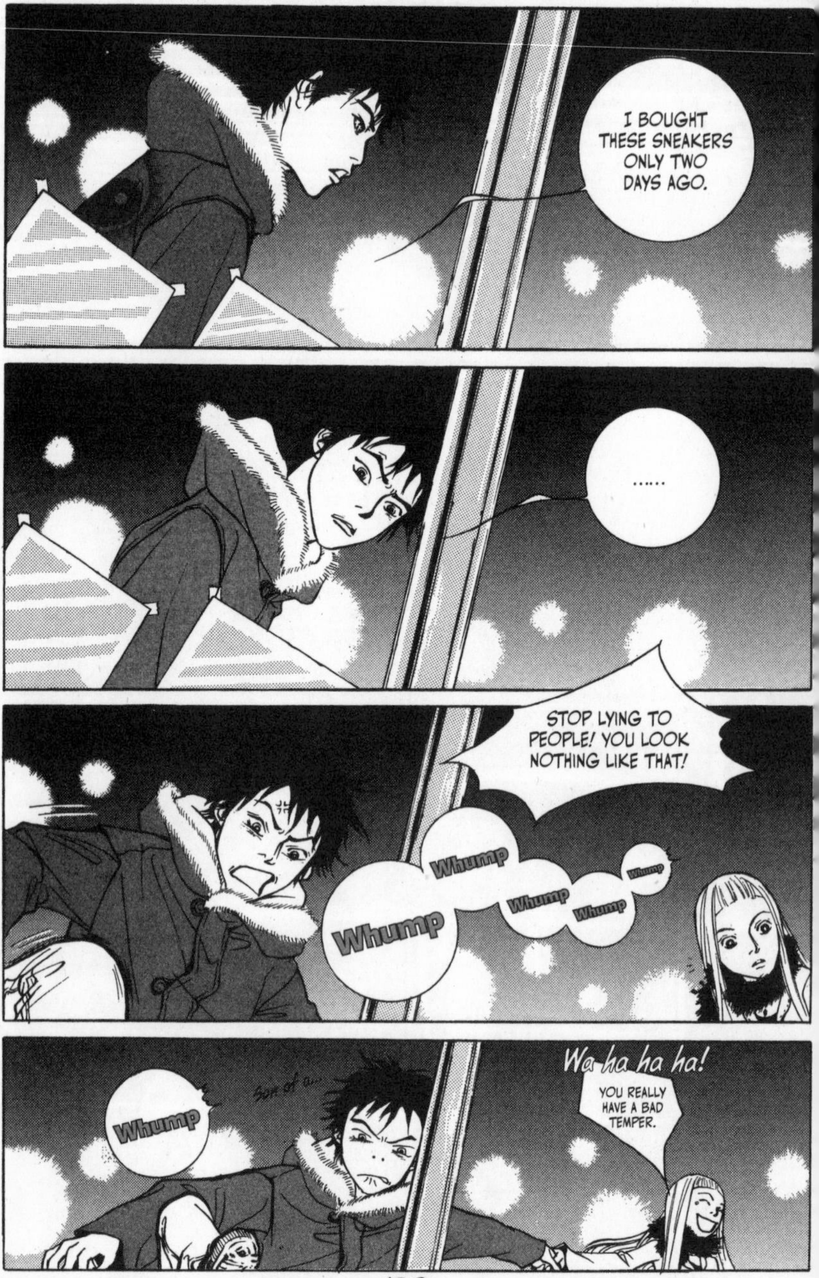
I BOUGHT THESE SNEAKERS ONLY TWO DAYS AGO.
……
STOP LYING TO PEOPLE! YOU LOOK NOTHING LIKE THAT!
Whump
Whump
Whump
Whump
Whump
Whump
Wa ha ha ha!
YOU REALLY HAVE A BAD TEMPER.

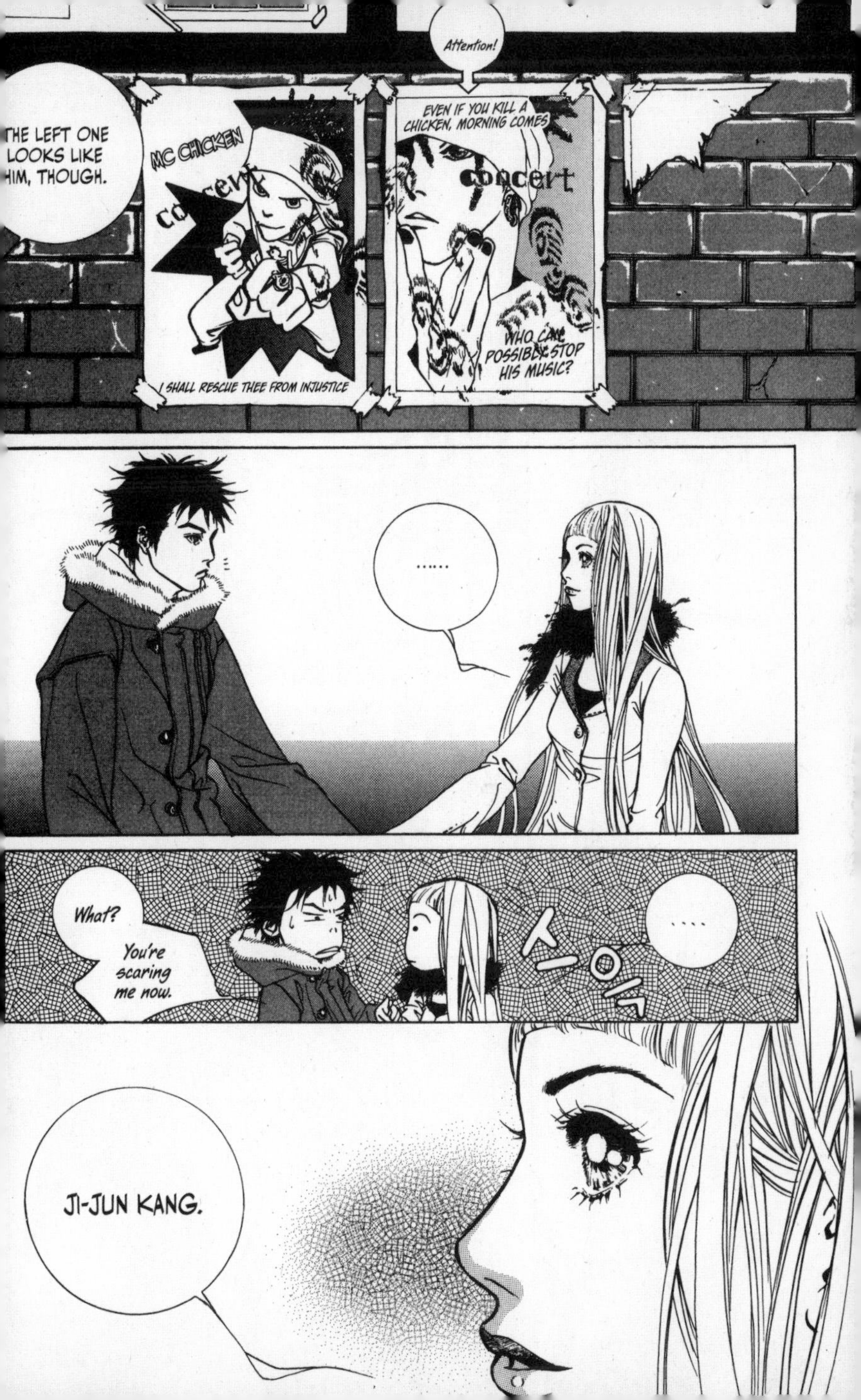
THE LEFT ONE LOOKS LIKE HIM, THOUGH.
MC CHICKEN
concert
I SHALL RESCUE THEE FROM INJUSTICE
Attention!
EVEN IF YOU KILL A CHICKEN, MORNING COMES
concert
WHO CAN POSSIBLY STOP HIS MUSIC?
......
What?
You're scaring me now.
....
JI-JUN KANG.

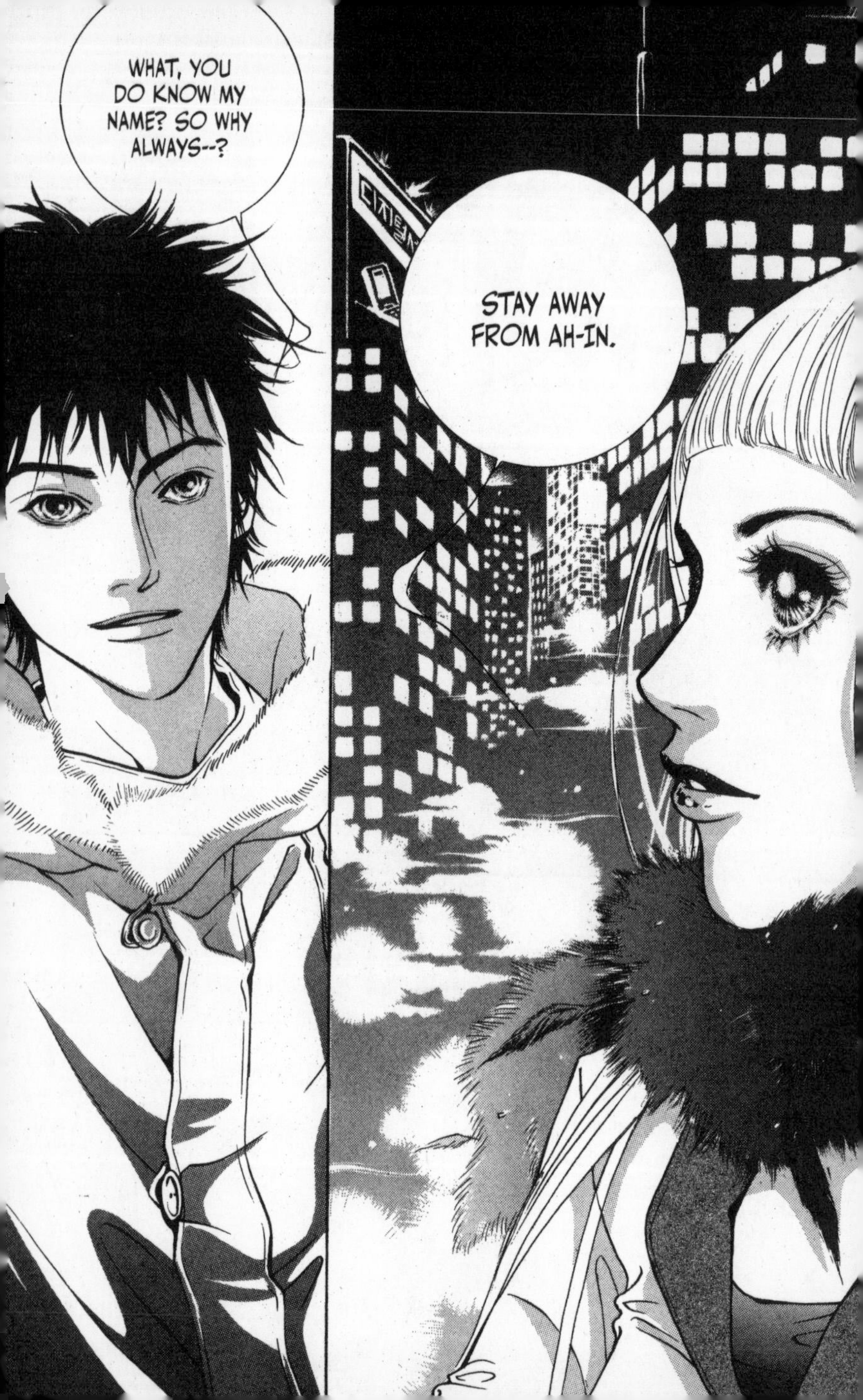
WHAT, YOU DO KNOW MY NAME? SO WHY ALWAYS--?
STAY AWAY FROM AH-IN.

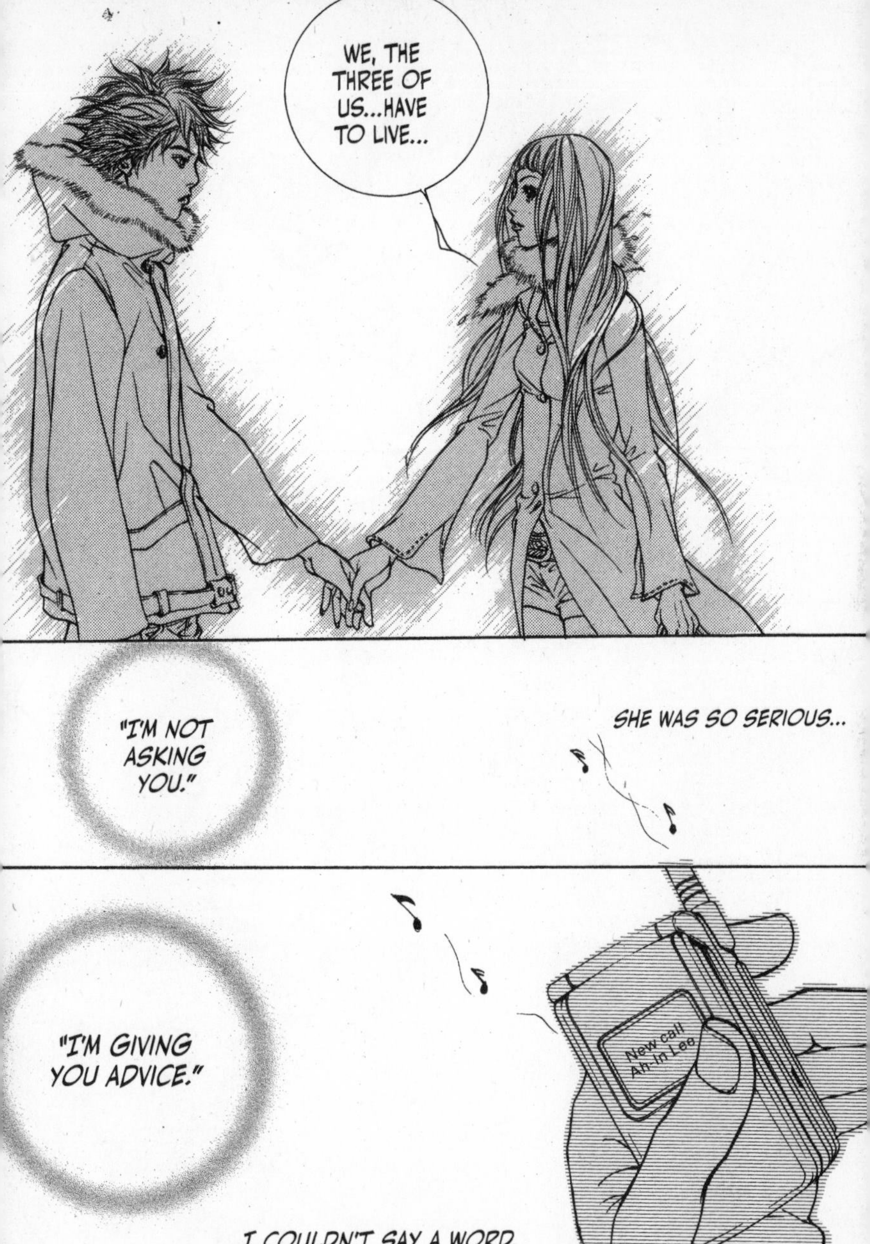
WE, THE THREE OF US...HAVE TO LIVE...
"I'M NOT ASKING YOU."
SHE WAS SO SERIOUS...
"I'M GIVING YOU ADVICE."
New call
Ah-In Lee
...I COULDN'T SAY A WORD.

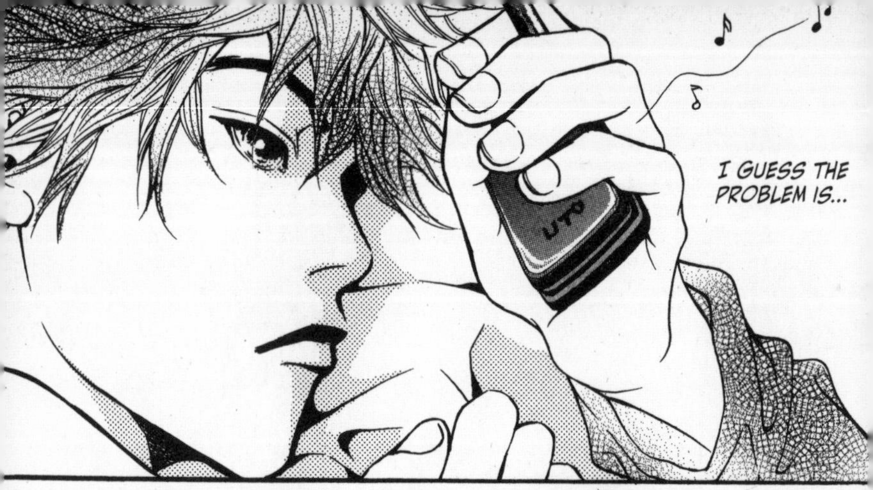
I GUESS THE
PROBLEM IS...

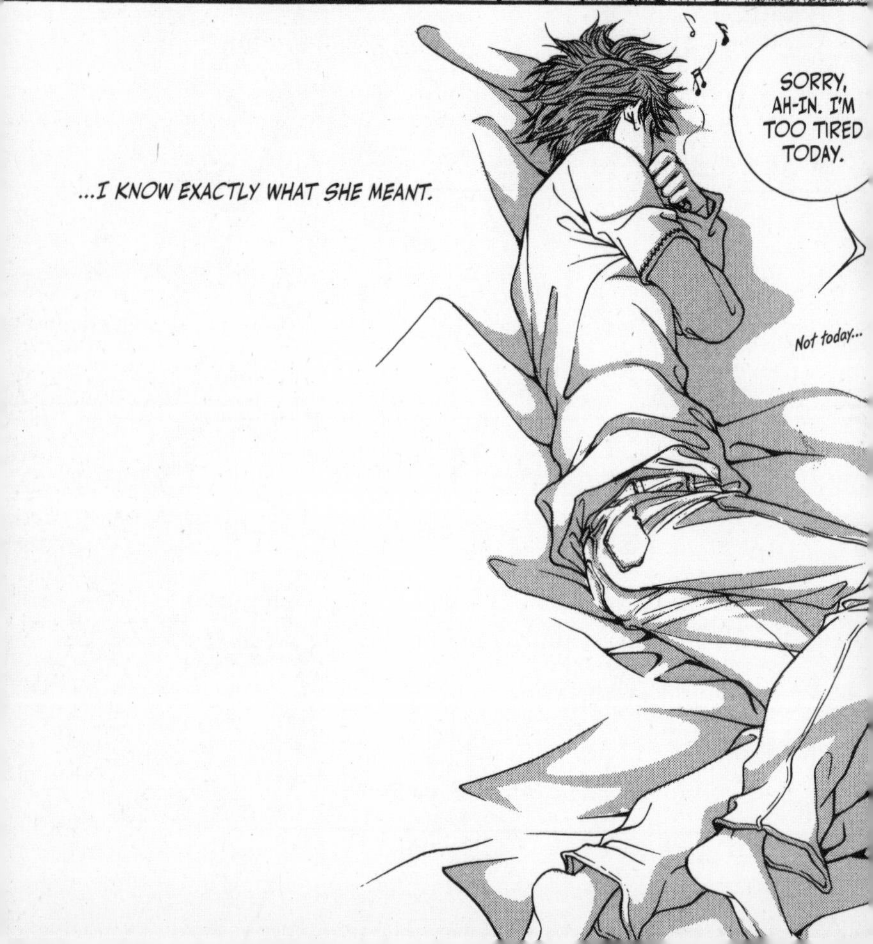
...I KNOW EXACTLY WHAT SHE MEANT.
SORRY, AH-IN. I'M TOO TIRED TODAY.
Not today...

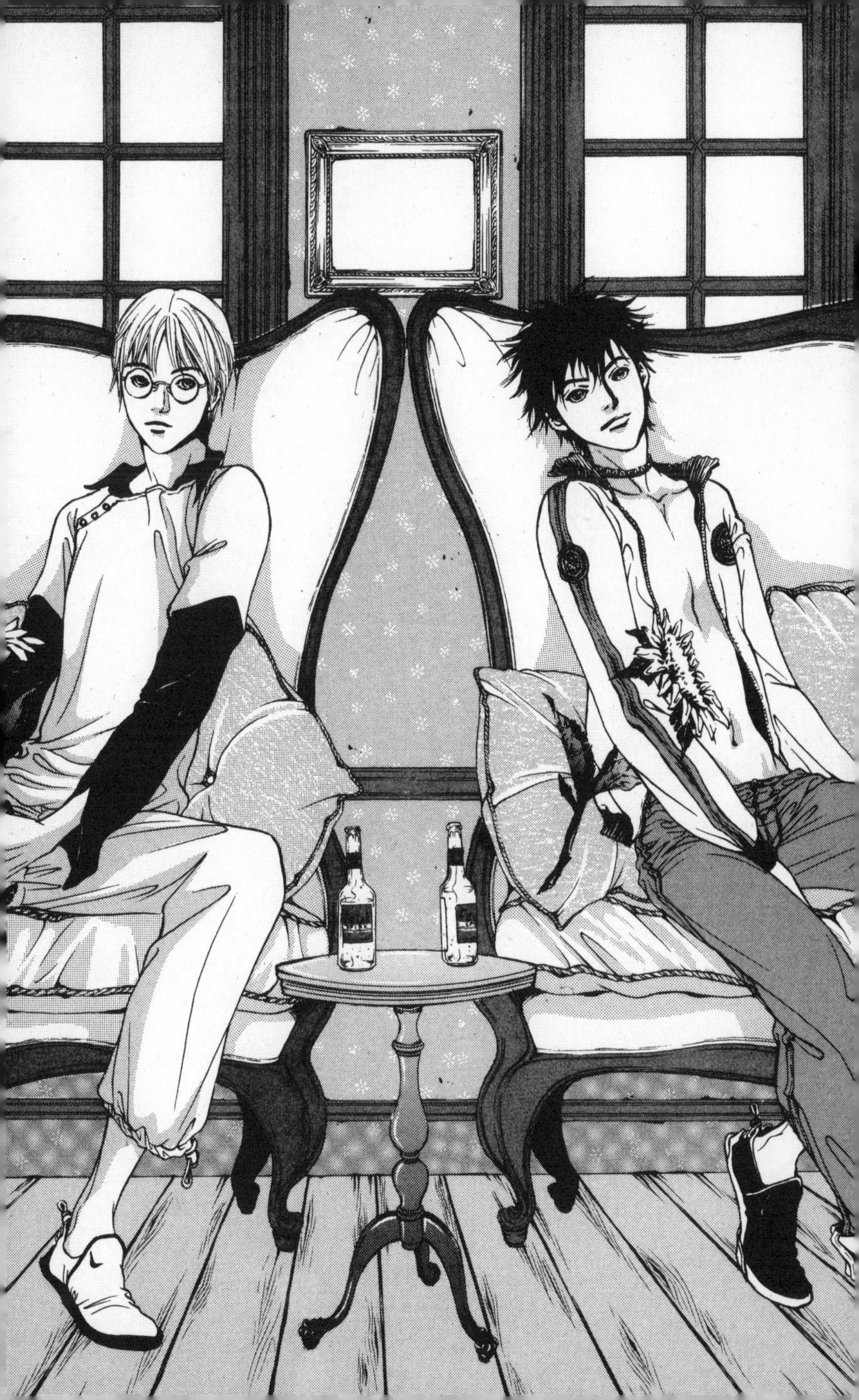

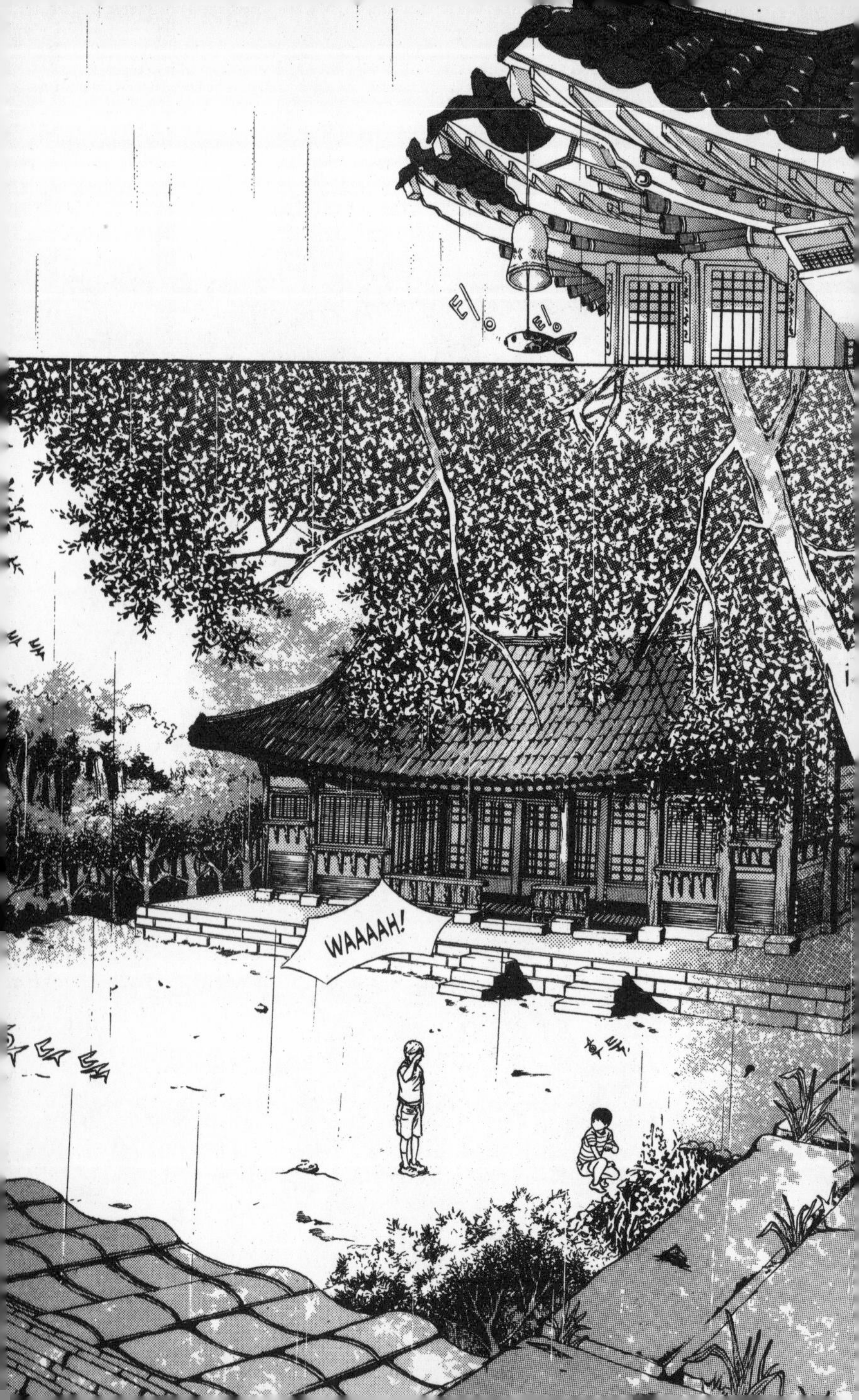
WAAAAH!

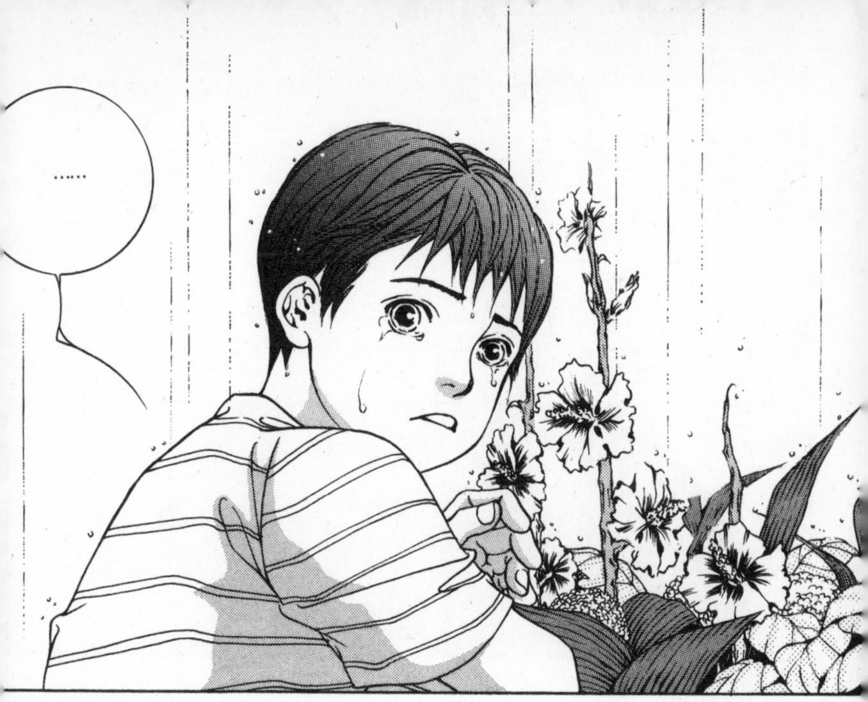
......

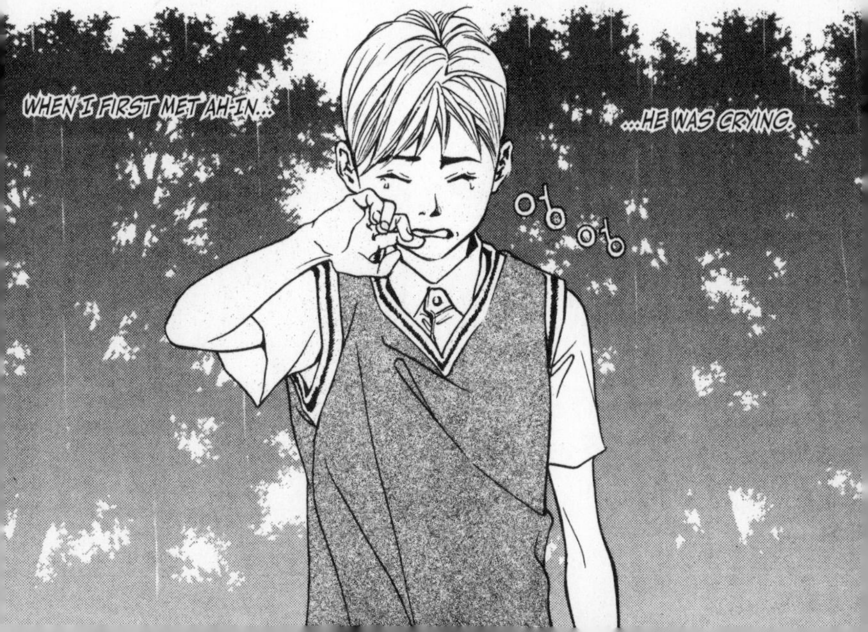
WHEN I FIRST MET AH-IN...
...HE WAS CRYING.

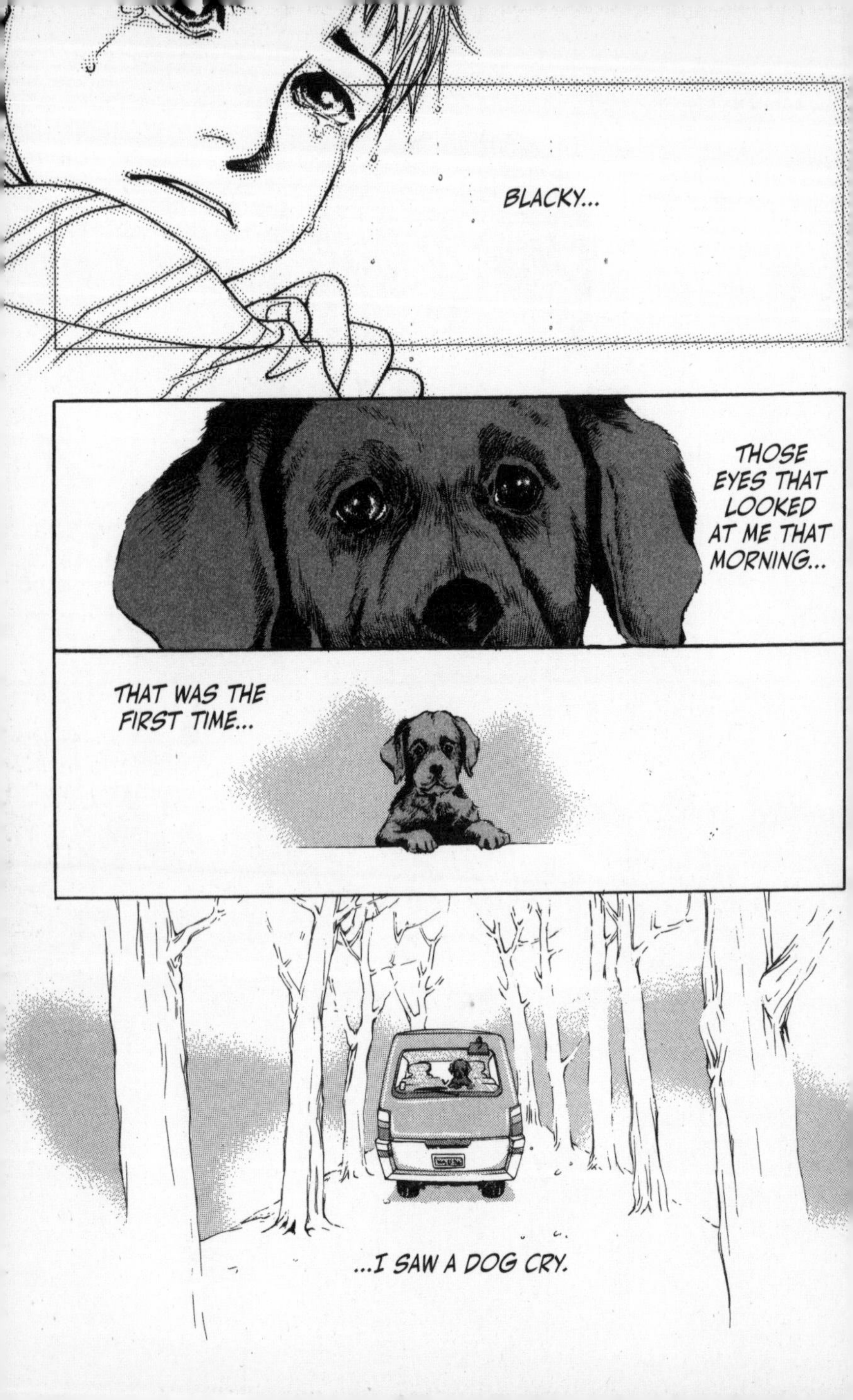
BLACKY...
THOSE EYES THAT LOOKED AT ME THAT MORNING...
THAT WAS THE FIRST TIME...
...I SAW A DOG CRY.

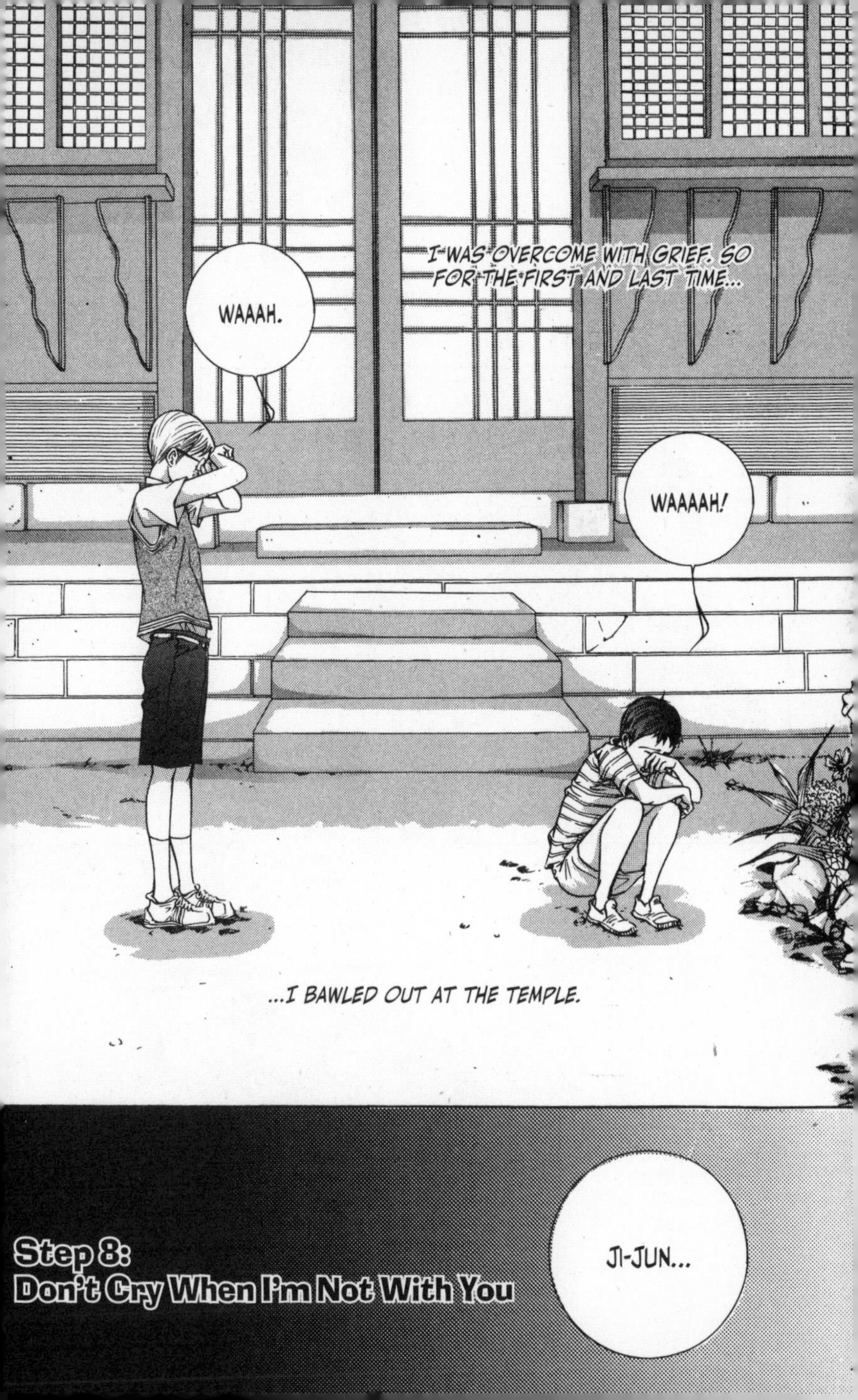
I WAS OVERCOME WITH GRIEF. SO FOR THE FIRST AND LAST TIME...
WAAAH.
WAAAAH!
...I BAWLED OUT AT THE TEMPLE.
Step 8:
Don't Cry When I'm Not With You
JI-JUN...

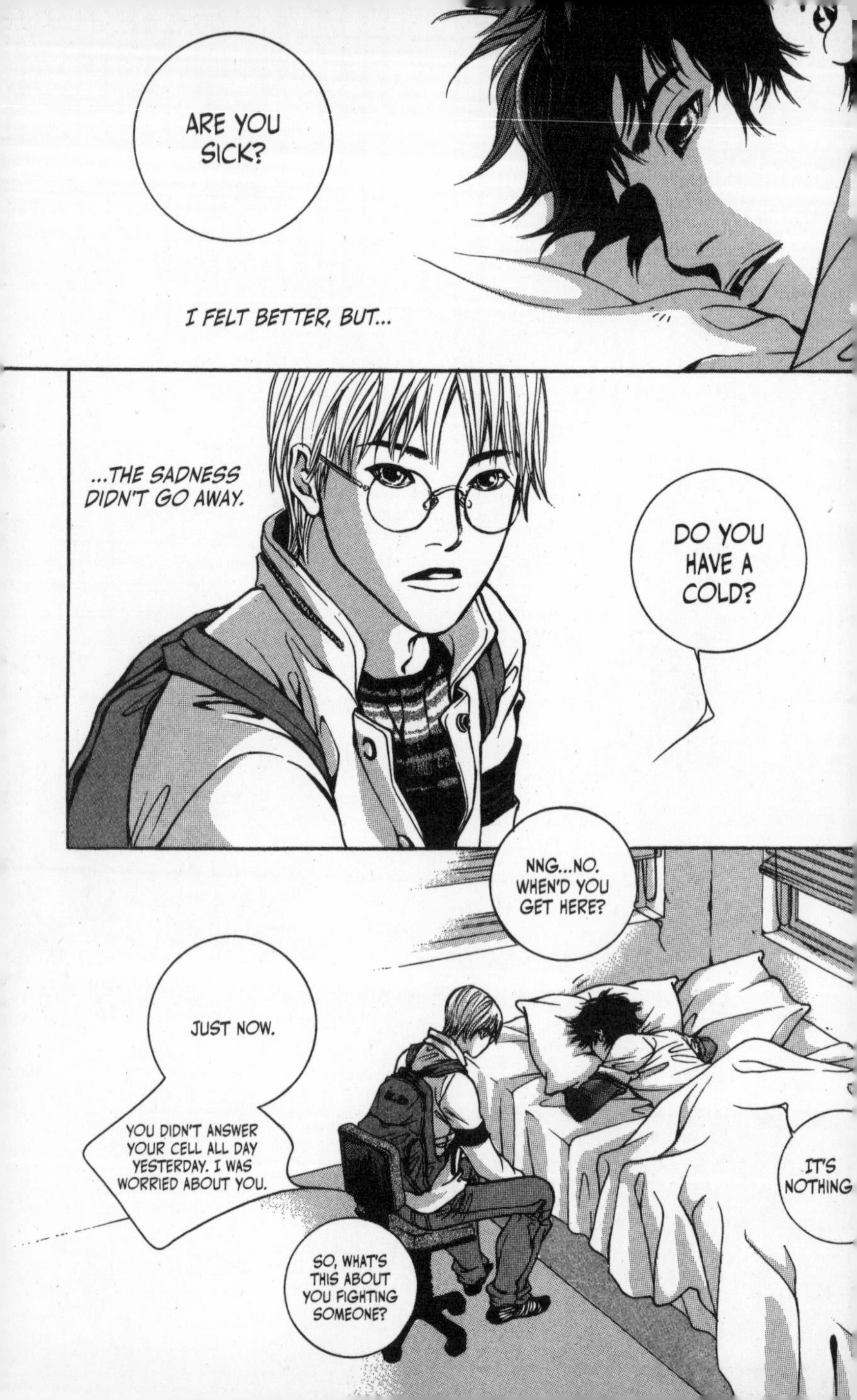
ARE YOU SICK?
I FELT BETTER, BUT...
...THE SADNESS DIDN'T GO AWAY.
DO YOU HAVE A COLD?
NNG...NO. WHEN'D YOU GET HERE?
JUST NOW.
YOU DIDN'T ANSWER YOUR CELL ALL DAY YESTERDAY. I WAS WORRIED ABOUT YOU.
SO, WHAT'S THIS ABOUT YOU FIGHTING SOMEONE?
IT'S NOTHING

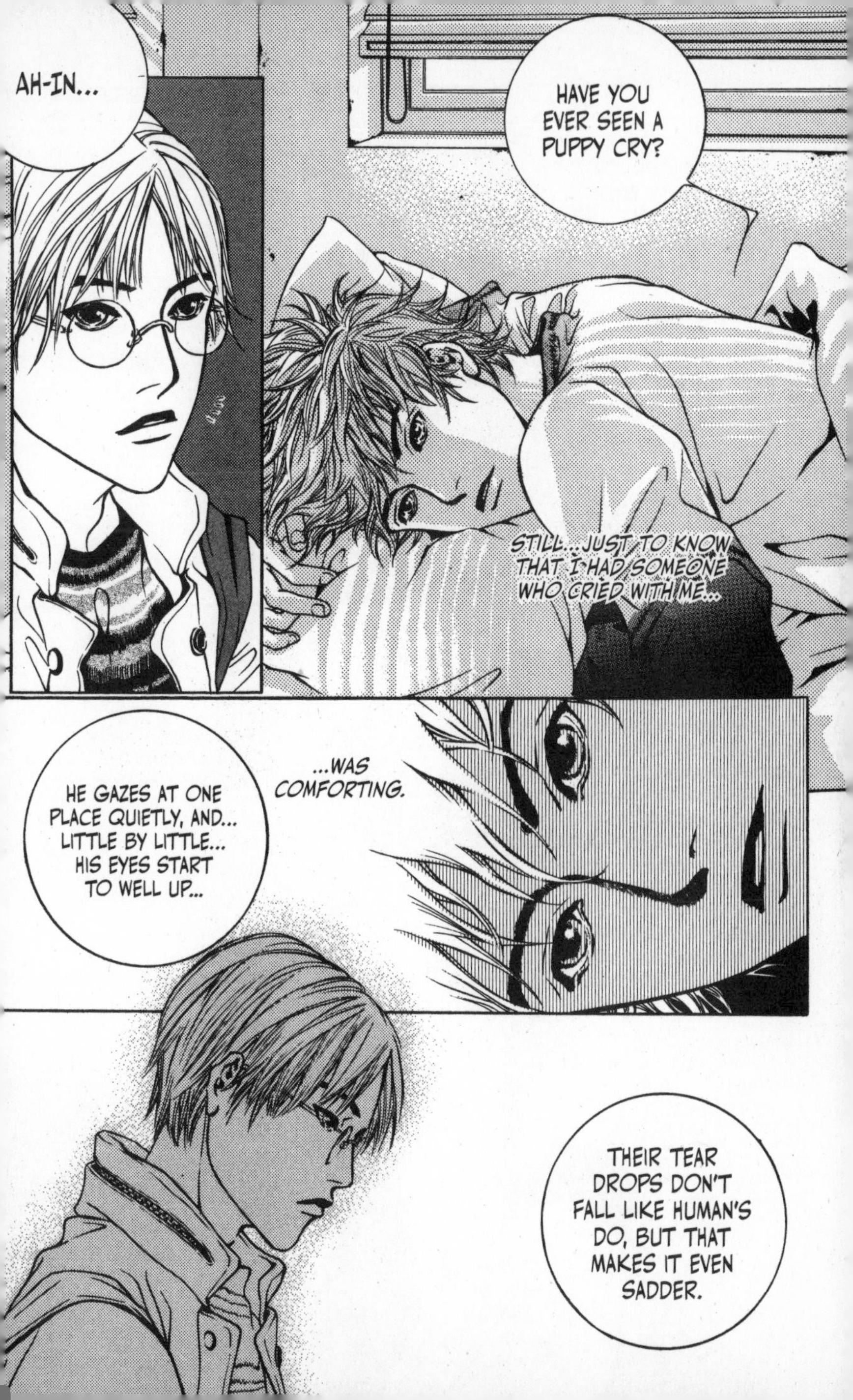
AH-IN...
HAVE YOU EVER SEEN A PUPPY CRY?
STILL...JUST TO KNOW THAT I HAD SOMEONE WHO CRIED WITH ME...
HE GAZES AT ONE PLACE QUIETLY, AND... LITTLE BY LITTLE... HIS EYES START TO WELL UP...
...WAS COMFORTING.
THEIR TEAR DROPS DON'T FALL LIKE HUMAN'S DO, BUT THAT MAKES IT EVEN SADDER.

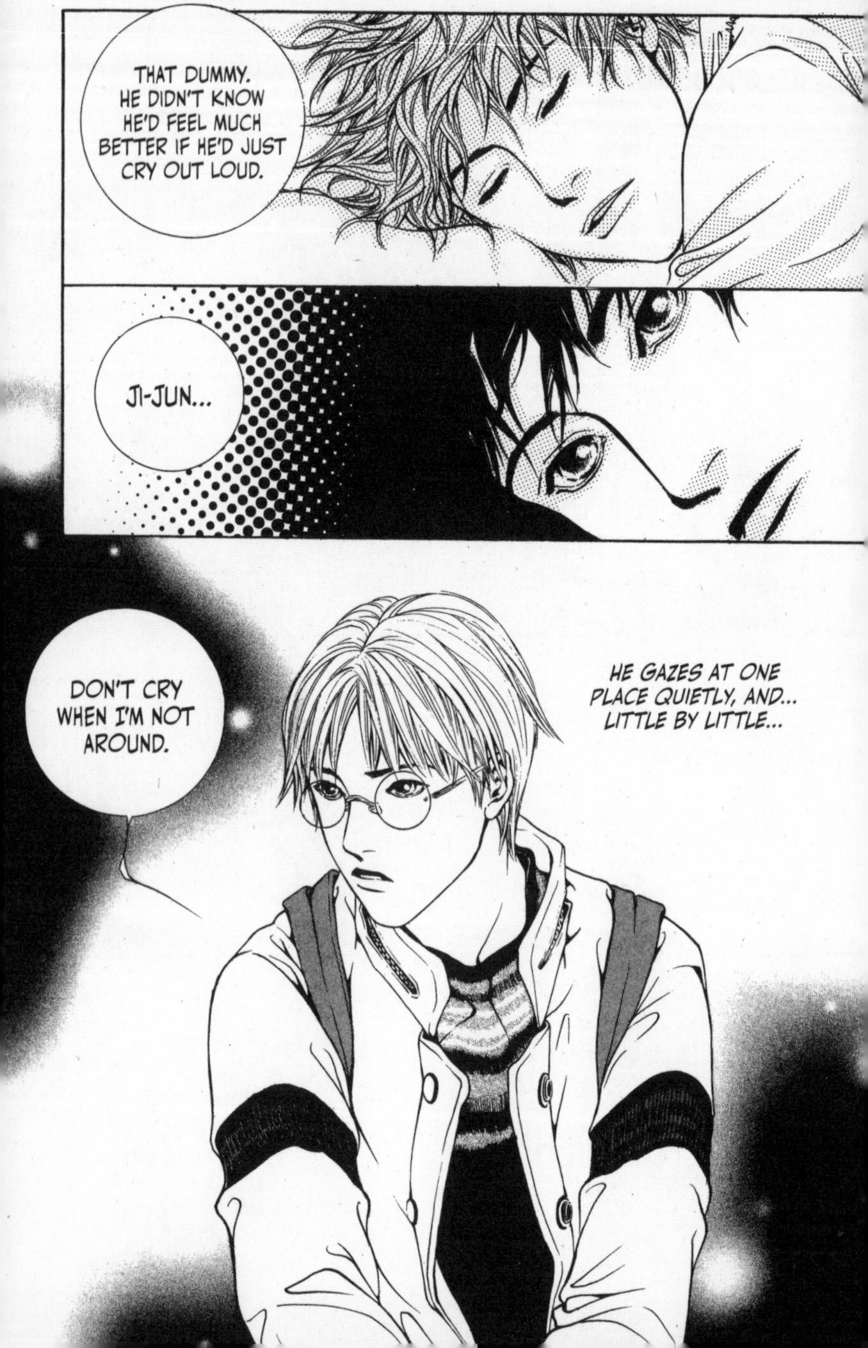
THAT DUMMY. HE DIDN'T KNOW HE'D FEEL MUCH BETTER IF HE'D JUST CRY OUT LOUD.
JI-JUN...
DON'T CRY WHEN I'M NOT AROUND.
HE GAZES AT ONE PLACE QUIETLY, AND... LITTLE BY LITTLE...

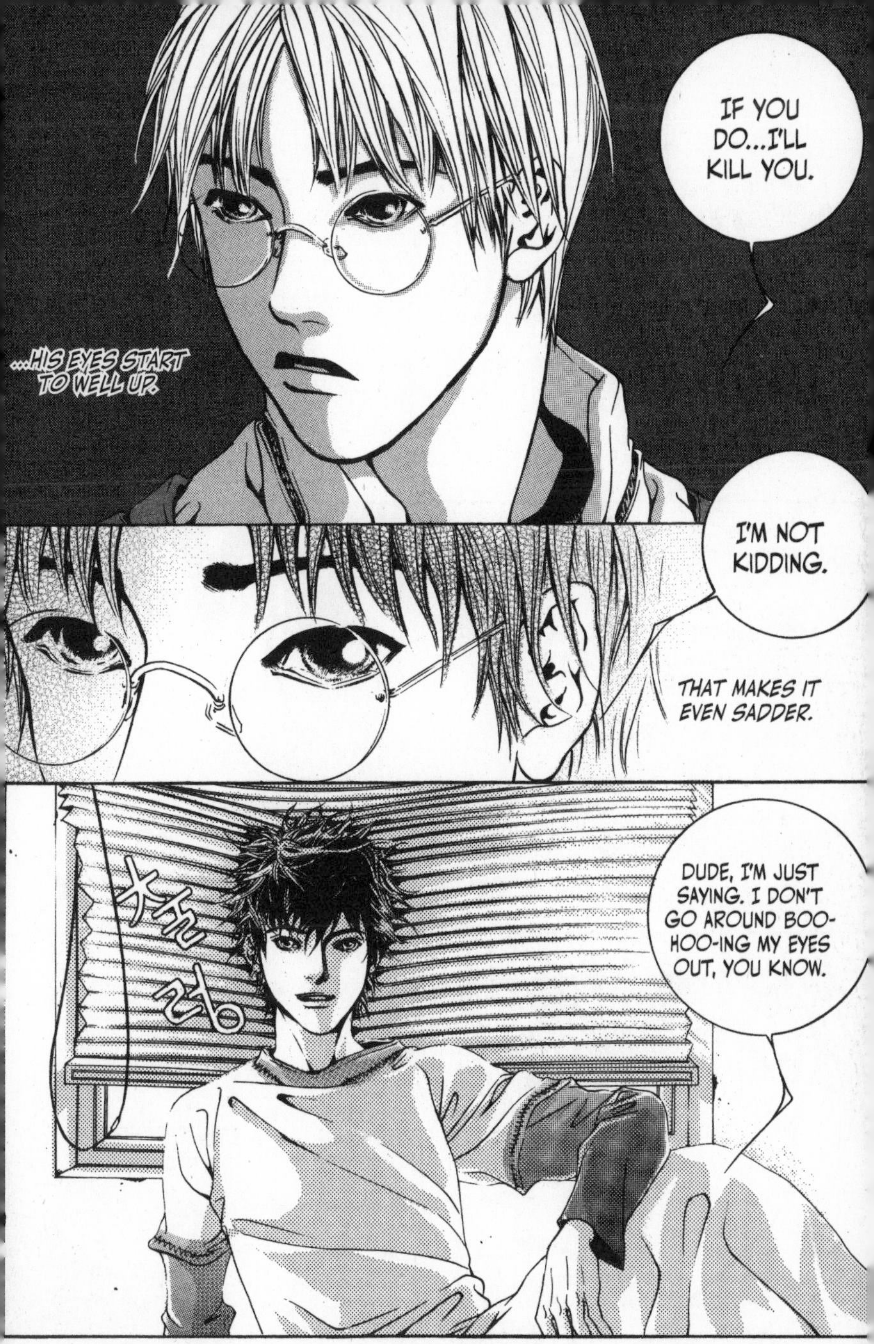
...HIS EYES START TO WELL UP.
IF YOU DO...I'LL KILL YOU.
I'M NOT KIDDING.
THAT MAKES IT EVEN SADDER.
DUDE, I'M JUST SAYING. I DON'T GO AROUND BOO-HOO-ING MY EYES OUT, YOU KNOW.

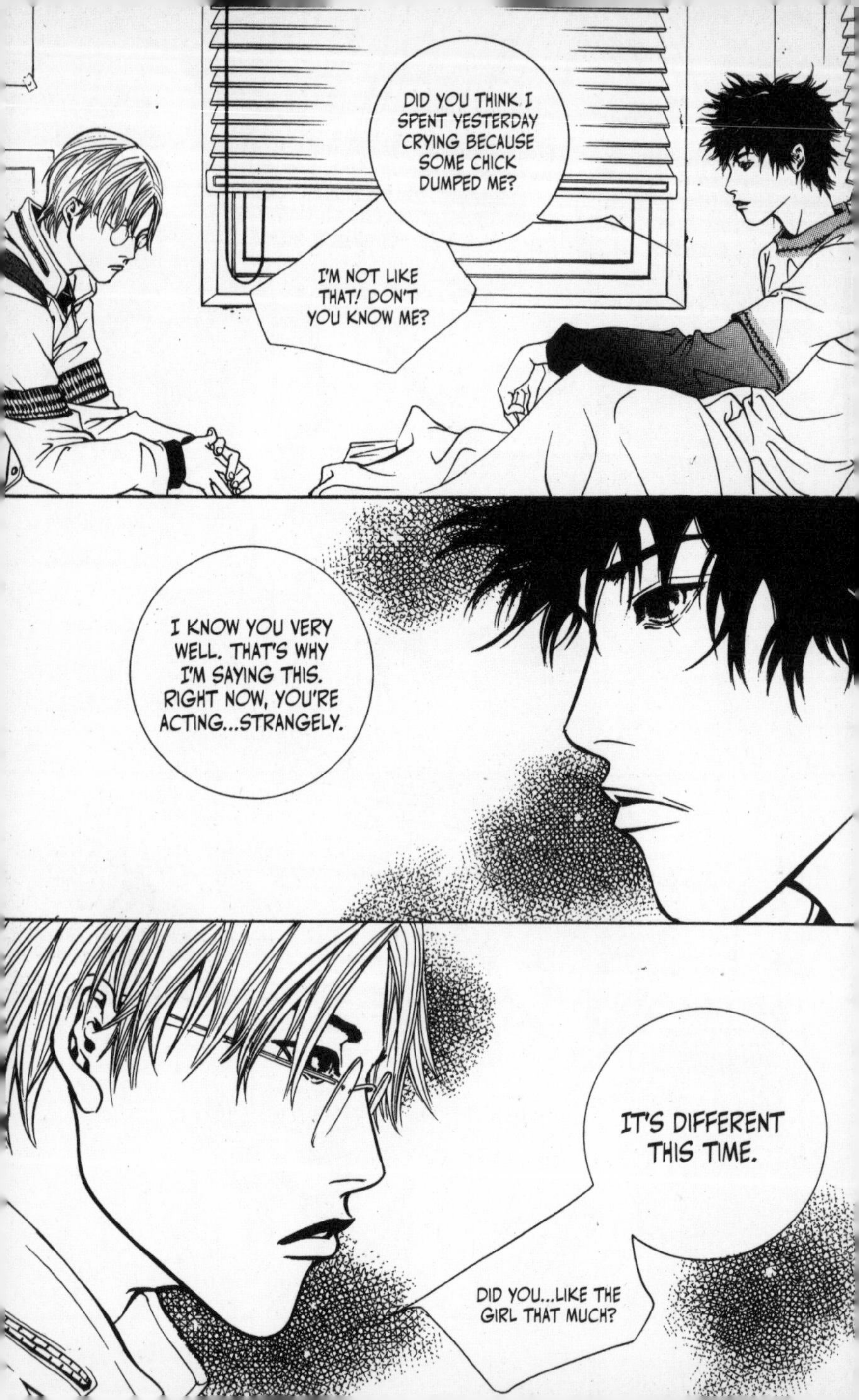
DID YOU THINK I SPENT YESTERDAY CRYING BECAUSE SOME CHICK DUMPED ME?
I'M NOT LIKE THAT! DON'T YOU KNOW ME?
I KNOW YOU VERY WELL. THAT'S WHY I'M SAYING THIS. RIGHT NOW, YOU'RE ACTING...STRANGELY.
IT'S DIFFERENT THIS TIME.
DID YOU...LIKE THE GIRL THAT MUCH?

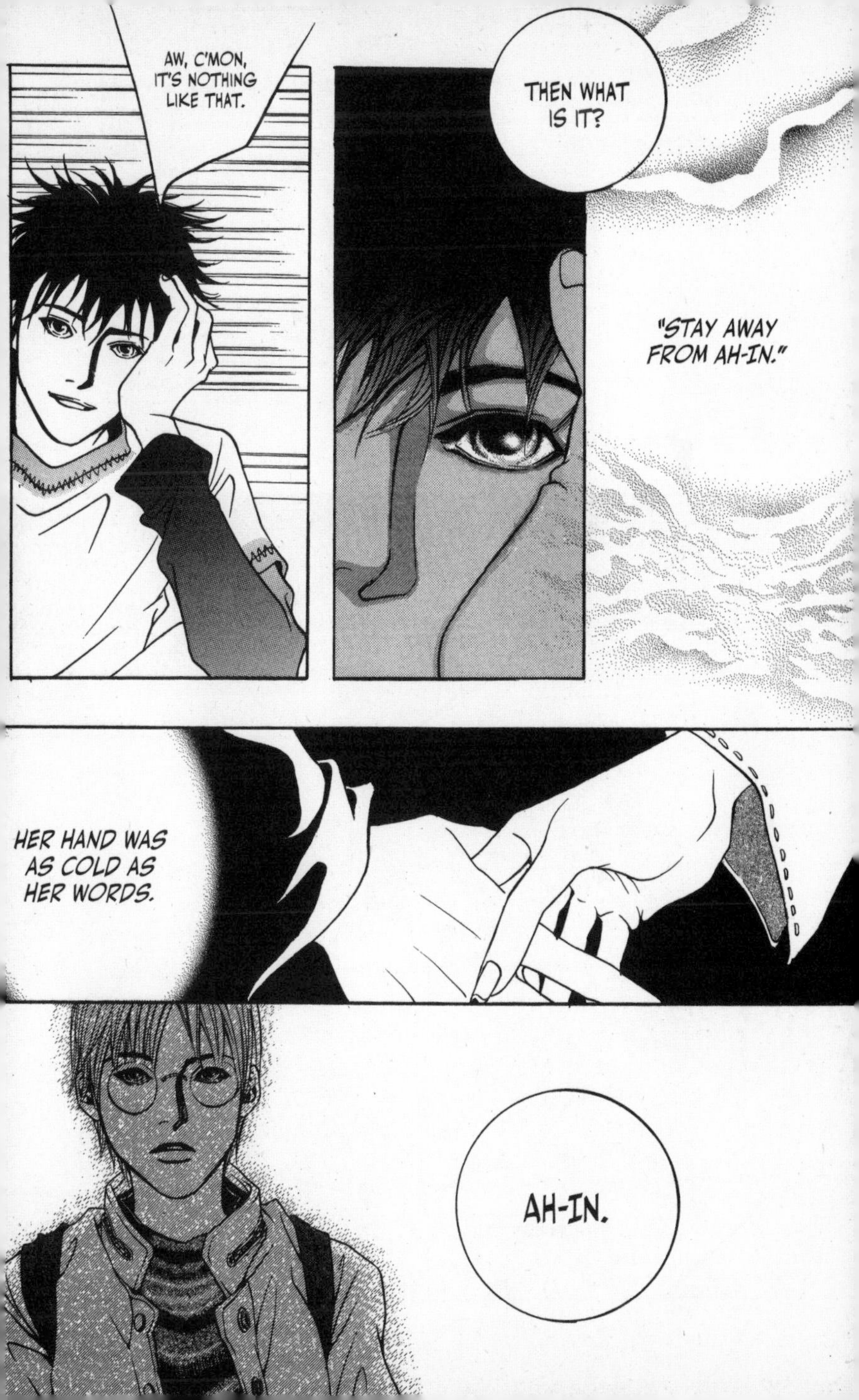
AW, C'MON, IT'S NOTHING LIKE THAT.
THEN WHAT IS IT?
"STAY AWAY FROM AH-IN."
HER HAND WAS AS COLD AS HER WORDS.
AH-IN.

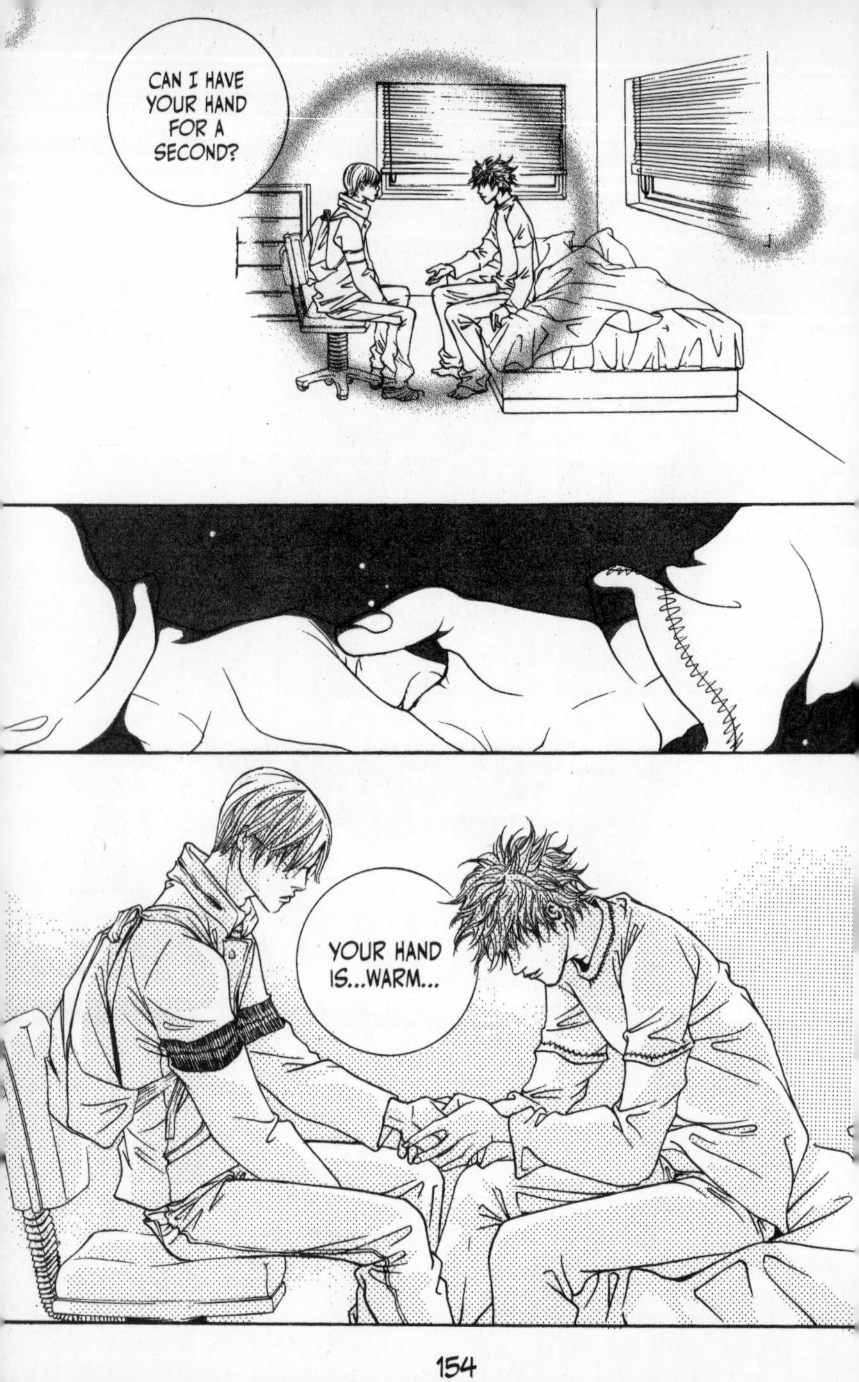
CAN I HAVE YOUR HAND FOR A SECOND?
YOUR HAND IS...WARM...

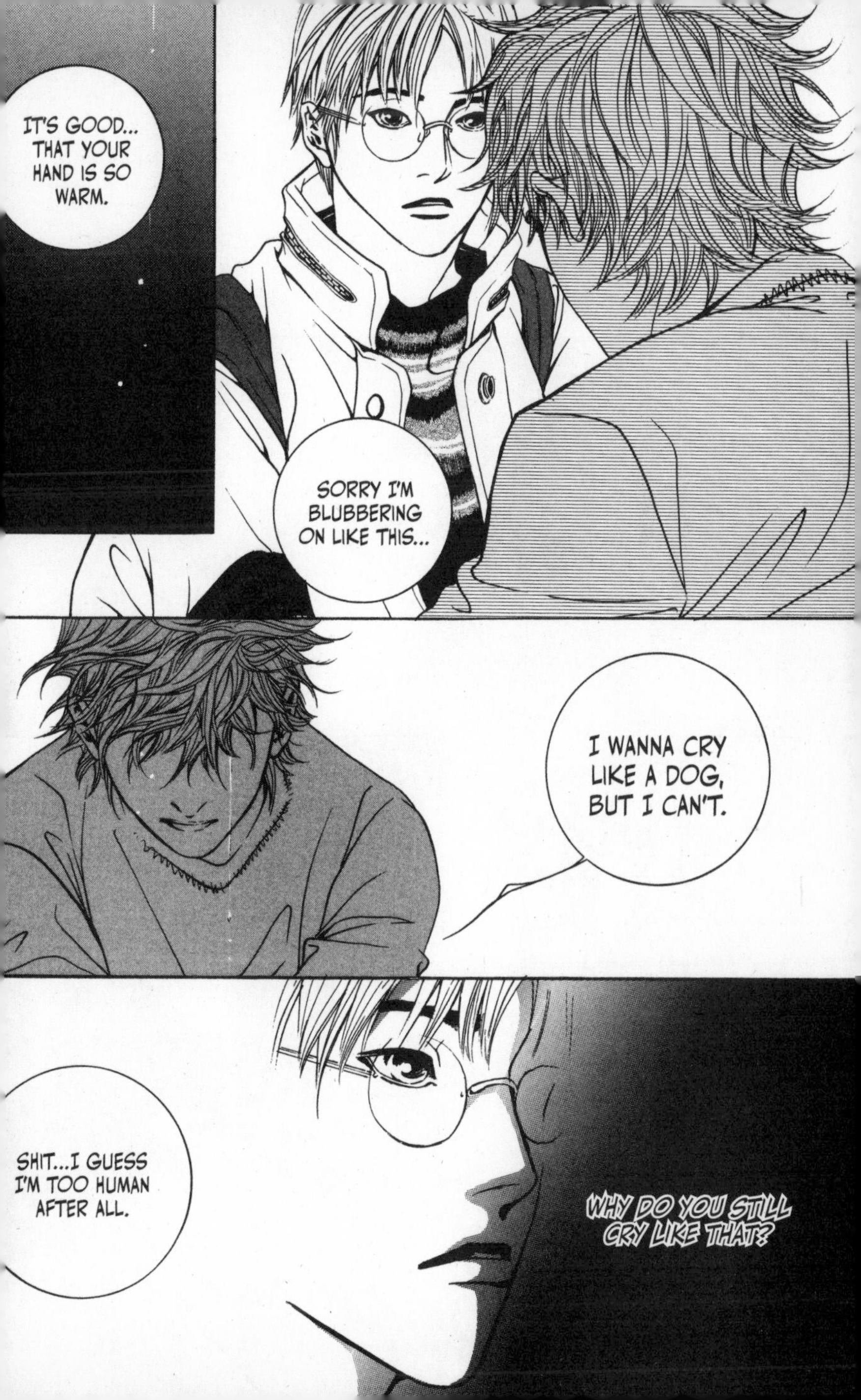
IT'S GOOD... THAT YOUR HAND IS SO WARM.
SORRY I'M BLUBBERING ON LIKE THIS...
I WANNA CRY LIKE A DOG, BUT I CAN'T.
SHIT...I GUESS I'M TOO HUMAN AFTER ALL.
WHY DO YOU STILL CRY LIKE THAT?

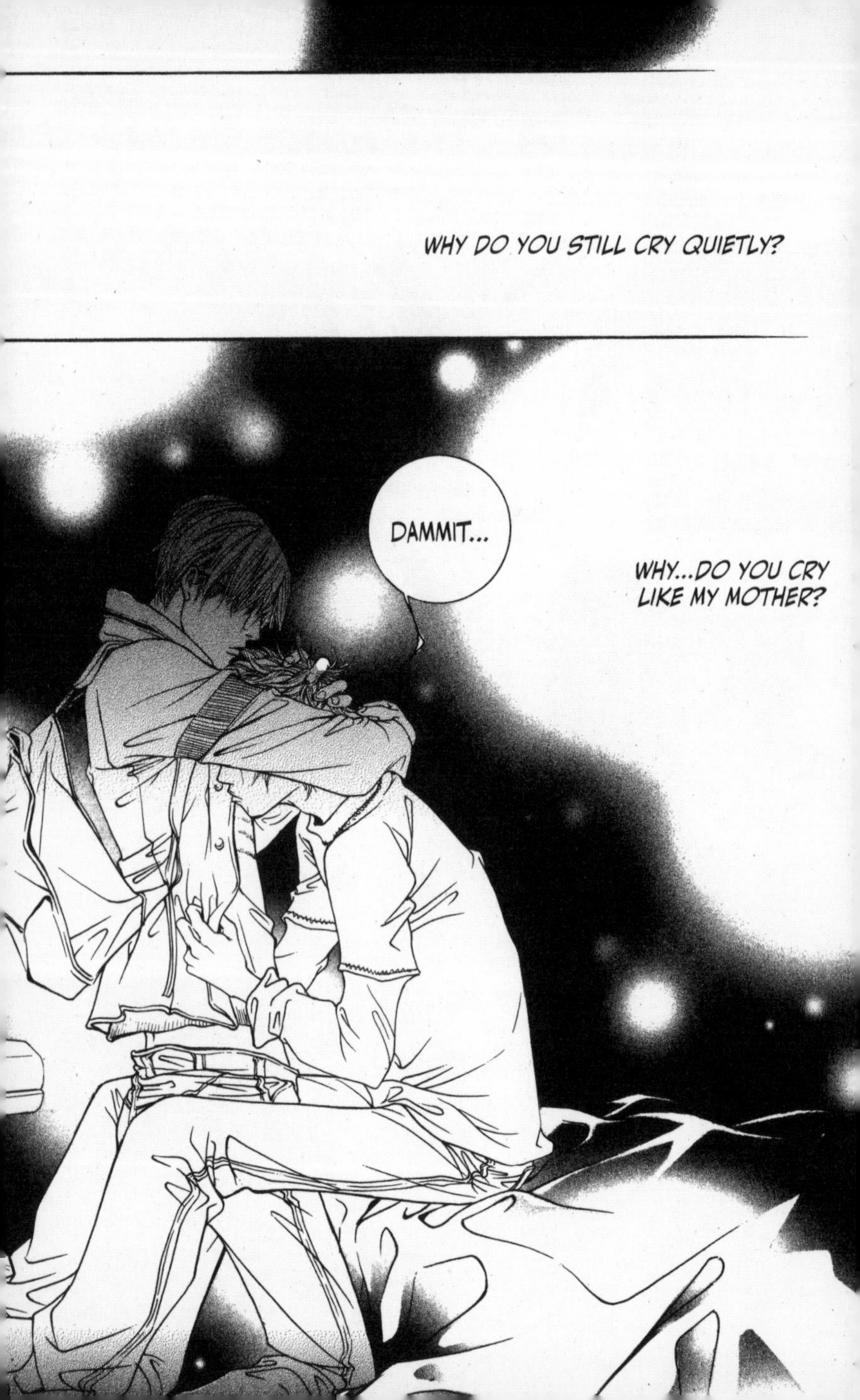
WHY DO YOU STILL CRY QUIETLY?
DAMMIT...
WHY...DO YOU CRY LIKE MY MOTHER?

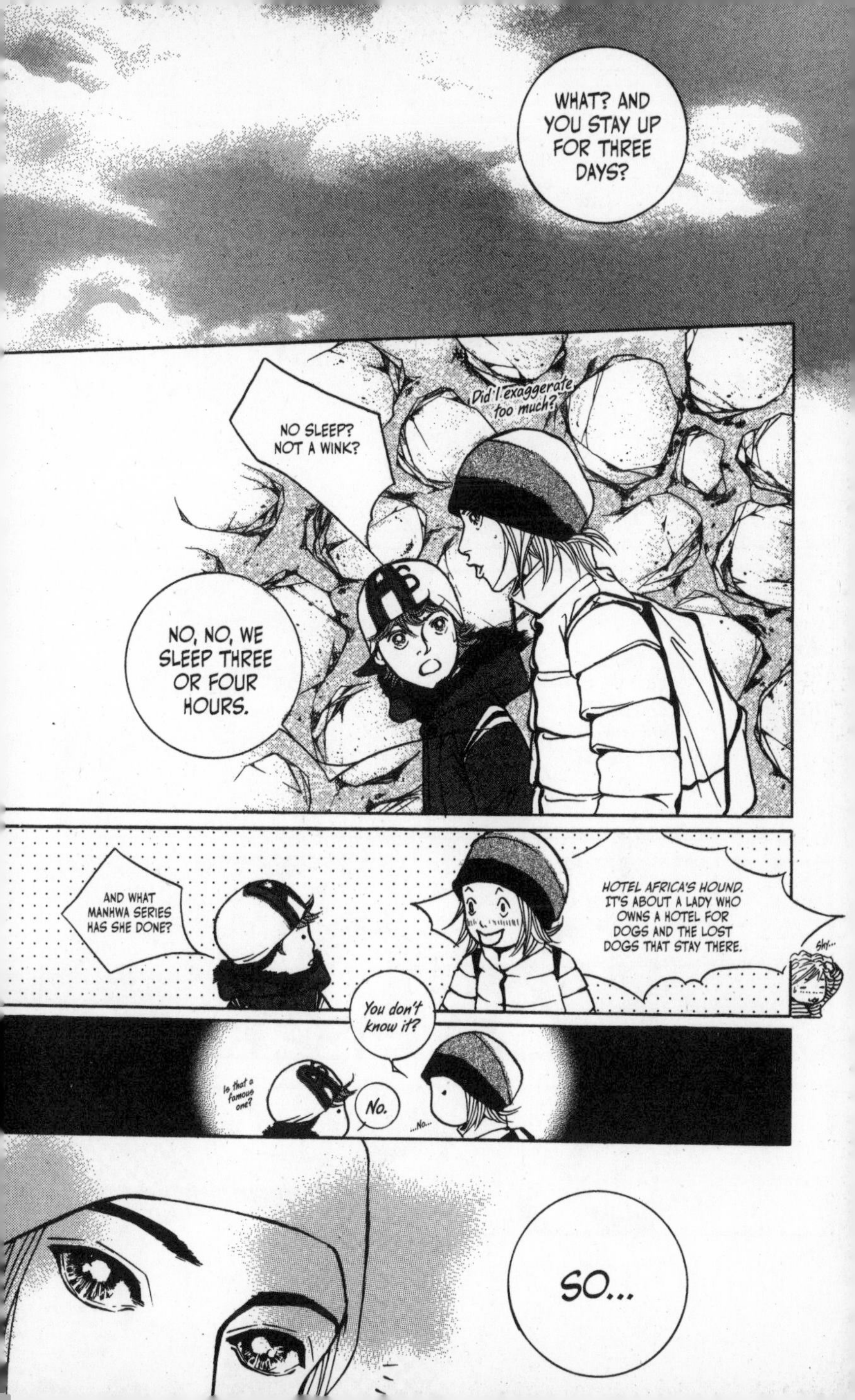
WHAT? AND YOU STAY UP FOR THREE DAYS?
NO SLEEP? NOT A WINK?
Did I exaggerate too much?
NO, NO, WE SLEEP THREE OR FOUR HOURS.
AND WHAT MANHWA SERIES HAS SHE DONE?
HOTEL AFRICA'S HOUND. IT'S ABOUT A LADY WHO OWNS A HOTEL FOR DOGS AND THE LOST DOGS THAT STAY THERE.
Shy...
You don't know it?
Is that a famous one?
No.
...No...
SO...

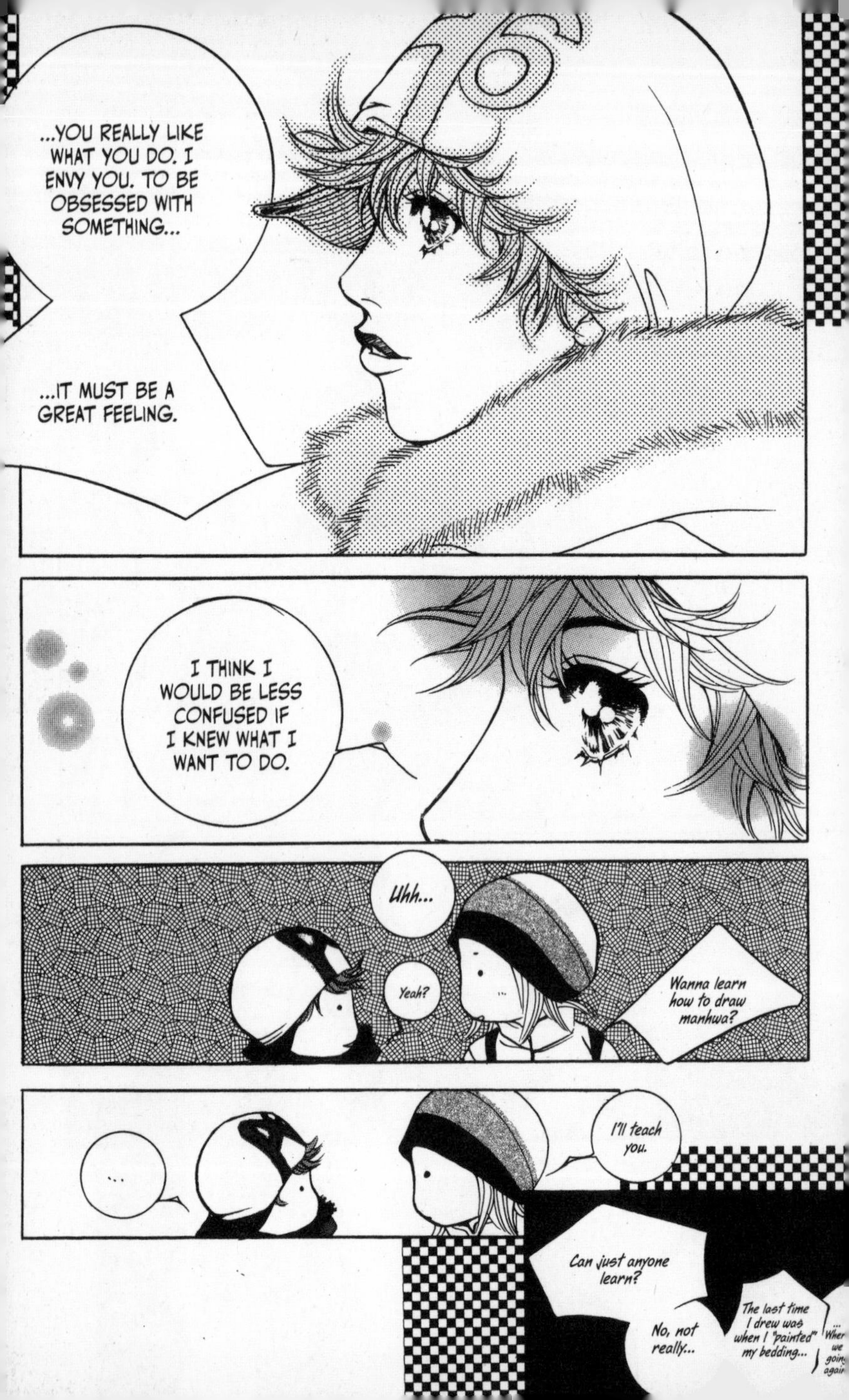
...YOU REALLY LIKE WHAT YOU DO. I ENVY YOU. TO BE OBSESSED WITH SOMETHING...
...IT MUST BE A GREAT FEELING.
I THINK I WOULD BE LESS CONFUSED IF I KNEW WHAT I WANT TO DO.
Uhh...
Yeah?
...
Wanna learn how to draw manhwa?
...
I'll teach you.
Can just anyone learn?
No, not really...
The last time I drew was when I "painted" my bedding...

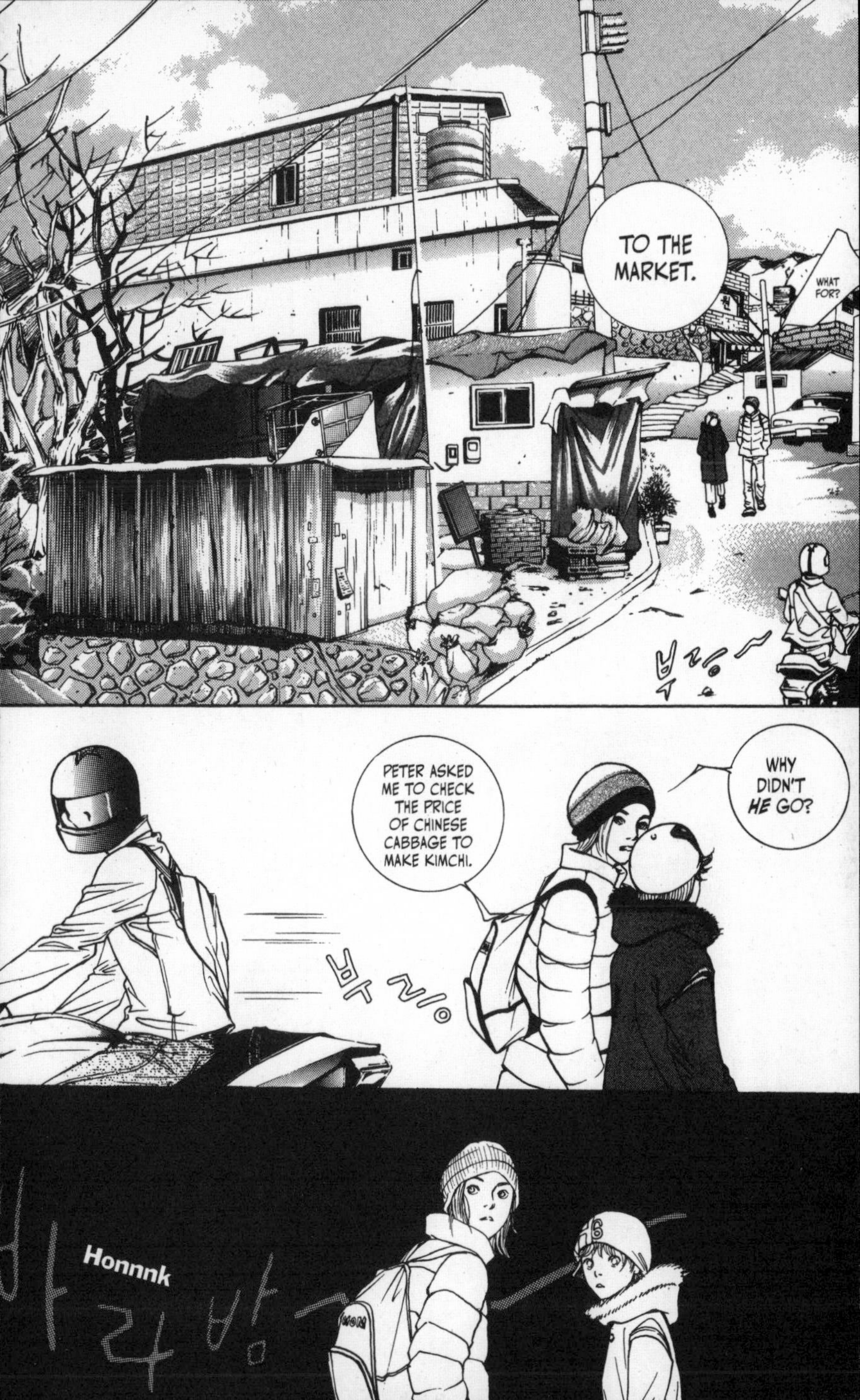
TO THE MARKET.
WHAT FOR?
PETER ASKED ME TO CHECK THE PRICE OF CHINESE CABBAGE TO MAKE KIMCHI.
WHY DIDN'T *HE* GO?
Honnnk

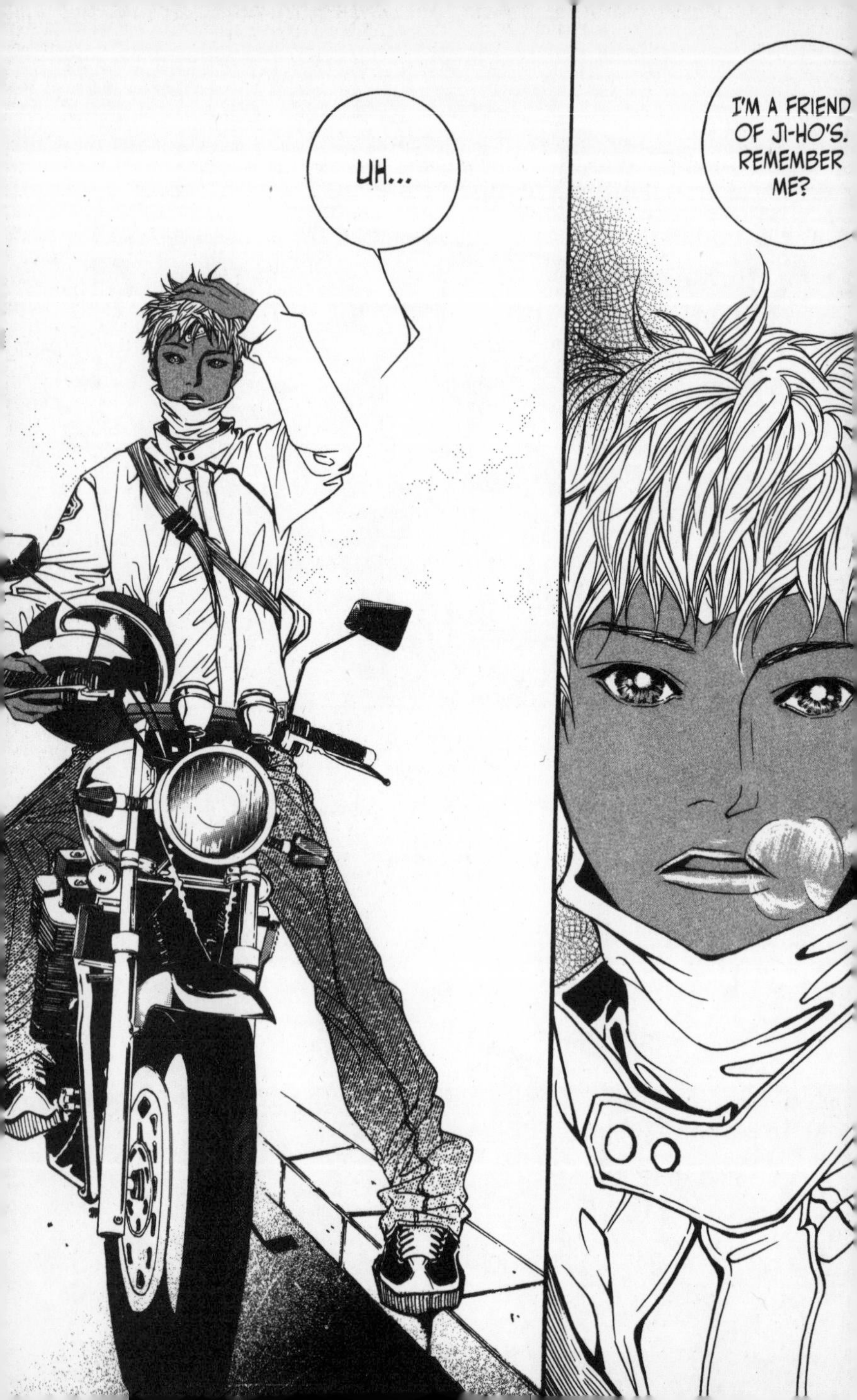
UH...
I'M A FRIEND OF JI-HO'S. REMEMBER ME?

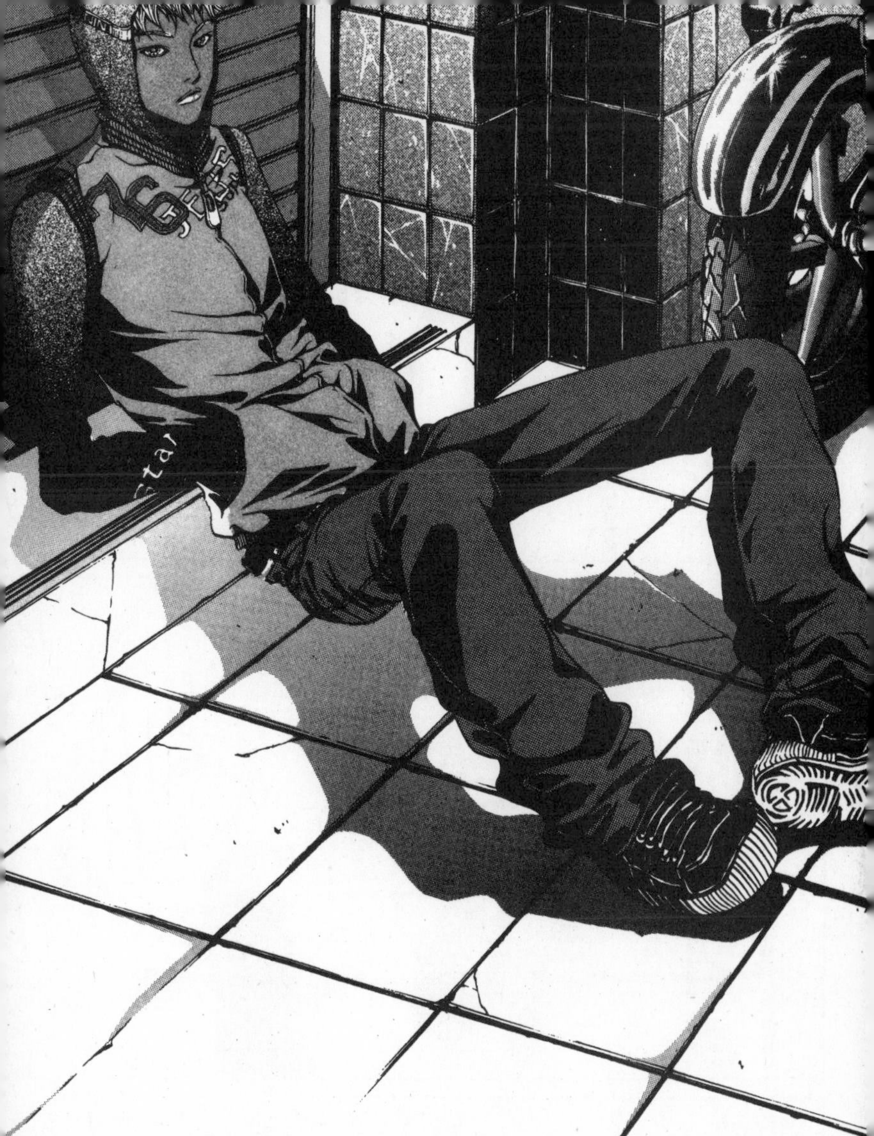

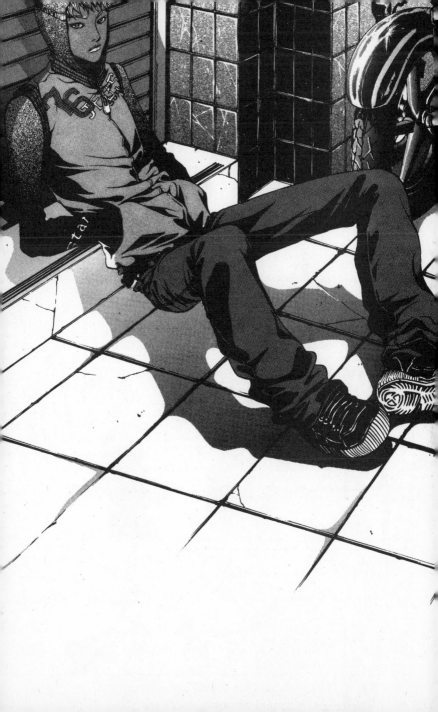

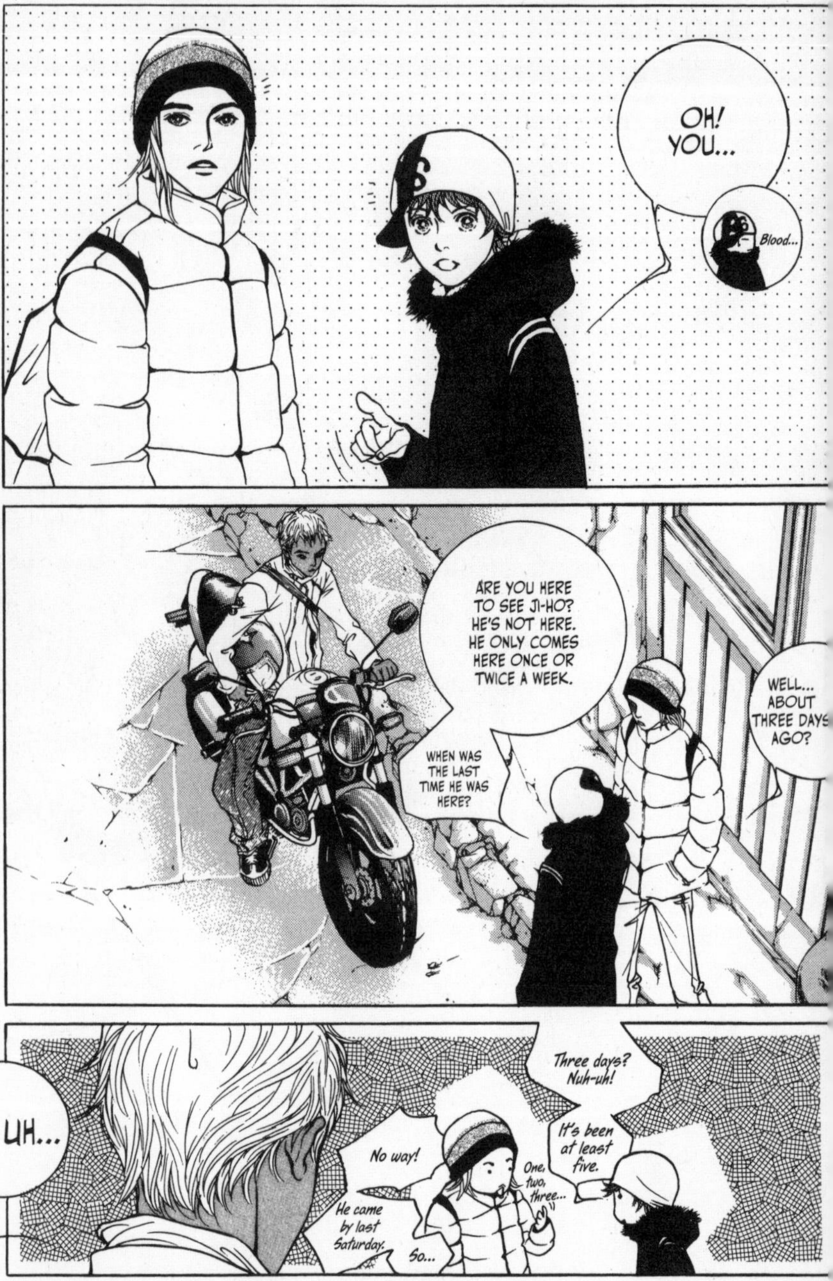
OH! YOU...
Blood...
ARE YOU HERE TO SEE JI-HO? HE'S NOT HERE. HE ONLY COMES HERE ONCE OR TWICE A WEEK.
WHEN WAS THE LAST TIME HE WAS HERE?
WELL... ABOUT THREE DAYS AGO?
UH...
Three days? Nuh-uh!
No way!
It's been at least five.
One, two, three...
He came by last Saturday.
So...

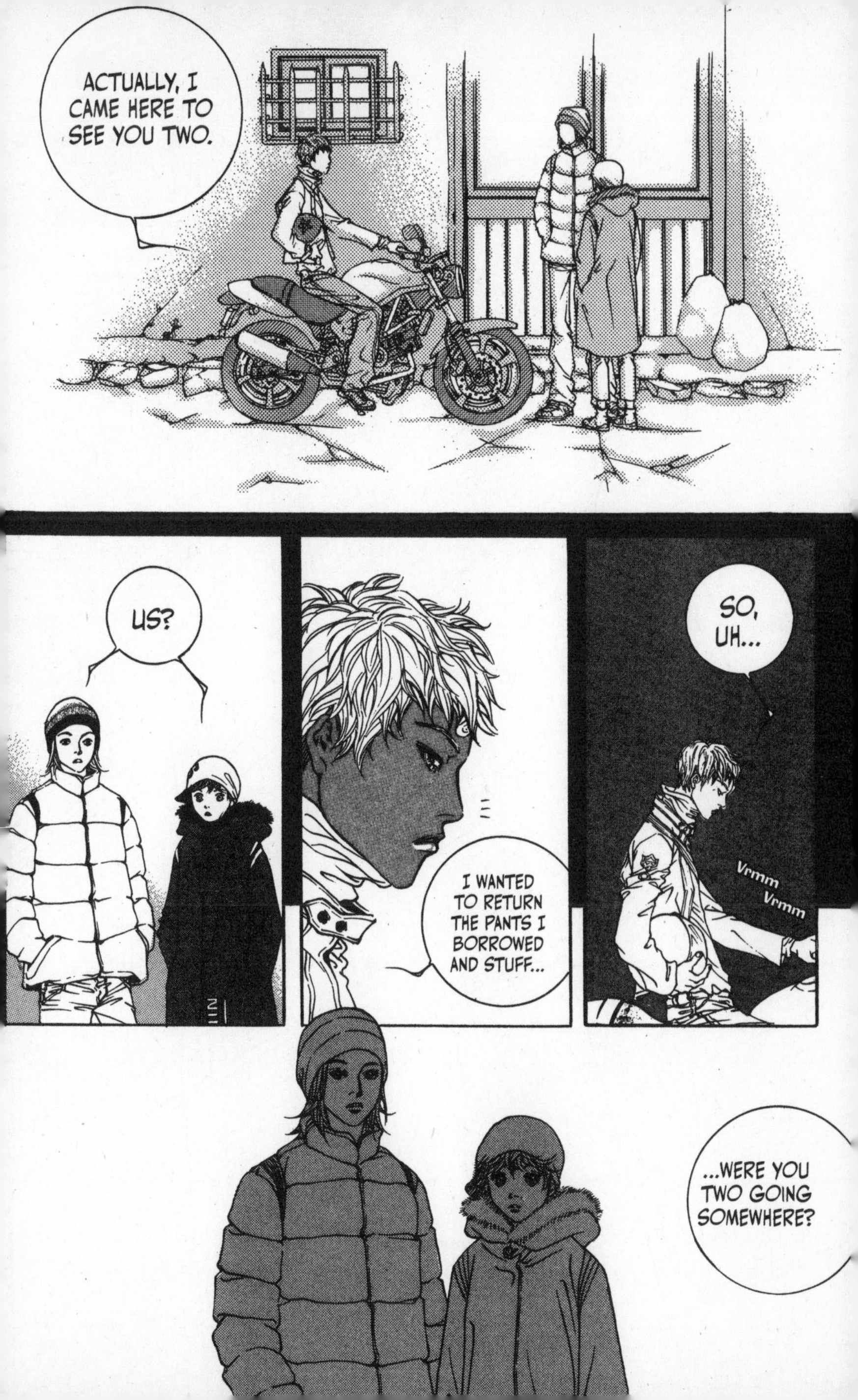
ACTUALLY, I CAME HERE TO SEE YOU TWO.
US?
I WANTED TO RETURN THE PANTS I BORROWED AND STUFF...
SO, UH...
Vrmm Vrmm
...WERE YOU TWO GOING SOMEWHERE?

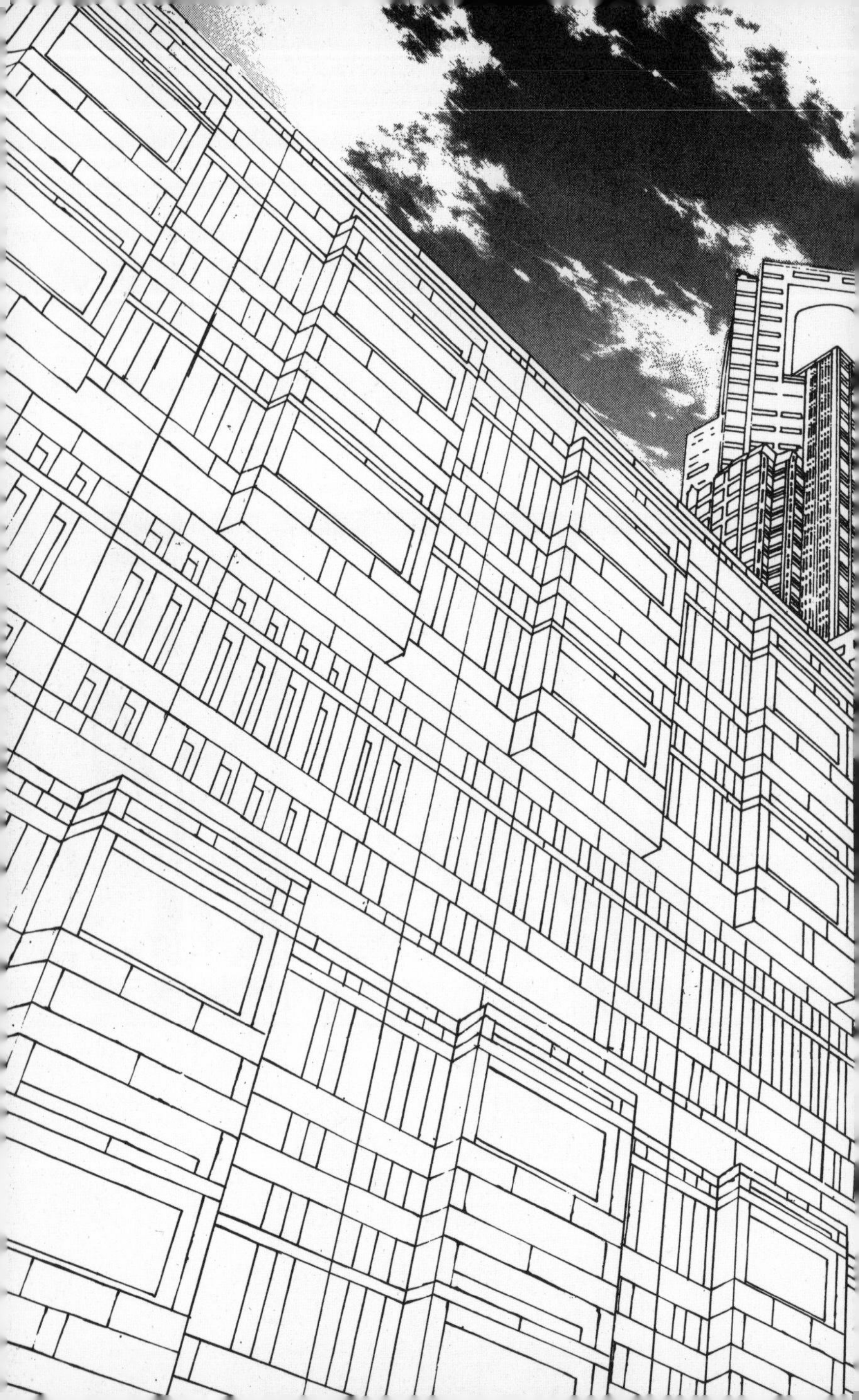

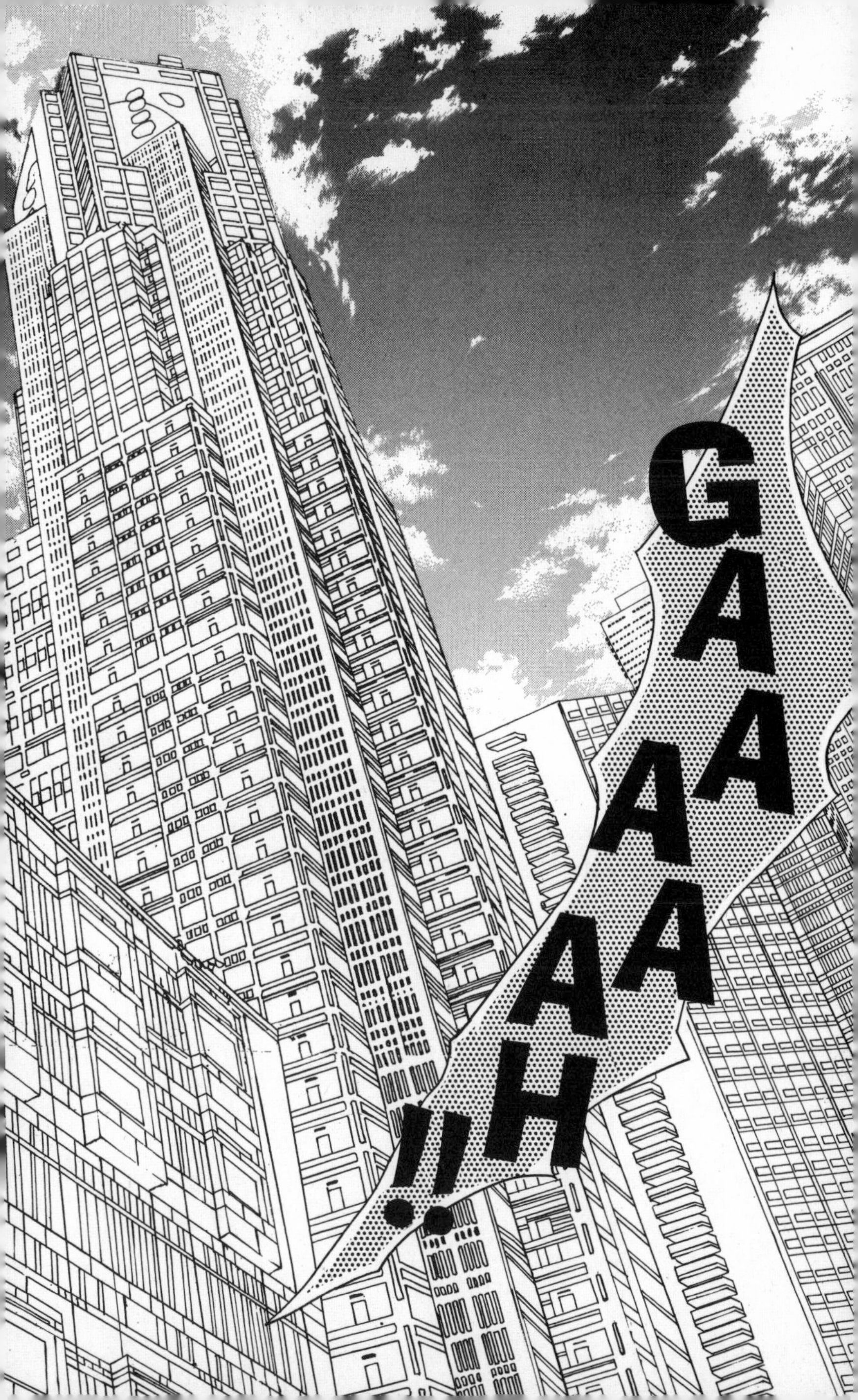

GAAAAAH!!

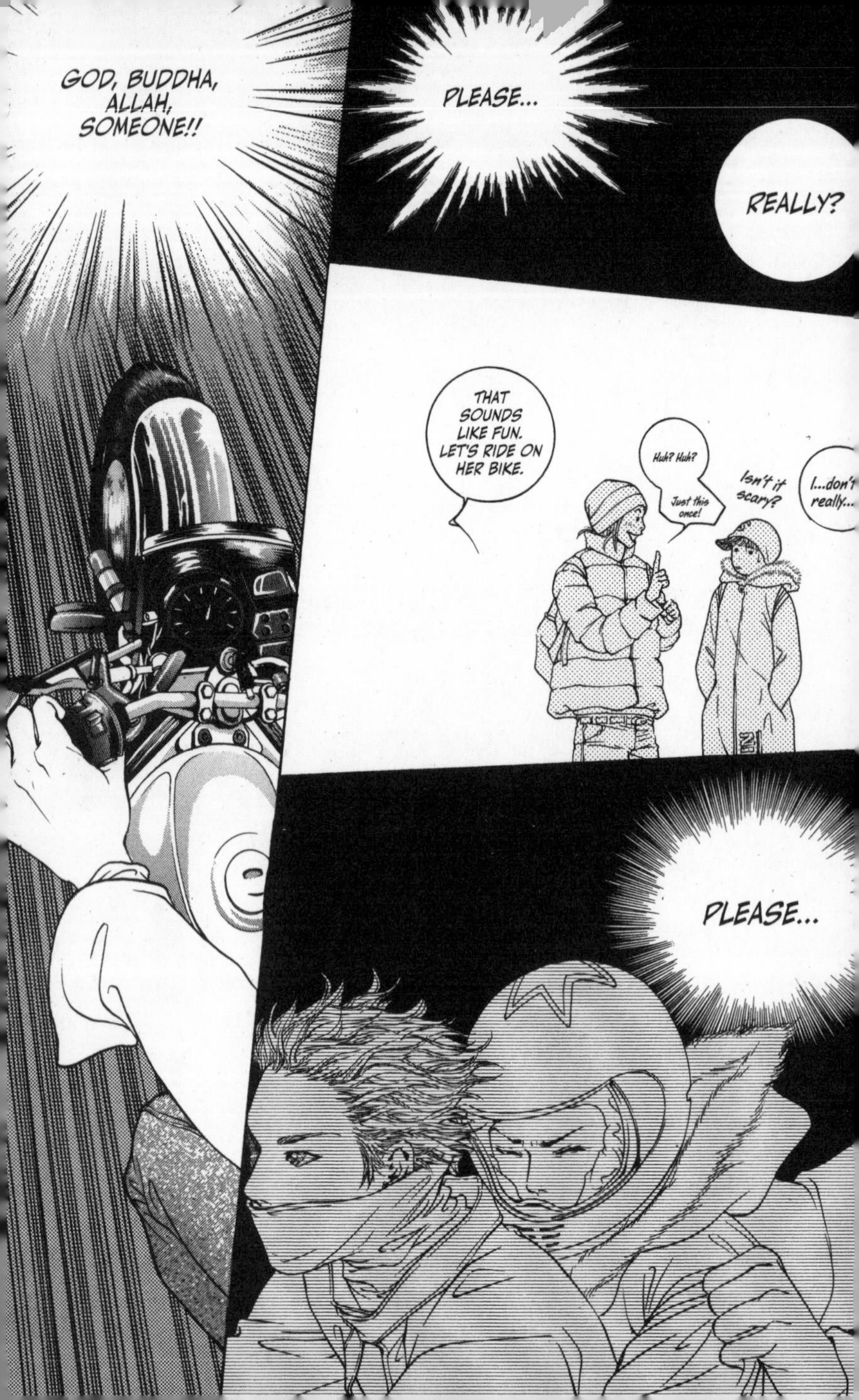
GOD, BUDDHA, ALLAH, SOMEONE!!
PLEASE...
REALLY?
THAT SOUNDS LIKE FUN. LET'S RIDE ON HER BIKE.
Huh? Huh?
Just this once!
Isn't it scary?
I...don't really...
PLEASE...

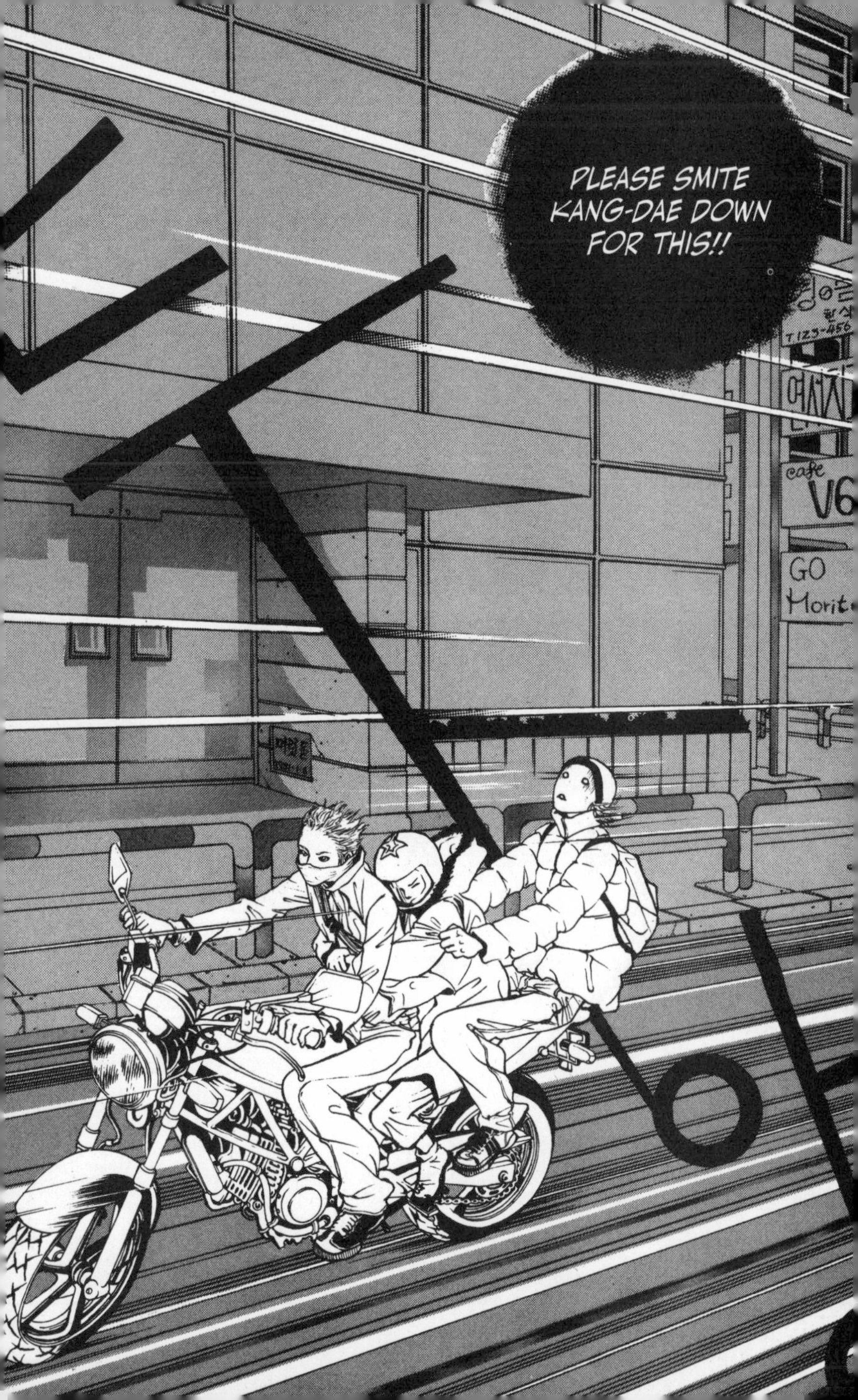
PLEASE SMITE KANG-DAE DOWN FOR THIS!!
cafe
V6
GO

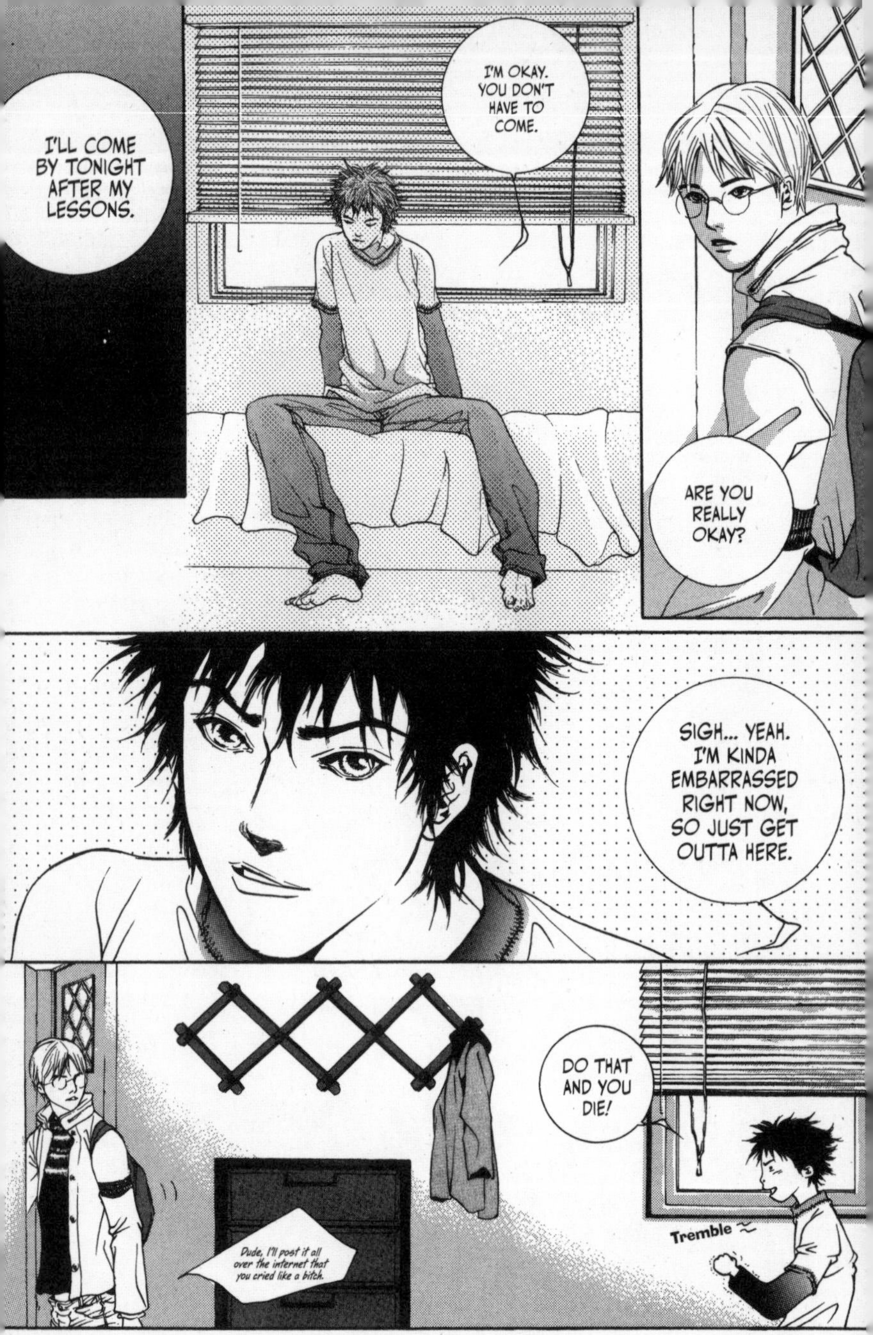
I'LL COME BY TONIGHT AFTER MY LESSONS.
I'M OKAY. YOU DON'T HAVE TO COME.
ARE YOU REALLY OKAY?
SIGH... YEAH. I'M KINDA EMBARRASSED RIGHT NOW, SO JUST GET OUTTA HERE.
Dude, I'll post it all over the internet that you cried like a bitch.
DO THAT AND YOU DIE!
Tremble ~

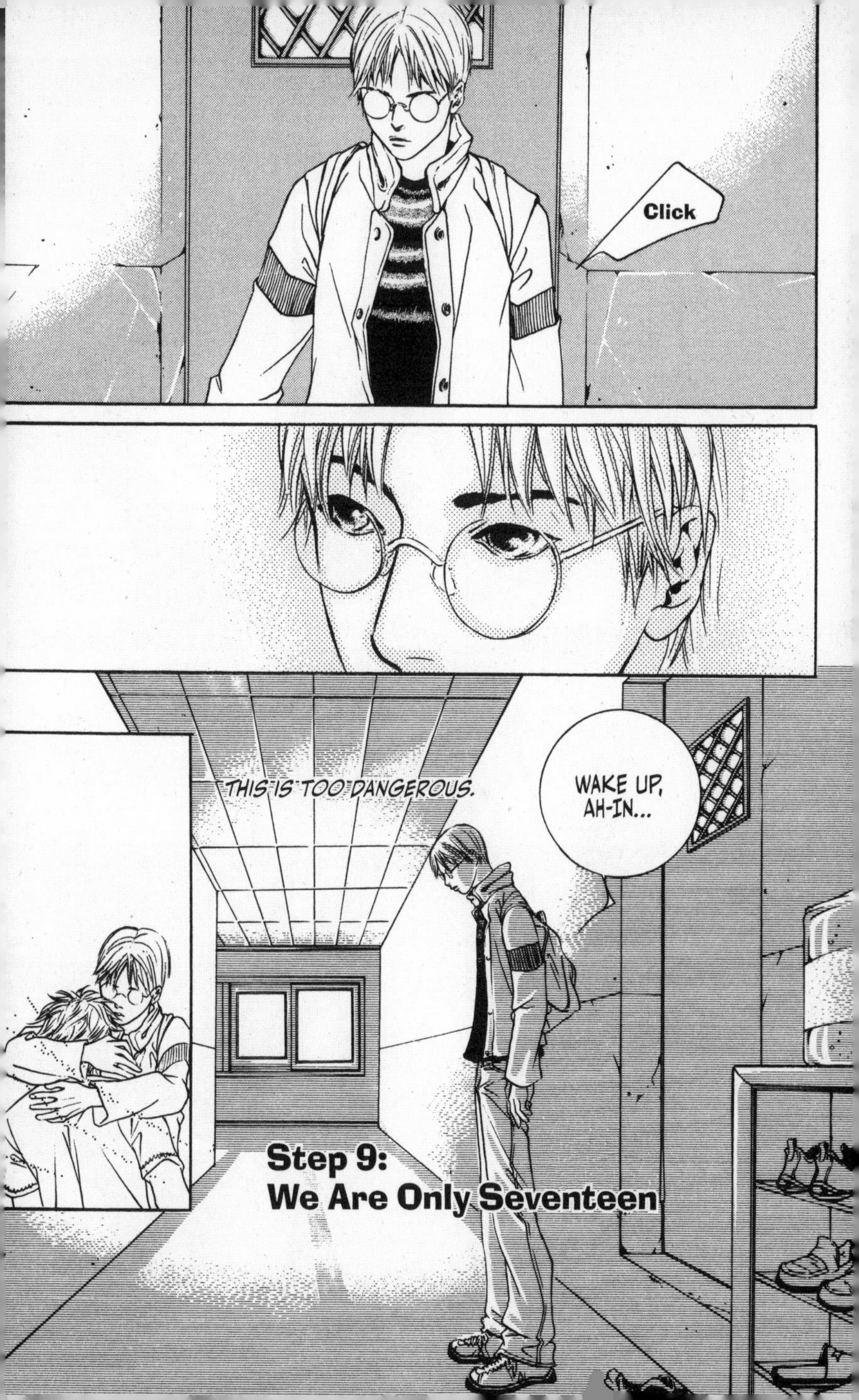
Click
THIS IS TOO DANGEROUS.
WAKE UP, AH-IN...
Step 9:
We Are Only Seventeen

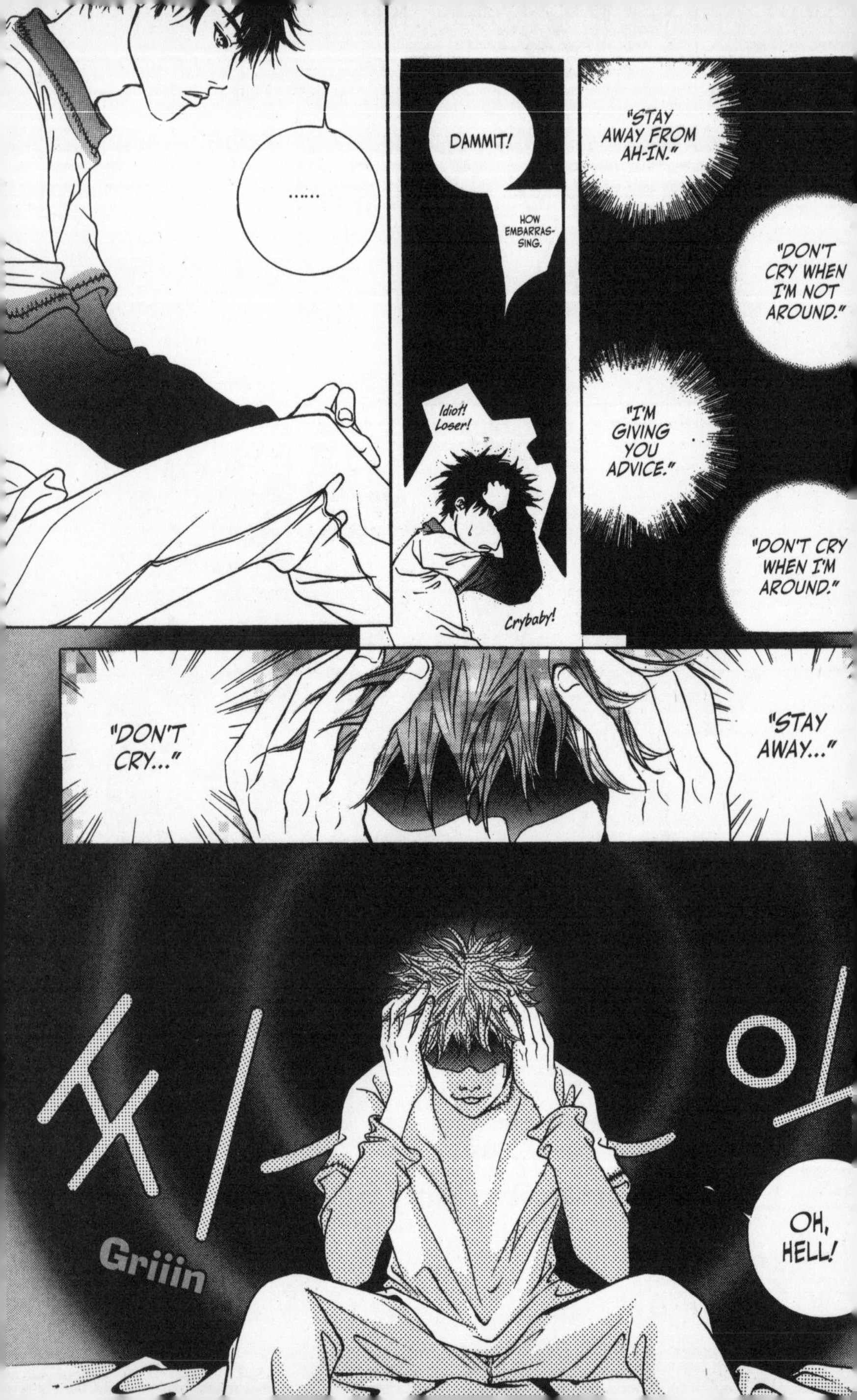
......
DAMMIT!
HOW EMBARRAS-SING.
Idiot! Loser!
Crybaby!
"STAY AWAY FROM AH-IN."
"DON'T CRY WHEN I'M NOT AROUND."
"I'M GIVING YOU ADVICE."
"DON'T CRY WHEN I'M AROUND."
"DON'T CRY..."
"STAY AWAY..."
Griiin
OH, HELL!

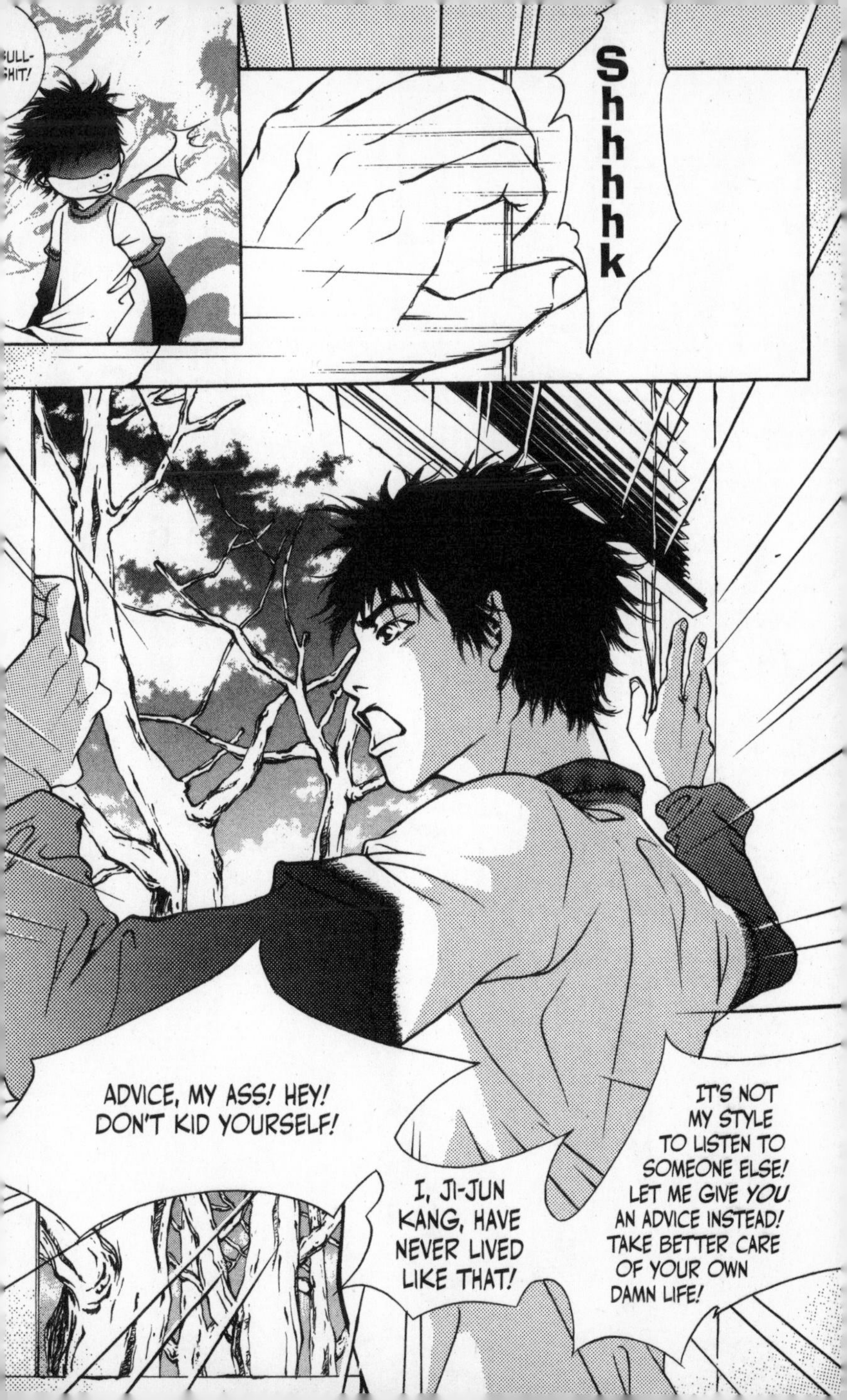
BULL-
SHIT!
Shhhhk
ADVICE, MY ASS! HEY!
DON'T KID YOURSELF!
I, JI-JUN
KANG, HAVE
NEVER LIVED
LIKE THAT!
IT'S NOT
MY STYLE
TO LISTEN TO
SOMEONE ELSE!
LET ME GIVE *YOU*
AN ADVICE INSTEAD!
TAKE BETTER CARE
OF YOUR OWN
DAMN LIFE!

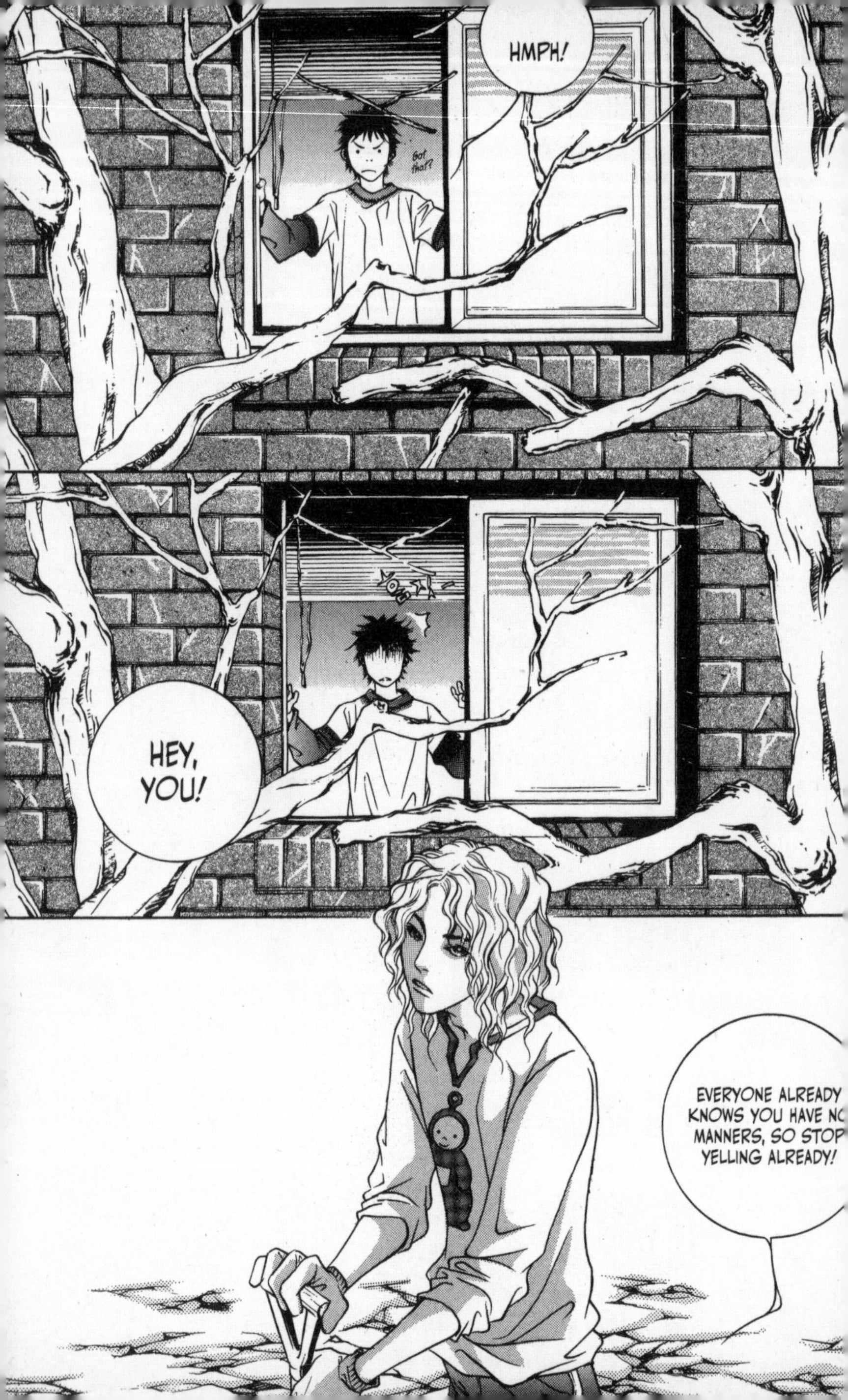
HMPH!
Got that?
HEY, YOU!
EVERYONE ALREADY KNOWS YOU HAVE NO MANNERS, SO STOP YELLING ALREADY!

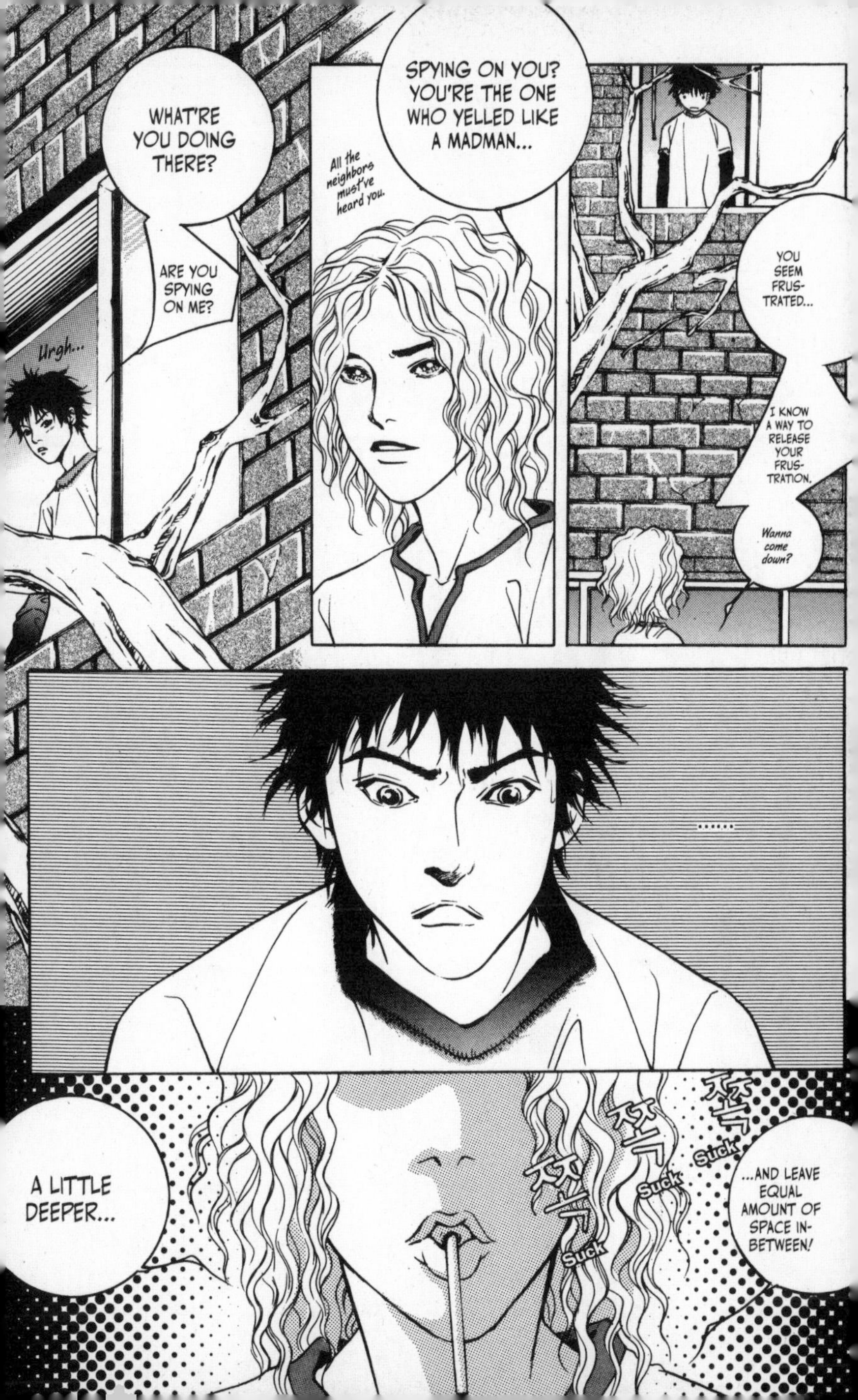
WHAT'RE YOU DOING THERE?
ARE YOU SPYING ON ME?
Urgh...
SPYING ON YOU? YOU'RE THE ONE WHO YELLED LIKE A MADMAN...
All the neighbors must've heard you.
YOU SEEM FRUS-TRATED...
I KNOW A WAY TO RELEASE YOUR FRUS-TRATION.
Wanna come down?
......
A LITTLE DEEPER...
Suck
Suck
Suck
...AND LEAVE EQUAL AMOUNT OF SPACE IN-BETWEEN!

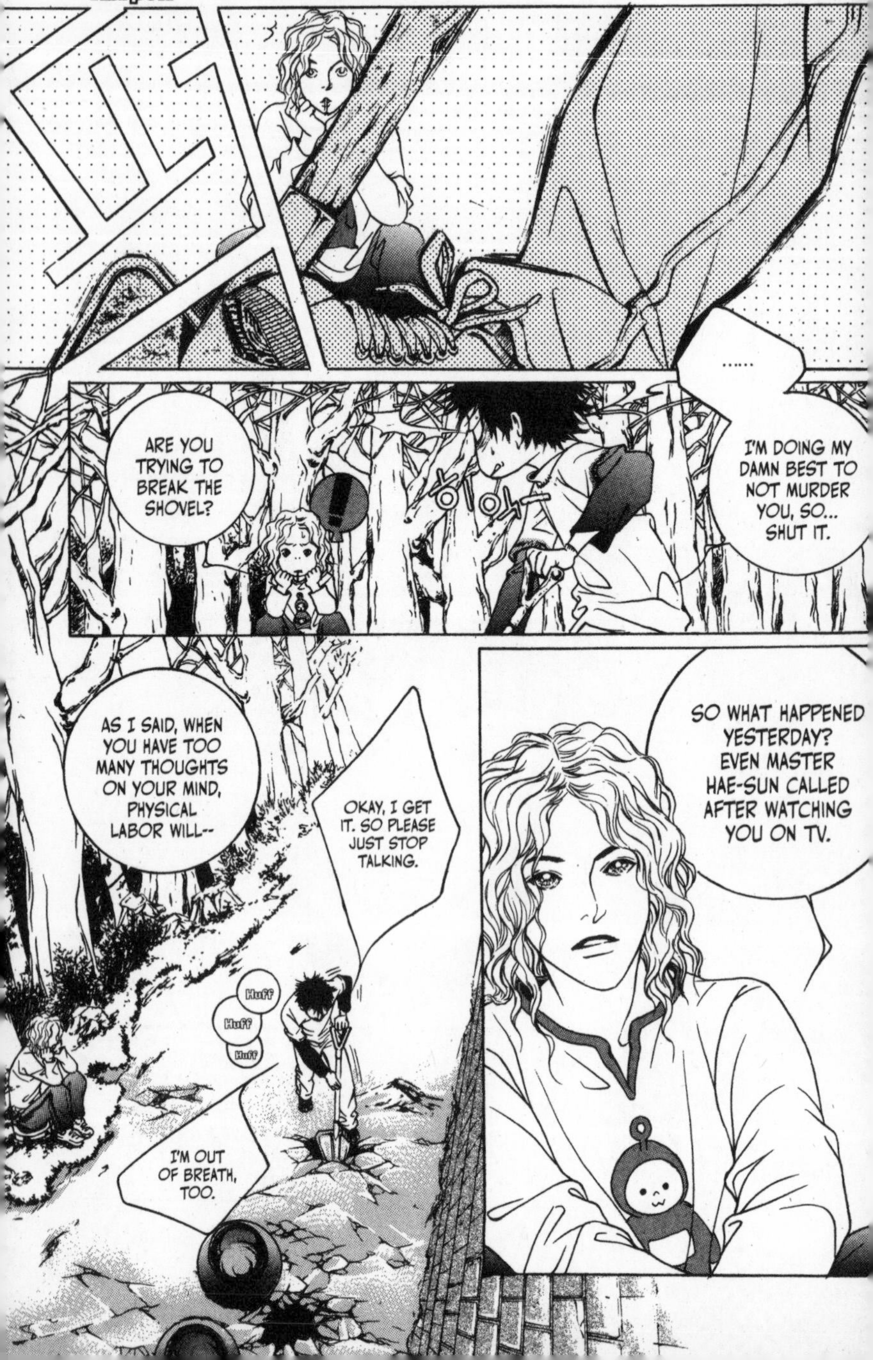
ARE YOU TRYING TO BREAK THE SHOVEL?
......
!
I'M DOING MY DAMN BEST TO NOT MURDER YOU, SO... SHUT IT.
AS I SAID, WHEN YOU HAVE TOO MANY THOUGHTS ON YOUR MIND, PHYSICAL LABOR WILL--
OKAY, I GET IT. SO PLEASE JUST STOP TALKING.
Huff
Huff
Huff
I'M OUT OF BREATH, TOO.
SO WHAT HAPPENED YESTERDAY? EVEN MASTER HAE-SUN CALLED AFTER WATCHING YOU ON TV.

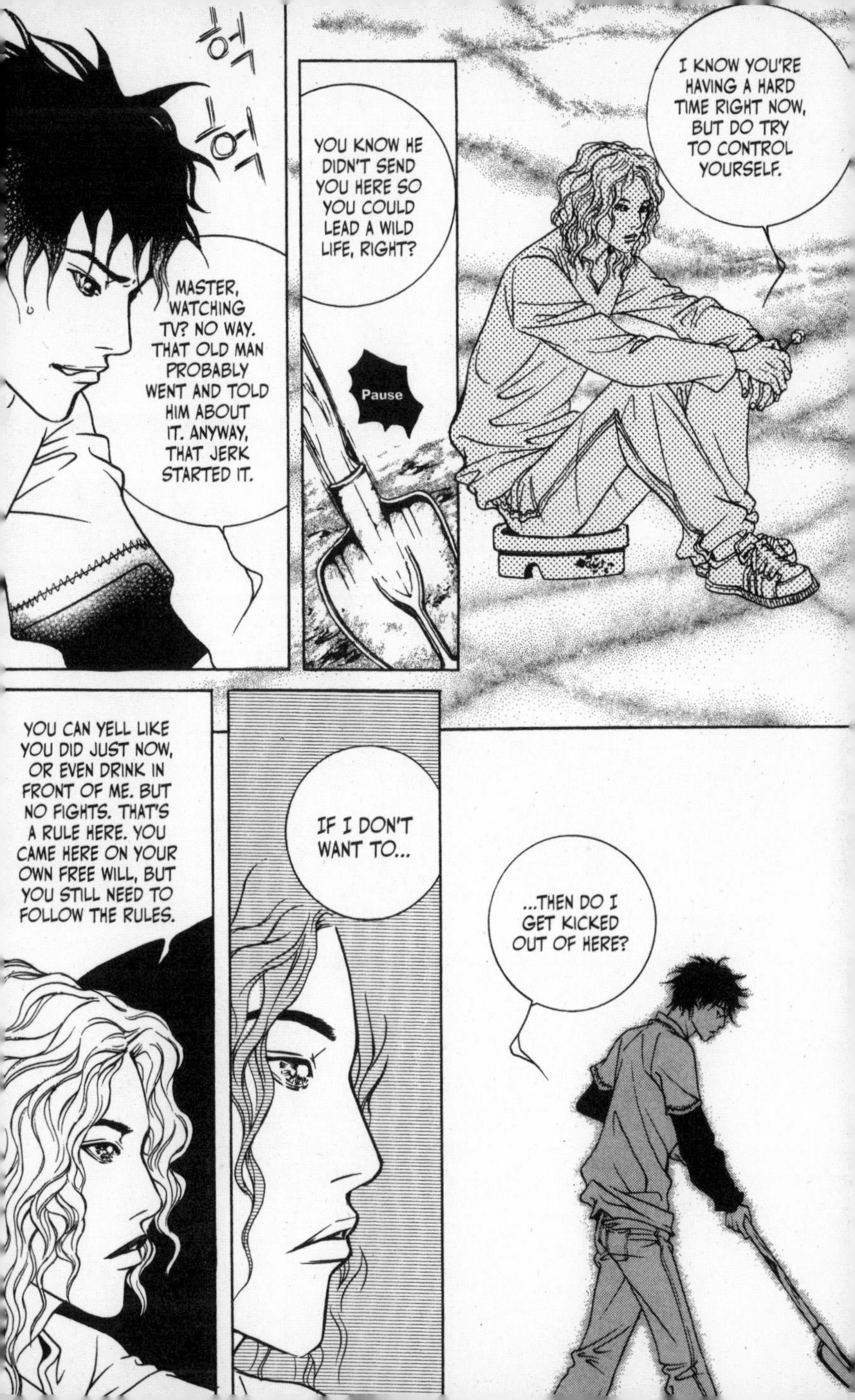
헉 헉
MASTER, WATCHING TV? NO WAY. THAT OLD MAN PROBABLY WENT AND TOLD HIM ABOUT IT. ANYWAY, THAT JERK STARTED IT.
YOU KNOW HE DIDN'T SEND YOU HERE SO YOU COULD LEAD A WILD LIFE, RIGHT?
Pause
I KNOW YOU'RE HAVING A HARD TIME RIGHT NOW, BUT DO TRY TO CONTROL YOURSELF.
YOU CAN YELL LIKE YOU DID JUST NOW, OR EVEN DRINK IN FRONT OF ME. BUT NO FIGHTS. THAT'S A RULE HERE. YOU CAME HERE ON YOUR OWN FREE WILL, BUT YOU STILL NEED TO FOLLOW THE RULES.
IF I DON'T WANT TO...
...THEN DO I GET KICKED OUT OF HERE?

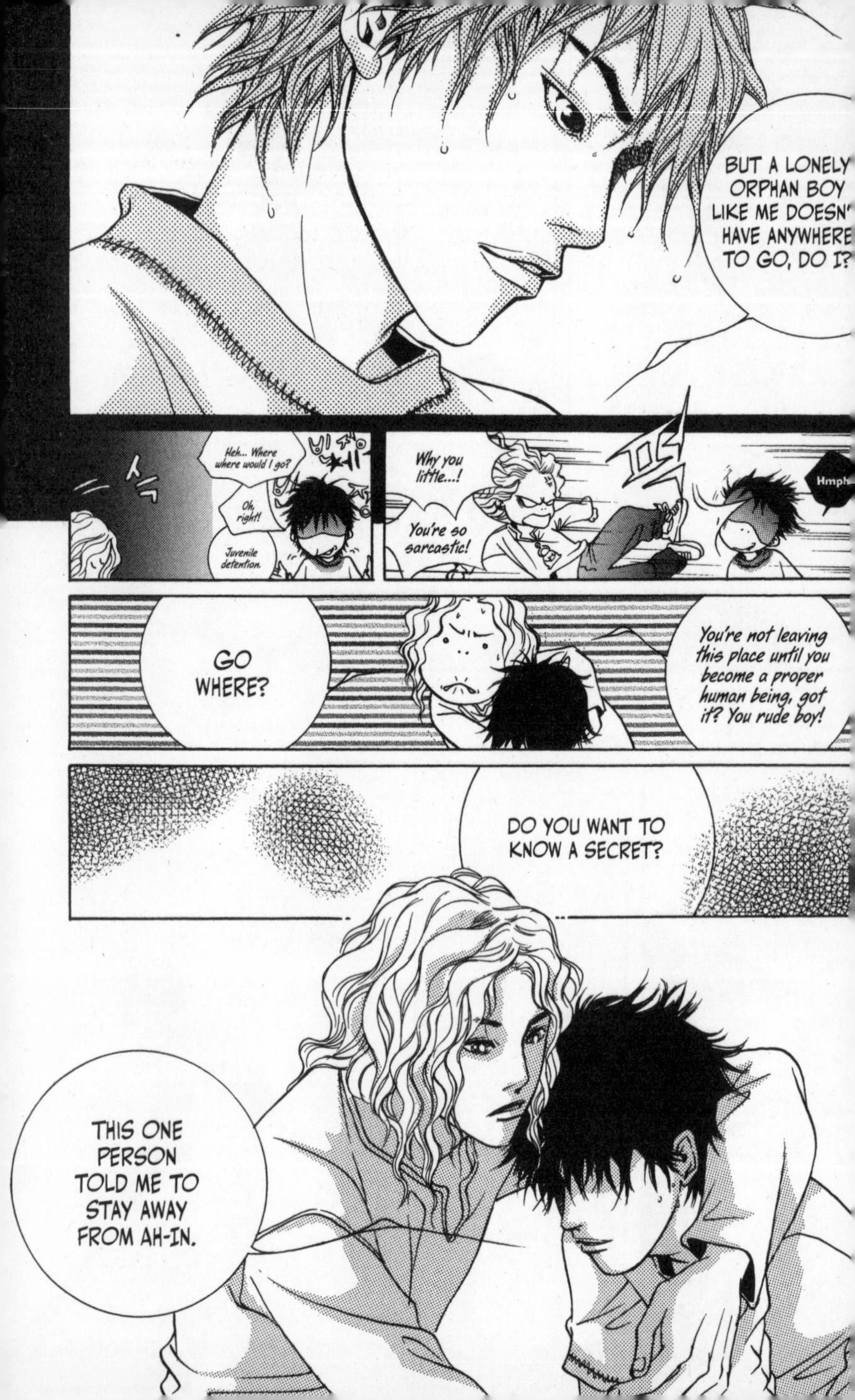
BUT A LONELY ORPHAN BOY LIKE ME DOESN' HAVE ANYWHERE TO GO, DO I?
Heh... Where where would I go?
Oh, right!
Juvenile detention.
Why you little...!
You're so sarcastic!
Hmph
GO WHERE?
You're not leaving this place until you become a proper human being, got it? You rude boy!
DO YOU WANT TO KNOW A SECRET?
THIS ONE PERSON TOLD ME TO STAY AWAY FROM AH-IN.

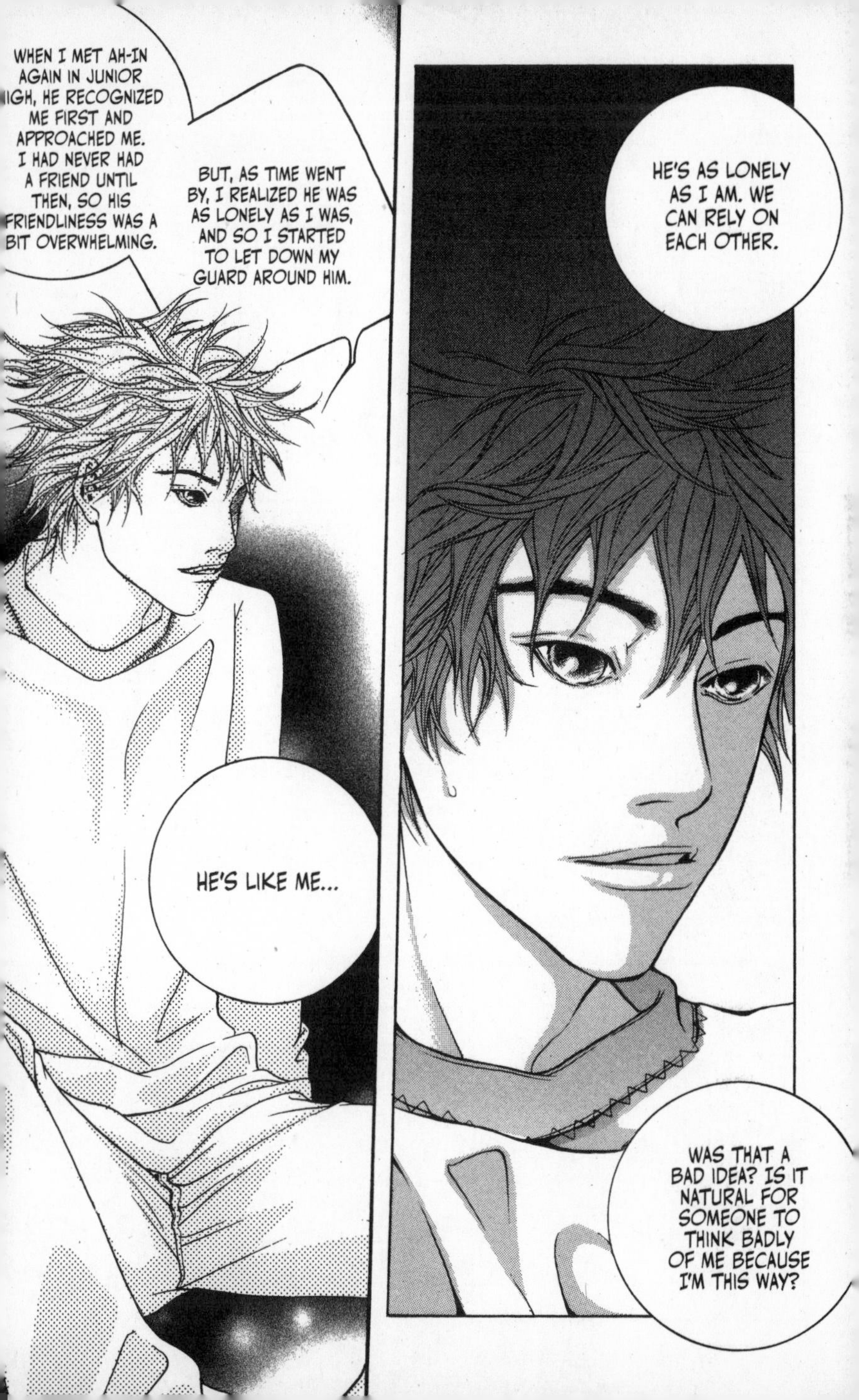
WHEN I MET AH-IN AGAIN IN JUNIOR IGH, HE RECOGNIZED ME FIRST AND APPROACHED ME. I HAD NEVER HAD A FRIEND UNTIL THEN, SO HIS FRIENDLINESS WAS A BIT OVERWHELMING.
BUT, AS TIME WENT BY, I REALIZED HE WAS AS LONELY AS I WAS, AND SO I STARTED TO LET DOWN MY GUARD AROUND HIM.
HE'S LIKE ME...
HE'S AS LONELY AS I AM. WE CAN RELY ON EACH OTHER.
WAS THAT A BAD IDEA? IS IT NATURAL FOR SOMEONE TO THINK BADLY OF ME BECAUSE I'M THIS WAY?

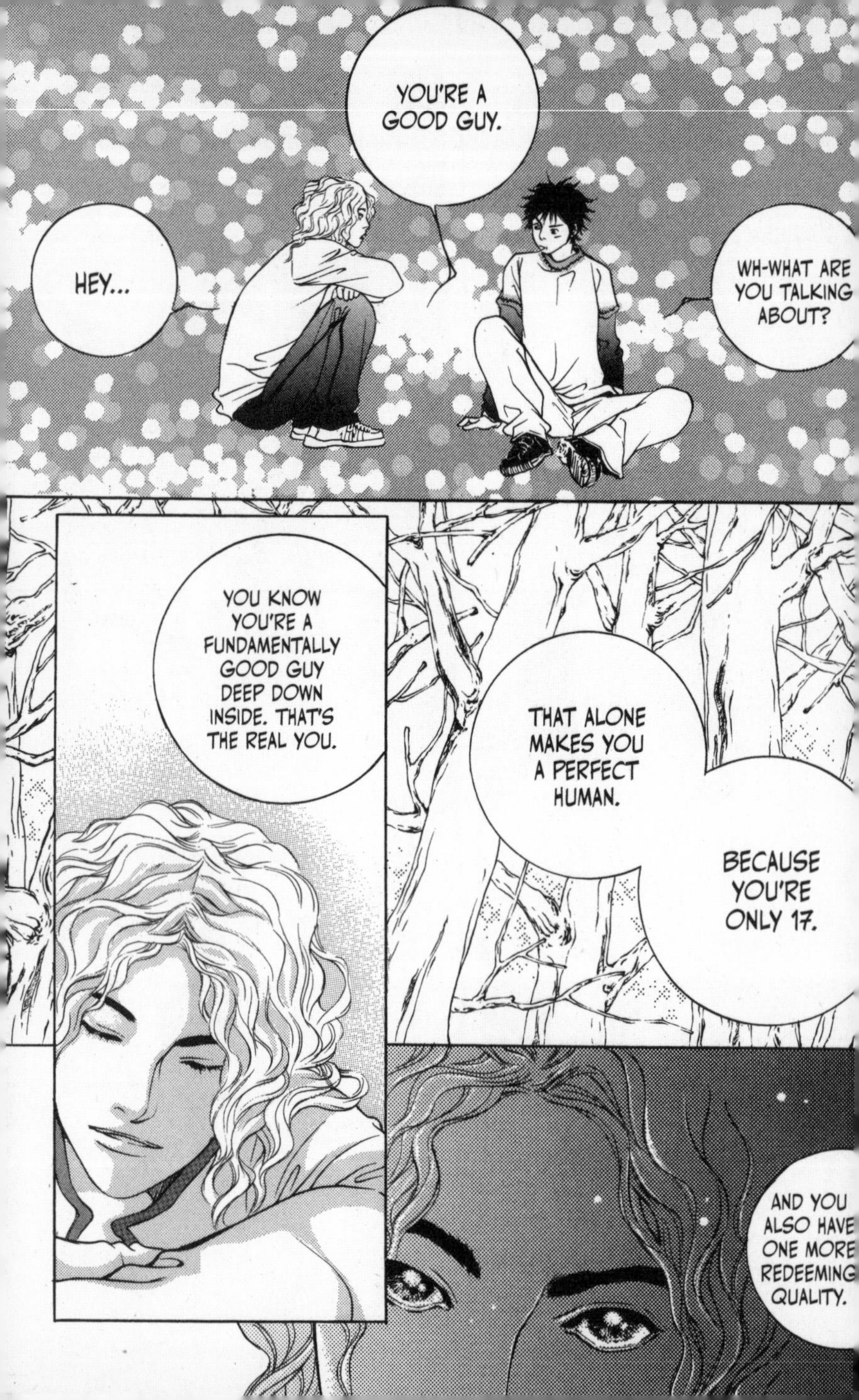
HEY...
YOU'RE A GOOD GUY.
WH-WHAT ARE YOU TALKING ABOUT?
YOU KNOW YOU'RE A FUNDAMENTALLY GOOD GUY DEEP DOWN INSIDE. THAT'S THE REAL YOU.
THAT ALONE MAKES YOU A PERFECT HUMAN.
BECAUSE YOU'RE ONLY 17.
AND YOU ALSO HAVE ONE MORE REDEEMING QUALITY.

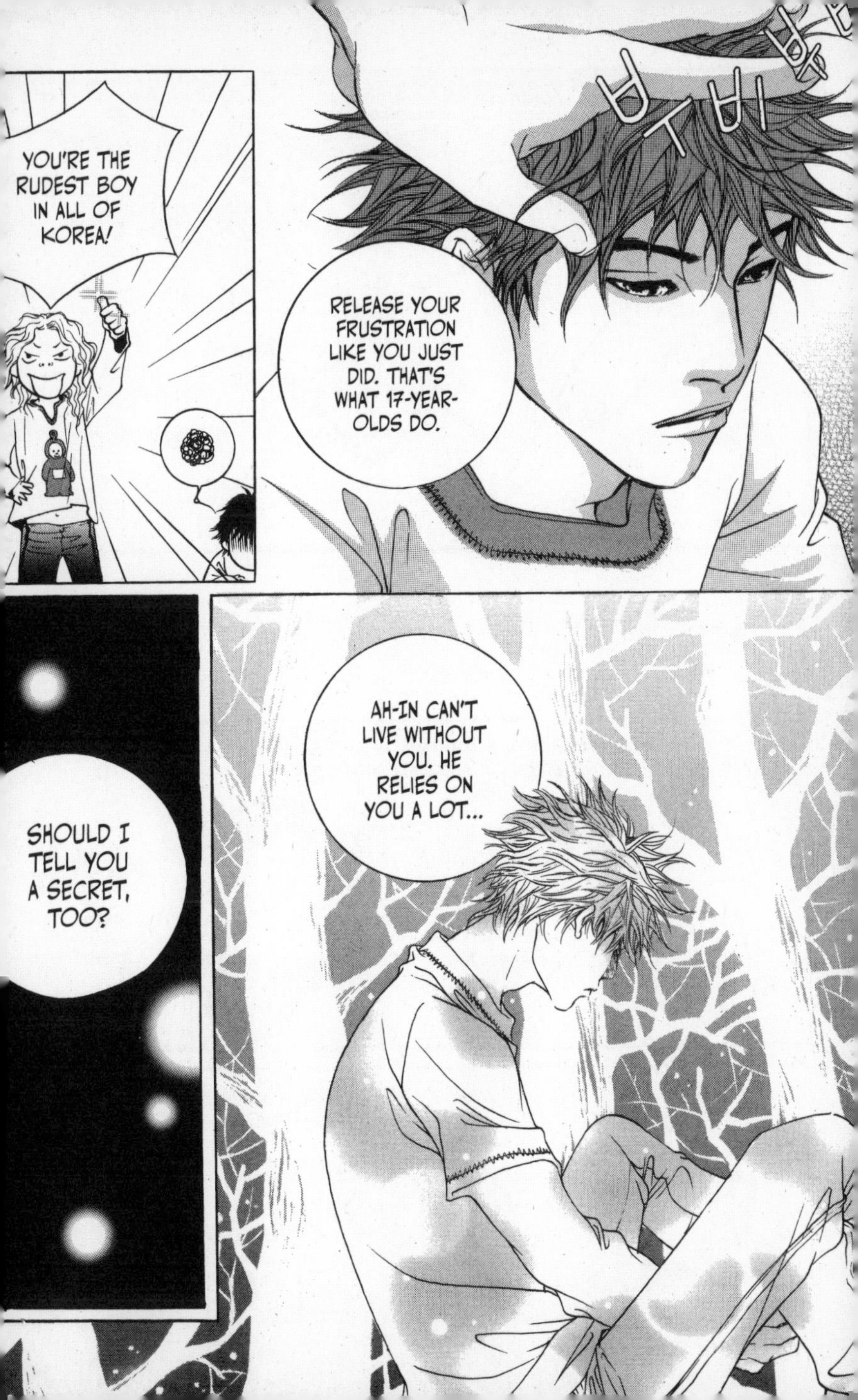
YOU'RE THE RUDEST BOY IN ALL OF KOREA!
RELEASE YOUR FRUSTRATION LIKE YOU JUST DID. THAT'S WHAT 17-YEAR-OLDS DO.
SHOULD I TELL YOU A SECRET, TOO?
AH-IN CAN'T LIVE WITHOUT YOU. HE RELIES ON YOU A LOT...

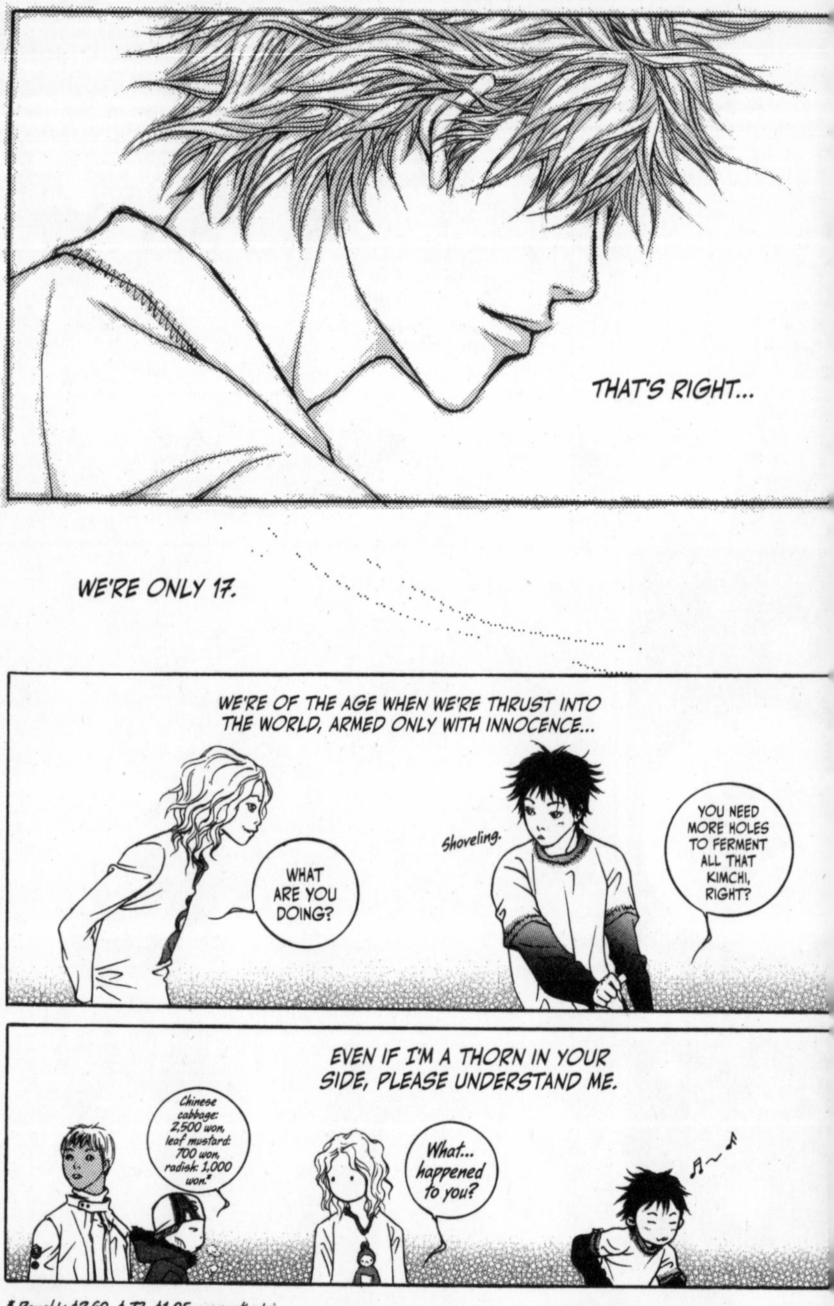
THAT'S RIGHT...
WE'RE ONLY 17.
WE'RE OF THE AGE WHEN WE'RE THRUST INTO THE WORLD, ARMED ONLY WITH INNOCENCE...
WHAT ARE YOU DOING?
Shoveling.
YOU NEED MORE HOLES TO FERMENT ALL THAT KIMCHI, RIGHT?
EVEN IF I'M A THORN IN YOUR SIDE, PLEASE UNDERSTAND ME.
Chinese cabbage: 2,500 won, leaf mustard: 700 won, radish: 1,000 won.*
What... happened to you?

* Roughly $2.60, $.73, $1.05 respectively.

I CAN'T HELP IT.

PRETTY HYUNG-IN?

NUH?

Mumble Mumble

Cabbage: 2,500 won...leaf...

WHERE'S KANG-DAE?

Shovel Shovel

Should we fire him?

Dazed

Yo...

Kang-Dae is here. ➔

Yes.

WE HAVE ONLY LIVED FOR 17 YEARS...

SNOW...

SNOW!

...

Cabbage...

...SO WE HAVE TO LEAN AGAINST EACH OTHER TO LIVE.

WE ARE...

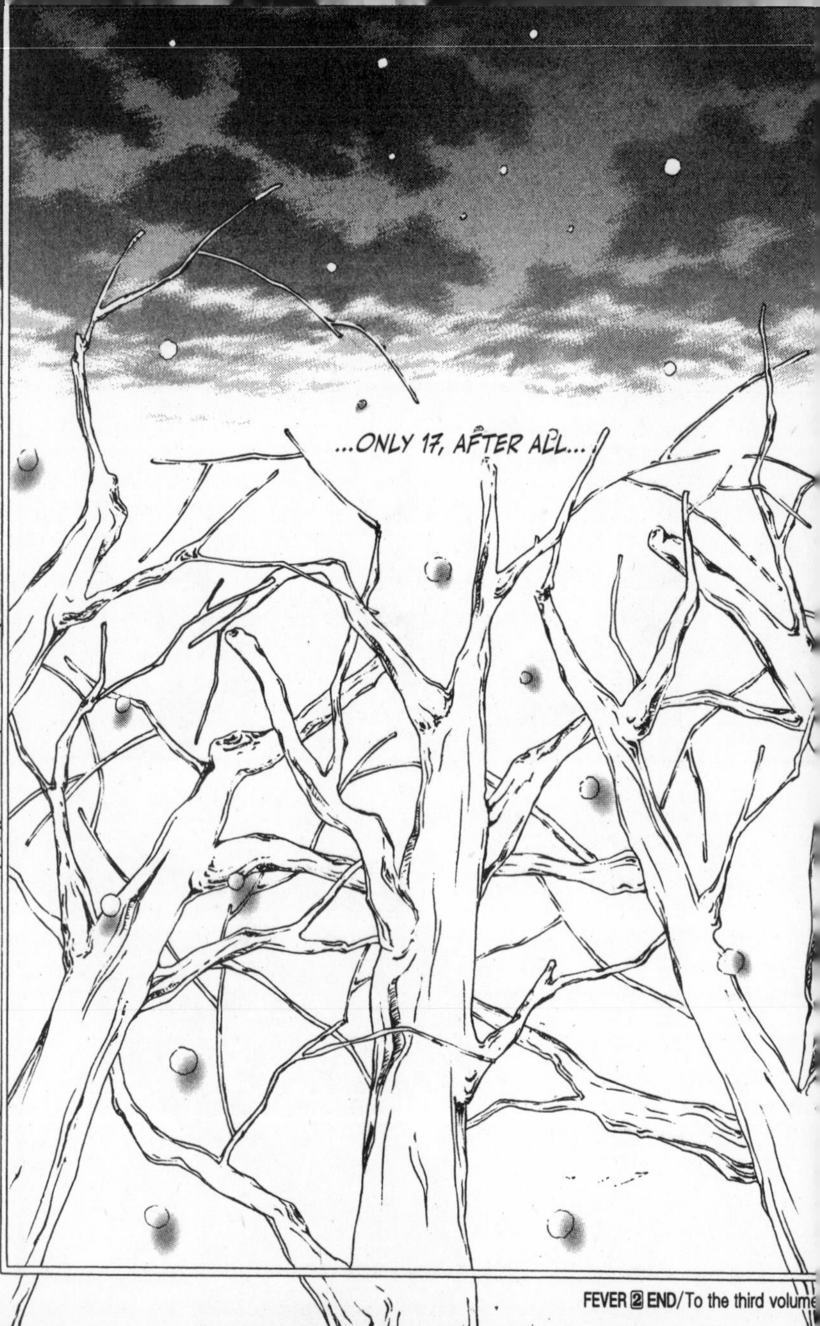
...ONLY 17, AFTER ALL...

FEVER 2 END/To the third volume

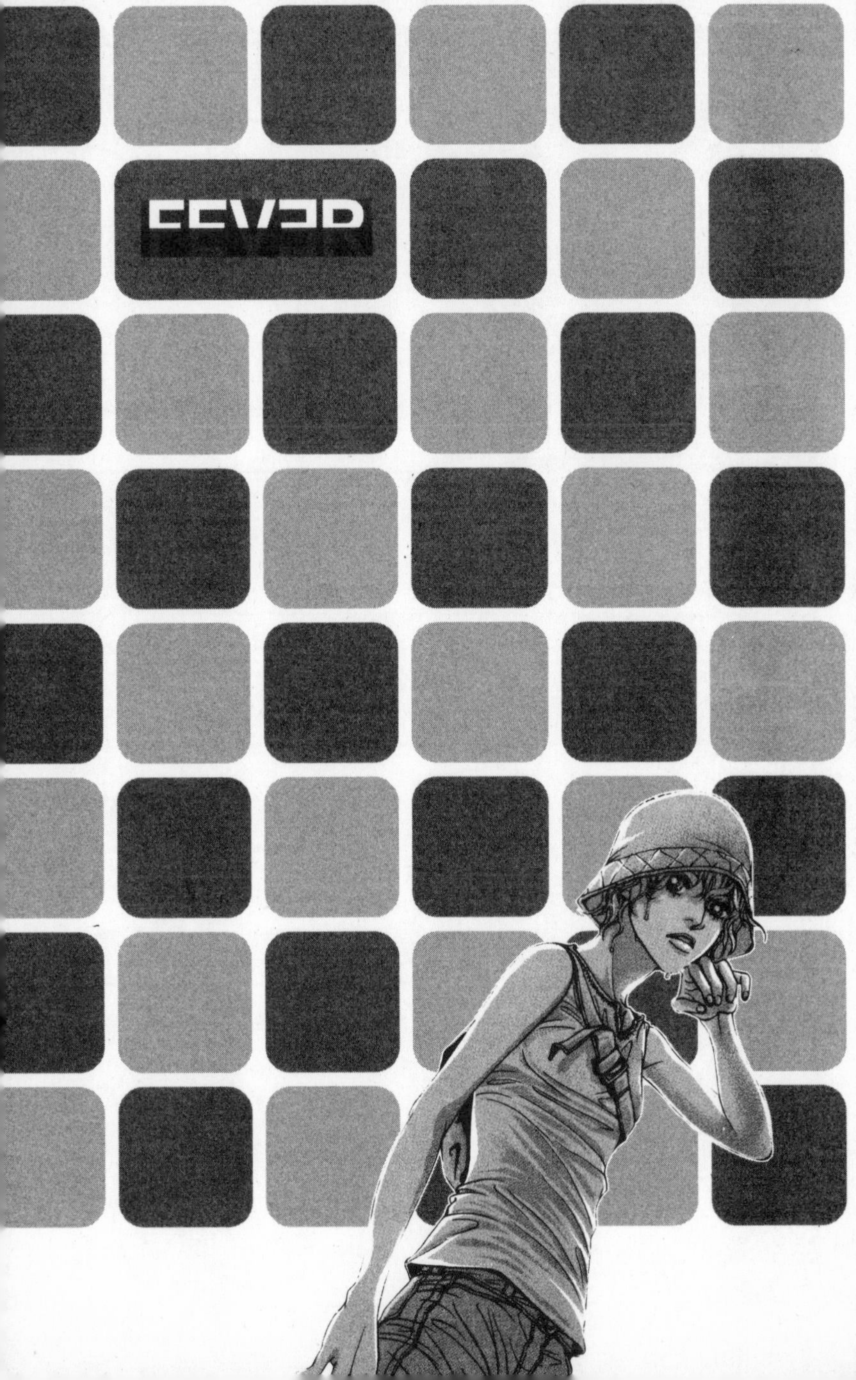

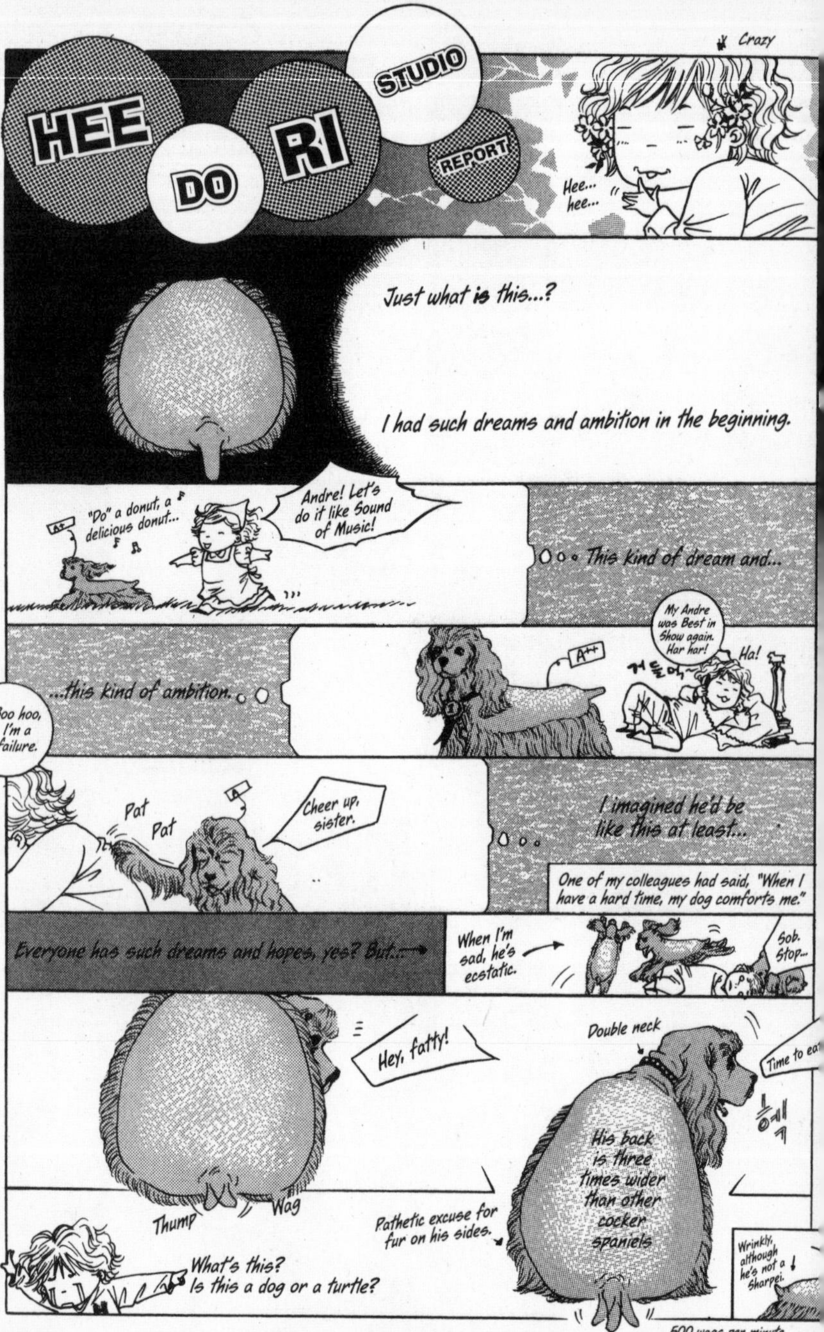
HEE DO RI STUDIO REPORT
Crazy
Hee... hee...
Just what is this...?
I had such dreams and ambition in the beginning.
A+
"Do" a donut, a delicious donut...
Andre! Let's do it like Sound of Music!
This kind of dream and...
...this kind of ambition.
A++
My Andre was Best in Show again. Har har!
Ha!
Boo hoo, I'm a failure.
Pat
Pat
A
Cheer up, sister.
I imagined he'd be like this at least...
One of my colleagues had said, "When I have a hard time, my dog comforts me."
Everyone has such dreams and hopes, yes? But...
When I'm sad, he's ecstatic.
Sob. Stop...
Hey, fatty!
Thump
Wag
What's this? Is this a dog or a turtle?
Double neck
Time to ea
His back is three times wider than other cocker spaniels
Pathetic excuse for fur on his sides.
Wrinkly, although he's not a Sharpei.
500 wags per minute.
His tail never stops wagging.

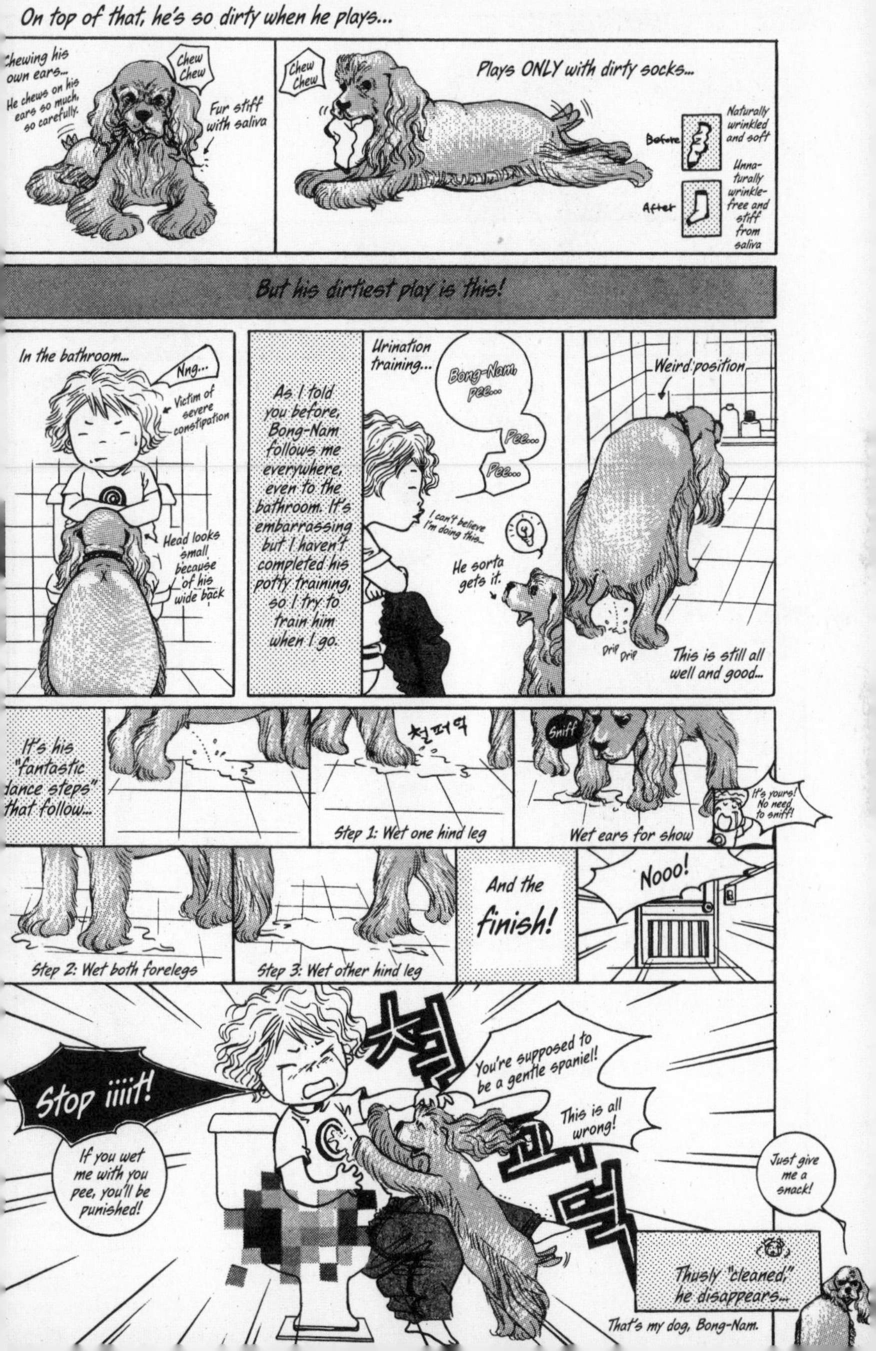
On top of that, he's so dirty when he plays...
Chewing his own ears...
He chews on his ears so much, so carefully.
Chew Chew
Fur stiff with saliva
Chew Chew
Plays ONLY with dirty socks...
Before
Naturally wrinkled and soft
After
Unnaturally wrinkle-free and stiff from saliva
But his dirtiest play is this!
In the bathroom...
Nng...
Victim of severe constipation
Head looks small because of his wide back
As I told you before, Bong-Nam follows me everywhere, even to the bathroom. It's embarrassing but I haven't completed his potty training, so I try to train him when I go.
Urination training...
Bong-Nam, pee...
Pee...
Pee...
I can't believe I'm doing this...
He sorta gets it.
Weird position
Drip Drip
This is still all well and good...
It's his "fantastic dance steps" that follow...
철퍼덕
Step 1: Wet one hind leg
Sniff
Wet ears for show
It's yours! No need to sniff!
Step 2: Wet both forelegs
Step 3: Wet other hind leg
And the finish!
Nooo!
Stop iiiiit!
If you wet me with you pee, you'll be punished!
You're supposed to be a gentle spaniel!
This is all wrong!
Just give me a snack!
Thusly "cleaned," he disappears...
That's my dog, Bong-Nam.

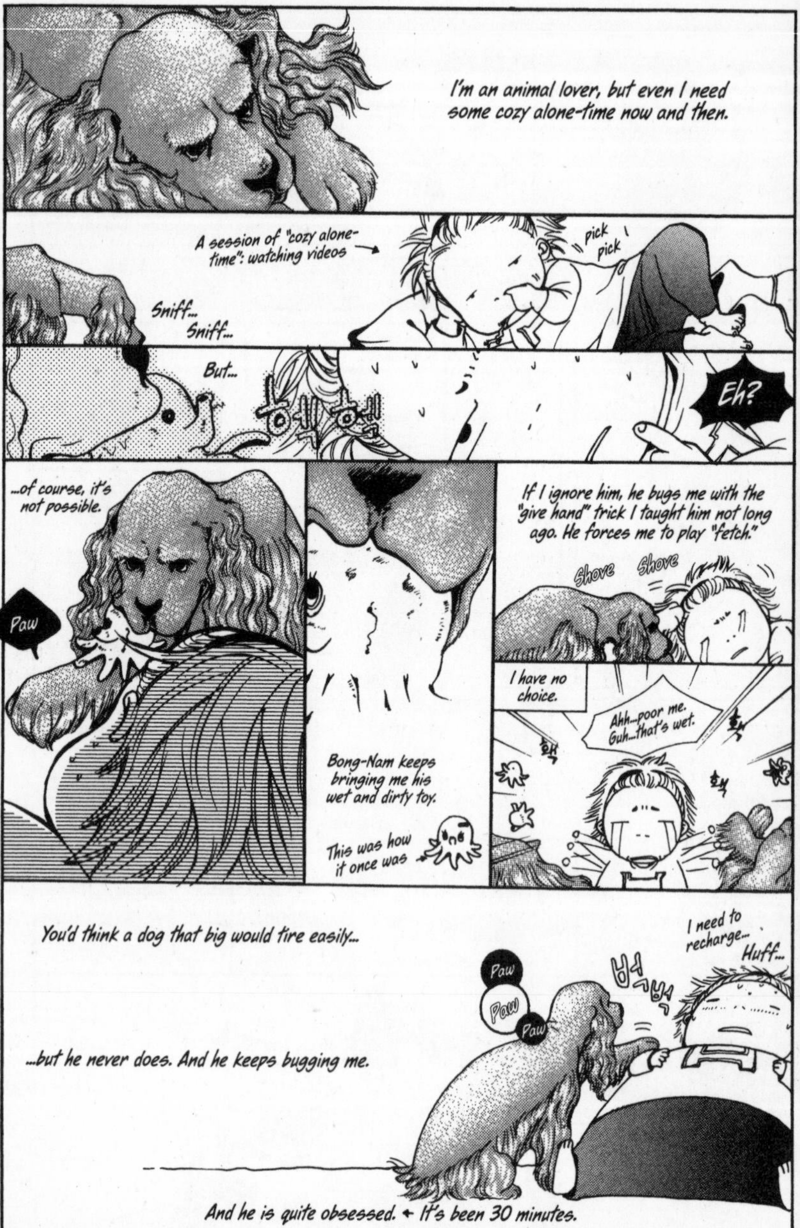
I'm an animal lover, but even I need some cozy alone-time now and then.
Sniff... Sniff...
A session of "cozy alone-time": watching videos
pick pick
But...
Eh?
...of course, it's not possible.
Paw
Bong-Nam keeps bringing me his wet and dirty toy.
This was how it once was
If I ignore him, he bugs me with the "give hand" trick I taught him not long ago. He forces me to play "fetch."
Shove
Shove
I have no choice.
Ahh...poor me. Guh...that's wet.
You'd think a dog that big would tire easily...
...but he never does. And he keeps bugging me.
Paw
Paw
Paw
I need to recharge...
Huff...
And he is quite obsessed.
It's been 30 minutes.

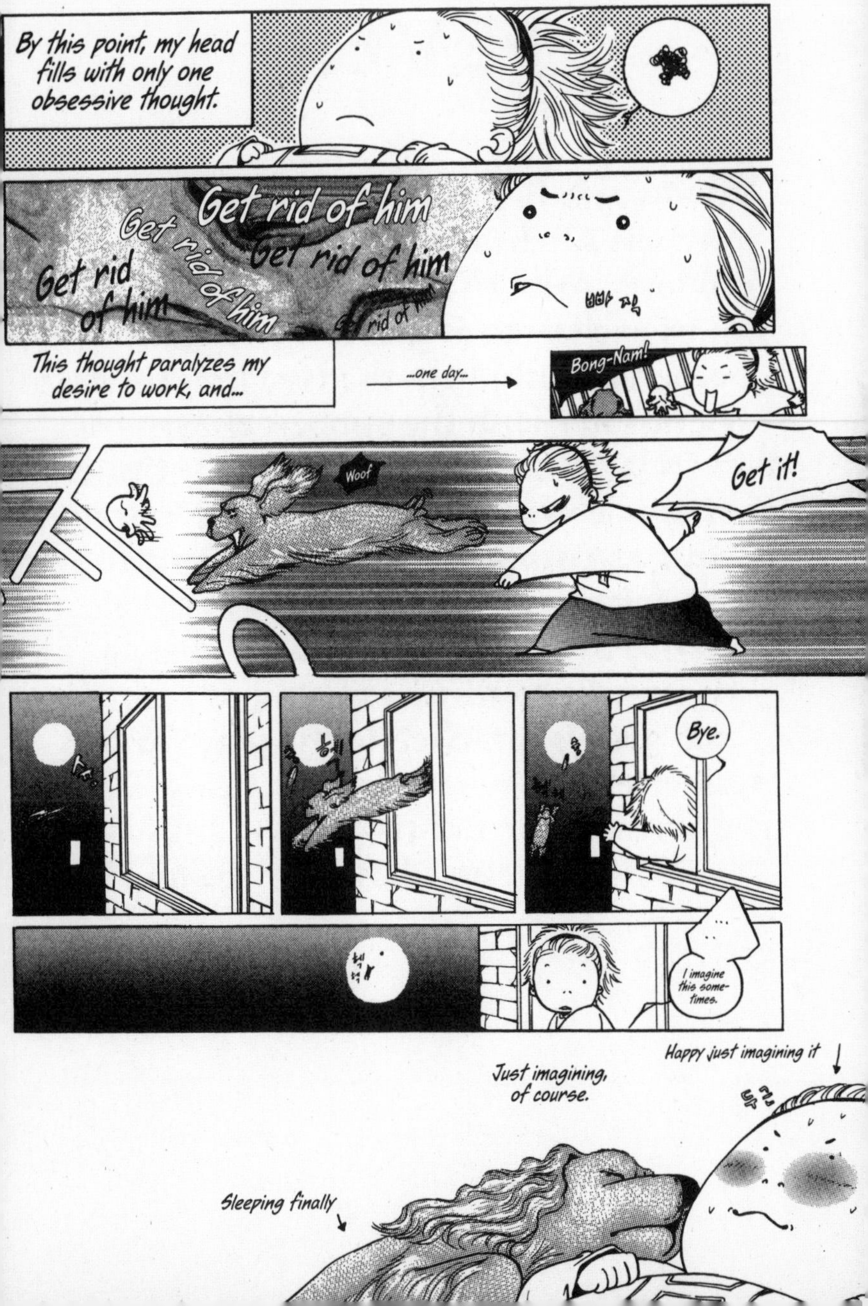
By this point, my head fills with only one obsessive thought.
Get rid of him
Get rid of him
Get rid of him
Get rid of him
Get rid of him
This thought paralyzes my desire to work, and...
...one day...
Bong-Nam!
Woof
Get it!
Bye.
...
I imagine this sometimes.
Just imagining, of course.
Happy just imagining it
Sleeping finally

In the next volume of :

FEVER

Ah-In and Ji-Jun's friendship is tested when Ah-In's feelings become too obvious. And Ah-Rip's offer to date Ji-Jun in exchange of granting her a favor doesn't exactly help the two longtime friends to mend the sudden chasm in their relationship, either. Ji-Ho continues to struggle with his self-loathing hatred, but attempts to heal himself with good friends at Fever...although his old friends aren't yet ready to let him go. Hyung-In continues to stay at Fever and grows attached to the place and residents, but when she and Kang-Dae are arrested for fighting in the subway, will her parents allow her to stay?

Hotel AFRICA™

Anything can happen at the Hotel Africa

Tales of heartbreak, irony, and redemption are in store when you check in a second time to the Hotel Africa. Continue along with Elvis as he reveals more tales of the desolate hotel and its strange guests.

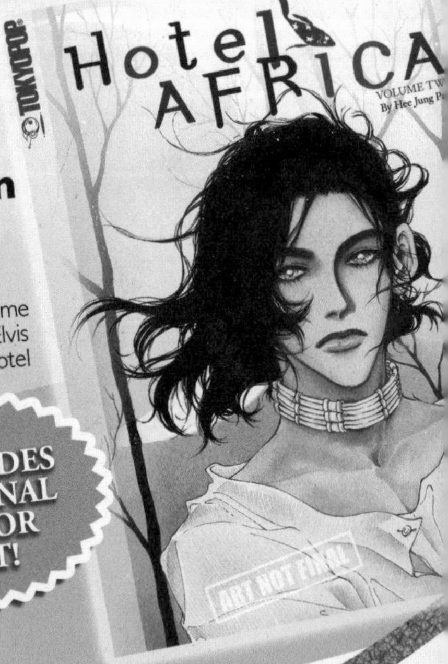
TOKYOPOP
Hotel AFRICA
VOLUME TW
By Hee Jung P
ART NOT FINAL

INCLUDES ORIGINAL COLOR ART!

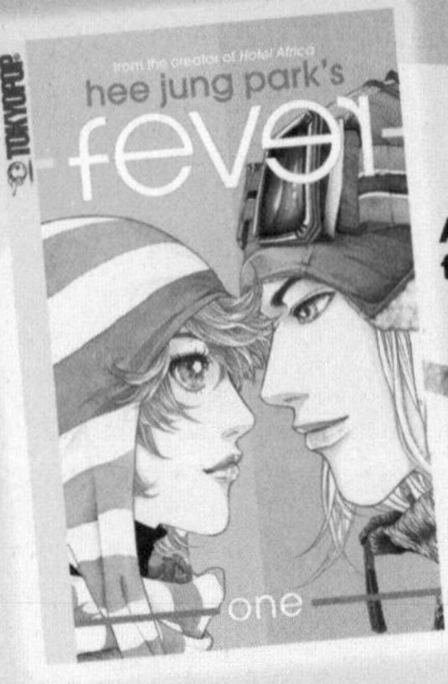
TOKYOPOP
from the creator of Hotel Africa
hee jung park's
fever
one

Also available from Hee Jung Park

Fever

Once you go to Fever, you will never be the same...

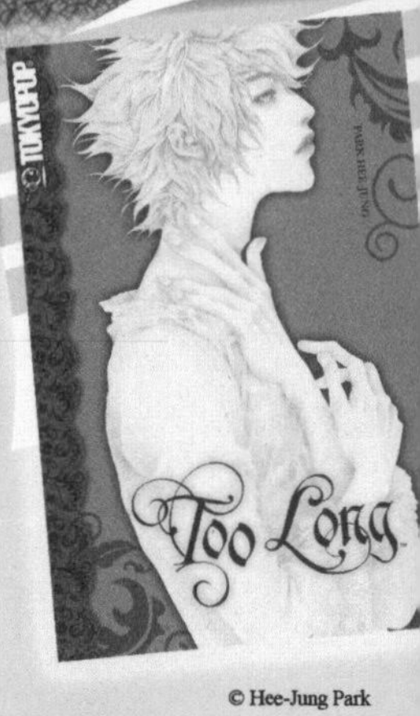
TOKYOPOP
Too Long

Too Long

A girl who attracts suicide victims, a shy record store customer, and the star of a rock band... what could these three have in common? Find out in this moving collection of short stories.

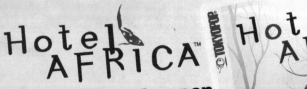

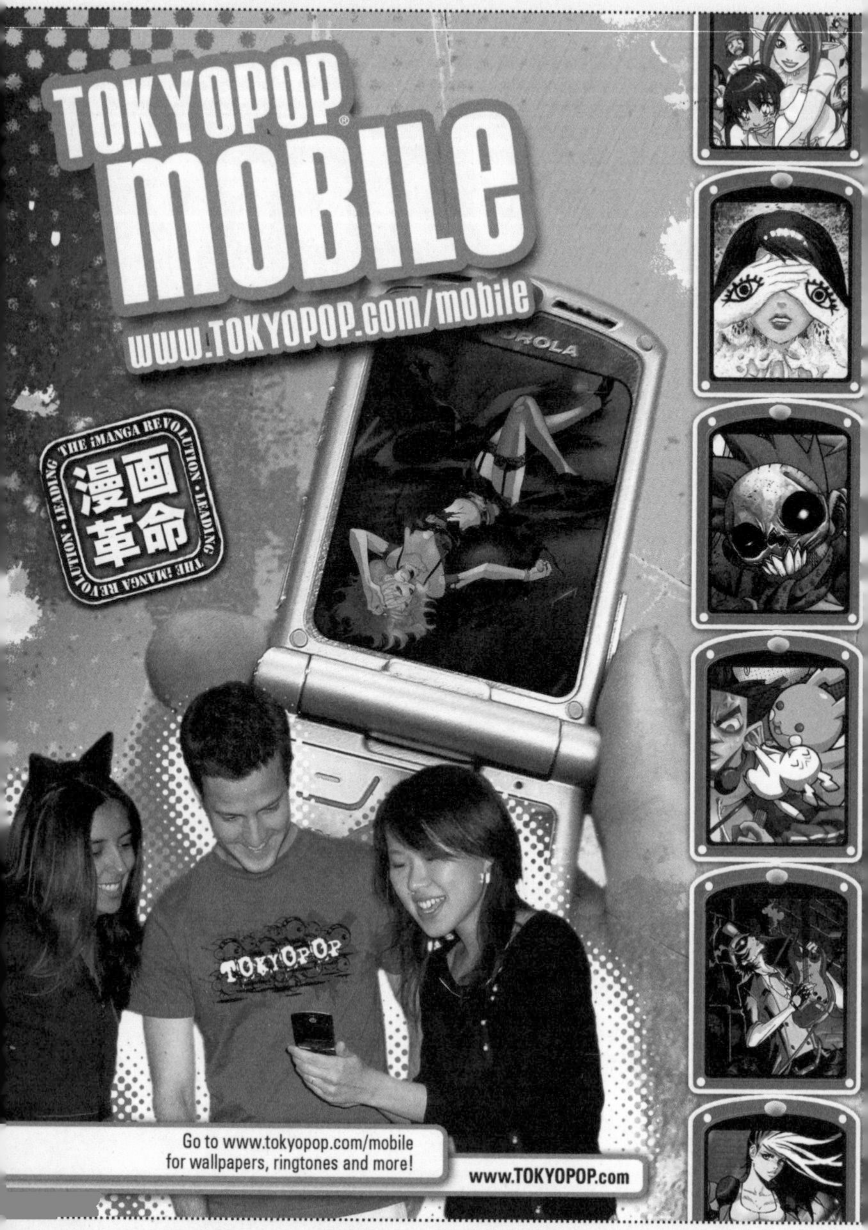
TOKYOPOP®
MOBILE
www.TOKYOPOP.com/mobile
THE iMANGA REVOLUTION · LEADING
漫画革命
THE iMANGA REVOLUTION · LEADING
TOKYOPOP
Go to www.tokyopop.com/mobile
for wallpapers, ringtones and more!
www.TOKYOPOP.com